The United States and the Rule of Law in International Affairs

John Murphy offers a careful and insightful analysis of why the United States does not always accept the rule of law in international affairs, even though it has made immense contributions to its creation, adoption, and implementation. Examining the reasons for this failure, John Murphy analyses a number of cases, not to make a case that the United States has been an international outlaw, but to illustrate the wide-ranging difficulties standing in the way of US adherence to the rule of law. He explains how the nature of the US legal system and the idiosyncrasies of the international legal process combine to compound problems for the United States, and he explores several alternative scenarios for the position of the United States vis-à-vis international law. This timely book offers a much needed examination of US attitudes and practices and makes a major contribution to the contemporary literature on international law and international relations.

JOHN F. MURPHY is Professor of International Law and Business, Villanova University School of Law, Pennsylvania. He is author or editor of numerous books and monographs and has served as a consultant to the US Departments of State and Justice, the American Bar Association Committee on Law and National Security, and the United Nations Crime Bureau. He is currently the American Bar Association's Alternate Observer at the US mission to the United Nations.

The United States and the Rule of Law in International Affairs

John F. Murphy

PUBLISHED BY THE PRESS SYNDICATE OF THE UNIVERSITY OF CAMBRIDGE
The Pitt Building, Trumpington Street, Cambridge, United Kingdom

CAMBRIDGE UNIVERSITY PRESS
The Edinburgh Building, Cambridge, CB2 2RU, UK
40 West 20th Street, New York, NY 10011-4211, USA
477 Williamstown Road, Port Melbourne, VIC 3207, Australia
Ruiz de Alarcón 13, 28014 Madrid, Spain
Dock House, The Waterfront, Cape Town 8001, South Africa

http://www.cambridge.org

First published 2004
Reprinted 2005

Printed in the United Kingdom at the University Press, Cambridge

Typeface Plantin 10/12 pt *System* LaTeX 2ε [TB]

A catalogue record for this book is available from the British Library

ISBN 0 521 82256 4 hardback
ISBN 0 521 52968 9 paperback

To Arthur T. Downey, nonpareil international lawyer, matchless friend

Contents

Acknowledgments

This book has been three years in the making. Along the way I have had the great good fortune to have the assistance and encouragement of some long-standing friends who also happen to be first-rate international lawyers. Richard B. Bilder, Arthur T. Downey, and John Lawrence Hargrove were colleagues of mine when I was an attorney in the Office of the Legal Adviser, US Department of State, during the 1960s. All have gone on to great success in various endeavors and have remained good friends. Each has made a major contribution to this book by reading and commenting on draft chapters, advancing numerous suggestions for improvement, and encouraging me to see the project through to completion. Henry H. Perritt, Jr., a former colleague of mine at the Villanova University School of Law, now at the Chicago-Kent School of Law, also read draft chapters and provided helpful comments. Larry D. Johnson, former Legal Adviser to the International Atomic Energy Agency and current Chef de Cabinet, Office of the President, International Criminal Tribunal for the former Yugoslavia, provided extremely helpful comments on the section in chapter 5 discussing the Nuclear Non-Proliferation Treaty. I am deeply grateful to all five of these gentlemen, although it should be understood that none is responsible for any errors or infelicitous language there may be in this book. Sole responsibility for these lies with me.

I am also grateful to Dean Mark A. Sargent for steadfast support of scholarship and other intellectual activities at the Villanova University School of Law. Similarly, I am grateful to William James, Associate Dean for Information Services at Villanova, and his excellent staff for numerous services. My secretary, Terri Laverghetta, has helped me in so many ways in my work on this book that I have lost count of them. I have benefited greatly, to understate the matter, from the good work of my research assistants – Alexis Cocco, Kevin Jarboe, Brya Keilson, Andrew Kenis, Charles Kocher, and Heath Lynch.

Lastly, a special note of gratitude goes to my wife, Laura Sunstein Murphy, for her infinite patience with me while I pursued my "obsession" to completion. Her love and support have sustained me throughout these three years.

Introduction

Philip Allott, a former Legal Counselor in the British Foreign and Commonwealth Office and a prominent scholar, recently suggested that the United States is a "law-state," that is, the "transformation of the American colonies into a new kind of society at the end of the eighteenth century was achieved through law."[1] This "new kind of society," moreover, has been grounded on the concept of the rule of law. In the words of former US Supreme Court Justice Hugo Black, the United States is "dedicated" to the rule of law.[2]

Recently, this "dedication" to the rule of law has taken the form of efforts, by the US government and others, to promote the rule of law in foreign countries, especially in the third world and the former Soviet bloc countries. Reflecting this new emphasis, in 1999 Secretary of State Madeleine Albright created the position of Senior Coordinator for the Rule of Law in the State Department.[3]

At the same time the precise meaning of the term "rule of law" has been a topic of sharp debate, and it has been suggested that its meaning "may be less clear today than ever before."[4] Also, although the rule of law as an ideal has enjoyed near universal support, some have criticized the very concept. For example, Morton J. Horwitz, a leader in the critical legal studies movement, has contended that the rule of law "[b]y promoting procedural justice . . . enables the shrewd, the calculating, and the wealthy to manipulate its forms to their own advantage. And it ratifies and legitimates an adversarial, competitive, and atomistic conception of human relations."[5]

For my part I join the nearly universal support for the rule of law as an ideal, even if the ideal is seldom realized in practice, and do not intend to join the debate over its precise meaning. Rather, for purposes of this study, I will use the term in the sense of Chief Justice Marshall's famous dictum in *Marbury v. Madison* that American government would cease to deserve the name of "a government of laws, and not of men," if its "laws furnish no remedy for the violation of a vested legal right."[6] The rule of law also requires that it guide its subjects in their affairs and that they understand

and comply with it. Officials as well as ordinary citizens should be subject to its dictates. Impartial instrumentalities of justice, including courts, should be available to enforce the law and should employ fair procedures. It may also be useful to keep in mind the observations of Richard H. Fallon:

> Perfectly realized, the Rule of Law would be rule: (i) in accordance with the originally intended and understood meaning of the directives of legitimate, democratically-accountable lawmaking authorities, (ii) cast in the form of intelligible rules binding on citizens, governmental officials, and judges alike, (iii) as identified and elucidated in any interpretive process guided by publicly accessible norms and characterized by reason-giving, and (iv) consistent with legitimate public purposes and sound, shared principles of political morality. When law, in the positivist sense, fails to satisfy any of these elements, the Rule of Law is less than completely realized, but still may (or may not) be more nearly approximated than it is scorned or abandoned.[7]

The United States has often proclaimed its support for the rule of law in international affairs.[8] In particular, at the close of World War II, when it was truly the "sole superpower," the United States engaged in strenuous efforts to create an international order based on legal principles. These efforts resulted in a post-World War II international system, still very much with us, that presupposed at every stage of its development a dominant power that would be essentially non-imperial, nonaggressive and committed to the proliferation of law-based international institutions.

The United States played the leading role in the creation of the United Nations and strongly supported the attempt in the United Nations Charter to reintroduce a system of collective security against aggression, one that improved upon the arrangements set forth in the Covenant of the League of Nations and that was based on a rule of law paradigm. It also strongly supported a veritable explosion of international organizations designed to encourage cooperation among member states to address a broad range of ills plaguing the world community. With the International Labor Organization serving as a forerunner, these international organizations included such specialized agencies of the United Nations as the Food and Agriculture Organization, the International Bank for Reconstruction and Development (World Bank), the International Civil Aviation Organization, the International Development Association (an affiliate of the World Bank), the International Fund for Agricultural Development, the International Finance Corporation (an affiliate of the World Bank), the International Maritime Organization, the International Telecommunication Union, the United Nations Educational, Scientific and Cultural Organization, the United Nations Industrial Development Organization, the Universal Postal Union, the World Health Organization, the

World Intellectual Property Organization, and the World Meteorological Organization. The United States also strongly supported the creation of two institutions that are not technically specialized agencies but are closely related to the United Nations: the General Agreement on Tariffs and Trade (succeeded in 1995 by the World Trade Organization) and the International Atomic Energy Agency. Some of these international organizations, such as the United Nations Educational, Scientific and Cultural Organization, primarily serve social welfare or cultural purposes rather than lawmaking or law-applying functions, but as we shall see in chapter 1 of this study, many of these institutions have significant lawmaking capability. Many other significant international organizations, such as the Organization of American States, the Organization for Security and Cooperation in Europe, and the Organization for Economic Cooperation and Development (OECD), have similarly enjoyed strong US support and participation. The United States was also early in accepting the so-called compulsory jurisdiction of the International Court of Justice (ICJ), the successor to the League of Nations Permanent Court of International Justice, whose jurisdiction the United States never recognized because it failed to join the League. To be sure, even as early as 1946, the United States had reservations about the ICJ and hedged its acceptance of the Court's jurisdiction with the disabling "Connally Reservation," which reserved to the United States rather than the Court the authority to determine whether a matter was essentially within the domestic jurisdiction of the United States and therefore outside the jurisdiction of the Court.

The very existence of the United States as *the* superpower was an indispensable element for its strong support of the rule of law concept in international affairs. As the predominant authority in world affairs, with a so-called "automatic majority" in the United Nations and overriding influence in other international institutions, the United States was in a position to ensure that the law would develop in a way acceptable to it and, to a considerable extent, that decisions taken regarding the interpretation and application of that law would be compatible with its interests. With the passage of time, however, the United States gradually began to lose the control it had over the international legal process. With the emergence of the Soviet Union as a key adversary, and the communist takeover in China, it became clear that the Security Council would not be able to maintain international peace and security through the collective security system envisaged by the drafters of the UN Charter because there would be no unanimity of view among the permanent members of the Council. Also, as the so-called "third world" states became a majority in the United Nations, a majority strongly influenced by Soviet views, US influence in the General Assembly sharply declined during the 1960s and

1970s to the point where that organ came to be regarded as a "dangerous place." Further, communist aggression in various parts of the world or state-sponsored acts of international terrorism sometimes resulted in unilateral action by the United States of questionable legality. In general the Cold War created numerous barriers to the rule of law in international affairs.

In the 1990s, with first the less aggressive foreign policy of Mikhail Gorbachev's Soviet Union, and then the dissolution of the Soviet Union and the rollback of communist control in eastern and central Europe, the situation changed dramatically. Now, it appeared, the rule of law international institutions, especially those created after World War II, would be able to function in the manner envisaged by their creators. The high point of this optimism, perhaps, was the performance of the Security Council in response to Iraq's invasion of Kuwait in 1990, when the Council adopted numerous resolutions demanding that Iraq withdraw from Kuwait and ultimately authorized the use of force by coalition forces to force a withdrawal and imposed an unprecedented cease-fire regime on Iraq. This optimism was soon dispelled, however, as UN efforts with respect to keeping the peace in Bosnia-Herzegovina, Somalia, and Kosovo, among others, ran into extreme difficulties.

For its part, during the 1990s and early in the new millennium, the United States has found itself in uncharted territory. While proudly proclaiming itself the "sole surviving superpower," the United States has experienced a "power shift" that has resulted in a significant loss of autonomy and its sharing power with a variety of nongovernmental actors.[9] Moreover, as Samuel P. Huntington has noted, "[t]he settlement of key international issues [including, of course, legal issues] requires action by the single superpower but always with some combination of other major states."[10] The United States, however, has often acted more or less unilaterally, with the result being that:

> On issue after issue, the United States has found itself increasingly alone, with one or a few partners, opposing most of the world's states and peoples. These issues include UN dues; sanctions against Cuba, Iran, Iraq, and Libya; the land mines treaty; global warming; an international war crimes tribunal; the Middle East; the use of force against Iraq and Yugoslavia; and the targeting of 35 countries with new economic sanctions between 1993 and 1996.[11]

For these and a host of other reasons the United States has found it increasingly difficult to adhere to the rule of law in international affairs. This study explores these reasons. The primary goal of the study is *not* to search out cases where the United States violated its international obligations, much less to make a case that the United States has been an international outlaw. Rather, such cases are examined only to the extent that they are illustrative of wide-ranging difficulties standing in the way of US adherence to the rule of law. A primary focus of the study is on reasons for the declining US support for the rule of law institutions it was instrumental in creating and on US unwillingness to support new initiatives in international law enjoying the support of most other members of the world community.

As a first step toward understanding why the United States has deviated from the rule of law concept in international affairs, chapter 1 considers the nature of international law and international institutions. These differ markedly from the law of the United States and from US institutions. For example, there is no legislative body in the international arena. The UN General Assembly has no authority to bind its members except with respect to budgetary and internal matters. By contrast, the UN Security Council, if it finds a threat to or a breach of the peace, has the authority to adopt resolutions that member states are bound to carry out, but this authority is limited in scope and has recently been exercised in a questionable manner. Unlike that of the US Supreme Court, the jurisdiction of the International Court of Justice depends on the mutual consent of the states parties to the dispute, and the Court has played a modest, although sometimes highly controversial, role in international affairs.

The nature of law in the international arena also differs greatly from its domestic counterpart. Treaties, the first primary source of international law, create binding obligations for those countries that become parties to them, but their terms are often ambiguous, and, more often than not, they contain no requirement that parties to a dispute over their interpretation or implementation refer the dispute to a court or some other dispute settlement mechanism for a binding resolution. To be sure, most contracts governed by national law contain no such requirement either. But in national legal orders, especially in that of the United States, there is a court system available for the resolution of contractual disputes, and one whose jurisdiction is not necessarily dependent on the consent of all parties to the dispute.

Customary international law, the second primary source of international law, is by definition unwritten and the product of interactions between countries undertaken with a sense of legal obligation. With the advent of over 190 countries ("states") constituting the international community, the process whereby customary international law is created has arguably become unwieldy, and debate over what degree of agreement among states is necessary to constitute a norm of customary international law has been sharp. Some decisions of international tribunals based primarily on the interpretation and application of alleged norms of customary international law – such as the decision of the International Court of Justice in *Nicaragua v. United States* holding that the United States had violated various norms of customary international law – have been highly criticized.

Finally, chapter 1 examines how the nature of international law has changed dramatically during the last few decades. Ironically, perhaps, one of the reasons why the United States has found it increasingly difficult to adhere to the rule of law in international affairs has been the explosive increase in the scope of international law. With the "globalization" of the world economy, and the externalization of matters that once were considered to be purely national, international law now applies to many subjects and fields of law – such as criminal law, environmental law, family law, the jurisdiction and judicial procedures of US courts, human rights, and economic, political, and social activities of states in the United States – that previously were regulated mostly or even solely by domestic law. Partly in response to the greatly expanded scope of international law, new international legal institutions – the World Trade Organization, ad hoc and permanent international criminal tribunals, and the Law of the Sea Tribunal – have been created, or existing international legal institutions – the United Nations, the International Court of Justice, the World Bank, and the International Monetary Fund – have become more active and have assumed greater responsibilities. As a result of this emergence of international law and international legal institutions, new actors have demanded, and have often been granted, the right to participate in their development. Besides the governments of the many states that have been created with the end of colonialism and the collapse of the Soviet Union and of Yugoslavia, these new actors have included transnational or multinational corporations, nongovernmental organizations (NGOs), prominent individuals, and state governments in the United States. On numerous occasions these new actors have had interests contrary to the official position of the US government, and at times they have worked assiduously and successfully in international conferences to bring about a final product that the United States has opposed. Recent examples include the statute for a permanent international criminal court and the treaty banning land mines.

Under the dualist approach long favored by the United States, international law and domestic US law are two entirely separate legal systems and each operates independently of the other. In accordance with the dualist approach international law becomes part of and is applied by the US legal system only to the extent that it is incorporated into the US legal system. Accordingly, chapter 2 of this study considers the status of international law under US law.

As chapters 1 and 2 attempt to demonstrate, the ambiguity of international law, its greatly expanded scope of coverage, its unsettled status as the law of the land, and the difficulty in invoking it in US courts as a constraint on the actions of the US government all undermine the likelihood that the United States will adhere to the rule of law in international affairs.

Besides the great expansion in the scope of international law, another recent development that has had a profound impact on US adherence to the rule of law in international affairs is the collapse of the Soviet Union. This has left the United States as the "sole remaining superpower" and has encouraged an attitude of triumphalism that has irritated the governments of other countries and may have undermined US initiatives toward the development of international law and policy. Accompanying this triumphalism and closely related to it is an attitude of "exceptionalism," that is, that the United States bears special burdens and is entitled to special privileges because of its status as the sole surviving superpower. The collapse of the Soviet Union has also brought about a recrudescence of US provincialism and isolationism as well as of a preference to act unilaterally rather than multilaterally. In short, certain attitudes currently characteristic of the US policy stand in the way of US support of the rule of law in international affairs.

US triumphalism, exceptionalism, and provincialism are especially well illustrated by the position taken by the executive branch and by Congress on the recently concluded statute for a permanent international criminal court. Although President Bill Clinton and other members of his administration had professed support for the creation of a permanent international criminal court, during the deliberations on the draft statute for a permanent international criminal court at the Rome Conference in the summer of 1998, it became clear that under no circumstances was the United States willing to contemplate that US soldiers or private citizens would be tried before such a court. In support of this position US executive representatives argued that because only the United States had global responsibilities for maintaining the peace, it could not risk subjecting its troops to possible politically motivated prosecution before a permanent international criminal court of uncertain integrity. For their part members of Congress decried the failure of the Court's Statute to incorporate all of the protections of the US Bill of Rights, although in practice the alternative to prosecution before the international criminal court would likely be a trial before an adversary's military tribunals, where protection of the rights of defendants would be utterly lacking, rather than trial before a US court or military tribunal. As we shall see in chapter 8, for its part the Bush administration has waged a "holy war" against the Court.

Similarly, the United States cited its responsibilities for the defense of South Korea and for maintaining the peace in refusing to become a party to the Convention on the Prohibition of the Use, Stockpiling, Production and Transfer of Anti-Personnel Mines and Their Destruction (the Landmines Treaty). It did so despite the publication of a full-page advertisement in the *New York Times* containing an open letter by General Norman Schwarzkopf and fourteen other retired generals and admirals stating that anti-personnel land mines were not essential to military effectiveness and the safety of US forces in South Korea. Primarily because of strenuous efforts by NGOs, 122 nations ultimately found the US arguments unconvincing and agreed to ban a weapon that previously most states had viewed as an essential part of their military inventory.

Most striking are US actions or inactions that undermine the integrity of international institutions that the United States was instrumental in creating. The US failure to pay its UN dues, despite a clear international obligation to do so, is perhaps the best-known example. Another example is the withdrawal by the United States from the proceedings in *Nicaragua v. United States* before the International Court of Justice after it lost the jurisdictional phase of the case.

As noted above, the availability and use of impartial instrumentalities of justice, including courts, is an indispensable component of the rule of law.

As we shall see in this study, there are increasing signs of rebellion at the US state level against the limitations of international law. For example, various states have enacted or threatened to enact rules imposing economic sanctions on foreign countries that displease them or on individuals or businesses that do business with such countries. In response, some of our closest allies have threatened to challenge these rules through the World Trade Organization's dispute settlement mechanism. Most strikingly, the collapse of OECD negotiations on a draft multilateral agreement on investment came about in part because of concerns that the agreement would disrupt state and local lawmaking capacity.[12]

Paradoxically, as Robert Keohane has observed, foreign policy considerations may counsel against US compliance with international law.[13] A reputation for compliance with international law is not necessarily the best means, and certainly not the only means, for accomplishing certain foreign policy objectives. States can also benefit from a reputation for toughness or even for irrationality or unpredictability. Powerful states, like the United States, are less likely than most to pay a high price when they violate international law, so they may conclude that they would do better by violating international law when doing so shows that they will retaliate against threats to national security. These and other attitudes that hinder US adherence to the rule of law in international affairs will be highlighted throughout this study.

With chapter 3 the focus of this study shifts from an overview of the nature of law and legal process in international affairs and of the treatment of international law in the domestic legal order of the United States to a detailed examination of some salient examples of US difficulties with the rule of law in international affairs. Chapter 3 begins with the US refusal to pay its UN dues. Subsequent chapters address the following subjects and US difficulties in adhering to the rule of law with respect to them: the use of force (ch. 4), arms control, disarmament, and nonproliferation (ch. 5), the law of the sea (ch. 6), the International Court of Justice (ch. 7), the prevention, prosecution, and punishment of international crimes (ch. 8), and human rights and international environmental issues (ch. 9). The final chapter includes a summary and conclusions, and some possible future scenarios (ch. 10).

A major challenge throughout this study will be how to assess the likely impact of the September 11, 2001, bombing of the World Trade Center and the Defense Department (Pentagon) on US attitudes towards the rule of law in international affairs. With President George W. Bush's declaration of a "war" on terrorism, the United States strenuously engaged in efforts to build a coalition of states to support its measures against terrorism, including the use of force in Afghanistan or other states deemed to be sponsors of terrorism. To this end the US House of Representatives voted to release $582 million that the United States owes in back dues to the United Nations, in part because "[t]he UN is the world's premier forum and will be one of the primary theaters for US diplomacy on this matter."[14] Prior to September 11, a bill to release the funds had been blocked in the House for reasons we shall explore in chapter 3. There have been and are likely to be other changes in US policy, having implications for the rule of law in international affairs, flowing from the events of September 11.

One caveat. It is my hope that both the trained international lawyer and a wider readership will benefit from this study. As a consequence, some parts of it may be of more immediate interest to some readers than to others. Thus some may wish to skim descriptions of the international legal process and concentrate instead on those sections that suggest how changes in and challenges to the international legal process have compounded the difficulties the United States has had in adhering to the rule of law model. Conversely, others may not be interested in the occasional technical or theoretical discussions, although I have tried to keep these to a minimum.

Notes

1. Philip Allott, *The True Function of Law in the International Community*, 5 IND. J. GLOBAL LEGAL STUD., 391, 392 (1998).
2. Bell v. Maryland, 378 US 226, 346 (1964) (Black, J., dissenting).
3. Remarks by the Under Secretary of State for Global Affairs, Frank E. Loy, at the Vice President's Conference on Corruption, Organization of American States, Washington, D.C., February 25, 1999, at 2, US Dept. of State Listserver, *at* UO9885@UICVM.UIC.edu.
4. Richard H. Fallon, Jr., *"The Rule of Law" as a Concept in Constitutional Discourse*, 97 COLUM. L. REV. 1 (1997).
5. Morton J. Horwitz, *The Rule of Law: An Unqualified Human Good?*, 86 YALE LJ 561, 566 (1977).
6. Marbury v. Madison, 5 US (1 Cranch) 137, 163 (1803).
7. Fallon, *supra* note 4, at 38.
8. Remarks made by President George H. W. Bush to a joint session of Congress in September 1990 in the wake of the coalition's victory over Iraqi forces in the Gulf offer a recent and prominent example. At that time President Bush said that a new world was emerging, "a world where the rule of law supplants the rule of the jungle. A world in which nations recognize the shared responsibility for freedom and justice. A world where the strong respect the rights of the weak . . . America and the world must support the rule of law. And we will." Transcript of President's Address to Joint Session of Congress, NY TIMES, Sept. 12, 1990, at A20. See also Excerpts from President's News Conference on Gulf Crisis, NY TIMES, Aug. 31, 1990, at A11.
9. See Jessica T. Mathews, *Power Shift*, FOREIGN AFF., Jan.–Feb. 1997, at 50.
10. Samuel P. Huntington, *The Lonely Superpower*, FOREIGN AFF., March–April 1999, at 35, 36.
11. *Id.* at 41.
12. For an extensive discussion of this issue, see Robert Stumberg, *Sovereignty by Subtraction: The Multilateral Agreement on Investment*, 31 CORNELL INT'L LJ 491 (1998).
13. Robert O. Keohane, *International Relations and International Law: Two Optics*, 38 HARV. INT'L LJ 487 (1997).
14. See statement of Representative Tom Lantos, quoted in Lizette Alvarez, *House Approves $582 Million for Back Dues Owed to U.N.*, NY TIMES, Sept. 25, 2001, at A8, col. 1.

1 Law and legal process in international affairs

"And now for something completely different"
Lead-in to each program in the *Monty Python* BBC television series

Law and legal process in international affairs are truly "something completely different" from their counterparts in domestic legal orders, especially, perhaps, that of the United States. One seldom finds, for example, allegations that what is called law in domestic societies is not really "law" but rather only "positive morality" giving rise to at most "political obligations."[1] By contrast, such allegations are frequently advanced with respect to international law. Prior to assuming his present position, John R. Bolton, currently US Under Secretary of State for Arms Control and International Security, claimed that treaties are "'law' only for US domestic purposes. In their international operation, treaties are simply 'political' obligations."[2]

In response Robert F. Turner, Associate Director of the Center for National Security Law at the University of Virginia Law School, refuted Bolton's claim with the following observations:

How do we know that international treaty commitments are legally binding? Because every single one of the 185 [now 191] states that are members of the United Nations, and every single one of the few states that are not, acknowledge that fact. Article 26 of the Vienna Convention on the Law of Treaties recognizes the fundamental and historic principle of *pacta sunt servanda*: "Every treaty in force is binding upon the parties to it and must be performed by them in good faith."

To be sure, like some of our own citizens, members of the international community of states do on occasion violate their legal obligations. But when they do, they never assert that treaty commitments are merely non-binding "political" undertakings. Stalin, Hitler, Kim II Sung, Gadhafi and Saddam Hussein all either denied the allegations against them, pretended that their acts of flagrant international aggression were really in "self-defense" to a prior attack by their victims, or proffered some other legal basis for their conduct. Not one of them asserted that treaties were "not binding," because they realized that no country would accept such a patently spurious assertion – it simply would not pass the straight-face test.[3]

The issue of whether international law really is "law" has been discussed extensively in other forums,[4] and will be addressed further from time to time throughout this study. At this point it is simply worth noting that the skepticism regarding the binding nature of international law expressed by John Bolton reflects a view held by other members of the US foreign policy elite. Even for those who recognize that international law creates legal and not just "political" obligations, there are some in positions of power who attach such low importance to treaty and other international legal obligations that they believe that they can and should be trumped by our perception of our national self-interest whenever the need arises. Such views constitute a primary reason why the United States has difficulty in adhering to the rule of law in international affairs.

Although international law has undergone dramatic changes in recent years, it is still primarily law that governs relations between nations or states. Moreover, international law is created primarily through interactions between the states themselves, resulting in tacit agreement that certain state practices are to be undertaken, or to be refrained from, as a matter of legal obligation or according to written international agreements setting forth the rights and obligations of the parties. Because the rules of international law are created by sovereign independent states, and therefore normally cannot be enforced through the kind of coercive measures available in domestic legal orders, those who follow the positivist school of jurisprudence and define law as the commands of a sovereign backed by the threat of coercive measures, including the use of armed force, deny that there can be law governing sovereign states. Skeptics also argue that there can be no international law because there is no international legislature to make it, no international executive to enforce it, and no effective international judiciary to interpret it and resolve disputes about it. However, as we shall see, the positivists' definition of law is arguably too narrow and dysfunctional as an approach to understanding how nations behave with respect to law.

Be that as it may, there is no question that international law and the international legal process differ substantially from their domestic counterparts, although, as we shall see, these differences are becoming less pronounced. This chapter turns first to the kinds or "sources" of international law and the methodology of its creation. Then it examines how international law is interpreted and applied in practice. It concludes with a discussion of compliance (or its lack) with international law. Throughout the chapter some of the dramatic changes that have recently occurred in international law and institutions, and the implications of these changes for US adherence to the rule of law in international affairs, are examined.

The "sources" of international law

The classic statement of the "sources" or kinds of international law is set forth in Article 38 of the Statute of the International Court of Justice (ICJ):

1. The Court, whose function is to decide in accordance with international law such disputes as are submitted to it, shall apply:
   a. international conventions, whether general or particular, establishing rules expressly recognized by the contesting states;
   b. international custom, as evidence of a general practice accepted as law;
   c. the general principles of law recognized by civilized nations;
   d. subject to the provisions of Article 59 [which provides that decisions of the Court have no binding force except between the parties to the dispute], judicial decisions and the teachings of the most qualified publicists of the nations, as subsidiary means for the determination of rules of law.
2. This provision shall not prejudice the power of the Court to decide a case *ex aequo et bono*, if the parties agree thereto.[5]

By way of elaboration Section 102 of the Restatement (Third) of the Foreign Relations Law of the United States provides with respect to the sources of international law:

1. A rule of international law is one that has been accepted as such by the international community of states:
   a. in the form of customary law;
   b. by international agreement; or
   c. by derivation from general principles common to the major legal systems of the world.
2. Customary international law results from a general and consistent practice of states followed by them from a sense of legal obligation.
3. International agreements create law for the states parties thereto and may lead to the creation of customary international law when such agreements are intended for adherence by states generally and are in fact widely accepted.
4. General principles common to the major legal systems, even if not incorporated or reflected in customary law or international agreement, may be invoked as supplementary rules of international law where appropriate.

From an examination of the Court's Statute and the Restatement's elaboration, one may conclude that states are both the creators and the primary subjects of international law. As revealed in these two authorities, it is the "will" of states, manifested in their practices accepted as law and in their international agreements, that creates the law. In domestic legal systems (at least those of a democratic nature) it is the legislature that is the primary lawmaking institution. By contrast, no such legislature exists at the international level, although, as we shall see later in this chapter, international law does possess institutions and procedures for generating new rules of law, not only by multilateral treaty making, but also by institutions with specialized rule-making competence. Moreover, subject to a few possible exceptions, and contrary to domestic legislation applicable to individuals, international law does not appear to bind states that have played no role in its creation through the ratification of a treaty or engaging in state practice accepted as law. One must be cautious, however, in accepting sweeping generalizations about international law and the international legal process, because almost any general statement that one might make is usually subject to arguable exceptions. Moreover, the Court's Statute and the Restatement's elaboration are at best an introduction to an understanding of the international legal process. With this point in mind we turn to a consideration of the most ambiguous and controversial source of international law, customary practices of states accepted as law.

Customary international law

As we shall see, dramatic changes in the nature of international relations have made the process of creating customary international law particularly problematic. Nonetheless, it is useful to begin our consideration with the classic description by Manley O. Hudson, a judge on the International Court of Justice and an eminent authority on international law, of the essential elements of the customary international law process:

1. concordant practice by a number of States with reference to a type of situation falling within the domain of international relations;
2. continuation or repetition of the practice over a considerable period of time;
3. conception that the practice is required by, or consistent with, prevailing international law; and
4. general acquiescence in the practice by other States.[6]

When this description of the customary international law process was published (1950), the United Nations had sixty member states. The international legal process, including the actions of the United Nations, was dominated by Western states, particularly the United States. Many of the states now constituting the third world were under colonial rule, and the Soviet Union had relatively little influence in the United Nations and other international institutions. Hence the number of states that had to engage in a concordant practice as part of the customary international law practice were relatively few. Today, by contrast, there are 191 member states of the United Nations and close to 200 states in the world community, and these states have raised a serious challenge to the dominance of the international legal process by the West. As a result, it is now by no means clear how many states must participate to constitute the number required by Manley Hudson.

Moreover, there is no agreement on what constitutes state practice.[7] The US Department of State emphasizes the acts of governments but not UN resolutions. This approach supports the claims of states, such as the United States, with strong centralized governments. In contrast, some scholars and less powerful states would include as state practice normative statements in drafts of the International Law Commission (ILC), resolutions of the UN General Assembly and recitals in international instruments.[8] If statements such as those found in General Assembly resolutions adopted by majority vote can alone create international law, the less powerful states can play a strong if not dominant role in the process of creating customary international law. By contrast, as noted by J. Patrick Kelly, the "'acts-only' jurisprudence gives lawmaking authority to the more powerful states while disenfranchising other members of the world community."[9] To be sure, smaller and weaker states may also by their conduct and pronouncements shape international law, but often lack the economic, political, or military resources to act effectively. The "acts-only" jurisprudence, however, favored by the United States, is increasingly under attack.

It is noteworthy that Article 38 of the ICJ's Statute, set forth above, in paragraph 1(d) treats judicial decisions and the writings of scholars not as sources of international law but rather as "subsidiary means for the determination of rules of law." Although the Restatement (Third) of the Foreign Relations Law of the United States and some scholars would ascribe considerable importance to the decisions of domestic courts, others have argued that decisions of domestic courts are of minimal value in determining customary international law because the judges of such courts generally lack the knowledge and expertise to do so or reflect a parochial view supporting the political position of the country's executive branch.[10] They also would argue that domestic court decisions cannot constitute state practice but only opinions about the existence of customary international law.[11]

The same may be said about international judicial and arbitral decisions, including ICJ decisions. To be sure, all would concede that ICJ decisions carry great weight, but the Court lacks the authority to create customary international law. Nonetheless, some commentators have claimed that the ICJ has increasingly assumed a law-creating role.[12]

Although Article 38(1)(d) of the ICJ's Statute refers to the writings of scholars only as "subsidiary means for the determination of rules of law," because of evidentiary difficulties in determining the state practice and *opinio juris* components of customary international law, it is clear that prominent international law scholars exert a quite extraordinary influence upon decision makers in the customary international law process. Louis Sohn, an eminent international law authority, has even gone so far as to suggest, not entirely facetiously, that: "This is the way international law is made, not by states, but by 'silly' professors writing books, and by knowing where there is a good book on the subject."[13] In the same vein, it is worth noting that, at the time the US Constitution was written, domestic law, both in the United States and elsewhere, was determined largely by reference to the writings of scholars, with Blackstone being a conspicuous example.

According to Manley Hudson's approach, state practice – however defined and engaged in by however many states – must continue and be repeated over a considerable period of time. For its part, the ICJ has stated that: "Although the passage of only a short period of time is not necessarily . . . a bar to the formulation of a new rule of customary international law . . . State practice . . . should have been both extensive and virtually uniform."[14] It has also been suggested that the time period necessary may be shorter if there is no conflicting state practice and the proposed rule does not overturn existing rules.[15]

Other commentators have contended that Hudson's formulation reflects a time when international life was slower and communication primitive and that today custom may be formed rapidly because "every event of international importance is universally and immediately known."[16] According to Anthony D'Amato, "[t]his argument suggests a communications factor in custom, reminiscent of Mateesco's observation that in France a custom had to be 'notorious' in order to be valid. The idea of communication or notice indeed may be more basic to custom than the mere fact of duration."[17] Some commentators have gone so far as to suggest that there can be "instant" customary international law,[18] at least if there is close to unanimity among states that a particular rule is necessary and there is no state practice to the contrary.[19] It is worth noting, however, that the concept of "instant" customary international law has not been generally accepted by government officials of states, and would give a substantial measure of legislative power to such international organizations as the United Nations that has not been adopted in their constitutive charters or to international conferences with nearly universal participation by states. At the same time it should be noted that the Internet makes it much easier to find sources of international law and to determine state practice.

Also, there are some arguable counter-examples to the generalization that states have not accepted the concept of instant customary international law. One thinks, for example, of the Declaration of Legal Principles

Governing the Activities of States in the Exploration and Uses of Outer Space,[20] unanimously adopted by the UN General Assembly in 1963, which calls for all states to refrain from introducing weapons of mass destruction in outer space. To be sure, the Declaration was followed by the Assembly's adoption in 1967 of the Treaty on Principles Governing the Activities of States in the Exploration and Use of Outer Space, Including the Moon and Other Celestial Bodies,[21] which bans "nuclear weapons or any other kinds of weapons of mass destruction" anywhere in space. But there is considerable evidence that states had fully already accepted this obligation at the time the Declaration was adopted. Oscar Schachter has suggested that "instant custom" is "an unfortunate phrase which sounds self-contradictory and may be misleading. The fact remains that several resolutions have asserted rules or principles of general international law when practice was negligible or inconclusive and these resolutions have been regarded as sufficient evidence of the legal character of the norm asserted."[22] The concept of "instant custom" remains controversial, however.

Parenthetically, it should also be noted that some General Assembly declarations are regarded as definitive interpretations of certain provisions of the UN Charter. Perhaps the most authoritative example is the 1970 Declaration on Principles of International Law concerning Friendly Relations and Co-operation among States in accordance with the Charter of the United Nations (Friendly Relations Declaration).[23] Other, more controversial, examples include the General Assembly's "Definition of Aggression" resolution[24] and the Universal Declaration of Human Rights.[25]

Hudson's requirements that states engage in a practice with an understanding that it is required by, or consistent with, prevailing international law and that there be general acquiescence in the practice by other states raises the complex issue of *opinio juris*, which is the general acceptance of a norm as a legal obligation by the world community. The concept of *opinio juris* introduces a subjective element in the customary international law process because it requires that states when engaging in or refraining from a particular practice do so under an understanding that they have a legal right to engage in the practice or a legal obligation to refrain from engaging in the practice. For example, it is generally accepted that states have the right, subject to a few exceptions, to exercise jurisdiction over persons and property within their territorial boundaries, but are under an international obligation not to commit acts of genocide.

In many, perhaps most, instances of alleged customary international law norms, however, there may be little clear evidence that the vast majority of states have accepted the norm as a legal obligation.[26] With respect to the methodological problem of determining *opinio juris*, D'Amato has suggested that, as a requirement for a finding of *opinio juris*, an objective claim of international legality be articulated in advance of, or concurrently with, the state practice allegedly required or permitted by customary international law.[27] Interestingly, under D'Amato's approach, the articulation of a claim of legality could be made by either a state, a recognized writer, or a court.[28] To Kelly, however, this "'claims approach' defines away the requirement of the normative conviction of the community."[29] Moreover, D'Amato concedes that it is not possible to determine if a majority of states are conscious of any international obligation.[30]

The persistent objector rule holds that a state that persistently objects during the process of formation can opt out of an otherwise generally applicable rule of customary international law. US support for this proposition contrasts sharply with its insistence that new states are fully bound by customary law as new members of the world community. Kelly suggests that the persistent objector principle is a new concept and "one of doubtful pedigree."[31]

According to Kelly, there was no recognition of a persistent objector principle until recently. On the contrary, in the late nineteenth century and throughout the twentieth century Latin American nations were considered bound by customary international law, including the disputed law of state responsibility, despite continuous objections by a large number of states. But then, according to Kelly:

> In the 1960s and early 1970s, as the newly independent nations became a majority at the UN General Assembly, Western states began to lose control of the development of customary law regimes such as that of the territorial sea and the protection of foreign investment. Using democratic theory, the nonaligned nations challenged the Western control of the international legal process. The notion of the persistent objector can be seen as the Western counter-reformation to this revolution. The Reporter of the Restatement, after consulting with a State Department critical of the ICJ after the *Nicaragua* case, adopted the persistent objector principle for the first time.[32]

Despite the position of the US government and the Restatement, Kelly contends that the persistent objector principle is not a norm of customary international law because there is no evidence that non-Western states have accepted "this fundamental change in the structure of international law."[33] There has been substantial scholarly debate on this subject, and the status of the persistent objector principle in international law is uncertain.[34]

The issue of how customary international law can be changed is of substantial significance to the United States and other member states of the world community. D'Amato has suggested that the "only way customary international law can change – and it certainly has changed significantly in the practice of states over the centuries – is by giving legal effect to departures from preceding customary norms . . . In particular, an 'illegal' act by a state contains the seeds of a new legality."[35] As noted further by D'Amato, "[u]nder the classical theory, change was impossible because each deviation was illegal, and hence there could be no *opinio juris* (no conviction that the actor was acting in conformity with existing law)."[36] It is unclear, however, precisely how and when the illegal "seed" blossoms into a new legality. Moreover, the process suggested by D'Amato would seem to ensure extensive illegal activity by states seeking to change the law, and this may have serious consequences for the rule of law in international affairs. At the least it would seem important to distinguish between state acts that amount simply to illegal behavior and state practice undertaken as part of an articulated challenge to existing law.

Another, less controversial, way to change customary international law is for states to conclude an international agreement. Unless a norm of customary international law has the status of a peremptory norm (*jus cogens*), from which no deviation is permitted, states may agree among themselves to opt out of acceptance of the norm or to change it in relations between them. Initially, the agreement between the parties may only bind them and have no wider significance. If a large number of states enter into bilateral agreements, or more likely conclude a multilateral agreement that is widely ratified, the act of ratification arguably constitutes a form of state practice that also contains the indispensable element of *opinio juris*, since the parties have chosen to incorporate the norm in a binding legal instrument.[37]

To be sure, not all provisions in treaties are potential norms of customary international law. Rather, the provisions must be "generalizable" to states that are not parties to the treaties. D'Amato cites a "most-favored-nation" provision as an example of a non-generalizable provision, pointing out that if this provision were generalized, it would give most-favored-nation status to all nations, which would destroy the intended meaning of the provision.[38]

As D'Amato has noted, treaties have become the preferred means of creating customary international law in recent years,[39] and the United States has been an enthusiastic participant in the treaty-making process. There is, however, substantial dispute over whether norms in particular bilateral and multilateral treaties are also norms of customary international law. Moreover, in the case of some widely ratified multilateral treaties which the United States has actively participated in negotiating but which it has not ratified, the United States has cited provisions in these treaties it strongly supports as representing customary international law. The Vienna Convention on the Law of Treaties and the Law of the Sea

Convention are prominent examples. US attempts to "pick and choose" among provisions in these two conventions have sometimes been strongly resisted by states parties to the conventions.

Although it is debatable whether *jus cogens*, or the concept of a peremptory norm, is a form of customary international law or rather a form of natural law,[40] there is substantial authority for the proposition that it is a form of customary international law and therefore deserves attention in this section of the chapter.[41] However classified, *jus cogens* is a highly problematic and controversial doctrine that raises substantial problems for the rule of law in international affairs.

In negotiations on the Vienna Convention on the Law of Treaties, the United States opposed incorporating the concept of a peremptory norm in the draft treaty prepared by the International Law Commission.[42] According to Richard D. Kearney and Robert E. Dalton, who represented the United States in negotiations on the Convention, there was little debate regarding the concept of *jus cogens*.[43] The problem was rather how to define the test for recognizing a rule of *jus cogens* and whether the Convention should identify examples of peremptory norms. It proved impossible to agree on examples of peremptory norms. Article 53 of the Convention, however, provides:

> A treaty is void if, at the time of its conclusion, it conflicts with a peremptory norm of general international law. For the purposes of the present Convention, a peremptory norm of general international law is a norm accepted and recognized by the international community of States as a whole as a norm from which no derogation is permitted and which can be modified only by a subsequent norm of general international law having the same character.

As a corollary to Article 53, Article 64 of the Convention provides:

> If a new peremptory norm of general international law emerges, any existing treaty which is in conflict with that norm becomes void and terminates.

The definition of a peremptory norm in Article 53 of the Convention leaves unclear the process whereby it is determined whether the international community of states as a whole has accepted and recognized a particular norm as being one from which no derogation is permitted. Indeed, the problems of identifying state practice and *opinio juris* as part of the process of creating a "normal" norm of customary international law, discussed above, would seem to loom especially large if one is attempting to identify a "supernorm" of international law from which no derogation is possible.

The failure of the drafters of the Vienna Convention on the Law of Treaties to agree on a list of *jus cogens* norms has not been followed by any greater success on the part of state representatives in other forums. For its part, the International Court of Justice, in *Nicaragua v. United States*, asserted that the international prohibition on the use of force was "a conspicuous example in a rule of international law having the character of *jus cogens*."[44] But as D'Amato has pointed out, the opinion in the *Nicaragua* case gives no indication as to how the judges reached this conclusion.[45]

The United States ultimately agreed to the inclusion of Articles 53 and 64 in the Vienna Convention. In doing so, however, it insisted that claims of *jus cogens* be subject to adjudication by the International Court of Justice or to arbitration, as provided in Article 66 of the Convention.[46] The United States has not become a party to the Vienna Convention. Accordingly, the procedures of Article 66 cannot be invoked either by or against the United States. Moreover, as pointed out by the Restatement (Third) of the Foreign Relations Law of the United States, although the principles of Articles 53 and 64 arguably are effective as customary international law, "there are no safeguards against their abuse. In such circumstances, the United States is likely to take a particularly restrictive view of these doctrines."[47]

Assuming that all "important elements" of the world community agree on a peremptory norm – say, the prohibition against genocide – it appears problematic at best that it would ever be possible (assuming, as is unlikely, a desire to do so) to change or get rid of it. Any attempt to do so by treaty would presumably be void *ab initio*, and the likelihood of all important elements of the world community ever agreeing to change a norm previously thought to enjoy *jus cogens* status is highly improbable.

Another kind of "supernorm" provision is found in Article 103 of the UN Charter, which declares that:

> In the event of a conflict between the obligations of Members of the United Nations under the present Charter and their obligations under any other international agreement, their obligations under the present Charter shall prevail.

There is disagreement among the commentators whether treaties contrary to the Charter are null and void as they would be if contrary to a *jus cogens* norm, or only suspended in effect because of their incompatibility with the Charter.[48]

As to the process of creating customary international law, there is substantial debate and disagreement among the scholars, and this debate often takes place at a high level of abstraction.[49] What is most striking, however, is that scholarly treatments of the subject usually cite the writings of scholars – both scholars from the United States and those from other countries – but not the pronouncements of governments.

Governments, it appears, have refrained from setting forth in detail their positions on the issues regarding the process of creating customary international law that animate the scholars and have made no effort to resolve these issues through negotiations in international forums. Rather, governments, including that of the United States, have been satisfied with contending as a matter of political rhetoric that a particular rule set forth in a treaty to which they are a party or in a nonbinding resolution of the United Nations is a norm of customary international law. Michael Reisman has noted that the Soviet Union defined the term "custom" for years to mean that it had to consent explicitly to the norms being prescribed, thus extending the veto power the Soviet Union enjoyed in the Security Council across the board. Although the United States resisted the Soviet position, Reisman points out, "now we have done them one better. We can stay in the world without the need for a veto and still have our way: We can use custom to get the international law we want without having to undergo the 'give' part of the 'give-and-take' of the legislative process."[50]

At this juncture it may be appropriate to consider the nature of the customary international law process, and its implications for the United States and the rule of law in international affairs. First, it is useful to note that most norms of customary international law are non-controversial, since they confirm power that states are already exercising and place few limits on state action.[51] These so-called "structural" or "constitutive" norms define and structure international relations and are empirically verifiable. Examples include international legal norms that sanction a state's dominion over its own territory, its people, the adjoining continental shelf, and its territorial sea, while imposing few limits on its sovereignty. Another example is the law of diplomatic immunity that provides a structural framework that facilitates communications between states and protects communicators from coercive pressures that might undermine their ability to perform. Immunity of diplomats from the exercise of civil and criminal jurisdiction by the receiving state is also necessary to promote stability in international relations.[52] Some have classified such norms as customary in nature, while others have suggested that they are an indispensable part of the concept of sovereignty or "associative norms" that are minimal conditions of membership in the world community.[53]

In contrast, substantive norms of liability or other rules that directly limit a state's sovereignty are much more controversial and problematic.[54] Many of these alleged norms, moreover, are strongly favored by the United States but equally strongly resisted, especially by non-Western states. Prominent examples include the standard of compensation for the expropriation of alien-owned property, the restrictive theory of foreign sovereign immunity, the requirement that a state ensure that activities within its territory do not cause harm to the environment of other states, and the Restatement's suggestion that a state may exercise jurisdiction over persons and property outside its territory only if such exercise would be reasonable under the circumstances.

Alleged customary norms of international human rights law pose especially perplexing problems for the United States. On the one hand, the United States actively promotes civil and political rights reflecting the Western tradition of individual rights against the state, but it rejects economic, social, and cultural rights based on a more communitarian or socialist set of values. Even with respect to the civil and political rights it promotes in other, especially non-Western countries, the United States resists any attempts to change US law to meet alleged international human rights requirements. More generally, as suggested by Kelly, it is arguable that, "[a]part from genocide and slavery, which are repugnant to any modern legal system, the civil, political, and social rights in the Universal Declaration of Human Rights reflect discrete cultural values that vary from country to country."[55] Hence it is debatable what norms found in the provisions of the Universal Declaration of Human Rights or the International Covenants on Civil and Political and on Economic, Social and Cultural Rights constitute general norms of customary international law in addition to binding treaty law for states parties.

The customary law of international human rights is perhaps the prime example of what some have called the "new customary international law." It is "new" in two senses. First, it governs relations between states and individuals as well as relations between states – the province of traditional customary international law – and second, at least according to some commentators, it would expand customary international law to include norms articulated in nonbinding resolutions adopted by international organizations, norms set forth in multilateral treaties ratified by substantially fewer than all states in the world community, and even norms widely espoused by international law scholars.[56] The United States has recently expressed its strong opposition to this approach. In 1994, the Human Rights Committee established to receive reports from states parties to the International Covenant on Civil and Political Rights on the steps they have taken to carry out their obligations under the Covenant issued its General Comment No. 24 on reservations to the Covenant.[57] According to the Committee, states parties to the Covenant may not make reservations to provisions therein that represent customary international law. Specifically, in the Committee's view,

> provisions in the Covenant that represent customary international law (and *a fortiori* when they have the character of peremptory norms) may not be the subject

of reservations. Accordingly, a State may not reserve the right to engage in slavery, to torture, to subject persons to cruel, inhuman or degrading treatment or punishment, to arbitrarily deprive persons of their lives, to arbitrarily arrest and detain persons, to deny freedom of thought, conscience and religion, to presume a person guilty unless he proves his innocence, to execute pregnant women or children, to permit the advocacy of national, racial or religious hatred, to deny to persons of marriageable age the right to marry, or to deny to minorities the right to enjoy their own culture, profess their own religion, or use their own language.[58]

The Committee's list of customary international law rights is far more expansive than the list set forth in Section 702 of the Restatement (Third) of the Foreign Relations Law of the United States and includes provisions to which the United States had submitted reservations (such as the duty to prohibit advocacy of national, racial, or religious hatred or to refrain from executing persons under eighteen years of age). Accordingly, the response of the United States was emphatic:

> The precise specification of what is contrary to customary international law . . . is a much more substantial question than indicated by the Comment[, which] asserts in wholly conclusory fashion that a number of propositions are customary international law which, to speak plainly, are not. It cannot be established on the basis of practice or other authority, for example, that the mere expression (albeit deplorable) of national, racial or religious hatred (unaccompanied by any overt action or preparation) is prohibited by customary international law . . . Similarly, while many are opposed to the death penalty in general and the juvenile death penalty in particular, the practice of States demonstrates that there is currently no blanket prohibition in customary international law. Such a cavalier approach to international law [raises] serious concerns about the methodology of the Committee as well as its authority.[59]

From the discussion so far in this section of the chapter, one may safely conclude that under present circumstances the customary international law process deviates in substantial measure from Richard Fallon's "perfectly realized" concept of the rule of law summarized in the Introduction to this study.[60] First, Fallon's requirement that the rule of law be rule "in accordance with the originally intended and understood meaning of the directives of legitimate, democratically-accountable lawmaking authorities" is hardly realized by a process increasingly characterized by debate over who the lawmaking authorities are and what acts constitute their directives. Similarly, as we have seen, in many instances the rules are unintelligible and it may be unclear whether they are binding on particular states. Also, the requirement that the rules be "identified and elucidated in any interpretive process guided by publicly accessible norms and characterized by reason-giving" is unfulfilled when much state practice is unavailable, only a few of the most developed states collect and publish their state practice, and, as we shall see later in this chapter, there is no generally accepted interpretive process. Finally, it is doubtful that customary rules of international law are "consistent with legitimate public purposes and sound, shared principles of political morality" when today's world is, in many instances, characterized by an absence of a broad base of shared values.

In short, the customary international law process fits uneasily at best within the rule of law paradigm. Whether it should therefore be discarded as a source of international law, as some have suggested,[61] is a debatable proposition.

Treaties

The primary method that the United States and other states have utilized as an alternative to the customary international law process for the creation of international law is the negotiation and conclusion of treaties. To be sure, the treaty-making process is "entangled" in various ways with customary international law. The binding effect of treaties depends on the doctrine of *pacta sunt servanda*, which was established through the customary international law process. Customary norms may serve to fill gaps in treaties and to guide the interpretive process. Treaties often have as their primary purpose the codification of customary norms. There is support for a general presumption that treaties are not intended to derogate from general custom – a presumption that prevails unless the terms of the treaty are clearly incompatible with it. Conversely, it is presumed that a treaty is not terminated or altered by subsequent custom in the absence of evidence that the parties had that intention. Subject to these presumptions of interpretation, the general rule is that treaties and custom have equal weight, with priority being accorded to the later in time. Also, certain kinds of treaties, especially multilateral treaties, may lay down broad rules of conduct for states generally and thereby serve as part of the customary international law process. In this respect they more closely resemble legislation rather than contracts on the national level. One must not stretch this analogy too far, however. Unlike legislators at the domestic level, the parties to a multilateral treaty cannot bind non-parties to the normative provisions in the treaty without their consent. Still, widespread ratification of certain kinds of multilateral treaties may constitute state practice and provide the *opinio juris* component of a norm of customary international law. In this case non-parties to such treaties may be bound by some of the norms they contain unless they object to them and do so persistently.

It is important to note that "treaties" are defined much more broadly for international law purposes than they are for purposes of US constitutional law. Under the US Constitution, the treaty process requires that the Senate advise and consent to ratification of the treaty by the president through a two-thirds vote of the senators present. As we shall see in chapter 2, it is unclear when, if ever, international agreements must be concluded in treaty form under the US Constitution, and in practice only a relatively small percentage of the international agreements entered into by the United States is submitted to the Senate for its advice and consent to ratification.

By contrast, at the international level the term "treaties" is highly inclusive. According to some prominent authorities, "[t]he term 'treaty' is used generally to cover the binding agreements between subjects of international law that are governed by international law."[62]

This definition, however, raises the question of what are the "subjects of international law" that are "governed by international law." In the *Anglo-Iranian Oil Co.* case[63] the International Court of Justice rejected a British contention that a contract signed between the Iranian government and the Anglo-Persian Oil Company, which was half-owned by the British government, had a "double character" of being both a concessionary contract between the government of Iran and the company and a treaty between the British and Iranian governments. According to the Court, the contract was nothing more than a concessionary contract between a government and a foreign corporation. In its dicta the Court implied that a treaty requires that two or more states become bound vis-à-vis each other.[64]

Parenthetically, it should be noted that a concessionary contract, or for that matter any contract between a government and a foreign corporation, could be "governed by international law" if a choice of law clause in the contract so provided. It would not follow, however, that the contract would thereby be transformed into a "treaty." There is no support in the jurisprudence of the International Court of Justice, and little to be found elsewhere, for the proposition that a corporation or an individual could be a party to a treaty, although they could be third-party beneficiaries of a treaty. On the other hand, it is clear that a "treaty" is not limited to an agreement concluded between two or more states. Decisions of the International Court of Justice, as well as other authoritative sources, have expanded the traditional definition of a treaty to include agreements between states and international organizations and between international organizations *inter se*. The modern definition also covers trilateral agreements involving two states and an international organization.[65]

The case for employing the treaty as the primary method of international lawmaking has been cogently presented by the late Richard Baxter, writing in 1970.

> As one looks at the present state of international law and attempts to see into the future, it should be quite clear that treaty law will increasingly gain paramountcy over customary international law. The treaty-making process is a rational and orderly one, permitting participation in the creation of law by all States on a basis of equity. Newly independent States, otherwise subject to a body of customary international law in the making of which they played no part, can influence the progressive development of the law or help to "codify" it in such a way as to make it more responsive to their needs and ideals. For the more established States, the codification process provides a welcome opportunity to secure widespread agreement upon norms which have hitherto been the subject of doubt or controversy or have been rejected by other States.
>
> Even in those cases in which customary international law is already clear and generally agreed upon, the treaty will strengthen that rule and simplify its application. Article 1 of the Chicago Convention confirms what is already agreed to be a State's sovereign right to exclude foreign aircraft from its airspace. The presence in bilateral treaties of a requirement of exhaustion of local remedies reminds us that the well-understood rule of customary international law has not lost its validity.[66]

As we shall see in later chapters of this study, however, the experience of the United States, especially in recent years, casts some doubt on the advantages of the treaty-making process set forth by Baxter. Specifically, the results of multilateral treaty making have often been unacceptable to the United States – either to the executive branch (the statute for a permanent international criminal court; the Landmines Treaty; initially the Law of the Sea Convention) or to the Senate (the Vienna Convention on the Law of Treaties; the Law of the Sea Convention; the Comprehensive Nuclear Test Ban Treaty) or to both. Moreover, the recent failure of the negotiations under the auspices of the Organization for Economic Cooperation and Development (OECD) to conclude a multilateral agreement on investment – an initiative strongly supported by the United States – came about largely because of strong opposition from various nongovernmental organizations and disagreements between the United States and other developed countries. The early expectation of the United States was that the OECD, a forum dominated by the developed countries, would be an appropriate place in which to conclude a multilateral agreement on investment and that the agreement concluded under OECD auspices could later be opened for accession by the developing countries. This in turn, it was hoped, would provide an opportunity to resolve the long-standing debate between the developed and developing world over the international norms governing foreign investment.

Not only has the United States been unwilling, rightly or wrongly, to become a party to a number of highly significant multilateral treaties, it is not clear that it has thereby avoided becoming bound by the norms set forth in these treaties. As Prosper Weil suggested in a notable article written in 1983, "in reality, the conventional norm itself may now create obligations incumbent upon all states, including those not parties to the convention in question."[67] Oscar Schachter, in commenting on Weil's analysis, has noted further:

> It is not only that non-parties become subject to rules they have not adhered to but also that the parties to a treaty may find themselves under obligations to non-parties in respect of the treaty rules. The mingling of treaty and custom may also be discerned in another respect – a tendency to consider treaty provisions as altered or superseded by State practice outside of the treaty itself.[68]

Schachter's and Weil's comments raise the issue, addressed earlier in this chapter, of US difficulties with the customary international law process. The relationship between treaty rules and norms of customary international law is especially complex and controversial. As Schachter has pointed out, there are three "well recognized" conditions under which a treaty rule may be considered as customary international law: "1) where the treaty rule is declaratory of pre-existing customary law; 2) where the treaty rule is found to have crystalized customary law in process of formation; 3) where the treaty rule has been found to have generated new customary law subsequent to its adoption."[69] Here, however, is where the agreement ends. Schachter summarizes the contending views:

> One view – probably a majority opinion – holds that all three conditions require proof of State practice and *opinio juris* outside of the application of the treaty in question. A different position – less precisely expressed – considers that in some circumstances the act of adopting the treaty and the ratifications and adherence of States constitute State practice and evidence of *opinio juris* for purposes of customary law. This would hold particularly for treaties of a declaratory character, but not only for them. A third view suggests that when a rule is included in a multilateral convention adopted at a conference of States and a number of interested States act in conformity with that rule and no States object to it, there is a strong presumption that the rule has become customary law, even though the treaty has not obtained the adherences necessary for its entry into force. A fourth position goes beyond this and maintains that an international conference of States, such as that on the Law of the Sea, may decide by consensus that treaty rules enshrine customary norms binding on states from the moment of their adoption by the conference.[70]

Under either the third or the fourth approaches summarized by Schachter, and perhaps the second as well, the United States could be subject to a wide variety of customary norms it found unacceptable in treaty form. Moreover, since it is debatable whether the persistent objector doctrine is part of general international law, it is unclear whether the United States would be able to avoid being bound by these norms.

On the other hand, as we have seen, the United States, having failed to become a party to such treaties as the Vienna Convention on the Law of Treaties and the Law of the Sea Convention, claims that provisions in these treaties of which it approves are also norms of customary international law. As Schachter has noted, "treaty and custom are not only alternative sources of international law but competitive with each other."

According to Schachter those of a "liberal" persuasion favor the treaty process, while conservatives are more inclined toward customary international law:

> The liberal approach, reflecting faith in reason and progress, tends to favour the treaty process because it involves deliberate and rational effort to meet perceived needs by general rules applicable to all. Written text brings clarity and precision in place of the obscurity and uncertainty of past precedents. In addition, multilateral treaty negotiations allow all governments the chance to participate and to express their consent in accordance with their constitutional processes. The treaty conferences generally are democratic in form, the participants are on an equal footing and the main decisions are taken openly and publicly. They are in keeping with the liberal ideal.
>
> Customary law, in contrast, tends to appeal to the conservative. Its case-by-case gradualism reflects particular needs in concrete situations. It avoids grand formulas and abstract ideals. The law that evolves is more malleable and more responsive to each State's individual interest. Not least in the minds of some of its supporters is that custom gives weight to effective power and responsibility whereas multilateral treaty-making unrealistically and unwisely, in their view, treats all States as equally capable.[71]

If the customary international law process does indeed favor the powerful states, it would seem to have considerable appeal for the United States. In light of the ambiguity and controversy surrounding customary international law at present, however, this proposition is debatable, and it is understandable that the United States would seek in the written text of treaties greater "clarity and precision in place of the obscurity and uncertainty of past precedents."

Besides being "entangled" with the customary international law process, treaties also serve as the constituent instruments, charters, or "constitutions" of international organizations, which, in some instances, may have lawmaking capacity. Traditionally a strong supporter of and participant in a host of international organizations, the United States appears lately to be much more ambivalent in its attitudes toward these institutions.

International organizations as law creators

The subject of lawmaking by international organizations is of vast proportions. As far as the United Nations, its specialized agencies, and the International Atomic Energy Agency (IAEA) are concerned, it has been exhaustively explored in a study sponsored by the American Society of International Law.[72] As one of the co-editors of that study, Oscar Schachter, has stated: "Neither the United Nations nor any of its specialized agencies was conceived as a legislative body."[73] Schachter and other contributors to the study go on, however, to demonstrate that the United Nations and its specialized agencies have created international law through a great variety of methodologies, some of which can fairly be classified as "legislative." The best known of these methodologies is the multilateral "norm creating" treaty. UN organs or international conferences sponsored by UN bodies have been the forum for the initiation, negotiation, and adoption of hundreds of such treaties. Some of these treaties, as we have seen, may bind states that choose not to become parties and refrain from acts that signify acceptance if the treaties "crystalize" emergent rules of law or generate customary state practice that follows the treaties' rules. The UN Convention on the Law of the Sea is an often cited example.

As we have also seen, some commentators and a few governments have argued that government statements made in UN bodies and resolutions of UN organs are evidence of state practice and *opinio juris.* UN resolutions that embody declarations of principles and rules of international law are a special case. As noted by Oscar Schachter:

> Lawyers have argued that resolutions and various other declarations may be authoritative evidence of binding international law on one or more of the following grounds: (1) as "authentic" interpretations of the UN Charter agreed by *all* the parties; (2) as affirmations of recognized customary law; and (3) as expressions of general principles of law accepted by states.[74]

Schachter also notes that studies of the International Law Commission, a subsidiary organ of the United Nations General Assembly responsible for codifying existing law and progressively developing new law, as well as comments of its members, are often invoked as evidence of general international law. At the same time he concludes that "[i]n the end, the 'law' is determined by the subsequent conduct of the states and their views of the law (*opinio juris*)."[75]

True legislative authority – in the sense of capacity to take action to bind member states without obtaining the consent of them all – is severely limited in the United Nations itself. With one exception this legislative authority is limited to the internal governance of the organization, in particular the law applicable to international personnel, the admission and exclusion of member states, and the principles of financial responsibility of member states. As we shall see later in this study, principles of the financial responsibility of member states of the United Nations have been severely challenged by the US refusal to pay its dues.

The one clear example of UN legislative authority that goes beyond the internal governance of the Organization is the power of the Security Council to take decisions binding on all members if it determines the existence of a threat to or breach of the peace under Chapter VII of the Charter.[76] Because as a permanent member of the Council the United States has a veto, it can control this exercise of legislative authority by the United Nations. As we shall see later in this study, however, the Security Council, and alleged US dominance of it, have recently come under severe criticism, and there have been numerous calls for reform of the process.

When one turns from the United Nations itself and to its specialized agencies, as well as to the International Atomic Energy Agency, one finds somewhat more legislative authority being exercised.[77] Frederic L. Kirgis, Jr. has exhaustively examined the nontraditional ways in which these organizations promulgate norms for the conduct of their members. As noted by Kirgis, although not all of these norms are binding, they generally "have the capacity to channel the conduct of members in ways that are designed to advance, or at least not impede, an organization's attempts to achieve its stated goals."[78] Some of the methods used to promulgate these norms have a distinctive legislative character.

One of these methods is the nontraditional or "super-treaty system" of the International Labor Organization (ILO). As described by Kirgis in detail, the ILO's treaty-making process is nontraditional in numerous respects.[79] Most significantly, the representation of members is unique among UN-related international organizations because it is tripartite. In the International Labor Conference, the ILO's plenary body, each member is represented by two government officials, one workers' representative, and one employers' representative. ILO conventions are adopted in plenary session by a majority of two-thirds of the votes cast, and all representatives have a vote. If a convention is adopted, an ILO member has an obligation to bring the convention before "the authority or authorities within whose competence the matter lies, for the enactment of legislation or other action,"[80] even if all four of the members' votes have been cast against it. If the domestic legislature approves the convention, the government is required to ratify it and to see that it is effective.[81] This imposes an international obligation on the United States that the US Constitution does not impose,[82] since normally the president is free to decide not to ratify a treaty even if the Senate has given its advice and consent to ratification. Even if the domestic legislature does not approve the convention, a government is required to report to the ILO at appropriate intervals on the extent to which its law and practice are consistent with the convention, "stating the difficulties which prevent or delay the ratification" of the convention.[83] If the member becomes a party to the convention, it is required to report periodically to the ILO on the measures it has taken to give effect to it, and to provide copies of its reports to representative associations of workers and employers in the reporting state, and these associations may submit their observations to the ILO.[84] Lastly, the ILO Conference often supplements its conventions with contemporaneously adopted recommendations that supply details to the more general provisions of the companion convention. These recommendations, too, are subject to reporting requirements.[85] The net result of all this, according to Kirgis, is that "a state – merely by being a member of the ILO – incurs significant responsibilities, and subjects itself to peer pressure, regarding not only conventions it ratifies, but also those of which it disapproves. In effect, the International Labour Conference, by two-thirds of the votes cast, channels all members' conduct in the direction of the norms embodied in an adopted convention."[86]

Although they are not as sophisticated as the ILO's super-treaty system, the constitutions of the World Health Organization (WHO) and of the UN Educational, Scientific and Cultural Organization (UNESCO) contain some parallel processes.[87]

Described by Kirgis as a "quasi-legislative" process, the constituent instruments of most specialized agencies have amendment procedures that bind all members if some fraction – usually two-thirds – of the total membership adopts and ratifies the amendment.[88] Although most of the amendments adopted by these procedures concern the internal workings of these organizations, some constituent instruments contain substantive duties for member states, going beyond institutional matters. Amendment of these duties by a process that binds all members on approval and ratification by fewer than all closely resembles a legislative process. The IAEA Statute, for example, specifies rights and duties regarding safeguards for Agency-assisted nuclear energy projects.[89] Amendments enter into force for all members when approved by two-thirds of those present and voting in the General Conference and accepted by two-thirds of all members under their constitutional processes.[90] The US Senate has given notice that the United States will not remain a member of the IAEA if the Senate refuses its advice and consent to an amendment that is nevertheless adopted[91] – thus negating a key process of the Agency whose constituent instrument it had previously approved for ratification.

Specialized agencies that have amendment procedures similar to that of the IAEA include the International Telecommunication Union, the

International Monetary Fund, and the International Bank for Reconstruction and Development.[92] Although the WHO Constitution does not contain substantive duties for member states, it does confer substantive regulatory authority on the Health Assembly. Under the WHO Constitution the Health Assembly can adopt regulations binding on member states, subject to an opt-out procedure, in such fields as sanitary requirements, nomenclatures for diseases, diagnostic procedures for international use, the safety and effectiveness of health products in international commerce, and advertising and labeling of such products.[93] Amendments to the Constitution enter into force for all members when adopted by two-thirds of the Health Assembly and accepted by two-thirds of the members.[94] Accordingly, as noted by Kirgis, "[t]he amendment process could be used, *inter alia*, to expand the Health Assembly's regulatory powers and thus to affect the substantive duties of member states."[95]

Several specialized agencies have so-called "tacit-consent/opt-out procedures."[96] The International Civil Aviation Organization (ICAO) is a prime example of such an agency. Under the Convention on International Civil Aviation (Chicago Convention), the ICAO Council can adopt international standards and recommended practices as Annexes to the Convention.[97] The measures cover various matters related to the safety and efficiency of civil aviation and become effective within a designated period after adoption by two-thirds of the Council, unless in the meantime a majority of ICAO member states disapprove of them.[98] Even if the measures become effective, however, a state may opt out of them by notifying the ICAO of the differences between its own practice and that contemplated by the measures.[99] Although no international standard has ever been rejected by a majority of the members, not all members have been willing to comply with all standards, and they have not always notified the ICAO of their discrepancies.[100] Similar procedures exist in the World Meteorological Organization, the International Maritime Organization, the International Telecommunication Union, and the Universal Postal Union.[101]

Kirgis offers the following observations on the "legislative" activities of the specialized agencies and of the International Atomic Energy Agency:

> The examples... illustrate both the constructive role that specialized agencies may play as true rule-makers and the reluctance of states to endow the agencies with broad, formal legislative powers. Nonterritorial ocean and air spaces beckon formal international regulation if chaos and severe environmental harm are to be avoided. International drug control does too. Regulation through treaty-making would be far too cumbersome, so a more streamlined method has been found. Of course, there is an intermediate method... that could have been

chosen: treaty-making, with a tacit-consent/opt-out procedure for new standards or amendments to standards, to keep pace with changing conditions. There is also a soft law method that could have been chosen: resolutions formally amounting only to recommendations . . . The streamlined legislative techniques . . . have been adopted because of (a) their limited scope, (b) the need for effective regulation in those limited areas, (c) the assurances provided by procedures that ensure careful preparation of the standards with significant input from governments, and (d) the relatively slight risks that the rules will impose significant disadvantages on governments or their important constituents vis-à-vis their foreign rivals, or will substantially impair other important interests sought to be protected by governments.[102]

For its part, as noted above, the US Senate has expressed its view that the authority of the IAEA to adopt an amendment to its Statute without the consent of the Senate could impair such significant US interests as to require withdrawal from the Agency. Since safeguards for Agency-assisted nuclear energy projects are viewed as a matter of national security, the Senate's view is perhaps not surprising. Kirgis suggests that one reason why governments are unlikely to yield significant, formal legislative authority to UN agencies in new areas is that to do so would be contrary to democratic principle, since UN agencies are not directly accountable to the people in their member states.[103] The issue of international law-making's compatibility with fundamental principles of democracy has recently arisen in sharp relief, and it is an issue we will consider at various places in this study, especially in chapter 2.

Soft law

The concept of "soft law" as part of the international legal process has given rise to considerable discussion and controversy. Indeed, there is little agreement on what the term means.[104] To some soft law is an oxymoron because at least one definition of soft law is that it is not legally binding. Others emphasize the capacity of soft law in the form of resolutions of international organizations to become hard law. Still others regard this capacity as "beside the point" and are of the view that "[e]ven if soft law does not harden up, soft law performs important functions, and, given the structure of the international system, we could barely operate without it."[105] For his part, Prosper Weil has suggested:

The term "soft law" is not used solely to express the vague and therefore, in practice, uncompelling character of a legal norm but is also used at times to convey the sublegal value of some non-normative acts, such as certain resolutions of international organizations . . . It would seem better to reserve the term "soft law" for rules that are imprecise and not really compelling, since sublegal obligations are neither "soft law" nor "hard law"; they are simply not law at all. Two basically different categories are involved here; for while there are, on the one hand, legal norms that are not in practice compelling, because too vague, there are also, on the other hand, provisions that are precise, yet remain at the pre- or sub-normative stage. To discuss both of these categories in terms of "soft law" or "hard law" is to foster confusion.[106]

Using the terms "soft law" as covering legally nonbinding norms, Geoffrey Palmer has suggested that governments often prefer "soft" in contrast to "hard" law because "it is so politically convenient."[107] By contrast, hard law, in the form of international custom, "takes time and often a lot of state practice before it hardens into a legally enforceable rule and treaties take a long time to negotiate and nations tend to shy away from the specificity they often involve."[108] Palmer further notes that resort to soft law leaves states with large amounts of discretion and is "often so vague that third party adjudication would be impossible even if it were provided for."[109]

Oscar Schachter has pointed out, however, that "not all nonbinding agreements are general and indefinite. Governments may enter into precise and definite engagements as to future conduct with a clear understanding shared by the parties that the agreements are not legally binding."[110] The key questions then become, according to Schachter, what is the nature of the commitment accepted by the parties in a nonbinding agreement, and what, if any, are the legal implications of such an agreement? As to the nature of the commitment, although it is generally agreed it does not engage the legal responsibility of the parties in the sense that noncompliance by a party would not be the basis for a claim for reparation or for judicial remedies, this point "is quite different from stating that the agreement need not be observed or that the parties are free to act as if there were no such agreement."[111] On the contrary, Schachter suggests that under certain circumstances parties to a nonbinding agreement may be barred from deviating from its terms:

> The conclusion that nonbinding agreements are not governed by international law does not however remove them entirely from having legal implications. Consider the following situations. Let us suppose governments in conformity with a nonbinding agreement follow a course of conduct which results in a new situation. Would a government party to the agreement be precluded from challenging the legality of the course of conduct or the validity of the situation created by it? A concrete case could arise if a government which was a party to a gentleman's agreement on the distribution of seats in an international body sought to challenge the validity of the election. In a case of this kind, the competent organ might reasonably conclude that the challenging government was subject to estoppel in view of the gentleman's agreement and the reliance of the parties on that agreement.[112]

Even if a party would not be barred from deviating from a nonbinding agreement by some legal principle as estoppel, the agreement may have significant legal effects. For example, a nonbinding agreement may create expectations that national law and practice will be modified to conform with the political commitment set forth in the agreement, and a failure to do so by one party may result in a strong reaction by other parties to the agreement. Soviet failure to carry out provisions of the Helsinki Accords relating to economic cooperation or to human rights, and the strong reaction of the United States and other Western countries to this failure, are a primary case in point. As the history of the Helsinki Accords illustrates, measures to ensure the carrying out of the political commitments in nonbinding agreements may be more elaborate and more effective than those available for treaties.

General principles of law

As we have seen, Article 38(1)(c) of the Statute of the International Court of Justice directs the Court to apply, as one of the sources of international law, "the general principles of law recognized by civilized nations." In this era of the sovereign equality of states, the adjective "civilized" has in practice been dropped. There is still, however, some question as to the precise meaning of the words "general principles of law."

Because of its positivist orientation the Soviet Union denied that general principles of law were an autonomous source of law, and argued that they could be international law only when drawn from customary international practice. In sharp contrast some scholars have argued that the concept is rooted in natural law and is the basis for the *jus cogens* doctrine. The most widely held view is that general principles of law are to be found in municipal law through the comparative law process. Under this approach, if some proposition of law is so fundamental as to be found in virtually every legal system, it will constitute a general principle of law.

Assuming *arguendo* the validity of the comparative law approach, some difficult questions remain to be resolved. Comparative law scholars suggest that the major legal systems of the world include (i) the Romanist–Germanic–civilist legal systems; (ii) the common law legal systems; (iii) the Marxist–socialist legal systems; (iv) the Islamic legal systems; and (v) the Asian legal systems.[113] It is unclear whether a general principle of law must be recognized by all of these legal systems or only some of them to become part of international law.[114] If the general principle of law must be recognized by all major legal systems, the problems of research become formidable.[115] Oscar Schachter has suggested that a municipal law principle must be not only general and recognized but also "appropriate" for international application to become part of international law.[116] In support of this proposition, Schachter cites the *Right of Passage Over Indian Territory* case (*India v. Portugal*),[117] where the International Court of Justice rejected arguments that the municipal law of easements found in most legal systems were appropriate principles for determining rights of transit over a country's territory. Similarly, the Court rejected a contention that the municipal law of trusts could be used to interpret the mandate of South Africa over South West Africa in the 1950 Advisory Opinion on the *International Status of South West Africa*.[118] In contrast, in the *Barcelona Traction, Light and Power Company* case,[119] the Court applied a general principle of municipal law that the corporate entity has legal personality. The Court's predecessor, the Permanent Court of International Justice, recognized in the *Factory at Chorzow* case that there is "a general conception of law that every violation of an engagement involves an obligation to make reparation."[120] Most often the International Court of Justice has used municipal law rules for international judicial procedure. In the *Corfu Channel* case (*United Kingdom v. Albania*),[121] the Court noted that the use of "indirect evidence is admitted in all systems of law and its use is recognized by international decisions." In other decisions the Court has recognized *res judicata* as applicable to international litigation,[122] it has approved the principle that legal remedies against a judgment are equally open to either party,[123] and it has applied the municipal law principle of estoppel.[124] In all, as Schachter notes, the use of general principles of law by international decision makers has been sparing, "nearly always as a supplement to fill in gaps left by the primary sources of treaty and custom."[125]

From a US perspective, a more enhanced role for general principles would seem highly undesirable. Some commentators have contended that general principles are the proper source for the *jus cogens* doctrine,[126] and the substantial uncertainty surrounding this concept would be considerably compounded if international decision makers were to render their decisions on a natural law basis. On the other hand, leaving the *jus cogens* issue aside, Schachter has suggested that "domestic law rules applicable to such matters as individual rights, contractual remedies, liability for extra-hazardous activities, or restraints on use of common property, have now become pertinent for recruitment into international law." He suggests further that "[i]t is likely that such rules will enter into international law largely through international treaties or particular arrangements accepted by the parties. But such treaties and arrangements still require supplementing their general provisions and such filling-in can often be achieved by recourse to commonly accepted national law rules."[127] It is also possible, even likely, that as national experience in these areas becomes richer, national law rules and arrangements will be formally incorporated into international treaties and institutions.

Interpreting and applying international law

Issues of interpreting and applying international law arise, of course, at both the international and national level. In this chapter we explore only issues arising at the international level. Chapter 2 examines in some detail the interpretation and application of international law in the US legal system, with a side-glance or two, for comparative purposes, at the experience in other national legal systems.

Turning first to the interpretation of international law, we should note that our primary focus will be on issues surrounding the interpretation of treaties. For participants in the international legal process, issues of interpreting customary norms or general principles tend to conflate with issues of whether such norms or general principles exist. How to interpret treaties, however, has been and remains a topic of considerable discussion and debate.

Principles of interpretation

Articles 31 and 32 of the Vienna Convention on the Law of Treaties, which contain the Convention's rules on treaty interpretation, were adopted without a dissenting vote at the conference and have been considered as declaratory of customary international law.[128] This lack of a dissenting vote, however, masked the divergence of views that arose at the conference concerning the proper approach to the interpretation of treaties.

Richard Kearney and Robert Dalton suggest that "[t]he articles on interpretation demonstrate that a quite conservative (even old-fashioned) series of rules would be accepted by the conference if endorsed by the [International Law] Commission."[129] The "old-fashioned" series of rules endorsed by the International Law Commission and accepted by the conference read as follows:

Article 31

General Rule of Interpretation

1. A treaty shall be interpreted in good faith in accordance with the ordinary meaning to be given to the terms of the treaty in their context and in the light of its object and purpose.
2. The context for the purpose of the interpretation of a treaty shall comprise, in addition to the text, including its preamble and annexes:

a. any agreement relating to the treaty which was made between all the parties in connection with the conclusion of the treaty;
b. any instrument which was made by one or more parties in connection with the conclusion of the treaty and accepted by the other parties as an instrument related to the treaty.

3. There shall be taken into account, together with the context:
   a. any subsequent agreement between the parties regarding the interpretation of the treaty or the application of its provisions;
   b. any subsequent practice in the application of the treaty which establishes the agreement of the parties regarding its interpretation;
   c. any relevant rules of international law applicable in the relations between the parties.
4. A special meaning shall be given to a term if it is established that the parties so intended.

Article 32

Supplementary Means of Interpretation

Recourse may be had to supplementary means of interpretation, including the preparatory work of the treaty and the circumstances of its conclusion, in order to confirm the meaning resulting from the application of article 31, or to determine the meaning when the interpretation according to article 31:

a. leaves the meaning ambiguous or obscure; or
b. leads to a result which is manifestly absurd or unreasonable.

Articles 31 and 32 of the Vienna Convention are a quintessential example of the textual approach to the interpretation of treaties.[130] Under this approach a hierarchy of means of interpretation is established. First and foremost in this hierarchy is the text of the treaty itself, and the fundamental objective of the interpretive process is to establish what the text means according to the ordinary meaning of its terms. To aid in determining the ordinary meaning of the treaty's terms Article 31 permits reference to the context of the treaty which is limited to agreements or similar instruments related to the treaty or to subsequent practice in the application of the treaty or relevant rules of international law – all objective factors relatively easy to discover. In contrast, under Article 32 the preparatory work of the treaty (*travaux préparatoires*) and the circumstances of the treaty's conclusion occupy a much lower rank in the hierarchy and are to be resorted to only if the means specified by Article 31 leave the meaning ambiguous or obscure or lead to a manifestly absurd or unreasonable result.

During the early stages of the conference the United States favored a distinctly different approach. In particular it objected to the hierarchy that the ILC's draft text established between the sources of evidence for interpretation of treaties, and criticized treating the *travaux préparatoires* as a secondary means of interpretation. To eliminate this hierarchy the United States introduced an amendment to the Commission's draft that would have combined the articles containing the general rule and the supplementary means of interpretation.[131]

This amendment reflected both the traditional US position in favor of according equal weight to *travaux* and the influence of Myres S. McDougal, an eminent international law scholar and a member of the US delegation. McDougal was a proponent of the so-called "policy-oriented and configurative approach" to treaty interpretation.[132] This complex and controversial approach asserts that it is the intentions of the parties that should be the primary focus of the interpretive exercise and that anything that sheds light on these intentions should be consulted. Although the text of the treaty is to be included as evidence of these intentions, it is only one, and not necessarily the most important, factor to be considered. Also, and most important, the McDougal approach would subject the interpretation process to a host of "principles of content and procedure" to give effect to "goals of a public order of human dignity."[133] Because of the ambiguity and seemingly open-ended nature of this approach, it has been the object of sharp controversy.[134]

The US amendment made no reference to McDougal's "goals of public order and dignity," nor did McDougal, in introducing the amendment. Rather, he stressed the practice of ministries of foreign affairs in looking at the *travaux* when considering issues of treaty interpretation, as well as the practice of international tribunals, including the Permanent Court of International Justice and the International Court of Justice, of examining preparatory work before reaching a decision on the interpretation of a treaty.[135]

Despite McDougal's efforts, the US amendment received "scant support."[136] In 1950 the Institute of International Law, a transnational nongovernmental organization founded in 1873 for the purpose of developing and codifying international law and composed of persons chosen as a result of their contributions to international law, had adopted the textual approach. Many of the arguments made during the Institute's debates were advanced during the Vienna Conference against the US amendment. It was argued, for example, that recourse to preparatory materials would favor wealthy states with large and well-indexed archives, that non-negotiating states would hesitate to accede to multilateral conventions because they would not be aware of or wish to have their rights based on materials in the *travaux*, and that the International Law Commission's text was a "neutral and fair formulation of the generally recognized canons of treaty interpretation."[137] There was also a concern that the approach represented by the US amendment would undermine the principle of *pacta sunt servanda* and thereby cause instability in the enforcement of treaties. Especially persuasive to many delegates to the Vienna Conference were the views expressed by Sir Eric Beckett in the Institute's debates:

> [T]he task of [a] Tribunal is that of interpreting a written document, a statute, a will, a contract in writing, or a treaty, and it has to proceed on the assumption that it finds the intention expressed in the words of the document which it has to interpret. There is a complete unreality in the references to the supposed intention of the legislature in the interpretation of the statute when in fact it is almost certain that the point which has arisen is one which the legislature never thought of at all. This is even more so in the case of the interpretation of treaties. As a matter of experience it often occurs that the difference between the parties to the treaties arises out of something which the parties never thought of when the treaty was concluded and that, therefore, they had absolutely no common intention with regard to it. In other cases the parties may all along have had divergent intentions with regard to the actual question which is in dispute..., possibly hoping that this point would not arise in practice, or possibly expecting that if it did the text which was agreed would produce the result which it desired... [I]t is unrealistic to attempt to find a common intention of the parties when, in fact, they never had a common intention on the point that has arisen, but simply agreed on a text.[138]

According to Kearney and Dalton, the rejection of the US amendment and the adoption of Articles 31 and 32 by the conference did "not seriously weaken the value of the convention." In their view, "[i]t seems unlikely that Foreign Offices will cease to take into consideration the preparatory work and the circumstances of the conclusion of treaties when faced with problems of treaty interpretation, or that international tribunals will be less disposed to consult Article 32 sources in determining questions of treaty interpretation."[139]

It seems clear that Kearney's and Dalton's prediction is correct with respect to the work of Foreign Offices, at least those with access to preparatory materials. As to international tribunals, it is less clear whether, in recent years, they, especially the International Court of Justice, have been more willing to resort to preparatory work.[140]

However interpreted, at the international level international law is most often applied in diplomatic practice through the representations of diplomats or other representatives of the state. In many of these situations, perhaps most, there may be agreement on the law to be applied but disagreement on the facts. As pointed out by Ian Johnstone, there is a substantial "need for new institutions and procedures, not for authoritative legal interpretation, but for fact-finding and fact-assessment."[141]

If there is a disagreement between states as to what the law is, or how it should be interpreted, the arguments of the contending states only constitute partisan claims that may or may not be accepted by the other side or by an impartial third-party decision maker. Resolution of the dispute by agreement between the parties may be based on factors other than agreement on the law – such as a desire to resume or improve diplomatic relations between the parties – and therefore be uncertain evidence of a norm of customary international law. Agreements for lump-sum payments to compensate US citizens for expropriations of their property after World War II, concluded between the United States and various Eastern European countries, are prominent examples.[142] Although claims and counterclaims regarding the law and their resolution are an integral part of the customary international law process,[143] as noted earlier in this chapter they constitute an uncertain and arguably unreliable guide for the international decision maker.

The role of international courts and tribunals

At the national level, of course, third-party decision makers in the form of courts and, increasingly, arbitral tribunals are actively involved in the interpretation and application of law. In sharp contrast international courts and tribunals play a much more modest role at the international level, although there has been an increase in judicial and arbitral activity in recent years. The United States, for reasons we note elsewhere in this study, has become increasingly suspicious of international courts and tribunals, except for those over whose establishment and proceedings it can exercise significant control. Thus, the United States has withdrawn its acceptance of the compulsory jurisdiction of the International Court of Justice and attempts to limit its appearances before the Court to situations where it has agreed on an ad hoc basis with another state to submit a dispute to a chamber of the Court whose composition is acceptable to both parties.[144] The United States has also strongly opposed the statute of a permanent international criminal court and has declined to become a party to the American Convention on Human Rights and to accept the jurisdiction of the Inter-American Court of Human Rights. In contrast, it was instrumental in the UN Security Council's establishing an international criminal tribunal for the former Yugoslavia, and it agreed to the establishment of and has been an active participant in the proceedings of the Iran–US Claims Tribunal, the UN Compensation Commission, the International Centre for the Settlement of Investment Disputes, and the innovative dispute settlement procedures of the North American Free Trade Agreement (NAFTA) and the World Trade Organization (WTO).

The United States has also been a strong supporter of international arbitration between private parties and has ratified and implemented in its domestic law the Convention on the Recognition and Enforcement of Foreign Arbitral Awards.[145]

Other countries besides the United States have been leery of appearing before the International Court of Justice. Currently only the United Kingdom among the permanent members of the UN Security Council has accepted the Court's compulsory jurisdiction, and only with significant reservations. Oscar Schachter has identified some salient problems with international adjudication generally:

> Litigation is uncertain, time-consuming, troublesome. Political officials do not want to lose control of a case that they might resolve by negotiation or political pressures. Diplomats naturally prefer diplomacy; political leaders value persuasion, manoeuvre and flexibility. They often prefer to "play it by ear," making their rules to fit the circumstances rather than submit to pre-existing rules. Political forums, such as the United Nations, are often more attractive, especially to those likely to get wide support for political reasons. States do not want to risk losing a case when the stakes are high or be troubled with the litigation in minor matters. An international tribunal may not inspire confidence, especially when some judges are seen as "political" or hostile. There is apprehension that the law is too malleable or fragmentary to sustain "true" judicial decisions. In some situations, the legal issues are viewed as but one element in a complex political situation and consequently it is considered unwise or futile to deal with them separately. Finally we note the underlying perception of many governments that law essentially supports the status quo and that courts are [not] responsive to demands for justice or change.[146]

As Schachter notes, states often prefer to submit their disputes to political forums such as the United Nations rather than to international adjudication. The result is that the United Nations plays a major role in the interpretation and application of international law. As we have seen, the International Court of Justice, the "principal judicial organ of the United Nations,"[147] interprets and applies various sources of international law in its proceedings. In contrast, the political organs of the United Nations, especially the General Assembly and the Security Council, primarily interpret and apply the UN Charter to the disputes that come before them.

At the 1945 San Francisco United Nations Conference on International Organization which established the United Nations, participating states were faced with the issue of "how and by what organ or organs of the Organization the Charter should be interpreted."[148] Some representatives proposed that the General Assembly, as the most "democratic" organ of the United Nations, should have this competence. Others proposed that the International Court of Justice, as the principal judicial organ of the United Nations, should perform that function. In the end the San Francisco Conference rejected both of these proposals. Instead, as summarized by Louis Sohn,

> The process of Charter interpretation involves, therefore, the following elements: (a) each United Nations organ interprets such parts of the Charter as are applicable to its functions; (b) if two organs of the United Nations differ concerning the correct interpretation of a provision of the Charter, a request may be made by them jointly or by one of them, to the International Court of Justice for an advisory opinion; (c) alternatively, they can set up an *ad hoc* committee of jurists to examine the question and report its views; or (d) they can follow the practice of the Congress of the United States and have recourse to a joint conference which may devise a compromise solution; (e) finally, if it is desirable to establish a formally binding authoritative interpretation, it would be necessary to embody it in an amendment to the Charter... No such interpretative amendment was ever adopted.[149]

Unlike the Supreme Court of the United States, which can determine that an action of the Congress or the president is unconstitutional, the International Court of Justice has no formal power of judicial review of actions taken by UN political organs. The ICJ has, however, interpreted and applied the UN Charter in contentious cases between states – most notably in the *Nicaragua v. United States* case.[150] Most significantly, in the *Lockerbie* case[151] Libya has contended that Security Council resolutions demanding that Libya surrender to the United States or to the United Kingdom its nationals accused of causing the explosion of Pan Am Flight 103 over Lockerbie, Scotland, are *ultra vires* and therefore do not bar its claim that the United States and the United Kingdom violated Libya's rights under the Montreal Convention for the Suppression of Unlawful Acts against the Safety of Civil Aviation by demanding such surrender rather than allowing it to choose between extradition or submission of the accused for purposes of prosecution to Libyan law enforcement officials. Having rejected the US and UK preliminary objections to jurisdiction, the Court is scheduled to proceed to a decision on the merits. In view of Libya's surrender of the accused to the Netherlands for trial by a Scottish court, and a determination of guilty for one of the accused and of not guilty for the other, however, it is not clear whether a final decision on the issue of the validity of the Security Council's resolutions will ever be rendered.

Under Article 96(1) of the UN Charter "[t]he General Assembly or the Security Council may request the International Court of Justice to give an advisory opinion on any legal question." Paragraph (2) of Article 96 permits the General Assembly to authorize other organs of the United Nations and specialized agencies to request advisory opinions of the Court on "legal questions arising within the scope of their activities." Through the advisory opinion process the Court has engaged in a number of significant interpretations of the UN Charter. For example, in its very first advisory opinion the Court refused to accept an argument that the admission of a member state could be made dependent on conditions not expressly provided for in Article 4(1) of the Charter,[152] and two years thereafter issued an opinion that the United Nations possesses international personality and therefore could bring claims for injuries suffered in the service of the Organization.[153] Most significantly, especially for the United States, in 1962 the Court issued its advisory opinion in the *Certain Expenses of the United Nations* case.[154] In this landmark opinion, which we shall consider in detail later in this study, the Court was asked by the General Assembly to advise on the dividing line between the powers of the General Assembly and those of the Security Council with regard to issues relating to both the maintenance of international peace and security and the financing of peacekeeping operations. The Court advised, *inter alia*, that certain expenses which were authorized by the General Assembly to cover the costs of the UN operations in the Congo and of the operations of the United Nations Emergency Force in the Middle East constituted "expenses" of the United Nations under Article 17(2) of the Charter[155] and that member states were therefore bound to pay these expenses as apportioned by the General Assembly.[156]

More recently, in 1994, over the opposition of the United States and many others, the General Assembly voted to request an advisory opinion from the ICJ on the question: "Is the threat or use of nuclear weapons in any circumstances permitted under international law?"[157] Earlier the World Health Organization, also over the opposition of the United States and many others, had voted to request that the Court give an advisory opinion on the question: "In view of the health and environmental effects, would the use of nuclear weapons by a State in war or other armed conflict be a breach of its obligations under international law including the WHO Constitution?"[158]

On July 8, 1996, the Court handed down its responses to both of these requests. It declined to give the advisory opinion requested by the WHO, on the ground that the question raised did not arise within the scope of the WHO's activities.[159] The Court thus agreed with the arguments the United States and others had made during the debate in the World Health Assembly over whether to request the opinion.[160] The Court also decided, however, that it would grant the General Assembly's request, holding that it raised a legal question within the Assembly's competence.[161]

For its part the United States, along with others, had not challenged the competence of the General Assembly to request the opinion from the Court. It did, however, suggest that the Court "should exercise its discretion to decline to provide an opinion because of the unusual character of the question that had been presented."[162] Specifically, according to the United States, the unusual character of the request consisted of the following elements. First, the request did not relate to any specific dispute or operational problem but rather raised a purely hypothetical question. Second, the request did not involve the interpretation of a particular agreement or instrument but instead presented "a very abstract and vague question about international law in general."[163] Third, the request came about because of the efforts of a coalition of governments and nongovernmental organizations who were pushing a political agenda, namely, the elimination of nuclear weapons. We have already noted and shall discuss later in this study the difficulties for the US government created by the efforts of nongovernmental organizations.

These arguments were overwhelmingly rejected by the Court when it voted, by a thirteen to one margin,[164] to accept the Assembly's request. Although it recognized that it has the discretion to decline such a request, the Court confirmed its traditional position that it should do so only for "compelling reasons" and found that none of the reasons advanced by the United States and other opponents of the request constituted such reasons.[165] In commenting on the Court's decision, Michael J. Matheson, Principal Deputy Legal Adviser, US Department of State, opined: "Unlike US courts, where such attempts would be routinely screened out under doctrines of justiciability, case or controversy, ripeness, standing and the like, the International Court of Justice will apparently have to be protected by the members of the General Assembly from these inappropriate requests."[166]

In sharp contrast to Matheson's opinion, Richard A. Falk has praised the Court's acceptance of the General Assembly's request as "an expression of judicial independence by the Court."[167] He notes that all of the permanent members of the Security Council except China strongly opposed the request, both in the debates on the General Assembly's resolution and in the written and oral pleadings before the Court.

Judicial independence is, of course, a salient characteristic of the rule of law. It is not at all clear from the record, however, that the United States favors the judicial independence of the International Court of Justice, especially in cases involving matters affecting the vital interests of the United States. On the contrary, as illustrated by the US withdrawal from the compulsory jurisdiction of the Court and its recent use of the Court's chamber procedures, the United States would appear to prefer to choose on a case-by-case basis judges who are unlikely to deviate in their decisions from strongly held US political positions. No such option was available to the United States in the case of the Court's advisory opinion on the compatibility of the threat or use of nuclear weapons with international law, an issue implicating major national security concerns. Because of the sensitivities of the issues addressed by the Court, this chapter discusses the Court's opinion, reactions to it, and the possible long-term significance of the opinion at some length.

Having decided to accept the General Assembly's request for an advisory opinion, the Court then turned to a consideration of the questions presented to it. The Court first rejected arguments that the use of nuclear weapons would violate the "right to life" guaranteed by Article 6 of the International Covenant on Civil and Political Rights and certain other human rights instruments and various principles of environmental law.[168] It next focused on the law on the use of force as the basis on which the legality of the threat or use of nuclear weapons should be judged.

By a vote of eleven to three, the Court concluded that "[t]here is in neither customary nor conventional international law any comprehensive and universal prohibition of the threat or use of nuclear weapons as such."[169] The Court also rejected arguments that prohibitions in the law of armed conflict, of poisonous weapons, or provisions in agreements on nuclear weapons taken together amounted to a general prohibition on all use of nuclear weapons.[170] Similarly, the Court rejected the proposition that a prohibition on the use of nuclear weapons had become part of customary international law since 1945. In the Court's view, "the members of the international community are profoundly divided on the matter of whether non-recourse to nuclear weapons over the past fifty years constitutes the expression of an *opinio juris*. Under these circumstances the Court does not consider itself able to find that there is such an *opinio juris*."[171] Significantly, the Court accepted the argument of the United States and others that the adoption of a series of UN General Assembly resolutions which declared, over the opposition of many states, the use of nuclear weapons to be contrary to international law cannot create international law but can only constitute evidence of preexisting international law if generally accepted by states, which was not the case with these resolutions.[172]

After an examination of certain basic rules of the law of armed conflict, such as the principle of neutrality, the requirement to distinguish between civilian and military targets, and the prohibition on the use of weapons causing unnecessary suffering to combatants,[173] the Court concluded, by a vote of seven to seven, decided by the vote of the president, that: "It follows from the above mentioned requirements that the threat or use of nuclear weapons would *generally* be contrary to the rules of international law applicable in armed conflict, and in particular the principles and rules of humanitarian law."[174] As noted by Matheson, the Court's use of the word "generally" indicated that it was not asserting that all uses of nuclear weapons would be illegal, but "it is not clear what types of uses [the Court] believed would or would not be prohibited."[175] Specifically, the Court expressly stated that it had reached no conclusions about three fundamental dimensions of the debate surrounding nuclear weapons of particular interest to the United States: "(1) the case of 'an extreme circumstance of self-defence, in which the very survival of a State would be at stake'; (2) the 'policy of deterrence'; and (3) the use of nuclear weapons in belligerent reprisal."[176] On the basis of his reading of the votes of the judges and the statements of the various judges, Matheson is of the view that "the Court is uncertain and divided on whether and in what circumstances the use of nuclear weapons is prohibited, and only a minority appears to have taken the position that all uses are prohibited."[177]

In sharp contrast to their uncertainty and divided opinions on the legality of the use of nuclear weapons, the judges of the International Court of Justice were agreed on the scope of the duty of states to negotiate with a view to reaching an agreement on nuclear disarmament. Article VI of the Nuclear Non-Proliferation Treaty provides: "Each of the Parties to the Treaty undertakes to pursue negotiations in good faith on effective measures relating to cessation of the nuclear arms race at an early date and to nuclear disarmament, and on a treaty on general and complete disarmament under strict and effective international control."[178] Interpreting this provision the Court concluded unanimously that "[t]here exists an obligation to pursue in good faith and bring to a conclusion negotiations leading to nuclear disarmament in all its aspects under strict and effective international control."[179] Elaborating on its use of the phrase "and bring to a conclusion," the Court stated that "the obligation involved here is an obligation to achieve a precise result – nuclear disarmament in all its aspects – by adopting a particular course of conduct, namely, the pursuit of negotiations on the matter in good faith."[180]

In the wake of all this one may well ask, what are the practical implications, if any, of the Court's rulings, especially for the United States, the preeminent nuclear power? As to the Court's divided opinion on the use of nuclear weapons, Matheson has suggested that the practical result is that "[n]ational authorities that believe their policy is lawful and vital to national security are unlikely to change important elements of it simply because legal issues have been raised but not resolved."[181] For his part, Falk notes that "[s]tates are habitually resistant to legal challenges directed at their national security policies, and powerful states are especially so."[182]

With respect to the Court's ruling on the duty to seek nuclear disarmament, Matheson believes that it "was never reasonable" to think that the Court's opinion could hasten the days when nuclear weapons are eliminated. Rather, in Matheson's view, this result can only be achieved by negotiations among states, "which will require the resolution of very difficult technical, political and security problems."[183] Falk agrees that the Court's opinion will have little impact in the short term on the actions of nuclear weapons states. But he is of the view that it would be a mistake to focus solely on the short-term intergovernmental impact. He suggests that the Court's opinion may encourage antinuclear social and political forces to push for nuclear disarmament, will provide a legal grounding for the advocacy of antinuclear positions within government, and will strengthen the bargaining position of nonnuclear states in relation to the nonproliferation agenda.[184]

Falk may well be right. It is worth noting that, to meet the demands of the nonnuclear weapons states, the indefinite renewal of the Treaty on the Non-Proliferation of Nuclear Weapons in 1995 was explicitly made conditional on progress in nuclear disarmament and ratification of the Comprehensive Test Ban Treaty. According to Jonathan Schell, however, in a provocative article published in *Foreign Affairs*,[185] the US government has decided, despite the end of the Cold War, that the abolition of nuclear weapons is not so much difficult to achieve as it is undesirable, and therefore the United States has remained committed to retaining arsenals of thousand of warheads indefinitely. In Schell's view this attitude is fundamentally incompatible with a legal regime of nonproliferation of nuclear weapons, and the United States will therefore have to choose between a world of uncontrolled proliferation or a world with no nuclear weapons at all. Even if the choice facing the United States is not as stark as portrayed by Schell, a commitment to retaining substantial arsenals of nuclear weapons indefinitely is clearly incompatible with US obligations under Article VI of the Non-Proliferation Treaty as unanimously and authoritatively interpreted by the International Court of Justice.

The United States and the World Trade Organization

In contrast to its at best ambivalent attitude toward the International Court of Justice, the United States has been a strong supporter of dispute settlement procedures of the World Trade Organization, but recent developments may call this support into question. Under the new Dispute Settlement Understanding (DSU), contained in an annex to the WTO Charter,[186] disputes arising under WTO agreements, including the Understanding itself, are resolved in a formal process of international arbitration. The DSU effected a radical change from the process followed under the General Agreement on Tariffs and Trade (GATT) concluded in 1947. Under GATT 1947, panel decisions were advisory only and did not have the force of law until adopted by the contracting parties. GATT 1947 also operated under a consensus rule that gave the losing party an effective veto over the adoption of panel recommendations if it chose to exercise that veto. Under the DSU panel reports are still advisory and do not have the force of law until adopted by the Dispute Settlement Body (DSB), that is, the General Council of the WTO. The DSB must still act by consensus. However, under the Uruguay Round Understanding panel reports will be deemed adopted by the DSB, at a meeting within sixty days of issuance, unless a party to the dispute decides to appeal or the DSB decides by consensus not to adopt the report. In other words, unlike GATT 1947, under the WTO it takes a consensus to block adoption of a panel report. This effectively gives the winning party a veto over any effort at blockage.

The DSU also confers on any party to a panel proceeding the right to appeal the panel's decision to a permanent Appellate Body. This body is composed of seven members appointed by the DSB for four-year terms renewable for an additional four years. Each appeal is heard by three of the seven members of the Appellate Body and the scope of review is limited to issues of law covered in the panel report and to legal interpretations developed by the panel. Members of the Appellate Body are to be experts in law, international trade, and the subject matter of the covered agreements, are to be independent, must not be affiliated with any government, and must not participate in the consideration of any dispute that would create a direct or indirect conflict of interest.

As with panel reports, Appellate Body decisions must be approved by the DSB in order to have the force of law. Appellate Body reports are adopted by the DSB and unconditionally accepted by the parties to the dispute unless the DSB decides by consensus not to adopt the appellate report. Once again the winner is given the power to veto any move to reject the Appellate Body decision. The Appellate Body is to conduct its proceedings in a confidential manner and while members may, in the report, record differing opinions, those opinions are to remain anonymous.

It is a debatable proposition whether members have an international legal obligation to change their laws in response to adverse WTO rulings.[187] In any event, as a matter of national law, members have so far denied WTO rulings direct effect in national courts.[188] For its part, the United States, through its implementing legislation, denies effect to WTO rulings that are inconsistent with US law.[189] US law also prohibits challenges to government conduct on the ground that the conduct violates WTO obligations.[190]

Other provisions in the US implementing legislation evince considerable uneasiness with the WTO in general and the DSU in particular. For example, the legislation requires the president to report to Congress by March 1, 2000, on the first five years of US participation in the WTO.[191] After the report is submitted, Congress has ninety legislative days to vote on any member's joint resolution (the equivalent of legislation) to withdraw from the WTO. In the week of June 19, 2000, the House of Representatives overwhelmingly defeated a resolution that would have required the United States to end its membership of the organization.[192]

Legislation was introduced in the House of Representatives on June 21, 2000, that would establish a commission to review dispute settlement decisions taken by the World Trade Organization against the United States.[193] This legislation would revive "almost word-for-word" a proposal made in 1994 by former Senator Robert Dole and former Senator Daniel Patrick Moynihan.[194]

The so-called WTO Dispute Settlement Review Commission would consist of five federal appellate judges who would review all approved WTO dispute settlement reports. It would evaluate WTO rulings adverse to the United States using four criteria: whether the WTO dispute settlement panel had exceeded its authority; added to the obligations or diminished the rights of the United States under the Uruguay Round multilateral trade agreement; acted arbitrarily, engaged in misconduct, or departed from established procedures; or deviated from the applicable standard of review, including antidumping cases, set forth in the Uruguay Round Agreement under the General Agreement on Tariffs and Trade. If the commission reported that the WTO had acted improperly, any member of Congress would be able to introduce a joint resolution calling on the president to negotiate new dispute settlement rules aimed at correcting the problem. Any member would also be able to introduce a joint resolution calling for the United States to withdraw from the WTO if the commission handed down three determinations of improper rulings in any five-year period.

In the result this draft legislation suffered the same fate as that of the Dole/Moynihan proposal in 1994, that is, it was not enacted into law. In large part this was because, as pointed out by the Clinton administration in opposition, WTO dispute settlement panels had ruled heavily in favor of the United States since the organization's creation. On January 14, 2002, however, the United States suffered a major loss when the WTO Appellate Body ruled that US tax legislation, intended to satisfy an earlier panel ruling that benefits for foreign sales corporations constituted an export subsidy in violation of the WTO Agreement on Agriculture, continued to violate the applicable rules.[195] The Dispute Settlement Body adopted the Appellate Body's report on January 29, 2002. A subsequent arbitration proceeding authorized the European Union to apply trade sanctions against the United States in an amount of slightly more than $4 billion on an annual basis.[196] As of this writing the European Union has refrained from applying such sanctions while Congress considers possible new legislative measures to bring US legislation in compliance with its trade obligations.

This is not the only recent major US loss to the European Union (EU) under WTO dispute settlement procedures.[197] In particular, a WTO panel has ruled that steel tariffs imposed by the United States in 2002 violated trade rules.[198] The United States has announced that it will appeal to the Appellate Body, but the European Union has threatened to impose trade sanctions of $2.2 billion if the appeal fails.[199]

Even when the United States has won, it has sometimes suffered frustration by the willingness of the losing side, especially the EU, to resist complying with adverse rulings. Indeed, the ability of the losers to delay the implementation process has illustrated a present weakness in the DSU.[200] The United States has accordingly taken a lead position in negotiations on reform of the World Trade Organization's dispute settlement proceedings.

The debate on the DSU has been heated and promises to become more so as dispute settlement in the WTO has begun to impact on sensitive domestic policy issues.[201] Efforts are currently under way to reform the WTO dispute settlement process, but these are proving difficult and protracted. The critics contend that the DSU undermines national sovereignty and democratic control over trade policy. Regardless of the validity of these criticisms, the fervor with which they are advanced at the very least complicates the ability of the United States to support a dispute settlement process designed to enhance the rule of law in international trade.[202]

The United States and NAFTA

Even more far-reaching in terms of enhancing the rule of law in international trade and investment are the dispute settlement provisions of the North American Free Trade Agreement (NAFTA). Its chapters 19 and 20 contain the general dispute settlement procedures for NAFTA.[203] Chapter 19 concerns disputes over antidumping and countervailing duty matters. Chapter 20(B) pertains to the settlement of all other disputes in which one member state claims that another member state has adopted a measure that (i) is inconsistent with its NAFTA obligations or (ii) has nullified or impaired the claimant's expected benefits even though the measure is not inconsistent with the accused's obligations under NAFTA. Chapter 11(B) confers on a private investor from one member state the right to arbitrate a claim that it has been damaged by another member state's breach of its obligations under Chapter 11 (the investment chapter of NAFTA) or under certain enumerated provisions dealing with state enterprises. Arbitral awards under these provisions are enforceable in the courts of member states.[204]

Chapter 19 provides that each member state retains its own antidumping and countervailing duty laws and that these laws will be administered and applied by the appropriate administrative agency in each country. However, Chapter 19 introduces a revolutionary innovation in international dispute settlement by replacing national judicial review with binational panel review. This binational panel is to determine whether the member state's administering agency made its determination "in accordance with the antidumping or countervailing duty law of the importing Party." In doing so, it is to follow the "general legal principles" that a court in the importing member state would apply in reviewing the administering authority's determination. If it finds that the determination is inconsistent with the law of the importing member state, the binational panel remands the case for a determination by the administering authority in the importing member state not inconsistent with the panel's decision. The decision of the panel may not be appealed in a member state's courts but may be reviewed in an "Extraordinary Challenge Committee" procedure. This procedure is very limited, however, and not the same as a general judicial review. Specifically, as noted by Avi Gesser,

> appeals are only permitted when: (1) there has been gross misconduct, bias, serious conflict of interest, or other material misconduct on the part of a panelist; (2) there has been a serious departure from a fundamental rule of procedure; or (3) a Panel manifestly exceeds its powers, authority or jurisdiction, for example, by failing to apply the appropriate standard of judicial review. It must also be established that the action materially affected the Panel's decision, and that the decision threatens the integrity of the Binational Panel review process.[205]

The constitutionality of the Chapter 19 procedure has been a subject of debate in the United States, and, in January 1997, the American Coalition for Competitive Trade filed a constitutional challenge to the binational panel dispute settlement mechanism under NAFTA Chapter 19 and its predecessor in the US–Canada Free Trade Agreement. The complaint charged that the Chapter 19 panel system violates Articles I, II, and III of the US Constitution, as well as the Fifth Amendment, by divesting US courts of their constitutional powers and depriving individuals of their right to due process and equal protection under the law. However, the US Court of Appeals for the District of Columbia unanimously rejected the claim, holding that the group lacked standing because its members were not directly injured by the binational panels. In addition, the court found that the American Coalition for Competitive Trade had failed to exhaust its legal remedies, as required under section 1516a(g)(4)(C) of the NAFTA Act.[206]

The constitutionality of concluding NAFTA in the form of a congressional–executive agreement rather than as a treaty has been a subject of debate between eminent US constitutional law scholars.[207] In *Made in the USA Foundation v. United States*,[208] however, the Court of Appeals for the Eleventh Circuit held that the issue of whether NAFTA was a "treaty" requiring the Senate's advice and consent to ratification was a nonjusticiable political question.

Accordingly, US courts of appeals have not yet ruled on the merits of the challenges to the constitutionality of either NAFTA's Chapter 19 procedures or its conclusion as a congressional–executive agreement. The Chapter 19 procedures remain controversial as a policy matter as well, since some critics have contended that foreign panelists cannot adequately apply the national law of the importing country. The application of Mexican law by binational panels has been especially "problematic," because of differences between the legal systems of the United States and Canada, on the one hand, and that of Mexico on the other, and because Mexico's experience in trade matters is not as developed as that of the United States and of Canada.

Equally revolutionary, as compared with dispute settlement under traditional international law and procedures, are the provisions of NAFTA's Chapter 11(B) that confer on a private investor from a member state the right to arbitrate a claim that it has been damaged by another member state's breach of its obligations under Chapter 11 or under specified other NAFTA undertakings. Nothing comparable exists under any of the World Trade Organization agreements. The arbitration is under the aegis of the International Centre for the Settlement of Investment Disputes (ICSID) or ad hoc arbitration under the UN Commission for International Trade Law (UNCITRAL) Arbitration Rules as modified by the fairly elaborate procedural provisions of Chapter 11(B). To give effect to this right each of the member states, in Chapter 11, has expressly consented to the submission of the investor's claim to arbitration although without prejudice to the rights of member states under Chapter 20 of the general dispute settlement procedures for NAFTA.

It should be noted, however, that, at this writing, the regular facilities of ICSID are not available for the settlement of disputes under Chapter 11 of NAFTA. This is because neither Canada nor Mexico is a party to the Convention on the Settlement of Investment Disputes Between States and Nationals of Other States, and the Convention requires that both the host state and the state of the foreign investor's nationality be parties for there to be arbitration under the Convention's procedures. ICSID's Additional Facility Rules, by contrast, require only that either the host country or the state of nationality of the foreign investor be a party to the Convention. As a consequence, US corporations have instituted a number of actions against Canada and Mexico under the Additional Facility Rules, since the United States is a party to the Convention.[209]

NAFTA's Chapter 11's dispute settlement procedures are, however, a two-edged sword. In the *Loewen* case, a Canadian corporation lost a $500 million verdict in a 1995 suit in Mississippi over fraudulent business practices. Allegedly unable to afford the $625 million appeals bond that the Mississippi Supreme Court required it to post as a condition to reviewing its appeal, the Canadian corporation settled the case for $175 million. It then filed a claim under Chapter 11 against the United States asserting that the US government should pay it at least $725 million in damages because the Mississippi proceedings constituted a denial of justice under international law, caused serious injury to the corporation's business in the United States, and thus related to its investment in the United States.[210] On July 26, 2003, a three-member NAFTA panel dismissed the Chapter 11 claims in their entirety, on the basis that it had no jurisdiction over them.[211] At the same time, in dicta, the panel indicated that "judicial wrongs may in principle be brought home to the State Party under Chapter Eleven" and stated that there had been unfairness shown in the Mississippi courts toward the Canadian corporation.

As to NAFTA's Chapter 20 proceedings, although there have been only a limited number of cases pursued to binational panel resolution, to date the United States has a losing record.[212] Moreover, it is worth noting a case that arose under Chapter 20 but ultimately was not pursued to resolution by a binational panel. The so-called Helms-Burton Act provides, among other things, that whoever "traffics" in property that once belonged to US nationals faces the prospect of litigation in the United States, and of possible damages equal in the first instance to the value of the property at issue, and, if trafficking continues, to treble damages. "Trafficking" is defined to include not only selling, transferring, buying, or leasing the property in question, but also "engag[ing] in a commercial activity using or otherwise benefiting from confiscated property."[213] It also places restrictions on entry into the United States by persons who traffic in confiscated property or who are affiliated with such persons by ownership, employment, or family.[214] Canada and Mexico reacted sharply to the passage of this legislation and sought consultations with the United States as a first step in a Chapter 20 proceeding. Although there are strong arguments that the Helms-Burton Act is incompatible with US obligations under NAFTA,[215] Canada and Mexico ultimately did not attempt to establish a binational panel under Chapter 20 to hear the dispute. Instead both countries enacted or amended domestic laws to prevent or "block" and counter the extraterritorial effect of Helms-Burton. They also declined to initiate a claim under the WTO procedures. The European Union did so in February 1997, but suspended the action when the United States made promises to defer application of the "trafficking" provisions of the Act, which the president has done for successive six-month periods, and to seek from Congress modification of the immigration provision, which Congress has not done.

The WTO, NAFTA, and the rule of law

As noted by David Gantz, "[b]oth the WTO and the NAFTA mechanisms are at least nominally legalistic or 'rule oriented' systems, which incorporate a formal adjudicatory decision-making process and effective enforcement mechanisms, as distinct from more pragmatic and flexible models that rely upon diplomatic negotiations between treaty partners – or political power – to resolve conflicts over the interpretation and application of international agreements."[216] The United States strongly supported and was a leader in establishing such systems. At this juncture experience under the WTO and NAFTA dispute settlement mechanisms is rather limited. Already, however, some of the disputes that have arisen have touched sensitive US nerves and involved issues where the stakes have been high. The disputes over Helms-Burton, the foreign sales corporation provisions of US tax law, and the Canadian corporation's challenge to the fairness of a Mississippi jury award are prominent examples. If future cases involve equally or even more sensitive issues, and the United States is the losing party in a fair number of them, the opposition within the United States to the WTO and NAFTA dispute settlement procedures could grow in intensity and call into question whether the United States should continue to support such "rule of law" proceedings.

Compliance with and enforcement of international law

As Louis Henkin has noted, the extent of compliance with international law greatly exceeds that accorded law in national legal systems. In his words, "almost all nations observe almost all principles of international law and almost all of their obligations almost all of the time."[217] This is true, but hardly remarkable, because, as several scholars have noted, nations are the creators of international law and naturally create a law that serves their collective and individual interests.[218] In the same vein, Phillip R. Trimble has asserted that governments "love international law" because it "confirms much more authority and power than it denies."[219] States may also be "induced"[220] to comply with international law by the realization that, under the decentralized system of enforcement characteristic of international law, they may be deprived of their "entitlements" by reciprocal sanctions imposed by other states in response to a violation.[221]

Unfortunately, there are some areas of international law where the compliance record of states is not so impressive. One thinks, for example, of international human rights law, where standards and norms are established in numerous international instruments, but compliance with and enforcement of these standards and norms are spotty, especially on a global basis.[222] Most important, recent clear and arguable violations of international law constraints on the use of force and of arms control obligations have presented major challenges to compliance with and enforcement of international law.

It is important to note that no international institution has general responsibility for the enforcement of international law. For its part the United Nations has the authority to enforce international law when it takes action through the Security Council under Chapter VII of the Charter with respect to threats to the peace, breaches of the peace, and acts of aggression. Under Chapter VII the Security Council has imposed mandatory economic embargoes, authorized the use of force, and established international criminal tribunals for the former Yugoslavia and for Rwanda. As we shall see later in this study, some of the Council's actions have been highly controversial. Outside Chapter VII the United Nations can only attempt to induce states to comply with their Charter obligations.

In national legal systems the most usual way to induce compliance with legal obligations is to bring an action in a court. As we have already seen, however, the Statute of the International Court of Justice makes the competence of the Court dependent on its recognition by individual states. Partially as a result, the number of cases brought before the ICJ have been relatively few, although, as we have also seen, advisory opinions of the Court have addressed some major issues of international law and practice. Under Article 94 of the UN Charter, the Security Council has the authority to recommend or decide on measures to be taken to give effect to a judgment of the Court. Although this is a major Charter provision designed to induce compliance with international law, it has not yet been utilized in practice.

It is also noteworthy that the Law of the Sea Convention, which the United States has not ratified, establishes an International Tribunal on the Law of the Sea. The Convention, which was adopted after ten years of negotiation at a UN-sponsored conference, in an innovative twist allows states parties to choose between four different methods for settling disputes arising under the Convention. These include the International Court of Justice, arbitration, special technical commissions, and the International Tribunal for the Law of the Sea.[223] If the parties to the dispute have chosen different methods, however, the dispute may be submitted only to arbitration. The International Tribunal for the Law of the Sea has been active and has handed down decisions in several cases.[224]

From an overall perspective it also is noteworthy that there are other international institutions of a judicial or quasi-judicial nature that are playing an increasingly important role in implementing and enforcing international law. Besides those institutions discussed above, these include the International Criminal Tribunals for the former Yugoslavia and Rwanda, the UN Compensation Commission, the Iran–United States Claims Tribunal, the Claims Resolution Tribunal for Dormant Accounts in Switzerland and the International Commission on Holocaust Era Insurance Claims.[225]

Besides reference of disputes to the ICJ, there are a number of other means of inducing compliance with international law within the framework of the United Nations. Chapter VI of the Charter, for example, especially in Articles 33 and 37, sets forth a variety of means for the peaceful settlement of disputes. Although the Security Council has no authority under Chapter VI to impose these means on the parties to a dispute, they are obligated to employ one or more of the means specified to settle their disputes peacefully.

Another means of inducing compliance is not expressly provided for in the Charter, but has been developed in practice by the United Nations. These are the various forms of peacekeeping created in response to the long period of nonfunctioning of the collective security system envisaged in Chapter VII. At least in their traditional form, these UN peacekeeping forces required the consent of the parties to the dispute for their creation and their operations on the ground.[226] Recently, as we shall see later in this study, the dividing line between UN peacekeeping, dependent upon consent, and enforcement measures has become somewhat indistinct.

Still another means of inducing compliance that constitutes an innovation in international law is the various supervisory bodies established in the field of human rights. These are commonly classified as treaty and non-treaty bodies. The Human Rights Committee established under the International Covenant on Civil and Political Rights is probably the best known of these treaty-based supervisory bodies. The Human Rights Committee, along with some of its counterparts created under other human rights treaties, is authorized to receive reports from states parties on the steps they have taken to implement the convention, to ask questions of state party representatives about their reports, and, in some cases, to receive "communications" from states parties or from individuals alleging that a state party has violated its obligations under the convention.[227] As for non-treaty bodies, the UN Commission on Human Rights has established various procedures for dealing with situations which appear to reveal "a consistent pattern of gross and reliably attested violations of human rights" and for investigating gross violations of human rights and applying pressure to states engaging in such violations.[228] Most significantly, in December 1993, the UN General Assembly decided to establish the position of High Commissioner for Human Rights. As the leading UN official with responsibility for human rights, the High Commissioner heads the UN's Human Rights Center in Geneva. The first occupant of the office, an Ecuadorian diplomat, Jose Ayala Lasso, was sharply criticized for failing to take forceful action.[229] In 1997, however, Mary Robinson, a former president of Ireland and a human rights activist, was appointed to the post. She played a leading role on human rights matters. But as we shall see in chapter 9, her activism brought her into conflict with the United States.

How successful UN efforts have been in promoting and protecting human rights is a controversial issue.[230] It is generally agreed that regional efforts in Europe and the Americas have enjoyed greater success.

We have already noted in this study that increasingly participants other than states or international organizations play a major role in the international legal process. Nongovernmental organizations, or NGOs, in particular are an integral part of international rule making and enforcement.[231] As Henry H. Perritt Jr. has recently emphasized, the Internet has enabled these private actors to advocate effectively the development of new international law, to promote the acceptance of international law by states, and to detect violations of international law and impose sanctions for such violations.[232]

Institutions concerned with the implementation of treaties are using the Internet to publicize widely national decisions taken under treaties as an aid in the interpretation process and in order to enhance compliance with these treaties. As pointed out by Perritt, "[w]hen violations of international norms are detected by NGOs, they can focus attention, through Web pages and e-mail, on the violators through blacklists and organize secondary pressure against those maintaining relations with the violators."[233] He further notes, as an example of the effectiveness of private actors in enforcing international law, that "[a]s Serb atrocities against the Albanian minority in Kosovo escalated during the spring and summer of 1998, the first color photographs of murder victims usually were found on Web sites maintained by the Albanian Diaspora, not on CNN."[234]

There has been considerable academic discussion of *why* states comply with international law.[235] As Thomas Franck has suggested, "The surprising thing about international law is that nations ever obey its strictures or carry out its mandates."[236]

In an effort to answer the question implicit in Franck's statement, scholars have advanced various theories of compliance. Abram and Antonia Handler Chayes, for example, have argued that states are much more likely to comply with international law if "a cooperative, problem-solving approach" is followed than if coercive mechanisms such as sanctions are imposed.[237] Franck's legitimacy theory postulates that states obey rules that they perceive to have "come into being in accordance with right process."[238] Harold Koh has claimed that the "transnational legal process," which involves a wide set of decision makers in addition to states, including multinational corporations, nongovernmental organizations, international organizations, private individuals, and so on, results in the internalization of transnational legal norms, and this leads to compliance.[239] Institutionalists argue that international institutions can facilitate international cooperation and adherence to international norms by reducing verification costs in international affairs, reducing the cost of punishing cheaters, and helping states overcome prisoner's dilemma problems that often arise in international affairs.[240] Finally, liberal theory contends that compliance with international law is determined in significant part by the domestic structure of a country. According to Anne-Marie Slaughter, for example, states with a "liberal" structure, that is, representative government, protection of civil and political rights, and a judicial system guided by the rule of law, normally comply with international law, at least among themselves.[241]

All of these theories have been subject to criticism,[242] and none has won general acceptance. Andrew Guzman has recently presented his own creative theory of compliance with international law in an effort to explain both instances of compliance and instances of breach.[243] His approach assumes that states are rational and act in their own self-interest and that they are aware of the impact of international law on behavior. As explained by Guzman:

> The model of international law presented in this article is an infinitely repeated game that operates as follows. Any given international obligation is modeled as

a two-stage game. In the first stage, states negotiate over the content of the law and the level of commitment. In the second stage, states decide whether or not to comply with their international obligations. International law affects a state's self-interest, and thus its compliance decision, in two ways. First, it can lead to the imposition of direct sanctions such as trade, military, or diplomatic sanctions. Second, it can lead to a loss of reputational capital in the international arena. If the direct and reputational costs of violating international law are outweighed by the benefits thereof, a state will violate that law.[244]

In analyzing the role of reputation in compliance, Guzman notes that "a decision to violate international law will increase today's payoff but reduce tomorrow's."[245] When entering into an international commitment, a country offers its reputation for living up to its commitments as a form of collateral. To be sure, as Guzman points out, not all countries will want to preserve a reputation for honoring their commitments. "Countries that decide against developing a strong reputation for compliance with international obligations choose short-term benefits over long-term gains."[246]

Guzman also suggests that states can choose from a range of commitment levels and that, by choosing one form of international agreement over another, countries vary the reputational stake they have in the obligation. Thus treaties are more binding than informal agreements. Also, the clarity of the agreement is important. When the agreement is in the form of a treaty and a nation's commitment is clear, a breach is more easily observed and the reputational cost is higher. Countries that wish to increase the level of commitment prefer detailed, formal agreements. International trade agreements such as NAFTA are a good example. In sum, according to Guzman, the impact on a state's reputation of an international law violation may vary depending on the severity of the violation, the reasons for the violation (were there mitigating circumstances present?), the extent to which other states know of the violation, and the clarity of the commitment.

Guzman notes that the clarity of a commitment may be especially problematic if it is based on a customary international law. If the existence of a rule of customary international law is debatable, the reputational cost of a violation will be slight. The same may be said if the existence of an obligation is acknowledged, but there remains uncertainty regarding the exact content of the rule, the exceptions to the rule, the identity of persistent objectors, and so on.

To obviate this problem, Guzman proposes a new definition of international law, including customary international law. That is, international law is defined as "those promises and obligations that make it materially more likely that a state will behave in a manner consistent with those promises and obligations than would otherwise be the case."[247] According to Guzman, "[t]he theoretical problems with CIL [customary international law] stem from the commitment of legal scholars to the traditional definition that emphasizes *jus cogens* and *opinio juris*. A more useful definition turns on the extent to which other states believe that a country has a legal obligation and the extent to which that country's reputation is harmed by a failure to honor that obligation."[248]

Under the Guzman approach, the scope of international law would expand to include obligations that are neither treaties, nor customary international law, nor general principles of law. Specifically, it would cover other forms of international commitment that have an impact on country behavior, including the nonbinding forms of soft law discussed earlier. As an example, Guzman cites the Basel Accord, which establishes minimum capital–asset ratios for banks. Although the Accord is not a treaty or otherwise binding under traditional definitions of international law, it has had a major impact on country behavior. This is because "a central banker whose country failed to supervise banking activity in a manner consistent with the Basel Accord would surely face a loss of influence in the international regulation of banking and find it more difficult to enter into future negotiations."[249]

Guzman would not, however, define international law in an outcome-based fashion – "applying the label of international law to those international obligations that change behavior and denying it from obligations that do not."[250] Even domestic law, he notes, can do nothing more than alter the incentives of actors. It cannot determine outcomes.

In conclusion, Guzman suggests that "[a]long with the possibility of direct sanctions, reputation provides an incentive for states to comply with their obligations."[251]

We shall return to and examine in detail some of Guzman's propositions later in this study, especially as they may apply to actions of the United States. In the meantime, it is clear that one of the most effective ways to implement and enforce international law, if not the most effective, is through domestic law and procedures. We turn in the next chapter to an examination of how this is done (or not done) through US domestic law and practice.

Notes

1. See John R. Bolton, *US Isn't Obligated to Pay the UN*, WALL ST. J., Nov. 17, 1997, at A27.
2. *Id.*
3. Robert F. Turner, *US and UN: The Ties That Bind*, Letter to the Editor, WALL ST. J., Dec. 1, 1997, at A23, col. 1.

4. See, e.g., INTERNATIONAL LAW ANTHOLOGY 37–48 (Anthony D'Amato ed., 1994).
5. Under this provision, states parties to a dispute may authorize the International Court of Justice to disregard the otherwise applicable law on grounds that it is unreasonable or unfair under the circumstances and decide the case on the basis of non-legal criteria. Although some international arbitral tribunals have been authorized by the parties to act *ex aequo et bono,* the International Court of Justice has yet to receive such authorization.
6. M. O. Hudson, [1950] 2 YB. INT'L L. COMM'N. 26 UN Doc. A/CN.4/Ser.A/1950/Add.1.
7. See J. Patrick Kelly, *The Twilight of Customary International Law*, 40 VA. J. of INT'L L. 449, 500–507(2000).
8. *Id.* at 501.
9. *Id.* at 505.
10. *Id.* at 506.
11. For a contrary view, see the Report of the Committee on the Formation of Customary International Law, *National Court Decisions as State Practice*, by Philip M. Moremen, *in* PROCEEDINGS OF THE AMERICAN BRANCH OF THE INTERNATIONAL LAW ASSOCIATION 102 (1999–2000).
12. Kelly, *supra* note 7, at 505.
13. Louis Sohn, *Sources of International Law,* 25 GA. J. INT'L & COMP. L. 399, 401 (1996).
14. North Sea Continental Shelf (F. R. G. v. Den/F. R. G. v. Neth.), 1969 ICJ 3, 43.
15. Michael Akehurst, *Custom as a Source of International Law*, 47 BRIT. YB INT'L L. 1,18–19, 53 (1977).
16. KAROL WOLFKE, CUSTOM IN PRESENT INTERNATIONAL LAW 67–68 (1964).
17. Anthony D'Amato, *Customary Law Doctrine*, *in* INTERNATIONAL LAW ANTHOLOGY, *supra* note 4, at 61, 63–64.
18. Bin Cheng, *United Nations Resolutions on Outer Space: "Instant" International Customary Law?* 5 INDIAN J. INT'L L. 23 (1965).
19. See Akehurst, *supra* note 15.
20. Declaration of Legal Principles Governing the Activities of States in the Exploration and Uses of Outer Space, GA Res. 1962 (XVII), at 15 (1963).
21. Treaty on Principles Governing the Activities of States in the Exploration and Use of Outer Space, Including the Moon and Other Celestial Bodies, Jan. 27, 1967, 18 UST 2410, TIAS No. 6347, 610 UNTS 205.
22. OSCAR SCHACHTER, INTERNATIONAL LAW IN THEORY AND PRACTICE 88 (1991).
23. GA Res. 2625, UN GAOR, 25th Sess., Supp. No. 28, at 121, UN Doc. A/8028 (1970).
24. GA Res. 3314, UN GAOR, 29th Sess., Supp. No. 31, at 142, UN Doc. A/0631 (1974).
25. GA Res. 217A (III) (1948).
26. Kelly, *supra* note 7, at 469–75.
27. ANTHONY A. D'AMATO, THE CONCEPT OF CUSTOM IN INTERNATIONAL LAW 77, 85 (1971).
28. *Id.*
29. Kelly, *supra* note 7, at 479.
30. D'AMATO, *supra* note 27, at 82–85.
31. Kelly, *supra* note 7, at 508.
32. *Id.* at 514.
33. *Id.* at 512.
34. See, e.g., Jonathan I. Charney, *The Persistent Objector Rule and the Development of Customary International Law*, 56 BRIT. Y.B. INT'L L. 1 (1986) (opposing the rule), and Ted L. Stein, *The Approach of the Different Drummer: The Principle of the Persistent Objector in International Law*, 26 HARV. INT'L LJ 457 (1985) (supporting the rule).

35. Anthony A. D'Amato, *A Reformulation of Customary Law*, *in* INTERNATIONAL LAW ANTHOLOGY, *supra* note 4, at 72–73.
36. *Id.* at 73.
37. For useful discussion, see Anthony D'Amato, *Treaty-Based Rules of Custom*, *in* INTERNATIONAL LAW ANTHOLOGY, *supra* note 4, at 94. The classic article on this subject is Richard Baxter, *Treaties and Custom*, 1970–71 REC. DES COURS 25.
38. D'Amato, *supra* note 37, at 95.
39. *Id.* at 101.
40. See Anthony D'Amato, *Jus Cogens: Definition*, *in* INTERNATIONAL LAW ANTHOLOGY, *supra* note 4, at 115.
41. See OPPENHEIM'S INTERNATIONAL LAW 7–8 (9th ed., R. Y. Jennings and A. Watts eds., 1992).
42. E. MCWHINNEY, UNITED NATIONS LAW MAKING 73–75 (1984).
43. Richard D. Kearney & Robert E. Dalton, *The Treaty on Treaties*, 64 AM. J. INT'L L. 495, 536 (1970).
44. Military and Paramilitary Activities in and Against Nicaragua (Nicaragua v. United States), 1986 ICJ 14 (Judgment on Merits of June 27).
45. See Anthony D'Amato, *It's a Bird, It's a Plane, It's Jus Cogens!*, 6 CONN. J. INT'L L. 1 (1990).
46. Kearney & Dalton, *supra* note 43, at 547.
47. Restatement of the Law (Third) of the Foreign Relations Law of the United States 331, Reporters' Note 4 (1987).
48. See LOUIS HENKIN, RICHARD CRAWFORD PUGH, OSCAR SCHACHTER, & HANS SMIT, INTERNATIONAL LAW 94 (3rd ed., 1993).
49. See e.g., Anthea Elizabeth Roberts, *Traditional and Modern Approaches to Customary International Law: A Reconciliation*, 95 AM. J. INT'L L. 757 (2001).
50. W. Michael Reisman, *The Cult of Custom in the Late 20th Century*, 17 CAL. W. INT'L LJ 133, 134 (1987).
51. Phillip R. Trimble, *Globalization, International Institutions, and the Erosion of National Sovereignty and Democracy*, 95 MICH. L. REV. 1946 (1995).
52. Kelly, *supra* note 7, at 480.
53. *Id.*
54. *Id.* at 481–84.
55. *Id.* at 490.
56. *Id.* at 484–95.
57. General Comment No. 24, General Comment on issues relating to reservations made upon ratification or accession to the Covenant or the Optional Protocols thereto, or in relation to declarations under Article 41 of the Covenant, UN Doc. CCPR/C21/Rev. 1/Add.6(1994).
58. *Id.* at para. 8.
59. Letter of Hon. Conrad K. Harper, Legal Adviser, Department of State, to Hon. Francisco Jose Aguilar-Urbina, Chairman, Human Rights Committee, quoted in Richard B. Lillich, *Introduction: The Growing Importance of Customary International Human Rights Law*, 25 GA. J. INT'L & COMP. L. 1, 20n.101 (1996).
60. See Introduction to this study, at page 2.
61. See Kelly, *supra* note 7.
62. HENKIN ET AL., *supra* note 48, at 416.
63. 1951 ICJ 89.
64. For discussion see Eduardo Jimenez de Arechaga, *International Law in the Past Third of a Century*, 159 REC. DES COURS 35–37(1978-I).

65. See *Id.*
66. Richard Baxter, *Treaties and Custom*, 129 REC. DES COURS 25,101(1970-I).
67. Prosper Weil, *Towards Relative Normativity in International Law?*, 77 AM. J. INT'L L. 413, 438 (1983).
68. Oscar Schachter, *Entangled Treaty and Custom*, *in* INTERNATIONAL LAW AT A TIME OF PERPLEXITY 717, 718 (Yoram Dinstein ed., 1988).
69. *Id.* at 718.
70. *Id.* at 718–19.
71. *Id.* at 720–21.
72. See vols. 1 and 2 of UNITED NATIONS LEGAL ORDER (Oscar Schachter & Christopher C. Joyner eds., 1995).
73. Oscar Schachter, *The UN Legal Order: An Overview*, 1 UNITED NATIONS LEGAL ORDER, *supra* note 72, at 1, 2.
74. *Id.* at 4.
75. *Id.* at 7.
76. See, in particular, Article 39 of the UN Charter.
77. For a magisterial examination of the lawmaking capacity of the specialized agencies and the IAEA, see Frederic L. Kirgis Jr., *Specialized Law-Making Processes*, *in* 1 UNITED NATIONS LEGAL ORDER, *supra* note 72, at 109.
78. *Id.*
79. *Id.* at 112–16.
80. ILO Const. Art. 19(5)(b).
81. ILO Const. Art. 19(5)(d).
82. See Restatement (Third) of the Foreign Relations Law of the United States, Section 303, comment d (1987).
83. ILO Const. Art. 19(5)(e).
84. ILO Const. Art. 23(2).
85. ILO Const. Art. 19(6)(d).
86. Kirgis, *supra* note 77, at 115.
87. *Id.* at 116.
88. *Id.* at 121.
89. IAEA Stat., Art. XII.
90. *Id.*, Art. XVIII(C).
91. PAUL SZASZ, THE LAW AND PRACTICE OF THE INTERNATIONAL ATOMIC ENERGY AGENCY 76–77 (1970).
92. Kirgis, *supra* note 77, at 122–23.
93. WHO Const., Art. 21.
94. *Id.* Art.73.
95. Kirgis, *supra* note 77, at 123.
96. *Id.* at 124.
97. Chicago Convention, Arts. 37, 54(1).
98. *Id.* Art.90(a).
99. *Id.* Art. 38.
100. Kirgis, *supra* note 77, at 125.
101. *Id.* at 126–34.
102. *Id.* at 142–43.
103. *Id.* at 143.
104. See JORDAN J. PAUST ET AL., INTERNATIONAL LAW AND LITIGATION IN THE US 34 (2000).
105. Remarks by W. Michael Reisman, *A Hard Look at Soft Law*, 82 PROC. AM. SOC. INT'L L. 371, 376 (1988).

106. Weil, *supra* note 67, at 414, n. 7 (1983).
107. Geoffrey Palmer, *New Ways to Make International Environmental Law*, 86 AM. J. INT'L L. 259, 269 (1992).
108. *Id.*
109. *Id.*
110. Oscar Schachter, *The Twilight Existence of Nonbinding International Agreements*, 71 AM. J. INT'L L. 296, 299 (1977).
111. *Id.* at 300.
112. *Id.* at 301.
113. See BURNS H. WESTON, RICHARD A. FALK, & HILLARY CHARLESWORTH, INTERNATIONAL LAW AND WORLD ORDER 146 (3d ed., 1997).
114. *Id.*
115. To be sure, with the Internet available, the research problems become somewhat less formidable.
116. OSCAR SCHACHTER, INTERNATIONAL LAW IN THEORY AND PRACTICE 52 (1991).
117. Right of Passage Over Indian Territory (Port. v. India) (Merits), 1960 ICJ 6.
118. International Status of South West Africa, 1950 ICJ 128.
119. Case Concerning the Barcelona Traction, Light and Power Company, Ltd., 1970 ICJ 3.
120. Factory at Chorzow Case, PCIJ Ser. A, No.17 (1928).
121. Corfu Channel Case (United Kingdom v. Albania), 1949 ICJ 4.
122. Effect of Awards of compensation Made by the United Nations Administrative Tribunal, 1954 ICJ 47 (Advisory Opinion).
123. Judgments of the Administrative Tribunal of the ILO Upon Complaints Made Against UNESCO, 1956 ICJ 77, at 85–86 (Advisory Opinion).
124. Case Concerning the Temple of Preah Vihear (Cambodia v. Thailand), 1962 ICJ 6, and the French Nuclear Test Cases (New Zealand v. France) (Australia v. France), 1974 ICJ 253, 268, 457, 473.
125. SCHACHTER, *supra* note 116, at 52.
126. See, in particular, Gordon A. Christenson, *Jus Cogens: Guarding Interests Fundamental to International Society*, 28 VA. J. INT'L L. 585 (1988).
127. SCHACHTER, *supra* note 116, at 53.
128. Jimenez de Arechaga, *supra* note 64, at 42 (1978-I).
129. Kearney & Dalton, *supra* note 43, at 518.
130. To be sure, Anthony D'Amato has labeled the approach taken by the Vienna Convention as the "limited contextual approach" on the ground that it is more liberal than the strictly textual approach taken by the Institute of International Law. He concedes, however, that the Vienna Convention's approach "does seem to come down on the side of the principle of textuality." Anthony D'Amato, *Three Approaches to Treaty Interpretation*, *in* WESTON, FALK, & CHARLESWORTH, *supra* note 113, at 98–101.
131. Kearney & Dalton, *supra* note 43, at 519. The amendment introduced by the United States read as follows:

    A treaty shall be interpreted in good faith in order to determine the meaning to be given to its terms in the light of all relevant factors, including in particular:
    (a) the context of the treaty;
    (b) its objects and purposes;
    (c) any agreement between the parties regarding the interpretation of the treaty;
    (d) any instrument made by one or more parties in connection with the conclusion of the treaty and accepted by the other parties as an instrument related to the treaty;

(e) any subsequent practice in the application of the treaty which establishes the common understanding of the meaning of the terms as between the parties;
(f) the preparatory work of the treaty;
(g) the circumstances of its conclusion;
(h) any relevant rules of international law applicable in the relations between the parties generally;
(i) the special meaning to be given to a term if the parties intended such term to have a special meaning.

132. This approach is set out in full in MYRES S. MCDOUGAL, HAROLD D. LASSWELL, & JAMES C. MILLER, THE INTERPRETATION OF AGREEMENTS AND WORLD PUBLIC ORDER (1967). For a succinct summary see Anthony D'Amato, *Three Approaches to Treaty Interpretation*, *in* WESTON, FALK, & CHARLESWORTH, *supra* note 113, at 98, 99–101.
133. MCDOUGAL, LASSWELL, & MILLER, *supra* note 132, at 40. In the words of the authors: "The goals of interpretation that we propose take into consideration the obligation of any decision-maker to act rationally in harmony with the fundamental objectives of the community whose authoritative spokesman he is. Decision outcomes have consequences that can and ought to be affected by deliberate efforts to further the realization of the basic pattern of value distribution and the fundamental institutions that are compatible with the preferred system of public order." *Id.*
134. For a biting critique of the McDougal approach, see Gerald Fitzmaurice, *Vae Victis or Woe to the Negotiators! Your Treaty or our "Interpretation" of it?*, 65 AM. J. INT'L L. 358 (1971).
135. Kearney & Dalton, *supra* note 43, at 520. In particular, McDougal cited the well-known but controversial decision of the Permanent Court of International Justice in The S.S. *Lotus*, PCIJ Ser. A, No. 10 (1927).
136. Kearney & Dalton, *supra* note 43, at 520.
137. *Id.*
138. *Comments of Sir Eric Beckett on the Report of H. Lauterpacht (of the Second Commission of the Institute of International Law) on the Interpretation of Treaties*, 43-I ANN. INST. D. INT'L 437–38 (1950). According to Kearney and Dalton, Jimenez de Arechaga, an eminent international law authority, cited Sir Eric Beckett in the Institute's debates when he suggested that "too ready admission of the preparatory work" would afford an opportunity to states which had "found a clear provision of a treaty inconvenient" to allege a different interpretation "because there was generally something in the preparatory work that could be found to support almost any intention." Kearney & Dalton, *supra* note 43, at 520.
139. *Id.*, at 520.
140. See HENKIN ET AL., *supra* note 48, at 478, para. 1.
141. Ian Johnstone, *Treaty Interpretation: The Authority of Interpretive Communities*, 12 MICH. J. INT'L L. 371, 419 (1991).
142. For discussion of such agreements and their value as evidence of customary international law see ALAN C. SWAN & JOHN F. MURPHY, CASES AND MATERIALS ON THE REGULATION OF INTERNATIONAL BUSINESS AND ECONOMIC RELATIONS 1076–82, 1086–93(2d ed., 1999).
143. The most elaborate, if controversial, discussion of this claim and counterclaim process in the establishment of customary international law norms is set forth in MYRES S. MCDOUGAL & W. MICHAEL REISMAN, INTERNATIONAL LAW IN CONTEMPORARY PERSPECTIVE 1–20 (1981).

144. An excellent example is the Gulf of Maine case, Case Concerning Delimitation of the Maritime Boundary in the Gulf of Maine Area (Canada v. US), 1984 ICJ 246. In this case, Canada and the United States invoked Art. 26 of the ICJ Statute, which provides for use of a Special Chamber by agreement of the parties. A five-person panel was selected by consent of the parties to decide the disputed fisheries jurisdiction in the Gulf of Maine. Both parties agreed to submit drafts of their proposed methods for drawing the baselines and settling the dispute, which would determine each state's territorial waters and continental shelf rights. The Special Chamber, after accepting proposals from each party, independently determined the new line.
145. 21 UST 2517, TIAS No. 6997. The US enabling legislation for the convention is Chapter 2 of the Federal Arbitration Act, 9 USC Sections 201–8.
146. Oscar Schachter, *International Law in Theory and Practice – General Course in Public International Law*, 178 REC. DES COURS 9208 (1982-V).
147. Art. 92 of the UN Charter provides: "The International Court of Justice shall be the principal judicial organ of the United Nations. It shall function in accordance with the annexed Statute, which is based upon the Statute of the Permanent Court of International Justice and forms an integral part of the present Charter."
148. See Louis B. Sohn, *The UN System as Authoritative Interpreter of its Law*, in 1 UNITED NATIONS LEGAL ORDER, *supra* note 72, at 169, 171.
149. *Id.* at 173–74.
150. *Id.* at 176–83.
151. Questions of Interpretation and Application of the 1971 Montreal Convention Arising from the Aerial Incident at Lockerbie (Libyan Arab Jamahiriya v. United Kingdom and Libyan Arab Jamahiriya v. United States), Preliminary Objections, Judgments, at http://www.icj-cij.org. International Court of Justice, Feb. 27, 1998.
152. Advisory Opinion relating to Conditions of Admission of a State to membership in the United Nations, 1948 ICJ Rep. 57.
153. Advisory Opinion relating to Reparation for Injuries Suffered in the Service of the United Nations, 1949 ICJ Rep. 174.
154. Certain Expenses of the United Nations, 1962 ICJ Rep. 151.
155. Article 17 of the UN Charter provides:

    1. The General Assembly shall consider and approve the budget of the Organization.
    2. The expenses of the Organization shall be borne by the Members as apportioned by the General Assembly.
    3. The General Assembly shall consider and approve any financial and budgetary arrangements with specialized agencies referred to in Article 57 and shall examine the administrative budgets of such specialized agencies with a view to making recommendations to the agencies concerned.

156. For an excellent summary of the Certain Expenses case, see Sohn, *supra* note 148, at 198–203.
157. GA Resolution 49/75 K, operative paragraph 1 (Dec. 15, 1994). The resolution was adopted by a vote of 78–43 (US)–38.
158. The request was made by a resolution adopted by the World Health Assembly, Resolution WHA 46.40, operative paragraph 1 (May 14, 1993). The resolution was adopted by a vote of 73–40 (US)–10. An earlier US motion determining that the resolution was not within the competence of the WHO was rejected by a vote of 62–38–3.
159. Legality of the Threat or Use by a State of Nuclear Weapons in Armed Conflict, 1996 ICJ Rep. 226 (Advisory Opinion of July 8). The decision was adopted by a vote of 11–3.

160. For discussion of the US position, see Michael J. Matheson, *The Opinions of the International Court of Justice on the Threat or Use of Nuclear Weapons*, 91 AM. J. INT'L L. 417, 419 (1997).
161. Legality of the Threat or Use of Nuclear Weapons (Advisory Opinion of July 8, 1996), *supra* note 159.
162. See Matheson, *supra* note 160, at 420.
163. *Id.*
164. The one dissenting vote was by Judge Shigeru Oda of Japan, who argued that the request was not a genuine request for an advisory opinion but merely a request for a preconceived "legal axiom"; that the request was unclear; that it did not represent a consensus of the General Assembly; and that the request did not relate either to a concrete dispute or to a concrete problem that had to be resolved. Dissenting opinion of Judge Oda, paras. 43, 51.
165. Legality of the Threat or Use of Nuclear Weapons, *supra* note 159, paras. 13, 14, 15, 16, and 17.
166. Matheson, *supra* note 160, at 421.
167. Richard A. Falk, *Nuclear Weapons, International Law and the World Court: A Historic Encounter*, 91 AM. J. INT'L LAW 64, 66 (1997).
168. For discussion see Matheson, *supra* note 160, at 421–23.
169. Legality of the Threat or Use of Nuclear Weapons, *supra* note 159, para. 105.
170. See Michael J. Matheson, *supra* note 160, at 424–25.
171. Legality of the Threat or Use of Nuclear Weapons, *supra* note 159, para. 67.
172. *Id.* paras. 70–71.
173. For discussion of the Court's examination see Matheson, *supra* note 160, at 427–29.
174. Legality of the Threat or Use of Nuclear Weapons, *supra* note 159, para. 105(2)(E) (emphasis added).
175. Matheson, *supra* note 160, at 429.
176. *Id.* at 429–30.
177. *Id.* at 433–34.
178. Treaty on the Non-Proliferation of Nuclear Weapons, July 1, 1968, 21 UST 483, 729 UNTS 161.
179. Legality of the Threat or Use of Nuclear Weapons, *supra* note 159, para. 105(2)(F).
180. *Id.* para. 99.
181. Matheson, *supra* note 160, at 435.
182. See Falk, *supra* note 167, at 74.
183. Matheson, *supra* note 160, at 435.
184. Falk, *supra* note 167, at 74.
185. Jonathan Schell, *The Folly of Arms Control*, 79 FOREIGN AFF. 22 (2000).
186. Understanding on Rules and Procedures Governing the Settlement of Disputes, WTO Agreement Annex 2, 33 INT'L LEG. MATERIALS 1226 (1994). For an overview of the Dispute Settlement Understanding, see SWAN & MURPHY, *supra* note 142, at 591–96.
187. Compare John H. Jackson, *The WTO Dispute Settlement Understanding – Misunderstandings on the Nature of Legal Obligation*, 91 AM. J. INT'L L. 60, 61, 63–64 (1997) (obligation), with Judith Hippler Bello, *The WTO Dispute Settlement Understanding: Less is More*, 90 AM. J. INT'L L. 416, 416–17 (1996) (no obligation).
188. See Mark L. Movsesian, *Sovereignty, Compliance and the World Trade Organization: Lessons from the History of Supreme Court Review*, 20 MICH. J. INT'L L. 775, 787–88 and n.89 (1999).
189. See 19 USC Section 3512(a)(1).
190. See 19 USC Section 3512(c)(1)(B).

191. See 19 USC Section 3535.
192. See INT'L TRADE REPORTER 997 (June 29, 2000).
193. See HR 4706, introduced by Representative Benjamin L. Chardin (D-Md).
194. INT'L TRADE REPORTER 997–98 (June 29, 2000).
195. United States – Tax Treatment for "Foreign Sales Corporations" Recourse to Article 21.5 of the DSU by the European Communities, Report of the Appellate Body, WT/DS108/24 (Jan. 14, 2002).
196. United States – Tax Treatment for "Foreign Sales Corporations" Recourse to Arbitration by the United States under Article 22.6 of the DSU and Article 4.11 of the SCM *Agreement* Decision of the Arbitrator, WT/DS108/ARB (Aug. 30, 2002).
197. See Pascal Lamy, *Come on, America, Play By the Rules!*, WALL ST. J., March 3, 2003, at A16, col. 3.
198. World Trade Organization, *United States–Definitive Safeguard Measures on Imports of Certain Steel Products, Final Reports of the Panel,* July 11, 2003, at http://www.wto.org/english/tratop_e/dispu_e/steel_panel_pdf_files_e.zip.
199. Paul Meller, *WTO Formally Designates US Steel Tariffs as Illegal*, NY TIMES, July 12, 2003, at C3, col. 3.
200. For recent discussion, see Movsesian, *supra* note 188, at 783–91. For an extensive consideration of the WTO's overall performance, see *Symposium: The First Five Years of the WTO*, 31 L. AND PO'Y IN INT'L BUS. 549 (2000).
201. For a summary of this debate, see Movsesian, *supra* note 188, at 791–95.
202. For an argument that "the WTO presently represents neither the threat to sovereignty its critics decry, nor the advance for international compliance its advocates anticipate," see *id.* at 812–18. For an argument that the World Trade Organization enhances rather than undermines democratic control over trade policy, see John O. McGinnis & Mark L. Movsesian, *The World Trade Constitution*, 114 HARV. L. REV. 511 (2000).
203. This description of the NAFTA dispute settlement procedures is taken largely from SWAN & MURPHY, *supra* note 142, at 529, 600, and 966. For an extensive and recent discussion of these procedures, see RALPH H. FOLSOM, MICHAEL WALLACE GORDON, & DAVID LOPEZ, NAFTA: A PROBLEM-ORIENTED COURSEBOOK 321–50, 425–596 (2000).
204. In the United States, if the arbitration takes place under the auspices of the International Centre for the Settlement of Investment Disputes (ICSID), arbitral awards are enforceable under 22 USC Section 1650(a). If the arbitration is ad hoc under the UN Commission for International Trade Law (UNCITRAL), an award is enforceable under the Federal Arbitration Act, 9 USC Section 9.
205. Avi Gesser, *Why NAFTA Violates the Canadian Constitution*, 27 DENV. J. INT'L L. & PO'Y 121, 128–29 (1998).
206. American Coalition for Competitive Trade v. Clinton, 128 F. 3d 761 (DC Cir. 1997).
207. Compare Laurence H. Tribe, *Taking Text and Structure Seriously: Reflections on Free-form Method in Constitutional Interpretation*, 108 HARV. L. REV. 1221 (1995), with Bruce Ackerman and David Golove, *Is NAFTA Constitutional?*, 108 HARV. L. REV. 801 (1995).
208. 242 F. 3d 1300 (11th Cir. 2001).
209. See Jack J. Coe Jr., *Taking Stock of NAFTA Chapter 11 in its Tenth Year*, 36 VAND. J. TRANSNAT'L L. 1381 (2003).
210. See William Glaberson, *NAFTA Invoked to Challenge Court Award,* NY TIMES, Jan. 28, 1999, at C6. For discussion of the Loewen case, see William S. Dodge, *Loewen v. United States: Trials and Errors under NAFTA Chapter Eleven*, 52 DEPAUL L. REV. 563 (2002).

211. The Loewen Group Inc. v. United States, ICSID, No. ARB(AF) 98/3(6.23/03).
212. See David A. Gantz, *Dispute Settlement Under the NAFTA and the WTO: Choice of Forum Opportunities and Risks for the NAFTA Parties*, 14 AM. U. INT'L L. REV. 1025 (1999).
213. The Cuban Liberty and Democratic Solidarity (Libertad) Act, Pub. L. No. 104-114, 110 Stat. 785 (March 12, 1996), section 4(13).
214. For discussion of the Act see Andreas F. Lowenfeld, *Agora: The Cuban Liberty and Democratic Solidarity (Libertad) Act*, 90 AM. J. INT'L L. 419–40 (1996).
215. See Michael Wallace Gordon, *The Conflict of United States Sanctions Laws with Obligations under the North American Free Trade Agreement*, 27 STETSON L. REV. 1259 (1998).
216. Gantz, *supra* note 212, at1031.
217. LOUIS HENKIN, HOW NATIONS BEHAVE 47 (2d ed., 1979).
218. As an eminent British authority on international law has noted: "All legal systems correspond to some extent to the prevailing climate of opinion in the society in which they operate, but in national legal systems the concentration of legislative power in the hands of a small number of individuals may result in the enactment of rules which most people do not want and are reluctant to obey. In international law the absence of a legislature means that states very largely create law for themselves, and it is unlikely that they will create law which is not in their interests or which they will be tempted to break." MICHAEL AKEHURST, A MODERN INTRODUCTION TO INTERNATIONAL LAW 8 (5th ed., 1984).
219. Phillip R. Trimble, *International Law, World Order and Critical Legal Studies*, 42 STAN. L. REV. 811, 833 (1990).
220. See Carl-August Fleischhauer, *Inducing Compliance*, *in* 1 UNITED NATIONS LEGAL ORDER, *supra* note 72, at 231.
221. Examples of this "tit-for-tat" or "tit-for-a-different tat" process are discussed in Anthony D'Amato, *Is International Law "Law"?*, *in* INTERNATIONAL LAW ANTHOLOGY, *supra* note 4, at 45–47.
222. Two recent major publications of note are LOUIS HENKIN ET AL., HUMAN RIGHTS (1999), and HENRY J. STEINER & PHILLIP ALSTON, INTERNATIONAL HUMAN RIGHTS IN CONTEXT (2000). An earlier work which explores enforcement issues in detail is LOUIS HENKIN & JOHN LAWRENCE HARGROVE, HUMAN RIGHTS: AN AGENDA FOR THE NEXT CENTURY (1994).
223. For discussion, see Louis B. Sohn, *Peaceful Settlement of Disputes in Ocean Conflicts: Does UNCLOS III Point the Way?* 46 LAW & CONTEMP. PROBS. 195 (spring 1983).
224. For discussion of the activities of the Tribunal see Margaret L. Tomlinson, *Recent Developments in the International Law of the Sea,* 32 INT'L LAW. 599, 602–3 (1998), Barry Hart Dubner, *Recent Developments in the International Law of the Sea,* 33 INT'L LAW. 627, 629 (1999), and James E. Baily, *Recent Developments in the International Law of the Sea,* 34 INT'L LAW. 829 (2000).
225. For discussion of recent activity of these institutions, see articles contained in *International Legal Developments in Review:1999* (John F. Murphy ed.), 34 INT'L LAW. 365–835 (2000).
226. See Fleischauer, *supra* note 220, at 237.
227. For discussion and critical analysis of the treaty-based supervisory bodies, see Anne F. Bayefsky, *Making the Human Rights Treaties Work*, *in* HENKIN & HARGROVE, *supra* note 222, at 229.
228. Under ECOSOC Res. 1235(XLII), 42 UN ESCOR Supp. (No.1) at 17, UN Doc. E/4393(1967), the Human Rights Commission is authorized to receive petitions alleging situations involving a "consistent pattern of gross and reliably attested violations." Under ECOSOC Res. 1503(XLVIII), 48 UN ESCOR (No.1A) at 8,

UN Doc. E/4832/Add.1 (1970), a working group of the Sub-Commission on the Promotion and Protection of Human Rights, a body composed of independent experts and a subsidiary organ of the Commission, reviews the complaints that have been received in the preceding year, and decides which "situations" should be forwarded to the Sub-Commission in plenary which, in turn, can decide to refer the country concerned to the Commission, drop the situation, or reconsider it the following year. The government concerned is invited to defend itself before the Commission, but the proceedings are private and the complainant is not even advised of the action taken. The Commission considers all of the relevant material and then announces the names of the countries it has considered and those dropped from consideration. In the absence of a decision to go public, the entire procedure is shrouded in secrecy, with each of its stages being accomplished in confidential sessions by the bodies concerned.

Under ECOSOC Res. 1235, the Commission holds an annual public debate focusing on gross violations of human rights. In this context it has developed an array of methods by which to investigate and apply pressure to individual states. In 1995, the United States was the subject of substantial discussion under Res. 1235. A resolution was introduced which endorsed the report of the Special Rapporteur on Racism and Xenophobia regarding the situation in the United States, and expressed concern about persisting racial discrimination in the United States. The proposed resolution was rejected by a wide margin, with only three countries voting in favor. Commission on Human Rights, *Violation of Human Rights in the United States as a Result of Racism and Racial Discrimination Persisting in United States Society*, UN Doc.E/CN.4/1995/L.Rev.2(1995).

The Commission has also adopted a practice under Res. 1235 of appointing special rapporteurs, special representatives, experts, working groups, and other envoys to monitor human rights violations in particular countries. Similarly, the Commission has developed so-called "Thematic Procedures" focusing on particular kinds of human rights violations. The first of these procedures, the Working Group on Enforced or Involuntary Procedures was established in 1980 in response to developments in Argentina and Chile. Subsequently, Special Rapporteurs have been appointed to address, *inter alia*, summary or arbitrary executions, torture, religious intolerance, freedom of opinion and expression, racial discrimination and xenophobia, the sale of children, child prostitution and child pornography, internally displaced persons, the independence and impartiality of the judiciary, violence against women, and the effects of toxic and dangerous products on human rights.

229. See Aryeh Neier, War Crimes, Brutality, Genocide, Terror, and the Struggle for Justice 23–24 (1998).

230. See, e.g., The United Nations and Human Rights; A Critical Appraisal (Philip Alston ed., 1992); Stephen Marks, *The United Nations and Human Rights: The Promise of Multilateral Diplomacy and Action, in* The Future of International Human Rights 291 (Burns Weston & Stephen Marks eds., 1999).

231. See Steve Charnovitz, *Two Centuries of Participation: NGOs and International Governance,* 18 Mich. J. Int'l L. 183 (1997).

232. Henry H. Perritt Jr., *The Internet is Changing the Public International Legal System*, 88 Ky LJ 885, 895–911 (1999–2000).

233. *Id.* at 910.

234. *Id.* at 910–11.

235. A helpful survey of this discussion may be found in Andrew T. Guzman, *A Compliance-Based Theory of International Law*, 90 Cal. L. Rev. 1823 (2002).

236. Thomas M. Franck, *Legitimacy in the International System,* 82 AM. J. INT'L L. 705 (1988).
237. ABRAM CHAYES & ANTONIA HANDLER CHAYES, THE NEW SOVEREIGNTY: COMPLIANCE WITH INTERNATIONAL REGULATORY AGREEMENTS 3 (1995).
238. Franck, *supra* note 236, at 706.
239. Harold Hongju Koh, *Transnational Legal Process*, 75 NEB. L. REV. 181 (1996); Harold Hongju Koh, *Why Do Nations Obey International Law*? 106 YALE LJ 2599 (1997).
240. For a listing of some of the leading institutionalist contributions, see Guzman, *supra* note 235, at 1839, n.67.
241. See Anne-Marie Burley (now Slaughter), *Law Among Liberal States; Liberal Internationalism and the Act of State Doctrine*, 92 COLUM. L. REV. 1907, 1920–21 (1992).
242. For a survey of these criticisms that also advances some of the author's criticisms, see Guzman, *supra* note 235.
243. *Id.*
244. *Id.* at 1846.
245. *Id.* at 1849.
246. *Id.* at 1850.
247. *Id.* at 1882.
248. *Id.* at 1887.
249. *Id.* at 1880.
250. *Id.* at 1882.
251. *Id.* at 1886.

2 The status of international law under US law

The strength of a country's adherence to the rule of law in international affairs is linked in substantial measure to the extent to which international law can be enforced through national mechanisms. The enforcement of international law through national mechanisms is grounded in the relationship between international law and national law in national legal systems, and this relationship varies considerably from country to country.

From a theoretical perspective the basic distinction is between the monist and dualist (or pluralist) approaches to the relation of international law to national law. Monists consider international law and national law as parts of a single legal system. Monists also often see national law as deriving its validity from international law, which enjoys a higher status in a hierarchy of legal norms. Under the monist approach, international law overrides conflicting national law, including constitutional limitations, and individuals have international legal personality.

In sharp contrast, dualists regard international law and national law as two separate legal systems which operate on different levels. International law can be applied by national mechanisms, particularly courts, only when it has been "transformed" or "incorporated" into national law. Moreover, even when it has been incorporated into national law, international law is subject to constitutional limitations applicable to national law, and may be repealed or superseded by legislative action for purposes of national law. Dualists also stress the international legal personality of states and downgrade or deny that of individuals or other entities.[1]

Some states have constitutional provisions that specify the status of treaties and customary international law in their national legal orders. Most European states now have treaty implementation provisions in their constitutions that have at least some monist attributes, although not all of these states accord treaties an equal or superior place in relation to domestic sources of law within their legal systems. These constitutional provisions may also state that customary international law is an integral part of the national legal order and, in some cases, accord it a status superior to national legislation.[2] By contrast, the United Kingdom, with its unwritten constitutional order, is a classic example of a dualist state where treaties have no domestic force at all unless embodied in an Act of Parliament. For years, the 1953 European Convention for the Protection of Human Rights and Fundamental Freedoms was the classic example of a treaty that bound the United Kingdom internationally – and gave rise to numerous proceedings against the United Kingdom before the European Commission of Human Rights and the European Court of Human Rights – yet had no status whatsoever under national law. In 2000, however, the Human Rights Act incorporated the Convention into British law,[3] although it limited the domestic impact of the Convention in various ways. As to customary international law, British courts have applied it since before the American revolution, stating that the law of nations was "part of the law of England."[4] For its part, the Privy Council stated in 1938 that British courts would treat international law "as incorporated into the domestic law, so far as it is not inconsistent with rules enacted by statutes or finally declared by their tribunals."[5]

Unlike the United Kingdom, the United States has a written constitution, but it is quite elliptical in its references to international law and even more so as to the precise status of international law under US law. The primary exceptions are Article VI, which declares treaties of the United States (as well as the Constitution itself and the laws of the United States) to be "the supreme Law of the Land," and Article III, Section 2, which provides that cases arising under treaties are within the judicial power of the United States. Other provisions of the US Constitution that refer to international law will be discussed later in this chapter, but it is worth noting at this juncture that none of them clearly indicates the status of international agreements other than treaties or of customary international law.

As previously noted in this study, the status of customary international law in the United States has become a topic of hot debate. Before we address this complex topic, however, we need to examine the status of treaties and other international agreements under US law, a topic itself of considerable complexity and some controversy.

Treaties and other international agreements

The restrictive definition of treaties under the US Constitution

At the outset of discussion in this section, it may be useful to distinguish between use of the term "treaty" in international law and practice and its use under the US Constitution. Under Article 1 of the Vienna Convention on the Law of Treaties, a treaty "means an international agreement concluded between states in written form and governed by international law, whether embodied in a single instrument or in two or more related instruments and whatever its particular designation." Under United States constitutional law and practice a treaty has a more restricted meaning. That is, under Article II(2)(1), the term "treaty" is applied only to international agreements, however denominated, that become binding on the United States through ratification by the president with the advice and consent of the Senate through a two-thirds vote of that body.

Self-executing and non-self-executing treaties

As noted above, Article VI of the US Constitution explicitly makes "Treaties" the supreme law of the land and further provides that "the Judges in every State shall be bound thereby, any Thing in the Constitution or Laws of any State to the Contrary notwithstanding." In the 1829 case of *Foster and Elam v. Neilson*,[6] however, Chief Justice John Marshall interpreted Article VI in such a way as to distinguish between "self-executing" and "non-self-executing" treaties. In Justice Marshall's words:

> Our constitution declares a treaty to be the law of the land. It is, consequently, to be regarded in courts of justice as equivalent to an act of the legislature, whenever it operates of itself without the aid of any legislative provision. But when the terms of the stipulation import a contract, when either of the parties engages to perform a particular act, the treaty addresses itself to the political, not the judicial department; and the legislature must execute the contract before it can become a rule for the Court.

It is generally agreed that a treaty cannot take effect as domestic law without implementation by Congress if the agreement would achieve what lies within the exclusive lawmaking power of Congress. Examples include agreements providing for the payment of money by the United States, committing the United States to come to the armed defense of an ally, or creating an international crime and providing for its punishment under national law. Beyond these agreed areas, however, US courts have experienced considerable difficulty distinguishing between self-executing and non-self-executing treaties utilizing the deceptively simple test set forth by Justice Marshall.

Before turning to an examination of this difficulty, however, we should keep in mind some points made by Louis Henkin:

> The difference between self-executing and non-self-executing treaties is commonly misunderstood. Whether a treaty is self-executing or not, it is legally binding on the United States. Whether it is self-executing or not, it is supreme

law of the land. If it is not self-executing, Marshall said, it is not "a rule for the Court"; he did not suggest that it is not law for the President or for Congress. It is their obligation to see to it that it is faithfully implemented; it is their obligation to do what is necessary to make a rule for the courts if the treaty requires that it be a rule for the courts, or if making it a rule for the courts is a necessary or a proper means for the United States to carry out its obligation.

The status of a treaty as law of the land derives from, and depends on, its status as a valid, living treaty of the United States. It is not law of the land for either the President or for the courts to enforce if it is not made in accordance with constitutional requirements, or if it is beyond the power of the President and the Senate to make, or if it violates constitutional prohibitions. It is not law of the land if it is not an effective treaty internationally because it is not binding or is invalid under international law, or because it has expired, or has been terminated or destroyed by breach (whether by the United States or by the other party or parties).[7]

Not infrequently a treaty is said to be self-executing only if it gives rise to rights in private individuals. There are serious problems with this view. Rarely do treaties confer rights on individuals in so many words. It is typically a matter of interpretation based upon the subject matter of the treaty and the nature of the behavior toward that subject that the treaty enjoins upon the governmental signatories. The more thoroughly the subject of the treaty falls within an area reserved in the signatory countries to private action (e.g., treaties concerning the ownership and inheritance of property, family matters, the establishment and carrying on of business enterprises, trade, the patenting of inventions, etc.), the more readily the treaty may be read as conferring rights on private individuals. The same may be said the more specifically the signatory governments pledge themselves in the treaty to a course of conduct intended to facilitate, protect, or regulate such private matters. But it should be quite apparent that this line of interpretive inquiry does not and cannot answer the question of whether the treaty was intended to operate of its own force as a rule of domestic law. That a treaty creates private rights may be probative of an intent to have the treaty operate automatically as domestic law. But, so long as private rights can also be created by statute, the mere conclusion that the treaty was intended to create private rights does not also demonstrate that the treaty was intended to be the exclusive mode for accomplishing that result superseding the need for a statute.

Conversely, the mere fact that a treaty was not intended to create rights in private individuals does not demonstrate the absence of an intent for it to operate of its own force as domestic law. On this point there is a great deal of confusion and much careless language in the cases. There are many treaties that create no private rights at all and cannot be readily enforced in a court of law. The reason is that, absent the conferral of a private legal right, it will be difficult, often impossible, for any private individual to surmount the threshold of standing and other justiciability requirements that must be overcome before a court can entertain the case. But, as noted by Henkin in the excerpt above, it would be startling in the extreme to suggest that the mere lack of judicial enforceability deprives a treaty of its force as domestic law; that it was not legally binding on state officials under the Supremacy Clause and their oath of office, or upon executive officials under the Supremacy and "take Care" clauses. Thus, the only distinction between a self-executing and non-self-executing treaty is whether the treaty was intended to operate of its own force as domestic law binding upon public officials, or whether that effect was intended to be contingent on further legislative action.

This distinction, however, has been difficult for US courts to draw. A classic case in this area illustrating, in part, some of the confusion that attends the subject is *Sei Fujii v. State of California*,[8] which held that the provisions of the UN Charter dealing with human rights were non-self-executing. In pertinent part the California court stated that for a treaty to be self-executing "it must appear that the framers of the treaty intended to prescribe a rule that, standing alone, would be enforceable in the [national] courts" and concluded that the UN Charter "pledges the various countries to cooperate" and "represents a moral commitment," but its provisions "were not intended to supersede existing domestic legislation, and we cannot hold that they operate to invalidate the Alien Land Law [of California] . . . " The court did, however, proceed to hold the California Alien Land Law invalid on the ground that it violated the equal protection clause of the Fourteenth Amendment.

The validity of the California court's decision and its reasoning on the issue of whether the human rights provisions of the UN Charter are self-executing have been subject to sharp debate, but no US federal or state court that has addressed the issue since *Sei Fujii* was handed down has held that the Charter's human rights clauses are self-executing. On the contrary, many courts have ruled expressly that they are not.[9] Moreover, US courts have relied on the alleged non-self-executing nature of other UN Charter obligations to deny individual plaintiffs the opportunity to challenge governmental actions as being in violation of such obligations.

For example, in *Diggs v. Richardson*,[10] plaintiffs sought judicial enforcement of UN Security Council Resolution 301, which declared South Africa's continued presence in Namibia to be a breach of international obligations and called upon all states (i) to abstain from sending diplomatic or special missions to South Africa that included the territory of

Namibia in their jurisdictions; and (ii) to abstain from entering into economic or other forms of relationship or dealing with South Africa on behalf of or concerning Namibia which might entrench its authority over the territory. Plaintiffs contended that the resolution constituted a binding international obligation of the United States and that the resolution was self-executing. On the basis of the resolution plaintiffs challenged several visits to South Africa by officials of the US Department of Commerce, who met South African officials and discussed the harvesting of seal furs in Namibia, as a violation of US international obligations and asked that the district court enjoin any further contacts of this type.

For its part the US government argued that the plaintiffs lacked standing, that the case raised a political question not appropriate for judicial resolution, that the resolution was not legally binding on UN member states, and that, in any event, the resolution was not self-executing. The circuit court of appeals affirmed the district court's dismissal of the suit on the ground that, "even assuming there is an international obligation that is binding on the United States," the resolution was non-self-executing and therefore did not confer rights on the citizens of the United States that were enforceable in the United States. The court's reasoning in this case was highly questionable.[11]

As a final example of a US court decision holding a treaty provision with human rights implications to be non-self-executing, in *Haitian Refugee Center, Inc. v. Baker*,[12] a panel of the US Court of Appeals for the Eleventh Circuit held, by a 2–1 vote, that Article 33 of the UN Convention on the Status of Refugees, which prohibits state parties from expelling or returning a refugee "in any manner whatsoever to the frontiers of territories where his life or freedom would be threatened on account of his race, religion, nationality, membership in a particular social group, or political opinion," was non-self-executing. There was a forceful dissent.

The political branches intervene: US declarations that human rights treaties are non-self-executing

Although the United States is a party to only a few human rights treaties, the issue of the self-executing or non-self-executing nature of provisions in these treaties has loomed large. As noted previously, treaties that call for the prevention and punishment of crimes are generally regarded as being non-self-executing as a matter of constitutional requirement. Hence, the Convention on the Prevention and Punishment of the Crime of Genocide (the Genocide Convention) and the Convention Against Torture and Other Cruel, Inhuman or Degrading Treatment or Punishment (the

Torture Convention) were ratified only after Congress had enacted implementing legislation. In addition, the Senate's consent to ratification of the Torture Convention was accompanied by a declaration that the Convention was not self-executing.

Other human rights treaties that provide for no criminal punishment for violations of their terms are not constitutionally required to be non-self-executing. Nonetheless, reflecting a decision by the Senate and the executive branch that the human rights treaties should not be the basis for challenges against federal or state law in US courts, as a policy matter, the Senate's consent to ratification of such treaties as the International Covenant on Civil and Political Rights (ICCPR, or Civil and Political Rights Covenant) and the International Convention on the Elimination of All Forms of Racial Discrimination (the Race Convention) has been accompanied by declarations that the treaties are non-self-executing. Neither the Civil and Political Rights Covenant nor the Race Convention has been followed by legislation designed to implement its terms.

The Senate's consent to ratification of the Civil and Political Rights Covenant and the Race Convention has also been accompanied by a series of reservations, understandings, and declarations (RUDs) that have proven highly controversial. The RUDs accompanying the Senate's consent to ratification of the Civil and Political Rights Covenant, in particular, have been the subject of sometimes heated debate.

Some of these RUDs are incompatible with the concept of the rule of law in international affairs. As Louis Henkin has pointed out,[13] the US reservations to the Civil and Political Rights Covenant were designed to ensure that the United States was taking on no new obligations beyond what its constitution and laws already required. Since a primary purpose of human rights treaties is to change the laws of states parties in such a way as to improve them, Henkin argues, the US reservations are incompatible with the object and purpose of the Civil and Political Rights Covenant and therefore invalid under Article 19 of the Vienna Convention on the Law of Treaties.[14] The Human Rights Committee, in its consideration of the US report on the measures it has taken to give effect to the rights recognized in the Covenant, has also expressed its "regrets" on the extent of the US reservations.[15]

The views of Henkin and of the Human Rights Committee on the validity of the US RUDs, from both a legal and a policy perspective, have enjoyed considerable support among international law scholars. Recently, however, they have been subject to a strong challenge on both practical and jurisprudential grounds. From a practical perspective Curtis A. Bradley and Jack L. Goldsmith have argued in support of US declarations that the Civil and Political Rights Covenant and other human rights treaties are non-self-executing:

> the ICCPR, if self-executing, would have the same domestic effect as a congressional statute and thus would supersede inconsistent state law and prior inconsistent federal legislation. Literally hundreds of US federal and state laws – ranging from essential civil rights statutes like Title VII to rules of criminal procedure – would be open to reconsideration and potential modification or invitation by courts interpreting the vague terms of the ICCPR. Even if courts ultimately decided that each of the differently worded provisions in the ICCPR did not require a change in domestic law, there was concern that litigation of these issues would be costly and would generate substantial legal uncertainty. These concerns also arose, although on a narrower scale, for the other human rights treaties.[16]

From a jurisprudential perspective Bradley and Goldsmith point out that the non-self-execution clauses attached to human rights treaties have historical predecessors. In particular, during the nineteenth and early twentieth centuries, especially in bilateral trade agreements, US treaty makers consented to treaties on the condition that the treaties, or particular provisions in the treaties, would take effect only if and when Congress enacted legislation implementing them. They note further that in essence these conditions were *international* non-self-execution clauses and therefore differed from the modern non-self-execution clauses since they prevented the treaty provisions from binding the United States until Congress acted, while the modern non-self-execution clauses prevent the treaty provisions from being enforced in US courts until Congress acts. But the early conditions were designed "to accomplish precisely the same goal as the modern non-self-execution clauses – inclusion of the House of Representatives in the domestic implementation of treaties."[17]

As noted by Bradley and Goldsmith, prior to World War II, international law regulated primarily interactions between states and did not contain extensive individual rights protections. Because of the Holocaust and other atrocities committed during that conflict, however, soon thereafter the international community began to develop a comprehensive body of international human rights law. Although US officials played a prominent role in creating this emerging human rights regime, in the 1950s there was an intense debate over whether and to what extent the United States should participate in it. The main issue in the debates concerned the domestic implications of ratifying the human rights treaties. These debates led to efforts by leaders of the American Bar Association and by Senator John Bricker of Ohio to offer various proposed amendments commonly referred to collectively as the "Bricker Amendment." These proposed amendments would, among other things, have precluded treaties from being self-executing and ensured that treaties would not override the reserved powers of the states. One of the proposed amendments fell only one vote short of obtaining the necessary two-thirds vote in the Senate.[18]

Senator Bricker lost the battle but won the war. To support this thesis, Henkin has argued:

> For the package of reservations, understandings and declarations achieves virtually what the Bricker Amendment sought, and more. In pressing his amendment, Senator Bricker declared: "My purpose in offering this resolution is to bury the so-called Covenant on Human Rights so deep that no one holding high public office will ever dare to attempt its resurrection." By its package of RUDs, the United States effectively fulfilled Senator Bricker's purpose, leaving the Covenant without any life in United States law:
>
> - The policy of declaring human rights conventions non-self-executing achieves what Senator Bricker sought to do by constitutional amendment.
> - Senator Bricker sought to prevent Congress from adopting legislation to implement human rights treaties; United States reservations have made congressional legislation largely unnecessary.[19]

There are other US RUDs accompanying US ratification of human rights treaties that have serious implications for the rule of law in international affairs. Most particularly, the United States has consistently reserved to clauses in human rights treaties pursuant to which a state party may bring a dispute as to the interpretation or application of the convention to the International Court of Justice. Under these reservations the specific consent of the United States is required in each individual case for the ICJ to have jurisdiction over a dispute arising under the convention. The reservations are partly the result of strong US reaction to the ICJ's decision in the *Nicaragua* case. They have been defended by US officials as necessary "to retain the ability of the United States to decline a case which may be brought for frivolous or political reasons."[20] Henkin has suggested that such language may be interpreted as "meaning that the United States recognizes that it may not be in compliance with the provisions of those conventions, even with whatever obligations might be left for the United States after its reservations."[21] In any event, such language ensures that the United States shall never be a respondent (defendant) before the ICJ in a case alleging a breach of the convention. It also ensures that the United States will never be an applicant (plaintiff) in such a case because the respondent state would be able to invoke the US reservation against it and defeat the Court's jurisdiction.

Another RUD that raises serious rule of law issues is the "federalism" clause that has been denominated an "understanding" rather than a reservation. The modern version of the federalism clause provides that the convention shall be implemented by the federal government to the extent that it "exercises jurisdiction" over matters covered by the treaty, leaving to the states implementation of matters over which the states exercise jurisdiction. Such clauses have been justified on the basis that they are necessary to maintain the constitutional balance between the state and federal governments and to avoid "federalizing" matters now within the competence of the states.[22] In Henkin's view, such clauses are "another sign that the United States is resistant to international human rights agreements, setting up obstacles to their implementation and refusing to treat human rights conventions as treaties dealing with a subject of national interest and international concern."[23]

The challenge to Missouri v. Holland

A primary goal of the Bricker Amendment was to overrule the US Supreme Court's controversial decision in *Missouri v. Holland*.[24] In that case, to reverse an alarming decline in migrating ducks and geese, Congress had enacted a law to regulate the hunting of migrating birds. The law was vigorously attacked by conservatives on the ground that it invaded states' rights protected by the Tenth Amendment to the US Constitution, which provides that "The powers not delegated to the United States by the Constitution, nor prohibited by it to the States, are reserved to the States respectively, or to the people." Some lower federal courts had declared the Act of Congress to be unconstitutional. In response the federal government then concluded a treaty with Canada, and Congress passed legislation to implement the treaty obligations calling for such regulation by both states parties. The federal government defended the implementing legislation under Article I, Section 8 of the Constitution as necessary and proper to execute the laws of the United States, which include treaties as part of the "law of the land" by virtue of Article VI, the so-called Supremacy Clause. States' rights advocates, however, contended that the Tenth Amendment overrode the federal government's treaty power with respect to matters within the historical prerogative of state government. The Supreme Court rejected the states' rights arguments. Speaking through Justice Oliver Wendell Holmes, the Court stated that regardless of whether the lower court opinions holding the earlier congressional legislation unconstitutional were correct, they could not be accepted as a test of the treaty power. Rather, the Court's opinion stated, "there may be matters of the sharpest exigency for the national well being that an act of Congress could not deal with but that a treaty followed by such an act could, and it is not lightly to be assumed that, in matters requiring national action, 'a power which must belong to and somewhere reside in every civilized government' is not to be found."[25] The Court went on to note that the treaty did not violate any prohibitions in the Constitution and suggested that the only question was whether it was forbidden by some "invisible radiation" from the general terms of the Tenth Amendment. In the Court's view it was not.

During the debate on the Bricker Amendment *Missouri* was a focal point of concern, because if the United States ratified the proposed covenant on human rights, then under *Missouri* Congress would have the power to implement it by adopting a national anti-lynching law or even a law prohibiting racial segregation. It was thought at the time that Congress would not have that authority in the absence of a treaty.

Ironically, as recently noted by David M. Golove,[26] Senator Bricker himself initially opposed overruling *Missouri* because his experience in the Senate had led him to the view that the treaty power would necessarily have to deal sometimes with matters otherwise within state legislative competence. He ultimately agreed to include a provision overruling *Missouri* in his amendments only after he was subject to intense pressure to do so from strong opponents of the human rights treaties. President Eisenhower and Secretary of State John Dulles, however, strongly opposed any overruling of *Missouri* and "[i]n the climactic battle, none of the three contending versions of the amendment would have had any effect on *Missouri*."[27] Moreover, the version of the Bricker Amendment that came within one vote of passage dealt only with executive agreements and made no reference to the treaty power. Since the defeat of the Bricker Amendment the Supreme Court has explicitly reaffirmed *Missouri* on several occasions.[28]

Nonetheless, as we have seen, the Senate's resistance to provisions in human rights treaties that would overrule state law constitutes a limitation on or even a repudiation of *Missouri*.[29] Also, as part of a wide-ranging attack on the constitutional law of foreign affairs that he and others have waged in recent years, Curtis Bradley has argued strenuously that *Missouri* was wrongly decided and that if the federal government enters into a treaty beyond Congress's regulatory authority, the treaty does not create binding law on the states nor does the treaty afford Congress a basis for implementing it through legislation. The states would be free to adopt or reject legislation necessary to implement the treaty. In Bradley's words, "[u]nder this approach, the treaty power would not confer any additional regulatory powers on the federal government, just the power to bind the United States on the international plane."[30]

In a lengthy article drawing on various historical sources, Golove has sought to refute Bradley's arguments and, in my view, has succeeded admirably.[31] However, even if *Missouri* remains good law, it has been effectively neutralized through the Senate's use of the federalism clauses, declarations of non-self-executing status, and reservations to provisions inconsistent with state law accompanying US ratification of human rights treaties. Bradley and other scholars have especially objected to what they call "foreign affairs exceptionalism" – the idea that the federal government's foreign affairs powers are different from its domestic powers, especially when it comes to federalism issues. Golove's response to this objection is cogent and in keeping with some of the basic themes of this study:

> If *pace* Professor Bradley, "foreign affairs exceptionalism" has a long and venerable pedigree, stretching back to 1776, his own project can also claim a long, though perhaps less venerable, pedigree in another great American "ism", American exceptionalism, itself inextricably intertwined with yet another long pedigreed "ism" – American isolationism. The underlying notion seems to be that the United States is better off to the extent that the Constitution can be made to limit and frustrate full US participation in the burgeoning institutions and regimes of international society. But if the Constitution "does not enact Mr. Herbert Spencer's Social Statics," neither does it enact an isolationist foreign policy. Like other essentially political questions, foreign policy ought to be fought out in the political – not the judicial – forum. All the more so, given the Constitution's built-in preference, dramatically manifested in the two-thirds rule for treaty-making, for inaction over action. Why ought isolationism to be afforded not only an advantage but a trump?[32]

The "last-in-time" and "political question" doctrines

Other factors contributing to the lowly status of treaties under US law are the so-called "last-in-time" and "political question" doctrines. The last-in-time doctrine has been developed by the US Supreme Court in cases where there is a conflict between a self-executing treaty and a federal statute.[33] In the words of the leading decision on this issue:

> By the Constitution a treaty is placed on the same footing, and made of like obligation, with an act of legislation. Both are declared by that instrument to be the supreme law of the land, and no superior efficacy is given to either over the other. When the two relate to the same subject, the courts will always endeavor to construe them so as to give effect to both, if that can be done without violating the language of either; but if the two are inconsistent, the one last in date will control the other, provided always the stipulation of the treaty on the subject is self-executing.[34]

The last-in-time doctrine has been confirmed by a number of Supreme Court decisions and now is firmly established.[35] As Louis Henkin and others have pointed out, however: "As an original matter, the equality in US law of treaties and federal statutes seems hardly inevitable."[36] The reason is that the Supremacy Clause invoked by the Supreme Court provides only that treaties and statutes are both the law of the land and supreme over state law and binding on state courts. It simply does not address the issue of whether a treaty or a federal statute should prevail if in conflict with each other. As a result arguments have been advanced in favor of statutes enjoying supremacy over treaties and vice versa.[37]

Some commentators have noted that the early Supreme Court cases dealt mainly with problems relating to tariffs, customs, and property rights under treaties with France and Spain and that these cases in the main involved bilateral treaties and not multilateral treaties applying to subjects of international concern. In particular, Louis Sohn has argued that the UN Charter is completely different from the kinds of treaties considered by the Supreme Court and has a "special, almost constitutional character."[38] Accordingly, he contends, the UN Charter should not be subject to the last-in-time rule but should prevail in any case of conflict with a federal statute.

The Supreme Court has not had occasion to address the issue of the status of the UN Charter under US law. In *Diggs v. Shultz*,[39] however, the US Court of Appeals for the Second Circuit summarily rejected the argument that the UN Charter has a special status that allows it to prevail over later inconsistent federal legislation. In *Diggs*, legislation required that the executive permit the importation of chromium from the then Southern Rhodesia despite a binding UN Security Council decision based on the UN Charter to embargo all such trade with the regime in power in that country. The court disposed in a footnote[40] of the appellants' argument that Congress could override the Security Council resolution imposing the embargo only by withdrawing from the United Nations entirely, on the ground that there was no evidence that US membership of the Organization was intended to be on such an all-or-nothing basis.

The rationale behind the political question doctrine as applied to foreign affairs was set forth most explicitly by the US Supreme Court in *Chicago & Southern Air Lines Inc. v. Waterman Steamship Corp.*:[41]

> [Foreign affairs] decisions are wholly confided by our Constitution to the political departments.... They are delicate, complex, and involve large elements of prophecy... They are decisions of a kind for which the Judiciary has neither aptitude, facilities nor responsibility and which has long been held to belong in the domain of political power not subject to judicial intrusion or inquiry.

This rationale has arguably led to a situation where "the federal judiciary has largely abdicated its constitutional role as umpire in matters affecting foreign affairs."[42] It is noteworthy, moreover, that the refusal of US courts to examine the legality of US actions in foreign affairs has included not only their legality under international or general federal law, but also their constitutionality. Thus, for example, US courts have declined to consider whether troops are being sent lawfully into combat, or whether members of Congress have been deprived of their constitutional role in the decision to go to war, or whether the president may terminate treaties on his own initiative or must obtain the consent of the Senate or Congress.

US courts are especially unlikely to uphold a challenge to an act authorized by the president that allegedly violates a treaty, because the president has independent constitutional authority in foreign affairs that allows him to denounce or otherwise terminate a treaty even if this puts the United States in violation of international law. Similarly, as Henkin has noted, the president has the constitutional authority to take other measures that violate international law. For example, "[i]f, say, President Reagan had constitutional authority to bomb Libya (in 1986) because of its alleged responsibility for terrorist activities, his constitutional authority to do so was not diminished by the fact that the bombing may have violated US obligations under the United Nations Charter. Surely, the courts would not enjoin the bombing."[43]

International agreements other than treaties

Although it is the only kind of international agreement expressly mentioned in the US Constitution, the treaty form is utilized much less often by the United States than other forms of international agreement.[44] These forms are the executive (or presidential) agreement, which is an agreement concluded by the president under his independent constitutional powers, and the congressional-executive agreement, which is an agreement concluded pursuant to statutory authorization or ratified, after conclusion, by statute or joint resolution of Congress. Most international trade agreements, for example, are congressional-executive agreements concluded pursuant to advance congressional authorization and approved by Congress – not just the Senate – under the so-called "fast track" procedure (currently renamed "Trade Promotion Authority") that requires approval or disapproval of the agreement as a whole and precludes efforts to amend particular provisions of the agreement. The Bretton Woods Agreements Act, authorizing US membership of the International Monetary Fund and the World Bank, is an example of congressional ratification after negotiation of the agreement.

On the whole, until recently, there has been relatively little controversy over the use of the congressional-executive agreement in place of the treaty. Many (although by no means all) commentators have accepted the proposition that the two are "functionally equivalent," that there is no constitutional limit on the use of a congressional-executive agreement in lieu of a treaty. Under this reading of the Constitution, the decision to enter into an international agreement in the form of a treaty rather than congressional-executive agreement is based on political rather than constitutional considerations (including the ability to secure fifty-one but not sixty-seven votes in the Senate).

Perhaps ironically, however, in light of the long experience of concluding international trade agreements in congressional-executive form, the decision to conclude the Uruguay Round Amendments in 1994 provoked some controversy in the halls of academe and in Congress. Some denied that the congressional-executive agreement was the full equivalent of a treaty, and insisted in particular that the United States could constitutionally become a member of the new World Trade Organization *only* by treaty. In this view, approval by treaty was constitutionally required because the agreement would impinge on states' rights. Henkin has suggested that the final decision to have the United States adhere to the World Trade Organization by congressional-executive agreement may have revived a debate that had long appeared to be resolved.[45]

While most agree that the executive, and only the executive, may negotiate and ratify international agreements, the debate has been heated over the authority of the president to set policy by executive agreements independent of Congress, that is, through presidential executive agreements. No one denies that the president has power to make some agreements on his own authority. Indeed, the US Supreme Court has explicitly confirmed his authority to do so.[46] But some have claimed that the president has only such independent authority as he would otherwise have whether acting by executive order, proclamation, or agreement (i.e., the instrumental "agreement making" power adds nothing to his independent policy-making power). Others have relied on the president's authority as chief executive or "commander-in-chief" to support an expansive power in the president to conclude such agreements where otherwise he could not act unilaterally (e.g., by executive order).

During the 1950s, as we have seen, the version of the Bricker Amendment that came within one vote of obtaining the necessary two-thirds in the Senate would have curtailed or severely regulated executive agreements. However, the debate over presidential powers more generally reached its greatest intensity during the Vietnam War and the Watergate crisis. During this period Congress had before it many bills to limit or regulate executive agreements. The only one of these to be adopted was the Case Act of 1972,[47] named after Senator Case of New Jersey, which requires the president to transmit to Congress all international agreements other than treaties within sixty days of their conclusion. If the president deems public disclosure prejudicial to national security, he need only transmit the text to the foreign affairs committees of both Houses. In such a case, the transmittal is made under an injunction of secrecy to be removed only upon notice from the president. The Case Act was amended in 1977 and 1978 to make it applicable to agreements made by any department or agency of the United States government and to oral as well as written agreements.

As to the scope of the president's constitutional authority to enter into presidential executive agreements, Henkin is "compelled to conclude that there are agreements which the President can make only with the consent of the Senate (or of both Houses), but [no one] has told us which are which."[48] The Supreme Court has never held any presidential executive agreement to be outside the president's constitutional authority, and as a practical matter the decision on the form a particular international agreement should take is made through the political process free from judicial constraint.

There remains to be considered the status of congressional-executive and presidential executive agreements under US law. Congressional-executive agreements, which find their constitutional support in the joint powers of Congress and the president, are clearly the supreme law of the land and prevail over inconsistent state law. They also enjoy the benefits of and are subject to the last-in-time rule, and can therefore prevail over earlier or be superseded by later federal legislation or treaty. The situation is more problematical with presidential executive agreements. Some have contended that, although they are internationally binding, presidential executive agreements can never be self-executing and cannot be effective as domestic law, unless implemented by Congress.[49] Supreme Court decisions, however, seem to refute this view and indicate that at least some presidential executive agreements are self-executing and are supreme over inconsistent state law.[50] But the Supreme Court has never ruled on the issue whether a presidential executive agreement can prevail over inconsistent prior federal legislation. At least one intermediate federal court has held that it cannot,[51] but the decision has been criticized.[52]

Whether they take the form of treaties, congressional-executive agreements or presidential executive agreements under US law, there is strong evidence that the United States is generally taking "treaties" as defined by the Vienna Convention on the Law of Treaties "less seriously" than the international commitments they contain would warrant.[53] For example, Congress has exhibited an increased willingness to rely on the last-in-time rule to adopt legislation that expressly overrides prior treaty commitments in place of calling on the executive branch to renegotiate the treaties.[54]

For their part, US courts have recently interpreted treaties in such a way as to minimize US obligations under them. According to one commentator the result in these cases was "to prevent treaty commitments from altering the way we are used to doing things."[55]

In later chapters in this study we shall examine specific examples of this attitude toward treaties in some detail. For present purposes we should just note that such factors as the distinction between self-executing and non-self-executing treaties, US RUDs to human rights treaties with their effect of undermining *Missouri v. Holland*, the last-in-time rule, the political question doctrine, the uncertain status of presidential executive agreements under US law, and the extensive constitutional authority of the president in foreign affairs to suspend, terminate, or deviate from treaty obligations have all contributed to "treaties" enjoying a lowly and problematical status under US law and practice. These factors constitute structural obstacles to US adherence to the rule of law in international affairs that transcend the transitory attitudes of Congress, the courts, or the executive branch.

Customary international law

In chapter 1 of this study we saw that the validity and practicality of customary international law as a source of international law have increasingly been challenged, and at least one critic has called for its elimination from international jurisprudence. Most recently, Jack L. Goldsmith and Eric A. Posner have advanced a so-called "rational choice" approach to customary international law that, if accepted, would effectively deny customary international law the status of law at both the international and national levels.[56] According to Goldsmith and Posner, states never act out of a motive to comply with an international norm, but only out of the desire of the state's political leadership to serve the self-interest of the state as determined by the leaders on an ad hoc basis depending on the circumstances faced at the time the decision is made. To support this thesis they identify three basic strategic positions: coincidence of interest, coercion, and cooperation. Coincidence of interest is "a behavioral regularity that occurs when nations follow their immediate self-interest independent of any consideration of the actions or interests of other nations."[57] Sometimes states act contrary to their self-interest in a way that results in behavioral regularities among nations because they are coerced into doing so by a more powerful state or states. Finally, according to the authors, behavioral regularities may result through cooperation induced by a bilateral prisoner's dilemma. The example given is when two states engaged in armed conflict refrain from seizing each other's fishing vessels.

The dilemma faced by each state is that it might refrain from seizing the other's vessels while the other state seizes its own, leaving the state that refrained worse off than if it had acted aggressively. To resolve the dilemma the two states may employ game theory. "Game theory shows that if both states value the future sufficiently, they may be able to cooperate to achieve the outcome of mutual restraint."[58] The authors argue further that "the bilateral prisoners' dilemma cannot, without implausible assumptions, be expanded to a multi-player prisoners' dilemma, where monitoring and other information costs rise, the incentives for any particular nation to defect from cooperation increases, and the incentives for any particular nation to punish deviation decreases."[59]

Interestingly, Goldsmith and Posner take an agnostic approach to the status of customary international law as law. In their words, "[t]he rational choice account seeks to explain accurately the behaviors associated with CIL [customary international law]. Whether CIL is or is not law is beyond its concern."[60] But, whether customary international law qualifies as law is a key issue with respect to the validity of their thesis that customary international law, as an independent normative force, has little if any effect on national behavior. If they are correct in suggesting that customary international law is "mostly aspirational," and amounts at most, at least in some circumstances, to a political or perhaps a moral obligation, then indeed customary international law would seem to have no independent normative force affecting national behavior. On the other hand, if it does qualify as law, and the authors admit that government officials, courts, and scholars do "continue to talk as if CIL had independent normative force,"[61] then it is considerably more likely that CIL has independent normative force that affects national behavior. If customary international law has the status of law, its normative provisions have a certain weight that nations will not lightly disregard. On the contrary, they will generally regard compliance with these norms to be in their interest, especially since clear violation of the norms is likely to be regarded by other states as a serious matter. To be sure, as the authors illustrate, states for a variety of reasons may conclude from time to time that the advantages of violation outweigh those of law observance or that outside coercion or internal pressures compel them to violate the customary international law norm. But it does not follow that customary international law has no independent effect on national decision making.

Goldsmith and Posner argue that "[w]hen nations decline to violate CIL, this is usually because they have no reason to violate it. Nations would act no differently if CIL were not a formally recognized source of law."[62] This is a highly questionable proposition. Customary international law develops only because states are of the view that it serves their interests. Because customary international law norms serve their interests, states expect general adherence to them and, as Henkin has famously noted, "almost all nations observe almost all principles of international law and almost all of their obligations all of the time."[63] When states violate customary international law norms, they do not do so on the ground that the norms are "aspirational" only. Rather, they argue that their actions are within the norm or, in a few cases, that the norm has changed. Indeed, as we have previously seen, violation of a customary international law norm under a claim of right to do so is one way that new customary international law norms develop.

This brings us to the question of the status and the role of customary international law in the US legal system. As an initial matter it is important to note that the US Constitution's only express reference to customary international law is in Article I, section 8, clause 10, which provides that Congress has the power "to define and punish . . . [o]ffenses against the Law of Nations." It is also important to note that customary international law may be applied in a variety of ways under US law and practice. The basic distinction is between the indirect and direct uses of customary international law.

Indirect uses

Indirect uses include the use of customary international law principles in interpreting provisions of the US Constitution, federal statutes, or treaties. As early as 1804 Chief Justice Marshall stated that "an Act of Congress ought never to be construed to violate the law of nations [customary international law] if any other possible construction remains,"[64] and the Restatement (Third) of the Foreign Relations Law of the United States provides: "[w]here fairly possible, a United States statute is to be construed so as not to conflict with international law or with an international agreement of the United States."[65] In several cases the Supreme Court has interpreted acts of Congress so as to avoid conflicts with earlier treaty provisions.[66]

Utilizing norms of customary international law in the process of interpreting the US Constitution has proven to be a more controversial proposition. As John Rogers has pointed out, even those persons who fully accept the concept of utilizing international law as a guide to interpreting an ambiguous statute may have difficulty with the idea that international law should be utilized in interpreting the US Constitution. "This is because it is much more difficult for the body politic to correct the Supreme Court in its constitution-interpreting function than it is for the legislature to correct the courts in their statute-interpreting function."[67]

Consequently, "[t]he Supreme Court is more willing to overrule a constitutional precedent than a statutory one because statutory interpretations that are perceived to be wrong by Congress can be easily corrected by Congress, and that is obviously not the case regarding constitutional amendment."[68]

Perhaps in part because of these considerations, the Supreme Court has never explicitly upheld the use of international law as a guide to interpreting the US Constitution. It had an opportunity to do so in *Boos v. Barry*,[69] but declined the invitation. In *Boos* the US Court of Appeals for the DC Circuit had upheld a DC statute prohibiting the display of signs bringing foreign governments into disrepute within 500 feet of an embassy and prohibiting persons from congregating within 500 feet of an embassy against a challenge that it violated First Amendment protections of freedom of speech and assembly.[70] Writing for the majority in the Court of Appeals, Judge Bork held the statute to be an exercise of Congress's power to "define and punish offenses against the Law of Nations."[71] Based on his analysis of international law and the legislative history of the US Constitution, Judge Bork concluded:

> We think it clear beyond quibble that since the founding of our nation adherence to the law of nations, and most particularly that branch of the law that demands security for the persons and respect for the dignity and peace of foreign emissaries, has been regarded as a fundamental and compelling national interest. It is also clear that the founders, who explicitly gave Congress the power to enforce adherence to the standards of the law of nations, which they understood well, saw no incompatibility between this national interest and any guaranteed individual freedom.[72]

The Court of Appeals went on to hold that this compelling national interest could not be served with a regulation that had any significantly smaller impact on freedom of speech. In short, Rogers has suggested, the Court of Appeals "balanced the First Amendment interest in freedom of expression with the need for the government to conform with its obligations under international law."[73]

The Supreme Court reversed. In her majority opinion Justice O'Connor expressly abjured deciding whether "the dictates of international law could ever require that First Amendment analysis be adjusted to accommodate the interests of foreign officials."[74] Rather, she decided that, even assuming that the interests protected by international law were compelling, the statute at issue was not sufficiently narrowly tailored to serve these interests and that another statute, not subject to challenge in the case, adequately protected these interests. On this point, Chief Justice Rehnquist, joined by Justices White and Blackmun, dissented, relying entirely on "the reasons stated by Judge Bork in his majority opinion below."[75] As a result, "the overall count of Supreme Court justices in *Boos* on the issue of whether international law should inform interpretation of the First Amendment was three, *yes definitely*, and five, *undecided.* (Justice Kennedy did not participate in the case.)"[76]

In the context of death penalty cases, as of this writing the challenges to the constitutionality of the death penalty have not involved customary international law. Rather the issue has been whether the views of the international community are relevant in determining whether a punishment is cruel and unusual and therefore prohibited by the Eighth Amendment to the US Constitution. In *Thompson v. Oklahoma*,[77] for example, a plurality of four justices on the Supreme Court concluded that it would be a violation of the Eighth Amendment to execute a defendant for a murder committed when he was less than sixteen years old. The writer of the plurality opinion, Justice Stevens, supported the opinion by stating: "The conclusion that it would offend civilized standards of decency to execute a person who was less than 16 years old at the time of his or her offense is consistent with the views that have been expressed by respected professional organizations, by other nations that share our Anglo-American heritage, and by the leading members of the Western European community," adding in a footnote, "We have previously recognized the relevance of the views of the international community in determining whether a punishment is cruel and unusual."[78] In sharp contrast Justice Scalia's dissent rejected the relevance of the international comparisons. While noting that 40 percent of US states permitted capital punishment for fifteen-year-old felons at the time, Justice Scalia argued that "where there is not first a settled consensus among our own people, the views of other nations, however enlightened the Justices of this Court may think them to be, cannot be imposed upon Americans through the Constitution."[79] A year later, in *Stanford v. Kentucky*,[80] in which the Court upheld the imposition of capital punishment for murder committed at the age of sixteen years plus six months, and seventeen years plus four months, Justice Scalia, writing for the majority, reiterated his rejection of comparative data.

Neither the majority in *Thompson* nor the dissent in *Stanford* considered whether there was a norm of customary international law that prohibited the execution of juveniles below a certain age. Rather, both opinions referred to foreign death penalty laws in various countries and to provisions in three international conventions – the International Covenant on Civil and Political Rights, the American Convention on Human Rights, and the Geneva Convention Relative to the Protection of Civilian Persons in Time of War – that prohibited the execution of persons who were under eighteen years of age at the time of the commission of the offense. At the time of the *Thompson* and *Stanford* decisions the United States was a party only to the Geneva Convention Relative to the Protection of Civilian Persons in Time of War, but it had not made a reservation to the provision prohibiting the execution of persons who committed their offenses when under the age of eighteen. When the United States later ratified the International Covenant on Civil and Political Rights, it specifically entered a reservation against the provision in the Covenant prohibiting the imposition of the death penalty for crimes committed by persons below eighteen years of age.[81]

Most recently, in *Lawrence v. Texas*,[82] a five-justice majority opinion of the Supreme Court cited an act of the British Parliament,[83] a decision of the European Court of Human Rights,[84] and an amicus curiae brief submitted to the Supreme Court by Mary Robinson and others[85] in ruling that a Texas statute making it a crime for two persons of the same sex to engage in certain intimate sexual conduct was unconstitutional as applied to adult males who had engaged in a consensual act of sodomy in the privacy of home, because it interfered with their exercise of liberty interests protected by the Due Process Clause of the Fourteenth Amendment to the US Constitution. The three-justice dissent, written by Justice Scalia, was of the view that "Constitutional entitlements do not spring into existence because . . . *foreign nations* decriminalize conduct . . . The Court's discussion of these foreign views (ignoring, of course, the many countries that have retained criminal prohibitions on sodomy) is therefore meaningless dicta."[86]

Direct uses

The direct use of customary international law as the basis for decision in US jurisprudence has taken one of two forms. The first, and most controversial, is the use of a norm of customary international law as the basis for decision without any express direction to do so by the political branches of government. The most celebrated but also the most ambiguous example is the Supreme Court's decision in *The Paquete Habana*.[87]

In *The Paquete Habana*, the United States Navy had seized a Cuban fishing vessel during the Spanish–American war. The Court held that customary international law excluded coastal fishing vessels from the general right of a belligerent to capture ships and goods at sea during times of war. In its most often quoted passage the Court stated:

> International law is part of our law, and must be ascertained and administered by the courts of justice of appropriate jurisdiction, as often as questions of right depending upon it are duly presented for their determination. For this purpose, where there is no treaty, and no controlling executive or legislative act or judicial

decision, resort must be had to the customs and usages of civilized nations; and, as evidence of these, to the works of jurists and commentators, who by years of labor, research and experience, have made themselves peculiarly well acquainted with the subjects of which they treat. Such works are resorted to by judicial tribunals, not for the speculations of their authors concerning what the law ought to be, but for trustworthy evidence of what the law really is.[88]

The Paquete Habana is a classic case that is reproduced in US international law casebooks for two primary purposes: to demonstrate the process of ascertaining a norm of customary international law and to raise the issue of the status of customary international law under US law. Ironically, Jack L. Goldsmith and Eric A. Posner have recently argued that the Supreme Court's decision that customary international law at the time prohibited the seizure of coastal fishing vessels was erroneous.[89] Be that as it may, our present concern is with what the Court had to say about the status of customary international law in the United States.

Note first the Court's statement that "International law is part of our law." The question that immediately arises is, how did this come to be? As Louis Henkin has pointed out,[90] it is clear when customary international law became part of US law. It was in 1776, when the United States became an independent nation. How it became part of US law is more questionable. Some claim that it came into US law as part of the common law the new state inherited from the former colonial power. Others contend that it came into US law not by "inheritance" but as an indispensable attribute of statehood. However it came into US law, courts have from the beginning of the nation treated customary international law as incorporated and applied it as domestic law.

The Court in *The Paquete Habana*, however, appeared to place significant limitations on the application of customary international law in the United States, because it indicated that there must be resort to it only "where there is no treaty and no controlling executive or legislative act or judicial decision." The ambiguity of this language is plain. What did the Court mean by a "controlling executive or legislative act or judicial decision"?

Since its decision in *The Paquete Habana* the Supreme Court has shed no light on the proper answer to this question. One lower court decision has suggested that a controlling executive act does not require action by the president but can come from one of his subordinates, in this case the Attorney General of the United States.[91] The decision has been sharply criticized,[92] but there is no US court decision to the contrary. There is, moreover, academic debate over whether the president is entirely free to violate customary international law as a matter of US law.[93] This issue, too, has not been squarely addressed by US courts.

There is no doubt that an act of Congress prevails as a matter of US law if it is in conflict with a customary international law norm that developed prior to the time the statute was enacted. It is unclear whether a rule of customary international law that developed after, and is inconsistent with, an earlier federal statute should be given effect as the law of the United States.[94] This is a highly questionable proposition, however, because a customary international law can develop simply by the executive branch failing to object to it during its formation. Giving effect to law created by the president acting or not acting on his sole authority over an act of Congress is arguably incompatible with basic democratic policy, and it is highly unlikely that a US court, if squarely faced with the issue, would hold that an act of Congress had been superseded by a rule of customary international law.

The conventional wisdom on the proper classification of customary international law as a specie of US law is that it is federal common law.[95] So classified, according to the conventional wisdom, customary international law preempts inconsistent state law under Article VI, the Supremacy Clause, of the Constitution.[96] In 1997, however, Curtis A. Bradley and Jack L. Goldsmith strenuously challenged this conventional wisdom, which they titled the "modern position."[97] To support their challenge the authors note that prior to 1938, when the US Supreme Court handed down the landmark decision of *Erie R.R. Co. v. Tompkins*,[98] customary international law was viewed as part of the general common law. As part of general common law, customary international law "lacked the supremacy, jurisdictional, and other consequences of federal law."[99] *Erie* eliminated the previous federal practice of applying general common law and held that, "[e]xcept in matters governed by the Federal Constitution or by Acts of Congress, the law to be applied in any case is the law of the State."[100] Under this formulation, according to the authors, "for several decades after *Erie*, it remained an open (and generally unaddressed) question whether CIL was part of this new federal common law . . . the recent ascendancy of CIL to the status of federal common law is the result of a combination of troubling developments, including mistaken interpretations of history, doctrinal bootstrapping by the Restatement (Third) of Foreign Relations Law, and academic fiat."[101] In the authors' view customary international law should not have the status of federal law to be applied by the courts unless there is an express authorization from the political branches of the federal government to do so.

Not surprisingly, Bradley's and Goldsmith's contentions precipitated a firestorm of protest from the academy.[102] At this juncture no US court has addressed the issues they raise. Their suggestion that customary international law not be applied by the courts in the absence of express authorization of the political branches to do so had previously been advanced by other commentators.[103] To my knowledge no federal court decision expressly supports this thesis, but it is significant that, in practice, US courts seldom apply customary international law in the absence of indications, if not express suggestions, from the political branches that they should do so. This is especially the case if customary international law is being invoked to challenge US governmental action.

Even in *The Paquete Habana* case, the Supreme Court noted that the president had issued two proclamations declaring that the United States would maintain the blockade of Cuba "in pursuance of the laws of the United States, and the law of nations applicable to such cases" and that it was desirable that the war against Spain "should be conducted upon principles in harmony with the present views of nations and sanctioned by their recent practice."[104] Accordingly, one way to analyze the Court's decision in *The Paquete Habana* is that the Court was simply carrying out the president's directive that the war should be conducted in accordance with the law of nations. To be sure, the Supreme Court struck down the US seizure of the Spanish fishing vessels even though the navy and the executive branch argued that the fishing vessels served a military purpose. But, as Goldsmith and Posner have noted, "*The Paquete Habana* remains an exception to the usual rule of judicial deference to the Executive's views, an exception rarely repeated, especially in cases with more significance than a determination . . . that occurred after a one-sided war that resulted in a decisive victory."[105]

Alien Tort Claims Act

Congressional directives to US courts to apply customary international law, in the form of federal legislation, occur with some frequency.[106] One particular federal statute, however, has generated considerable controversy. This is the Alien Tort Claims Act (ATCA), which gives US district courts "original jurisdiction of any civil action by an alien for a tort only, committed in violation of the law of nations or a treaty of the United States."[107] The ATCA was seldom invoked until 1980, when, in the landmark decision of *Filartiga v. Pena-Irala*,[108] the US Court of Appeals for the Second Circuit and, on remand, the US District Court for the Eastern District of New York[109] held that Paraguayan plaintiffs were entitled to recover damages against a Paraguayan official for torture committed in Paraguay, on the ground that torture constitutes a violation of the law of nations. *Filartiga* has been followed by a number of other US court decisions that awarded damages for torture or other violations of the law of nations.[110]

The Second Circuit in *Filartiga* ruled only that the ATCA gave US federal courts jurisdiction over a suit brought by an alien against another alien for a tort alleged to be a violation of customary international law. Upon remand the district court had to decide whether the "tort" to which the statute refers means a wrong in violation of the law of nations or merely a wrong actionable under the law of the appropriate foreign state. The court decided the statute intended the former rather than the latter. Shortly after the Second Circuit's decision on jurisdiction, however, its rationale on jurisdiction was challenged. According to Judge Irving Kaufman, the writer of the Second Circuit's opinion in *Filartiga*, the constitutional basis for the Alien Tort Claims Act was the law of nations, which had always been part of the federal common law, and the provision in Article III of the Constitution that the judicial power extends to all cases arising under "the Laws of the United States." Judge Kaufman interpreted the phrase "in violation of the law of nations" as referring to "international law not as it was in 1789 [the date of the statute], but as it has evolved and exists among the nations of the world today."[111] In sharp contrast, Judge Bork, in a concurring opinion of the Court of Appeals for the District of Columbia Circuit in *Tel-Oren v. Libyan Arab Republic*,[112] interpreted the phrase "in violation of the law of nations" as referring only to the law of nations as it stood in 1789. In addition, Judge Bork would require that the treaty provision or customary international law norm in question explicitly grant individuals a "cause of action."

In *Tel-Oren* neither of the two other judges involved in the case supported Judge Bork's position and voted to dismiss the plaintiffs' suit on other grounds. After the *Tel-Oren* decision, however, the US Department of Justice adopted Judge Bork's "cause of action" approach in a memorandum for the United States as amicus curiae in a suit pending before the Ninth Circuit[113] – even though the US Departments of Justice and State had earlier filed an amicus curiae memorandum in *Filartiga* supporting the position adopted by Judge Kaufman. Although the Ninth Circuit and other circuits have rejected this view, it has never been considered by the US Supreme Court.

Torture Victim Protection Act

The Torture Victim Protection Act of 1999[114] authorizes civil suits against persons who, under the color of law of any foreign nation, torture or summarily execute another person. Unlike the Alien Tort Claims Act, the Torture Victim Protection Act does not limit its coverage to alien plaintiffs. On the other hand the Act has been interpreted as "not intended to trump diplomatic and head-of-state immunities."[115] Also, as pointed out by Steven Ratner and Jason Abrams, the Torture Victim Protection Act has four basic requirements:

(1) the defendant must have committed torture or an extrajudicial killing;
(2) the defendant must have acted under actual or apparent authority, or color of law, of a foreign nation;
(3) the plaintiff must be a victim, their legal representative, or a person who may be a claimant in a wrongful death action; and
(4) the plaintiff must have exhausted remedies in the country where the conduct giving rise to the claim occurred.[116]

In part because of its substantive and procedural limitations, the Torture Victim Protection Act is, for Bradley and Goldsmith, a paradigmatic example of an express authorization from the political branches of government to the courts to apply a customary norm of international law that they favor.[117] Per contra they regard the Alien Tort Claims Act, and most of the cases decided under it, as the paradigmatic example of *The Current Illegitimacy of International Human Rights Litigation*.[118]

Unlike the Torture Victim Protection Act, the Alien Tort Claims Act, in the view of Bradley and Goldsmith, does not represent a sufficient authorization from the political branches of government to apply customary international law and has a shaky constitutional basis. The claim that the Alien Tort Claims Act has a shaky constitutional basis follows from their contention that, contrary to the "modern position," customary international law is not part of federal common law, and, absent specific incorporation by the political branches of government, is not part of US law at all. In *Filartiga*, it will be remembered, Judge Kaufman stated that customary international law is federal common law and therefore ruled that the court had jurisdiction on the basis of Article III of the Constitution, which extends the judicial power to all cases arising under "the Laws of the United States." Bradley and Goldsmith also reject the contentions that the Alien Tort Claims Act itself establishes a substantive federal cause of action for violations of customary international law or, alternatively, that, while the congressional grant did not create a cause of action itself, it authorized federal courts to do so. If either of these contentions were valid, the Alien Tort Claims Act would constitute congressionally authorized federal common law for purposes of Article III.

In a major response to Bradley's and Goldsmith's arguments, Harold Koh has noted that under their approach, "if customary international law is neither federal *nor* state law (unless specifically incorporated by the state or federal political branches), then in most cases, customary international law is not United States law at all!"[119] In a counter-response to Koh, Bradley and Goldsmith admit and attempt to defend this result, although they suggest that customary international law might not be US law at all only "in some instances" rather than, as Koh concludes, "in most cases."[120]

It is not necessary for present purposes to present an extensive analysis of the debate between Bradley and Goldsmith, on the one side, and Koh and a host of other international scholars, on the other. What does deserve further comment, however, is Bradley's and Goldsmith's reliance on their distinction between the "traditional" customary international law and the "new" customary international law represented by international human rights norms. As the authors correctly point out, traditional customary international law *primarily* (but not exclusively) governed relations between nations, while the "new" customary international law of human rights "almost exclusively regulates relations between a nation and its citizens on such matters as torture, capital punishment, inhuman and degrading treatment, prolonged arbitrary detention, and freedom of thought, conscience, and religion."[121] They then go on to argue, however, that "[t]raditional CIL was customary law that purportedly reflected the actual practices of the community of nations. The CIL of human rights does not arise in that fashion, however, because many nations continue to commit human rights violations."[122] This argument betrays a profound misunderstanding of the process of creating a norm of customary international law. Although, sadly, many states do engage in torture, for example, no state engages in torture under a claim of right to do so under international law. On the contrary, such states either deny that they engage in such practices or contend that the particular practice did not constitute torture. Moreover, most of these states have become parties to treaties banning torture or have enacted domestic legislation banning torture and making it a crime under their domestic law – part of the state practice that has resulted in a general acceptance of the proposition that torture is a crime under international law. As we have seen, one of the ways in which customary international law changes is for states to engage in a contrary practice under a claim of right to do so. Absent such a claim the practice simply constitutes a violation of customary international law. The problem, in other words, is one of enforcement of a customary norm, not of its lack of existence.

Bradley and Goldsmith are especially concerned that customary international law not be considered part of "the Laws of the United States" under the Supremacy Clause of the US Constitution. A major reason for their concern is that the customary international law of human rights governs subjects that are primarily a matter of state law in the United States.

Federalism and customary international law

According to the Restatement (Third) of the Foreign Relations Law of the United States, "[i]t is now established that customary international law in the United States is a kind of federal law, and like treaties and other international agreements, it is accorded supremacy over State law by Article VI of the Constitution."[123] In response to Koh's suggestion that it is settled that customary international law governs domestic state officials, however, Bradley and Goldsmith note that "he cites no decision (and we know of none) that has ever squarely held that CIL is federal law within the meaning of the Supremacy Clause."[124] They also respond to Koh's criticism that they failed to cite any examples of states complaining about a federal court ruling on international law invading their sovereignty by suggesting that "[b]ecause no federal court actually has applied CIL to invalidate a state law, it is not surprising that there are no such complaints. We suspect that there would be plenty of state complaints if courts were to begin using CIL to invalidate, for example, state capital punishment schemes otherwise consistent with the Constitution and enacted federal law."[125]

This suspicion is well founded. Concern over the possibility of such state complaints has undoubtedly been a major reason why the executive branch has supported the Senate's declarations that human rights treaties are non-self-executing, thus precluding individual suits against state laws allegedly inconsistent with the treaties' provisions. Also, as Bradley and Goldsmith point out, "to the best of our knowledge the executive branch has never argued that the new CIL of human rights trumps state law. This makes sense because the Executive has consistently insisted that the human rights treaties on which this CIL is based not be construed to preempt state law."[126]

Even assuming *arguendo* that the Restatement and Koh are right and customary international law is part of "the Laws of the United States" for purposes of the Supremacy Clause, the record indicates quite convincingly that this doctrine has little if any operational significance. There appears to be no inclination on the part of either the courts or the political branches of the federal government to invoke customary international law directly in order to strike down state law. It is at least theoretically possible, however, that customary international law might be utilized indirectly in a case challenging state law on the ground that it violated the "dormant" foreign affairs powers of the federal government.

The classic case on the question of whether a state's laws and practices interfere with US foreign policy is *Zschernig v. Miller.*[127] In *Zschernig* an Oregon statute provided that non-resident aliens could inherit only if

(i) there was a reciprocal right for a US citizen to take property in the foreign country; (ii) American citizens in the United States could receive payment from an estate in the foreign country; and (iii) foreign heirs would receive the proceeds of the Oregon estate "without confiscation." The statute had been applied by the state courts to deny an inheritance to the heir of an Oregon resident living in the former East Germany. The Supreme Court held the statute unconstitutional as applied on the ground that it was "an intrusion by the State into the field of foreign affairs which the Constitution entrusts to the President and the Congress."

In so ruling the Court distinguished *Clark v. Allen.*[128] There, in upholding a California inheritance statute that contained a general reciprocity clause, the Court stated that the clause did not on its face intrude on the federal domain and would have only "some incidental or indirect effect in foreign countries." Here, by contrast, the application of the Oregon statute "has led into minute inquiries concerning the actual administration of foreign law, [and] into the credibility of foreign diplomatic statements . . ." This, in the Court's view, had more than "some incidental or indirect effect in foreign countries" and had "great potential for disruption or embarrassment."

Zschernig has been subject to sharp criticism, in part because the majority's opinion failed to define clearly the scope of the new foreign affairs preemption doctrine and hence provided little guidance as to when state action may impair foreign policy. The result has been that lower courts have reached inconsistent results in interpreting and applying *Zschernig.*

It was widely expected that the Supreme Court would address some of the issues raised by *Zschernig* in its decision in *Crosby v. National Foreign Trade Council.*[129] The Court, however, declined the opportunity. In *Crosby* the state of Massachusetts had enacted a statute that broadly prevented companies and individuals that did business with Myanmar (formerly Burma) from doing business with the Commonwealth of Massachusetts and its agencies. In 1998 the National Foreign Trade Council, a 550-member trade group comprising corporations and financial institutions involved in overseas trade and international investments, filed suit in the federal district court challenging the constitutionality of the law. Both the district court and, on appeal, the US Court of Appeals for the First Circuit found the law to be unconstitutional, holding that the statute was inconsistent with the dormant foreign affairs power. The First Circuit also held that the statute had been preempted by federal legislation and that it was invalid under the dormant Foreign Commerce Clause doctrine. The Supreme Court unanimously affirmed, but solely on the ground that the state legislation conflicted with federal legislation, enacted shortly after the Massachusetts statute that imposed sanctions on Myanmar.

The First Circuit, however, in its opinion, addressed *Zschernig* and the issues of the dormant foreign affairs doctrine it raises at some length.[130] While acknowledging that the "precise boundaries of the Supreme Court's holding in *Zschernig* are unclear," the court upheld the district court's holding that the Massachusetts Burma Law was unconstitutional under *Zschernig* because it "has more than an 'indirect or incidental effect in foreign countries,'" and has a "great potential for disruption or embarrassment" in the conduct of foreign affairs. In so holding the First Circuit considered some arguments advanced by Massachusetts that raised "issues of first impression."

First, Massachusetts argued that the district court misinterpreted *Zschernig* to hold that a state law that goes beyond an incidental or indirect effect on foreign affairs is impermissible. Instead, according to Massachusetts, *Zschernig* should be read to require courts to weigh the decree of impact against the particular state interest at issue. The First Circuit disposed of this argument by stating: "We do not read *Zschernig* as instructing courts to balance the nation's interests in a unified foreign policy against the particular interests of an individual state. Instead, *Zschernig* stands for the principle that there is a threshold level of involvement in and impact on foreign affairs which the states may not exceed."[131]

Most significantly for our purposes, the First Circuit rejected the Massachusetts argument that it should ignore the protests launched by US allies and trading partners. In support of this argument Massachusetts noted that the US federal law implementing the Uruguay Round of the General Agreement on Tariffs and Trade (GATT) denied foreign governments and private persons the right to challenge state laws based on GATT. The court noted, however, that the action had not been brought under the GATT or any World Trade Organization agreement. Rather, the protests were relevant only to the issue whether the Massachusetts law was adversely affecting US foreign relations. In *Zschernig* the Supreme Court had expressly cited Bulgaria's objections to the Oregon law as evidence that the law was affecting foreign relations.

Similarly, it would appear that protests from foreign countries that a state law or action violated a norm of customary international law could be evidence of interference with the federal government's conduct of foreign affairs. If so, even if Bradley and Goldsmith are right that customary international law is not part of "the Laws of the United States" for purposes of the Supremacy Clause, and thus could not be used directly as the basis for invalidating state law and practice, it could play a role in a court's determination that state action was inconsistent with the dormant foreign affairs doctrine.

Massachusetts also relied on the Supreme Court's decision in *Barclays Bank PLC v. Franchise Tax Board*[132] and on the views of some academic commentators to contend that *Zschernig* should be treated as a highly limited holding. In *Barclays Bank* the Supreme Court refused to invalidate California's unitary corporate tax policy, despite arguments that it impaired the conduct of foreign policy. Jack Goldsmith, among others, interpreted this holding as evidence that the Court would not readily subordinate state concerns to federal foreign affairs concerns.[133] The First Circuit rejected the thesis of Goldsmith et al., favoring instead Harold Koh's analysis.[134] In Koh's view, Goldsmith reads too much into the Court's statements in *Barclays Bank.* He points out that the Solicitor General backed California's argument that there was no conflict between the state's tax laws and federal policy. Thus, Koh suggests, "the case reveals less about the Supreme Court's view of federalism than about the Court's traditional judicial deference to the executive branch in foreign affairs."[135]

Peter Spiro has put a provocative "spin" on the *Barclays Bank* decision. Arguing against the rule of federal exclusivity over foreign affairs (the "exclusivity principle"), Spiro notes that while the British government took up Barclays's cause and expressed its protests through the usual diplomatic channels, it also enacted retaliatory legislation – directed not against the United States as a whole, but only against the corporations registered in California and other states with the unitary taxing approach.[136] This targeted retaliation apparently was effective, because California abandoned its unitary tax approach. To Spiro this experience suggests the following:

> . . . the *Barclays Bank* episode demonstrates the efficacy of targeted retaliation . . . First the mechanism of targeted retaliation proves the path to vindicating state preferences without jeopardizing national ones. That was always the problem with the rule of federal exclusivity: it denied some states their preferences, sometimes on issues with deep moral implications. With targeted retaliation, balancing those interests becomes unnecessary; state preferences, to the extent that they are consistent with other constitutional restrictions, will find no bar in domestic law.
>
> They may, however, find a bar in international law. Retaliation at the international level is increasingly governed by norms rather than merely by interests, and indeed it is now being undertaken by a variety of actors beyond nation-states. US state officials will find it increasingly hard to hide behind the veil of national sovereignty, and will come (some the hard way) to understand that international law is now relevant to the exercise of their authorities. With no intention of romanticizing the substance of all international law – for the results will not always be progressive – this constraint on state-level action must presumptively be a good thing, for it will facilitate the rule of that law, make responsible actors accountable, and lead to the better formulation of international norms.[137]

In *Barclays Bank*, however, although there were protests from numerous foreign governments about California's unitary tax scheme, these were not based on an alleged violation of international law. Rather, the complaints were based on strong disagreement with California's approach to tax policy. Moreover, the British retaliatory legislation targeting California was an economic power play that did not involve international law or the international legal process in any way.

By contrast, international law and legal process were directly involved in the *Crosby* case. As a result of the Massachusetts law, the European Union, and Japan and other Asian countries lodged formal protests with the United States, alleging violations of World Trade Organization obligations. Most to the point, the European Union and Japan filed a formal protest with the World Trade Organization, which the United States itself was forced to defend since Massachusetts, as a constituent state of the United States, lacked standing to appear before the WTO. Spiro suggests that, if the Massachusetts statute were to be found GATT-illegal, "it is at least possible that the EU and Japan would propose retaliatory sanctions targeting Massachusetts entities or products."[138] Perhaps. But not before the United States government would have been exposed to international litigation and an embarrassing loss before a WTO panel.

To be sure, in theory the United States government could itself have brought an action against Massachusetts alleging a violation on the state's part of WTO obligations. The federal legislation implementing the results of the Uruguay Round of trade talks prohibits foreign governments and private persons from challenging state laws based on GATT, but not the federal government.[139] Such an action, however, would be highly unlikely. By bringing the action, the US government would be admitting the validity of the European Union and Japanese complaint, which for strategic and other reasons it would be unwilling to do. Such a suit would also be highly delicate from a domestic political perspective. It is worth noting that, despite considerable pressure from both opponents and proponents of the Massachusetts statute for early action, the Clinton administration did not become involved in *Crosby* until well after the Supreme Court had granted the writ of *certiorari* and there were two unanimous lower court decisions.[140]

Because of the narrow basis of its decision in *Crosby* it remains for another day for the Supreme Court to rule on the continued viability of *Zschernig* and the dormant foreign affairs doctrine. The Court may have an opportunity to do so in the near future. Reportedly, as of February 2000, twenty-nine state and local governments other than Massachusetts had passed or proposed forty-two sanctions against a variety of disfavored foreign governments.[141] Moreover, one interpretation of *Crosby* is that state and local governments are free to continue imposing such sanctions as long as Congress has not adopted a sanctions regime of its own, and reportedly many activists have chosen to read the decision in this manner.[142] If a suit challenging such state sanctions were to come before the Supreme Court, it could decide the case on the basis of the dormant foreign affairs doctrine, although alternatively it might rule on the basis of the dormant foreign commerce clause doctrine.

If the Supreme Court decides to revisit *Zschernig* and the dormant foreign affairs doctrine, it seems unlikely that the Court will accept the arguments advanced by Goldsmith et al. and rejected by the First Circuit in *Crosby*. With the world increasingly becoming interdependent, with international law through the globalization process increasingly governing aspects of US life previously regarded as matters solely of domestic concern, and with the United States increasingly being held accountable for alleged violations of international law in international forums, the need for the United States to speak with one voice is, if anything, greater than it was in the past.[143]

Moreover, as we have seen previously, the federal government has taken numerous and controversial measures to protect state interests from interference by international law and institutions. The specter of the federal government using international law – whether it be in the form of treaties and other international agreements or of customary international law – to ride roughshod over state law and practice is a chimera.

The status of international law in the United States and the rule of law in international affairs

To return to the "truism" posed at the beginning of this chapter, the strength of a country's adherence to the rule of law in international affairs depends in substantial measure on the extent to which international law can be enforced through national mechanisms. Judged by this criterion the strength of US adherence to the rule of law in international affairs would appear to be weak indeed. One of the primary reasons that international law is difficult to enforce through national mechanisms is the lowly status that international law has under US law.

From a theoretical perspective, of course, the United States strongly adheres to the dualist approach to the relationship between international and national law. Moreover, when the United States has incorporated international law into its national legal system, it has developed legal doctrines and taken other steps to minimize or eliminate the impact of this law. Thus, although treaties and other international agreements are the "supreme Law of the Land," the judicially established distinction between self-executing and non-self-executing treaties has resulted, especially in the case of human rights treaties, in the non-enforcement of many treaties through national means. Although a number of US scholars have recently challenged the constitutionality of a Senate declaration that a treaty is non-self-executing,[144] or even the validity of the Supreme Court decisions establishing the distinction between self-executing and non-self-executing treaties,[145] this challenge currently enjoys no support from the executive branch and has no basis in US court decisions. The same may be said of scholarly criticism of the last-in-time doctrine and the application of the political question doctrine in cases involving alleged violations of international law.

Customary international law constitutes a special case. Increasing skepticism of the customary international law process at the international level hardly promotes a willingness to accord customary international law much status and influence at the national level. This may contribute to the apparent unwillingness of the executive branch and the courts to recognize customary international law as the supreme law of the land. It is also clear that despite, or perhaps because of, the ambiguity of *The Paquete Habana* decision, customary international law places few if any constraints on executive branch action as a matter of US jurisprudence.[146]

In sharp contrast, there appears to be an increasing willingness on the part of Congress and US courts to hold foreign nationals or foreign states accountable for violations of customary international law. Despite the protestations of Bradley and Goldsmith and others, the Alien Tort Claims Act continues to be utilized frequently as the basis for civil litigation against foreign individuals who allegedly engaged in violations abroad of customary international law norms.[147] Also, Congress recently amended the Foreign Sovereign Immunities Act to permit a suit for money damages against a foreign state for personal injury or death that was caused by an act of torture, extrajudicial killing, aircraft sabotage, hostage taking, or the provision of material support or resources for such an act if the act or provision of support is engaged in by an official agent of the foreign state while acting within the scope of his or her duties.[148] US courts shall decline to hear such a claim, however, if the foreign state was not designated as a state sponsor of terrorism by the US government at the time the act occurred. At this writing the states designated as sponsors of terrorism include Cuba, Iraq, Iran, Libya, North Korea, Sudan, and Syria. The amendment has resulted in several judgments awarding damages.[149] It has also survived a challenge on constitutional grounds,[150] but its compatibility with the customary international law of foreign sovereign immunity is debatable, since no other state's law on foreign sovereign immunity provides for a loss of immunity under similar circumstances.

From the discussion set forth above in this chapter, one may conclude that there are two salient structural impediments that undermine the status of international law in the United States: the separation of powers doctrine and federalism. The separation of powers doctrine has resulted in periodic struggles for control over US foreign policy, not only between Congress and the executive branch but also between the two houses of Congress. Moreover, as Louis Henkin has noted:

> The respective powers of President and Congress are established in the large, but the division I have described has not been accepted in all respects by all Presidents and all Congresses (or all members of Congress) at all times; in any event, the generalizations leave ample areas of uncertainty. In principle as in fact, recurrent competition for power has punctuated relations between President and Congress, raising the dominant, least tractable constitutional issues of US foreign relations. That the Constitution is especially inarticulate in allocating foreign affairs powers; that a particular power can with equal logic and fair constitutional reading be claimed for the President or for Congress; that the powers of both President and Congress have been described in full, even extravagant adjectives ("vast," "plenary"); that instead of a "natural" separation of "executive" from "legislative" functions there has grown an irregular, uncertain division of each – all have served and nurtured political forces inviting struggle.[151]

For their part US courts have seldom intervened to resolve these "boundary disputes" and have invoked the political offense doctrine, the last-in-time rule, the distinction between self-executing and non-self-executing treaties, lack of standing or justiciability, questionable interpretations of treaties, or other grounds to reject challenges based on international law to actions undertaken by the political branches.

Heightened sensitivity to state prerogatives arising out of federalism concerns has led Congress and the executive branch to take steps, especially with respect to human rights treaties, to ensure that international law will not be the basis for a challenge to state law and practice. Doctrinal support for this approach has been provided by a profusion of academic writing. With rare exceptions US courts have been non-participants in this evolving debate.

Congress, in particular, has increasingly taken "less seriously" the fulfillment of US obligations under international law. One of the most striking examples has been (until recently) its refusal to authorize the payment of dues owed to the United Nations – a subject we turn to in the next chapter of this study.

Notes

1. There have been efforts to bridge the gap between monism and dualism and develop other approaches. See, e.g., Edward Borchard, *The Relation Between International Law and Municipal Law*, 27 VA. L. REV. 137 (1940). For a general discussion of the distinction between the two schools of thought, see STARKE'S INTERNATIONAL LAW 63–64 (I. Shearer, 11th ed., 1994).
2. Article 25 of the Basic Law of the Federal Republic of Germany is among the constitutional provisions in western Europe most favorable to the status of customary international law. It provides:

   The general rules of public international law shall be an integral part of federal law. They shall take precedence over the laws and shall directly create rights and duties for the inhabitants of the federal territory.

   Under decisions of the German Federal Constitutional Court the general rules of international law are norms recognized as binding by a predominant majority of states but not necessarily by the Federal Republic of Germany. They include customary international law (but not regional customary international law) and principles generally recognized by civilized states. In contrast, under Article 59(2) of the Basic Law, treaties require validity under national law only after a special transformation act. Treaty law, moreover, is not superior to national law and may be overruled by subsequent enacted legislation. The situation is very different in the Netherlands, however, where Article 94 of the Netherlands Constitution provides:

   Statutory regulations in force within the Kingdom shall not be applicable if such application is in conflict with provisions of treaties that are binding on all persons or of resolutions by international institutions.

3. For discussion see Clive Walker & Russell L. Weaver, *The United Kingdom Bill of Rights 1998: The Modernisation of Rights in the Old World*, 33 U. MICH. JL REFORM 497 (2000).
4. See Lord Mansfield in Triquet and Others v. Bath, 97 Eng. Rep. 936, 938, 3 Burr. 1478, 1481 (KB 1764).
5. Chung Chi Cheung v. The King, [1939] AC 160, 168 (Hong Kong) (1938).
6. 27 US (2 Pet.) 253, 7 L.Ed. 415 (1829).
7. LOUIS HENKIN, FOREIGN AFFAIRS AND THE US CONSTITUTION 203–4 (2d ed., 1996).
8. 3 Cal. 2d 718, 242 P. 2d 617 (1952).
9. See, e.g., Frolova v. USSR, 761 F. 2d 370, 374 (7th Cir. 1985).
10. 555 F. 2d 848 (DC Cir. 1976).
11. For a critique of this case, see ALAN C. SWAN & JOHN F. MURPHY, CASES AND MATERIALS ON THE REGULATION OF INTERNATIONAL BUSINESS AND ECONOMIC RELATIONS 1233–35 (2nd ed., 1999) and notes in 18 HARV. INT'L LJ 375 (1977); 24 KAN. L. REV. 395 (1976); 24 UCLA L. REV. 387 (1976).
12. 949 F. 2d 1109 (11th Cir. 1991), cert. denied 502 US 1122 (1992).
13. Louis Henkin, *US Ratification of Human Rights Conventions: The Ghost of Senator Bricker*, 89 AM. J. INT'L L. 341 (1995).
14. In pertinent part, Article 19 of the Vienna Convention on the Law of Treaties provides: "A State may, when signing, ratifying, accepting, approving or acceding to a treaty, formulate a reservation unless . . . the reservation is incompatible with the object and purpose of the treaty."

15. Consideration of Reports Submitted by States Parties Under Article 40 of the Covenant: Comments of the Human Rights Committee, 53d Sess., 1413th mtg., at 4, UN Doc. CCPR/C79/Add.50 (1995).
16. Curtis A. Bradley & Jack L. Goldsmith, *Treaties, Human Rights, and Conditional Consent*, 149 U. PA. L. REV. 399, 415 (2000).
17. *Id.* at 408.
18. For general discussion of the Bricker Amendment controversy, see NATALIE HEVENER KAUFMAN, HUMAN RIGHTS TREATIES AND THE SENATE (1990); DUANE TANANBAUM, THE BRICKER AMENDMENT CONTROVERSY: A TEST OF EISENHOWER'S POLITICAL LEADERSHIP (1988).
19. Henkin, *supra* note 13, at 349.
20. See International Convention on the Elimination of All Forms of Racial Discrimination, 103d Cong., 2d Sess., Exec.Rept. 103–29, at 8 (1994).
21. Henkin, *supra* note 13, at 345.
22. See Bradley and Goldsmith, *supra* note 16, at 422.
23. Henkin, *supra* note 13, at 346.
24. 252 US 416 (1920).
25. *Id.* at 433.
26. David M. Golove, *Treaty-Making and the Nation: The Historical Foundations of the Nationalist Conception of the Treaty Power*, 98 MICH. L. REV. 1075, 1273–78 (2000).
27. *Id.* at 1276.
28. *Id.* at 1270–72.
29. For an article making this point, see Peter J. Spiro, *The States and International Human Rights*, 66 FORDHAM L. REV. 567, 576–78 (1997).
30. Curtis A. Bradley, *The Treaty Power and American Federalism*, 97 MICH. L. REV. 390, 456 (1998).
31. Golove, *supra* note 26.
32. *Id.* at 1314.
33. The classic decision establishing the last-in-time doctrine is Whitney v. Robertson, 124 US 190 (1888).
34. *Id.* at 194.
35. In addition to Whitney v. Robertson, *supra* note 33, the leading decisions include The Chinese Exclusion Case, 130 US 581 (1889), Head Money Cases, 112 US 580 (1884), The Cherokee Tobacco Case, 78 US (11 Wall) 616 (1870), Moser v. United States, 341 US 41 (1951), and Foster & Elam v. Neilson, 27 US (2 Pet.) 253 (1829).
36. HENKIN, *supra* note 7, at 210.
37. *Id.* at 210–11.
38. Louis Sohn, *Remarks*, 63 ASIL PROC. 180 (1969).
39. 470 F. 2d 461, 465–67 (DC Cir. 1972).
40. *Id.* at 465, n. 4.
41. 333 US 103, 111 (1948).
42. Thomas M. Franck, *Dr. Pangloss Meets the Grinch: A Pessimistic Comment on Harold Koh's Optimism*, 35 HOUS. L. REV. 683, 696 (1998). For further consideration of this issue, see THOMAS M. FRANCK, POLITICAL QUESTION/JUDICIAL ANSWERS: DOES THE RULE OF LAW APPLY TO FOREIGN AFFAIRS? 4–9 (1992).
43. HENKIN, *supra* note 7, at 242.
44. According to Louis Henkin, as of 1996, presidents had made some 1,600 treaties with the consent of the Senate, but many thousands of other international agreements without seeking Senate consent. *Id.* at 215.
45. *Id.* at 218–19, n. **.

46. United States v. Belmont, 301 US 324 (1937). In 1981, in Dames & Moore v. Regan, 453 US 654 (1981), the Supreme Court upheld the president's authority to make presidential executive agreements settling international claims.
47. Pub. L. No. 92-403, 86 Stat. 619, codified as amended at 1 USC Section 112b (1994).
48. HENKIN, *supra* note 7, at 222.
49. For citations supporting this view, see *id.* at 503, n. 187.
50. For discussion of the Supreme Court decisions, see *id.* at 226–30.
51. United States v. Guy W. Capps, Inc., 204 F.2d 655 (4th Cir. 1953).
52. See HENKIN, *supra* note 7, at 228.
53. See Detlev F. Vagts, *Taking Treaties Less Seriously*, 92 AM. J. INT'L L. 458 (1998).
54. For example, Congress has shifted from provisions in tax legislation specifying that new legislation would not override prior tax treaty commitments to sections of the laws of 1986 and 1988 specifying that new rules would override prior commitments. *Id.*, at 459. Also, as pointed out by Vagts, several recent US court decisions have interpreted federal legislation as trumping treaty commitments. Thus, in Dole v. South African Airways, 817 F. 2d 119 (DC Cir.), cert. denied, 484 US 896 (1987), the court held that the Comprehensive Anti-Apartheid Act overrode the bilateral civil air agreement with South Africa; in Havana Club Holding, SA v. Galleon, SA, 974 F. Supp. 302 (SDNY 1997), the court placed the provisions of the Cuban Assets Control Regulations above provisions of an older Organization of American States treaty relating to transfers of intellectual property; and in Breard v. Greene, 523 US 371 (1998), the Supreme Court held that the Antiterrorism and Effective Death Penalty Act of 1996 trumped Art. 36 of the Vienna Convention on Consular Relations.
55. See Vagts, *supra* note 53, at 460.
56. See Jack L. Goldsmith & Eric A. Posner, *A Theory of Customary International Law*, 66 U. CHI. L. REV. 1113 (1999); Jack L. Goldsmith & Eric A. Posner, *Understanding the Resemblance Between Modern and Traditional Customary International Law*, 40 VA. J. INT'L L. 639 (2000).
57. Goldsmith & Posner, *Understanding the Resemblance, supra* note 56, at 655.
58. *Id.* at 658.
59. *Id.* at 659.
60. *Id.* at 662.
61. *Id.* at 663.
62. *Id.* at 672.
63. LOUIS HENKIN, HOW NATIONS BEHAVE 47 (1979).
64. Murray v. Schooner Charming Betsy, 6 US (2 Cranch) 64, 118, 2 L.Ed. 208, 226 (1804).
65. Restatement (Third) of the Foreign Relations Law of the United States, Section 114 (1987).
66. For a listing and brief discussion of some of these cases, see Reporters' Note 1, *id.*
67. JOHN M. ROGERS, INTERNATIONAL LAW AND UNITED STATES LAW 65 (1999).
68. *Id.*
69. 485 US 312 (1988).
70. *Finzer v. Barry*, 798 F.2d 1450 (DC Cir. 1986).
71. *Id.* at 1455.
72. *Id.* at 1458.
73. ROGERS, *supra* note 67, at 68.
74. 485 US at 324.
75. 485 US at 338 (Rehnquist, CJ, concurring in part and dissenting in part).
76. ROGERS, *supra* note 67, at 70.
77. 487 US 815 (1988).

78. 487 US at 830 and n.31 (citing Trop v. Dulles, 356 US 86 (1958); Coker v. Georgia, 433 US 584 (1977); and Enmund v. Florida, 458 US 782 (1982)).
79. 487 US at 868–69 n.4.
80. 492 US 361 (1989).
81. The second US reservation to the International Covenant on Civil and Political Rights reads in pertinent part as follows: "the United States reserves the right, subject to its Constitutional restraints, to impose capital punishment on any person (other than a pregnant woman) duly convicted under existing or future laws permitting the imposition of capital punishment, including such punishment for crimes committed by persons below eighteen years of age." 138 Congressional Record S4781-01 (1992).
82. Lawrence v. Texas, 123 S.Ct. 2472 (2003).
83. *Id.* at 2481. The British legislation is the Sexual Offences Act of 1967, section 1.
84. Lawrence v. Texas, *supra* note 82. The cited decision of the European Court of Human Rights is Dudgeon v. United Kingdom, 45 Eur. Ct. HR (1981) at para 52.
85. Lawrence v. Texas, 123 S.Ct. at 2483.
86. *Id.* at 2488, 2495 (Justice Scalia's dissent).
87. 175 US 677 (1900).
88. 175 US at 700.
89. Goldsmith & Posner, *Understanding the Resemblance Between Modern and Traditional Customary International Law, supra* note 56, at 641–54.
90. Louis Henkin, *International Law as Law in the United States*, 82 MICH. L. REV. 1555 (1984).
91. Garcia-Mir. v. Meese, 788 F. 2d 1446 (11th Cir. 1986).
92. See HENKIN, *supra* note 7, at 244–46.
93. See e.g., *Agora: May the President Violate Customary International Law?*, 80 AM. J. INT'L L. 913 (1986).
94. See Restatement (Third) of the Foreign Relations Law of the United States, Section 115, comment d.
95. For US court decisions stating this proposition, see, e.g., Kadic v. Karadzic, 70 F. 3d 232, 246 (2d Cir. 1995) (referring to the "settled proposition that federal common law incorporates international law"), cert. denied, 518 US 1005 (1996); *In re* Estate of Ferdinand E. Marcos Human Rights Litigation, 978 F. 2d 493, 502 (9th Cir. 1992) ("It is . . . well settled that the law of nations is part of federal common law."); Xuncax v. Gramajo, 886 F. Supp. 162, 193 (D. Mass. 1995) ("[I]t is well settled that the body of principles that comprise customary international law is subsumed and incorporated by federal common law"). Some examples of scholarly comment supporting this proposition include Lea Brilmayer, *Federalism, State Authority, and the Preemptive Power of International Law*, 1994 SUP. CT. REV. 295, 302–4; Henkin, *supra* note 90, at 1555, 1560–62.
96. See Restatement (Third) of the Foreign Relations Law of the United States, Section 111, comment d (1987).
97. Curtis A. Bradley & Jack L. Goldsmith, *Customary International Law as Federal Common Law: A Critique of the Modern Position*, 110 HARV. L. REV. 815 (1997).
98. 304 US 64 (1938).
99. Bradley & Goldsmith, *supra* note 97, at 820–21.
100. 304 US at 78.
101. Bradley & Goldsmith, *supra* note 97, at 821.
102. The most notable of these responses, perhaps, is Harold Hongju Koh, *Is International Law Really State Law?*, 111 HARV. L. REV. 1824 (1998). Koh's article in turn stimulated a counter-response, Curtis A. Bradley & Jack L. Goldsmith, *Federal Courts and the Incorporation of International Law*, 111 HARV. L. REV. 2260 (1998). See also, e.g., Gerald

L. Neuman, *Sense and Nonsense About Customary International Law: A Response to Professors Bradley and Goldsmith*, 66 FORDHAM L. REV. 371 (1997); Beth Stephens, *The Law of Our Land: Customary International Law as Federal Law After Erie*, 66 FORDHAM L. REV. 393 (1997). For a superb article proposing a (at least partial) reconciliation between the two camps, see Ernest A. Young, *Sorting Out the Debate Over Customary International Law*, 42 VA. J. INT'L L. 365 (2002).

103. See e.g., Phillip R. Trimble, A *Revisionist View of Customary International Law*, 33 UCLA L. REV. 665 (1986); A. M. Weisburd, *State Courts, Federal Courts, and International Cases*, 20 YALE J. INT'L L. 1 (1995). For a student comment on the Trimble article, see M. Erin Kelly, *Customary International Law in United States Courts*, 32 VILLANOVA L. REV. 1089 (1987).
104. *The Paquete Habana*, 175 US at 712.
105. Goldsmith & Posner, *Understanding the Resemblance Between Modern and Traditional Customary International Law, supra* note 56, at 666.
106. See HENKIN, *supra* note 7, at 508, n.16 (citing examples).
107. Judiciary Act of 1789, ch. 20, section 9, 1 Stat. 73, 77 (1789), as amended, 28 USC section 1350 (1994).
108. 630 F.2d 876 (2d Cir. 1980).
109. Filartiga v. Pena-Irala, 577 F. Supp. 860 (EDNY 1984).
110. For further discussion, see John F. Murphy, *Civil Liability for the Commission of International Crimes as an Alternative to Criminal Prosecution*, 12 HARV. HUM. RTS. J. 1, 30–32 (1999).
111. Filartiga, 630 F.2d at 881.
112. 726 F.2d 774, 798–823 (DC Cir. 1984).
113. The Department of Justice submitted its memorandum in Trajano v. Marcos, No. 86–207, slip opinion (d. Hawaii, July 18, 1986), appeal docketed No. 86–2448 (9th Cir. Aug. 20, 1986).
114. Torture Victim Protection Act of 1991, Pub. L. No. 102–256, 106 Stat. 73 (1992), 28 USC Section 1350.
115. Lafontant v. Aristide, 844 F. Supp. 128, 138 (EDNY 1994) (extrajudicial killing action against exiled president of Haiti dismissed on head-of-state immunity grounds).
116. STEVEN R. RATNER & JASON S. ABRAMS, ACCOUNTABILITY FOR HUMAN RIGHTS ATROCITIES IN INTERNATIONAL LAW: BEYOND THE NUREMBERG LEGACY 207 (1997).
117. Curtis A. Bradley & Jack L. Goldsmith, *The Current Illegitimacy of International Human Rights Litigation*, 66 FORDHAM L. REV. 319, 363–68 (1997).
118. *Id.* at 356–63.
119. See Koh, *supra* note 102, at 1828.
120. See Curtis A. Bradley & Jack L. Goldsmith, *Federal Courts and the Incorporation of International Law*, 111 HARV. L. REV. 2261 (1998).
121. *Id.* at 2264.
122. *Id.* at 2266.
123. Restatement (Third) of the Foreign Relations Law of the United States, Status of International Law and Agreements in United States Law, Introductory Note, at 43 (1987).
124. Bradley & Goldsmith, *supra* note 120, at 2265.
125. *Id.* at 2261, n. 31.
126. *Id.* at 2267, n. 34.
127. 389 US 429 (1968).
128. 331 US 503 (1947).
129. 530 US 363 (2000).

130. National Foreign Trade Council v. Natsios, 181 F. 3d 38, 49–61 (1st Cir. 1999).
131. *Id.* at 52.
132. 512 US 298 (1994).
133. See Jack L. Goldsmith, *Federal Courts, Foreign Affairs, and Federalism*, 83 VA. L. REV. 1617, 1698–705 (1997). For another analysis of Barclays Bank along similar lines, see Peter J. Spiro, *Foreign Affairs Federalism*, 70 U. COLO. L. REV. 1223, 1266–67 (1999).
134. National Foreign Trade Council v. Natsios, *supra* note 130, at 58, n. 12.
135. Koh, *supra* note 102, at 1848.
136. See Spiro, *supra* note 133, at 1265–67.
137. *Id.* at 1267.
138. *Id.* at 1268.
139. See Uruguay Round Agreements Act, Pub. L. No. 103–465, 108 Stat. 4809, 4815–19 (1994) (codified at 19 USC Section 3512 (West Supp. 1999)).
140. For discussion of this point, see Brannon P. Denning & Jack H. McCall, *International Decisions: Crosby v. National Foreign Trade Council*, 94 AM. J. INT'L L. 750, 758 (2000).
141. See Brannon P. Denning & Jack H. McCall, *States' Rights and Foreign Policy*, 79 FOREIGN AFF. 9, 11 (Jan./Feb. 2000).
142. See Denning & McCall, *supra* note 140, at 754.
143. For a contrary view, see Spiro, *supra* note 133. In American Insurance Association v. Garamendi, 123 S.Ct. 2374 (June 23, 2003), by a five to four vote, the US Supreme Court recently relied on Zschernig in ruling that the President's complex but voluntary international arrangements to compensate Holocaust victims for insurance assets confiscated by the Nazi regime preempted a Californian statute designed to compel European insurance companies either to divulge records of insurance policies they sold in Europe between 1920 and 1945 or to forfeit their state licenses.
144. See, e.g., Jordan J. Paust, *Self-Executing Treaties*, 82 AM. J. INT'L L. 760 (1988); Stefan A. Riesenfeld & Frederick M. Abbott, *The Scope of US Senate Control Over the Conclusion and Operation of Treaties*, 67 CHI.-KENT L. REV. 571, 631 (1991); Lori Damrosch, *The Role of the United States Senate Concerning "Self-Executing" and "Non-Self-Executing" Treaties*, 67 CHI.-KENT L. REV. 515 (1991).
145. Paust, *supra* note 144.
146. Apparently the only US decision invalidating action on the part of the executive branch solely on the basis of international human rights law is Fernandez v. Wilkinson, 505 F. Supp. 787 (D. Kan. 1980), *aff'd on other grounds sub nom.* Rodriguez v. Wilkinson, 654 F.2d 1382 (10th Cir. 1981). There the federal district court for Kansas granted Fernandez a writ of habeas corpus on the ground that his indeterminate detention in a maximum security prison pending deportation was a violation of customary international law and an abuse of discretion on the part of the Attorney General and his delegates.
147. Reportedly, as of early 2000, the Filartiga decision has been used as a reference point for over 100 cases. See HENRY J. STEINER & PHILIP ALSTON, INTERNATIONAL HUMAN RIGHTS IN CONTEXT 1049 (2d ed., 2000).
148. 28 USC Section 1605(A)(7) (1998).
149. For discussion, see Murphy, *supra* note 110.
150. See Socialist People's Libyan Arab Jamabiriya v. Rein, 162 F. 3d 748 (2d Cir. 1998), cert. denied, June 14, 1999.
151. HENKIN, *supra* note 7, at 84.

3 UN dues

In chapter 1 we examined the claim by John Bolton that treaties were simply "political obligations" rather than law in their international operation.[1] Bolton advanced this claim in an op-ed piece with the title "US Isn't Obligated to Pay the UN."[2] In sharp contrast to Bolton's contention that the United States is under no legal obligation to pay its UN dues, José Alvarez has pointed out "the conclusions of various former Legal Advisers to the Department of State as well as the vast majority of legal scholars: Article 17 of the UN Charter upholds a fundamental principle of 'collective financial responsibility' and imposes a legal obligation on members to pay the amount assessed by the General Assembly."[3]

Indeed, at least on paper, the capacity of the UN General Assembly to set and allocate dues among member states is the most far-reaching "legislative" authority the Assembly has. In theory the General Assembly could decide on a budget and allocate the responsibility to pay for it entirely to the United States or to the United States and a few other highly developed states. In realpolitik terms, of course, there is no possibility of the Assembly taking such an action.

Under Article 17(1) of the UN Charter, the General Assembly is authorized to "consider and approve the budget of the Organization." This decision of the Assembly is taken by a two-thirds majority of the member states present and voting, since it constitutes a decision on an "important question," as specified by Article 18(2) of the Charter.[4] Paragraph 2 of Article 17 in turn makes it clear that the budgetary decision of the Assembly creates an international obligation for member states when it provides: "The expenses of the Organization shall be borne by the Members as apportioned by the General Assembly."

As pointed out by Alvarez, however, the UN Charter "leaves the formula for determining the assessments, as well as the actual level," to be determined by the Assembly. Operating through its Committee on Contributions, the General Assembly "has varied the percentage of the regular UN budget assessed to individual states over the years but has adhered, at least in principle, to 'capacity to pay' as the basis for assessment."[5] Under

Article 19 of the Charter, member states overdue in their payments for two full years "shall" have no vote in the General Assembly, unless the Assembly is "satisfied that the failure to pay is due to conditions beyond the control of the Member." The result of these provisions is that two-thirds of the member states of the United Nations can adopt a budget over the strong objections of as many as one-third of the member states, thus creating a potential "tyranny of the majority." Moreover, although voting in the General Assembly is on the basis of one state/one vote, financial assessments have varied from the early US share of slightly under 40 percent to the current minimum of 0.001 percent.[6] At the same time, in practice the US percentage in the scale of assessments has been set through negotiations in the United Nations, and the US share has been, and continues to be, less than its rate would be if it fully reflected US economic strength.[7]

From its very beginning, the United Nations had problems collecting dues from member states. But timely payments by major contributors, including the United States, allowed the Organization to avoid financial crises. In the 1960s, however, a major financial and political crisis erupted when the Soviet Union and France refused to pay expenses the General Assembly had apportioned to them for peacekeeping operations by the UN Emergency Force (UNEF) in the Middle East and the UN Operation in the Congo (ONUC). By way of response the General Assembly requested an advisory opinion from the International Court of Justice on whether the expenses the Assembly had authorized for UNEF and ONUC constituted "expenses of the Organization" within the meaning of Article 17(2) of the Charter.

Certain expenses of the United Nations

In a sense the genesis of the crisis over UNEF and ONUC was the General Assembly's adoption, in 1950, of the Uniting for Peace resolution.[8] Adopted in response to the stalemate in the Security Council when the Soviet Union returned[9] and blocked any further action by the Council with respect to Korea, the resolution provided that the General Assembly would meet to recommend collective measures in situations where the Security Council was unable to deal with a breach of the peace or act of aggression. Under the resolution, whenever a veto prevented the Council from acting, a special emergency session of the General Assembly could be convened within twenty-four hours by a procedural vote of any seven members of the Security Council. By its terms, the resolution envisages the Assembly, which, unlike the Security Council acting under Chapter VII of the Charter, cannot take decisions binding on member states regarding the maintenance of international peace and security, making "appropriate recommendations to Members for collective measures, including in the case of a breach of the peace or act of aggression the use of armed force when necessary, to maintain or restore international peace and security."[10] It thus implicitly provides that the Assembly may act as an agent to enforce the peace against a state deemed (by the Assembly) to be an aggressor. The Uniting for Peace resolution was so utilized against North Korea and the People's Republic of China.[11] Thereafter, however, the Assembly assumed a more modest role and confined its recommendations regarding the use of armed force to the establishment of peacekeeping forces.

Specifically, in 1956, the Security Council adopted a resolution, not subject to the veto because it dealt with a matter of procedure,[12] that placed the question of the Suez crisis before the General Assembly. Once the question was on its agenda, the Assembly called on the parties to the conflict to agree to a cease-fire and to the withdrawal of all forces behind the armistice lines, and passed a resolution establishing "a United Nations Command for an Emergency International Force [UNEF] to secure and supervise the cessation of hostilities."[13] With Egyptian approval, the UNEF was established on its territory, Israel having refused categorically to accept the stationing of any foreign force on its territory.

In abstaining on the Assembly's resolution – the abstention rather than a negative vote was apparently due to a desire to avoid offending Egypt – the Soviet Union challenged the establishment of the UNEF. It argued, among other things, that the Assembly had no jurisdiction in matters involving "action," and that all UN forces, whether their function was "policing" or "enforcement," were engaged in action. The authority to take "action," according to the Soviet view, was reserved to the Security Council under the terms of Article 11(2) of the United Nations Charter.[14]

Immediately upon the establishment of the UNEF, a disagreement arose as to the allocation of costs of the force not borne by members sending troops or met by donations. In keeping with its legal position, the Soviet Union insisted that UNEF costs be borne by the United Kingdom, France, and Israel. The United States argued that the costs should be considered "expenses of the Organization" and financed on the usual scale of assessments. The General Assembly ultimately decided that assessments should be made on all members, but on a sliding scale with low-income members paying less than their usual share and the difference being made up by voluntary contributions.

The Soviet Union refused to accept the Assembly's decision and withheld payment of its share of the UNEF's expenses.

The backdrop to the dispute over ONUC is more complicated.[15] ONUC was created by the Security Council in 1960 in response to widespread violence and foreign intervention in the former Belgian Congo (now the Democratic Republic of the Congo) shortly after it declared independence. Initially the Council passed resolutions expanding the authority of ONUC to take action in the Congo. Later, however, disputes between then Secretary-General Dag Hammarskjold and the Soviet Union arose and ONUC took action that disfavored Prime Minister Patrice Lumumba, who was friendly to the Soviets, in his power struggle with President Joseph Kasavubu. The result was that the permanent members of the Security Council were unable to reach agreement. In particular, the Soviet Union was unwilling to accept a draft resolution introduced by the United States that would have required that all aid to the Congo be channeled through the United Nations because this limitation was so obviously directed against Soviet aid to Lumumba. When the Soviet Union rejected a draft resolution introduced by Tunisia and Ceylon (now Sri Lanka) that would have limited the channeling of aid through the United Nations to miliary aid, the United States submitted a draft resolution to convene an emergency session of the General Assembly under the procedure of the Uniting for Peace resolution. This resolution was adopted despite a Soviet negative vote, the veto not being applicable to a procedural matter.

Although the Security Council was later able to adopt resolutions with respect to the Congo, in the meantime the General Assembly adopted resolutions on the substance of the conflict as well as resolutions that classified ONUC expenses as "expenses of the Organization" within the meaning of Article 17(2) of the Charter and apportioned them according to the regular scale of assessments. Bulgaria, Czechoslovakia, France, Poland, Romania, and the Soviet Union, however, announced that they would not contribute to ONUC expenses.[16] This led in 1962 to the *Certain Expenses* Advisory Opinion of the International Court of Justice, requested by the General Assembly at the urging of the United States.

The ICJ Advisory Opinion

Some twenty governments submitted materials to the Court in the *Expenses* case, including the United States, France, and, for the first time, the Soviet Union. France argued that the General Assembly had only the limited authority to assess member states for "administrative" expenses and therefore peacekeeping expenses were not among the "expenses" included in Article 17.[17] The Soviet Union contended that only the Security

Council could fund peacekeeping operations and that even the Council could do so only by so-called Article 43 agreements with member states.[18] The Soviets further argued that since all resolutions of the General Assembly are only recommendations, they cannot create legal obligations for member states.

In sharp contrast, the United States strongly supported an expansive budgetary power for the General Assembly. According to the United States, the mandatory language and negotiating history of Article 17, as well as subsequent practice, confirmed the "exclusive character of the fiscal authority of the General Assembly." Moreover, the authority of the General Assembly to create "legally binding financial obligations" covers peacekeeping as well as "administrative" expenses. In response to French and Soviet concerns about the tyranny of the majority in the Assembly, the United States, in the person of Abram Chayes, suggested:

> Member States do not find their protection against such action – if protection is needed – in legal strictures of the Charter, but in the political requirement of a two-thirds majority in the General Assembly both to initiate action and to make the necessary financial arrangements. If these majorities can be mustered; if the activities engaged in are immediately related to the express purposes of the United Nations; if they are approved in due course according to the regular procedures of one of its organs having competence over the subject-matter; if they do not contravene any prohibition of the Charter nor invade the sovereign powers of individual States – if conditions such as these are satisfied, I can perceive no reason why the United Nations should be prohibited from levying assessments to pay for goods and services needed for those activities.[19]

In its majority Advisory Opinion, the Court basically accepted the US contentions.[20] By nine votes to five, the Court opined that expenditures for a General Assembly peacekeeping operation did constitute expenses of the Organization within the meaning of Article 17. The Court noted the absence of any modifying word like "regular" or "administrative" in the terms of Article 17 and decided that none was intended. In the Court's view the validity of expenditures authorized by the Assembly "must be tested by their relationship to the purposes of the United Nations." If an expenditure were not made for a purpose of the United Nations – as set forth in Article 1 of the Charter – it would not be considered an "expense of the Organization."[21] Although it acknowledged that the purposes of the United Nations are not "unlimited," the Court went on to suggest that "when the Organization takes action which warrants the assertion that it was appropriate for the fulfillment of one of the stated purposes of the United Nations, the presumption is that such action is not *ultra vires* the Organization."[22] For their part dissenting judges argued that such reasoning could authorize the Assembly to do virtually anything it wished through the assessment procedure, as long as it claimed to be acting to further a purpose of the United Nations.[23]

In other passages the majority opinion of the Court was even more far-reaching in its support of the budgetary powers of the General Assembly. To the majority, even if it is alleged that the expenditure in question relates to an *ultra vires* act on the part of a UN organ such as the General Assembly, "this would not necessarily mean that the expense incurred was not an expense of the Organization . . . each organ must, in the first place at least, determine its own jurisdiction."[24] In the situation before the Court, for reasons that have been examined elsewhere, the majority of the Court was of the view that the General Assembly had not acted *ultra vires* in its actions with respect to the UNEF and ONUC peacekeeping operations.[25]

In a provocative and critical article on the Court's majority opinion, Leo Gross aptly summed up exactly how far-reaching it was:

> It enhanced the "institutional effectiveness" of the United Nations immeasurably by attributing to it a virtually unlimited budgetary power. It affirmed specifically that the General Assembly could and did validly and with legally binding force authorize expenditures for the purpose of effectuating legally non-obligatory resolutions of either the General Assembly or the Security Council. It affirmed that financial resolutions were presumptively not *ultra vires* the Organization if they were geared to one of the purposes stated in the Charter.[26]

The opinion's aftermath: the Article 19 crisis

Following the Court's opinion, debate began in the General Assembly regarding what action, if any, the Assembly should take in response to it.[27] The United States and other countries proposed that the Assembly should formally accept the Court's opinion. France, the Soviet Union, and various communist countries argued that, since the opinion was not binding, Assembly acceptance would be tantamount to amending the Charter. Also, some member countries feared that accepting the opinion would lead to application of Article 19 sanctions against countries more than two years in arrears, which might result in a Soviet walkout.

The position of the United States prevailed, and on December 19, 1962, the Assembly adopted a resolution in which it accepted the Court's opinion.[28] It is worth noting that, following the announcement of the advisory opinion, the US Congress enacted an "expression of satisfaction" with the opinion, stating that it provided "a sound basis for obtaining prompt payment of assessments . . . by making them obligations of all members of the United Nations."[29]

In the General Assembly the question arose as to the application of sanctions against member states more than two years in arrears. By 1964 the Soviet Union was sufficiently behind in payments that the provisions of Article 19 of the Charter came into play. The position of the United States was that loss of vote was automatic under Article 19 if a member state was the requisite two years in arrears on its payments. Czechoslovakia, however, contended that only the General Assembly could decide to suspend the right of a member state to vote and that such a decision would be an "important question" requiring a two-thirds majority of those member states present and voting.[30]

When the General Assembly met for its nineteenth session in autumn 1964, the United States pressed hard to have member states in arrears on their dues automatically deprived of their vote. However, the president of the Assembly declined to rule that loss of vote was automatic, and the Assembly decided to avoid an immediate confrontation on the issue by proceeding to do as much business as it could without taking any votes. Albania attempted to upset this arrangement by insisting on a formal vote over the question of returning to a normal voting procedure. The vote on the Albania motion (which was defeated) was ruled "procedural" and hence not relevant to the issue whether delinquent member states could vote on Assembly business.[31]

Between the nineteenth and the twentieth sessions of the General Assembly, support for the United States' position regarding the deprivation of vote for those member states in arrears on payments for the UNEF and ONUC eroded markedly, in part because of the developing countries' strong reaction to the joint US–Belgian airlift into the Congo in 1964. As a result, before the start of the twentieth session of the Assembly in 1965, Arthur Goldberg, US permanent representative at the United Nations, announced that, while preserving its position on the legal issues, the United States would no longer press for adoption of its position and the Assembly could resume its normal business. At the same time, he noted, "the United States reserves the same option to make exceptions if, in our view, strong and compelling reasons exist for doing so. There can be no double standard among the members of the Organization." But Ambassador Goldberg emphasized that the United States still was of the view that the Assembly should be applying Article 19 to withholding states and that the United States "places the responsibility where it properly belongs – on those member states which have flouted the Assembly's will and the Court's opinion."[32]

Questions have arisen regarding the legal effect, if any, of this so-called "Goldberg reservation." Most commentators have been of the view that Ambassador Goldberg's statement has no legal effect, indeed that it was never intended to have legal effect. Elisabeth Zoller, for example, writing in 1987, points out that Goldberg "never acquiesced in exceptions to the principle of collective financial responsibility; he merely reserved US rights. On the whole, the United States has never ceased to support a rather strict interpretation of UN financial obligations."[33]

Others have suggested that the failure to apply Article 19 sanctions(or at least their infrequent application) may have caused the legally binding nature of Article 17 to have fallen "into desuetude."[34] Zoller, however, has pointed out that in the absence of a total lack of enforcement of Article 19, desuetude cannot operate and, in any event, "desuetude is not recognized as a legal basis for the extinction of treaties."[35]

Assuming *arguendo* that Article 17(2) retains its status as binding international obligation, the issue still remains: Under what circumstances, if any, are member states entitled to withhold payment of expenses assessed and allocated by the General Assembly? Alvarez suggests the following:

> The opinions rendered in the Expenses case, as well as pleadings in that case, have led most commentators to conclude that members have no legal duty to pay for *ultra vires* acts, that is, those involving "manifest" violations of the Charter, such as an expense which is not in accord with substantive purposes of the Charter or has been enacted in violation of the procedural requirements of the Charter, as, for example, an expense authorized by the wrong organ or by a less than two-thirds vote of the General Assembly. Nonetheless, the consequences which flow from this conclusion are far from clear. In particular, does "manifest" illegality render the organization's action void *ab initio* such that a member can unilaterally withhold payment corresponding to such action or is the action merely voidable if the organization or some third party, such as the World Court, makes a determination that the action is *ultra vires*?[36]

These issues came to the forefront when the United States and other member states issued new challenges to UN authorized expenses.

The United States as "Uncle Deadbeat"[37]

In the beginning: the late 1970s and the 1980s

The United States first began withholding or threatening to withhold portions of its assessed payments to the United Nations in 1979.[38] Ironically, one year earlier, in 1978, Herbert Hansell, then Legal Adviser to the US Department of State, had concluded that Article 17 of the UN Charter "impose[d] a legal obligation on members to pay the amount assessed to them by the General Assembly"[39] and gave no indication of any possible exception to this obligation.

The United States initially imposed "selective" withholdings targeted at specific UN programs included in the UN's regular budget of which the United States disapproved. These disfavored programs and projects provided certain benefits to the Palestine Liberation Organization (PLO), or entities associated with it; the South West Africa People's Organization (SWAPO); Libya, Iran, and Cuba; and certain communist countries specified by the president pursuant to US legislation.[40] Similarly, Congress mandated the withholding of US contributions for UN funds budgeted for the Second Decade to Combat Racism and Racial Discrimination and for implementation of the General Assembly's "Zionism is racism" resolution;[41] for the construction of a $73,500,000 conference center in Addis Ababa, Ethiopia, for the Economic Commission for Africa; for the UN's "post-adjustment allowance" for employees; and for the "biased" Department of Public Information.[42] For its part the executive branch withheld US contributions for the Preparatory Commission implementing the 1982 Law of the Sea Convention and for alleged "inadequacies" in the UN's system to equalize the effect of US income taxation on UN staff salaries.[43]

Next Congress imposed several types of contingent withholdings designed to take effect should certain events occur. The so-called "Kassebaum amendment," for example, adopted in 1985, required the US Secretary of State to seek the adoption of weighted voting on budgetary matters in the United Nations and the specialized agencies, and unilaterally reduced the US share of assessed contributions from 25 to 20 percent beginning with fiscal year 1987.[44] Further payments were contingent on the adoption of weighted voting on budgetary matters in the United Nations and its agencies, making voting rights proportionate to member states' contributions to the budget. As noted by Alvarez, weighted voting would have required an amendment to the UN Charter and was widely regarded as an "impossible" goal.[45]

Apparently Senator Kassebaum and other supporters of her amendment were primarily motivated by "the incredible array of salaries and benefits paid to UN employes"[46] and the alleged ineffectiveness of the executive branch since 1972 in controlling the UN budget through diplomatic channels. As to the latter point, Senator Kassebaum stated:

> During a 10-year period 1972–1982, during four administrations, the US executive branch fought UN budget increases within the system. The result? A 273 percent increase in the assessed contributions [of the United States]. When the Congress has acted, there have been results. In 1952 the Congress voted to reduce the maximum US contribution from 40-some percent to $33\frac{1}{3}$ percent. It was said that it could not be negotiated. It was negotiated. In 1972 a further congressional action reduced the maximum US contribution to 25 percent. Again we

were told that the United Nations would never accept it. In the end, our decision was accepted.[47]

The event that may have ensured enough support for Congress to pass the Kassebaum amendment was the General Assembly's aforementioned decision to build a $73 million conference facility in Addis Ababa, Ethiopia. In the biting words of one senator, "it will cost [the United States] $18.5 million to pay for that conference center in Ethiopia so that they can stand on the 29th floor and watch the rest of their countrymen starve to death."[48]

The "Kassebaum" withholdings did not result in a system of weighted voting, but in December 1986 the General Assembly adopted a resolution on "the Review of the Efficiency of the Administrative and Financial Functioning of the United Nations."[49] Although the resolution arguably constituted only a "gentlemen's agreement" with no binding legal effect,[50] it did contain four elements deemed essential by the United States: (i) a budget ceiling; (ii) an indication of program priorities; (iii) provision for a limited contingency fund limiting the possibility of add-ons to the budget; and (iv) a consensus-based decision-making process.[51]

The adoption of these reforms by the United Nations, especially the consensus-based decision-making process, apparently satisfied both Congress and the executive branch and led to a modification of the Kassebaum amendment. In its revised form the law made prospective US payments to the United Nations conditional upon a presidential determination of the status of three ongoing reforms: (i) implementation of a 15 percent reduction in UN Secretariat staff; (ii) progress in achieving a 50 percent limitation for nationals of any member state "seconded" to the UN Secretariat; and (iii) implementation of the consensus-based budget reform procedure. In 1988 the administration made the necessary certification, thereby allowing release of $44 million.[52]

Two other US contingent withholdings adopted during the 1980s are worthy of note. The first threatened US suspension of participation in the General Assembly or any specialized agency along with total withholding of all payments of assessed contributions to the United Nations or its specialized agencies should the General Assembly or any of its specialized agencies "illegally" expel, suspend, or deny the credentials of Israel.[53] The second was the executive branch's response to the PLO's announcement in 1989 that it intended to seek membership for the "state of Palestine" in the World Health Organization. In such an event, the executive branch announced, the United States would "make no further contributions – voluntary or assessed – to any international organization which makes any change in the PLO's present status as an observer organization."[54]

As noted by Zoller,[55] the timing of the Kassebaum amendment exacerbated the problem created by US withholdings. Other legislation adopted around the same time threatened to cut even more funds from US contributions to the United Nations. The so-called Gramm-Rudman-Hollings Act,[56] which had as its goal the elimination of the federal budget deficit by 1991, mandated a 4.3 percent sequestration of almost all federal appropriations, including those earmarked for international organizations. Also, the Sundquist amendment,[57] adopted in 1985, imposed a reduction in payment of US assessments corresponding to the US share of the salaries of UN employees who were compelled by their national governments to return a portion of their wages to their governments.

By 1988, however, the United States had changed its policy on payment of UN dues, and in 1989 it began to pay arrears that totaled nearly $1 billion.[58] Further, the Foreign Relations Authorization Act for fiscal years 1990 and 1991[59] extended the revised Kassebaum amendment, allowing the president to use his discretion in deciding whether to withhold 20 percent of US payments to the United Nations. This softening of congressional rhetoric against the United Nations may be attributable in part to the collapse of the Soviet Union and the reemergence of the United States as the sole superpower. This was soon to change.

The 1990s: Congress lays down the law

As indicated above, even with the softening of congressional attitudes towards the United Nations in the early 1990s, US pledges to repay its accumulated arrears and future assessed contributions remained contingent on continued UN progress on "budgetary restraint" and on the Organization continuing to adhere to consensus budget making.[60] This approach "led many to suggest that major contributors to UN system organizations are now exercising or threatening to exercise a financial veto never anticipated by the drafters of the UN Charter – often in addition to the Security Council veto given permanent members."[61]

Moreover, as the decade progressed, Congress upped the ante. The 1994–95 Foreign Relations Authorization Act,[62] for example, threatened to withhold 20 percent of US assessed contributions unless the United Nations established an Office of Inspector General to ferret out mismanagement and corruption. Then from 1997 to 1999, Congress attempted to tie payment of UN dues to the passage of legislation that would have barred federal spending for international family planning organizations that lobby foreign governments to change their abortion policies, but this effort was vetoed by President Clinton.[63] Similar riders held up payment of arrears during 1999 as well.[64]

In 1999 Congress passed the pièce de résistance, the United Nations Reform Act,[65] otherwise known as the Helms-Biden Act, which made the payment of $926 million of US assessed contributions and arrears contingent on the occurrence of specified reforms by the United Nations and its specialized agencies. Payment was to be made in three tranches, one each for fiscal years 1998, 1999, and 2000. Payment for each tranche was made conditional on the US Secretary of State certifying that the United Nations had met certain criteria. The criteria that were to be met for tranche one, for example, included the following:

1. The United Nations was to take no action that required the United States to violate the US Constitution and the United Nations was not to exercise sovereignty over the United States. Other sections of the Act specified that the United Nations must not exercise authority over the real property rights of the US government or its citizens.[66]
2. The United Nations was not to tax US nationals and was not to propose to develop taxes. There were exceptions to this requirement for the World Intellectual Property Organization and UN staff assessment costs.[67]
3. The United Nations was to have no standing army or plans to develop a standing army or to call upon the armed forces of a member state under UN Charter Article 43.[68]
4. No interest fees or penalties were to be levied against the United States for arrears on its annual assessments.[69]
5. The United Nations and its specialized agencies were not to amend any financial external borrowing, nor call upon the United States to pay any interest costs incurred from external borrowing made after 1984.[70]

The Secretary of State certified that these criteria had been met and the United States paid the $100 million of "tranche one" in December 1999.[71]

The criteria that must be met for payment of tranche two deal with the assessment rate and peacekeeping operations:

1. The United Nations must establish an account for all US "contested arrears," that is, those contested by the United States and therefore not included in the Helms-Biden Act. Failure to pay this account must not affect the application of Article 19 of the Charter to the United States.[72]

2. The assessed share of the UN peacekeeping budget must not exceed 25 percent for any single member state.[73]
3. The assessed share of the UN regular budget must not exceed 22 percent for any single member state.[74]

In its special millennium session the General Assembly approved a new scale of assessments for both the regular budget and the peacekeeping budget.[75] As demanded by the Helms-Biden legislation, the Assembly lowered the ceiling of the amount to be paid by any single country from 25 to 22 percent of the regular budget. For the least developed countries, a minimum assessment rate of 0.001 percent and a maximum assessment rate of 0.01 percent was also instituted.

The scale of assessments for peacekeeping operations was also revised, changing the system in place since 1973.[76] The US assessed rate was lowered from 31 percent of the annual peacekeeping budget to about 28 percent for the first six months of 2001.[77] For the second six months of 2001, the rate was 27.5 percent.[78] The 2002 rate was 26.5 percent and then the rate was dropped to approximately the 25 percent benchmark called for by the Helms-Biden legislation.[79] Although the UN scale was not in complete compliance with the categoric mandate of 25 percent of the Helms-Biden legislation, Senator Helms declared himself satisfied.[80]

Despite Senator Helms' satisfaction, payment of the $582 million for tranche two was for a time blocked in the House of Representatives by Tom Delay of Texas, the majority whip, who wanted assurances that Americans would be exempt from the jurisdiction of the permanent international criminal court. In the wake of the September 11, 2001, terrorist attacks against the World Trade Center and the Pentagon, however, Delay agreed to withdraw his opposition so as not to undermine US efforts to build a coalition against terrorism and states sponsoring or supporting terrorism. In the words of Representative Tom Lantos, the senior Democrat on the International Relations Committee, "this is no time to quibble with the United Nations over money or unrelated issues tying up the money."[81]

The criteria for tranche three are extensive and relate largely to budget and personnel reform:

1. The assessed share of the UN regular budget must not exceed 20 percent for any single member state.[82]
2. The United Nations and each of its specialized agencies must establish independent offices of an inspector general. The inspector general will have the authority to conduct audits, inspections, investigations, and reports relating to the administration of programs.[83]
3. The United Nations and its specialized agencies must adopt new budget procedures that require maintenance of a budget that will not

exceed the budget agreed to by consensus at the beginning of each budgetary biennium. Any changes in the budget must be made by consensus. Further, expenditures must be categorized by functional categories such as personnel, travel, and equipment.[84]

4. A sunset policy for certain programs of the United Nations and its specialized agencies must be implemented. The Office of Internal Oversight Services is responsible for creating a "standardized methodology" to evaluate the "continuing relevance and effectiveness" of programs.[85]
5. The United States must have a seat on the UN Advisory Committee on Administrative and Budgetary Questions, or the five largest member contributors each have a seat on the Advisory Committee.[86]
6. The United States General Accounting Office must have access to UN financial data in order to assist the US Office in reviewing UN operations.[87]
7. The United Nations must adopt specific reforms in the appointment of personnel and the personnel evaluation system. Appointments must be made according to Article 101 of the UN Charter (merit-based appointments). The General Assembly must establish a Code of Conduct that is binding on all UN employees and that requires financial disclosure statements for senior UN personnel.[88]
8. UN specialized agencies must achieve zero nominal growth in their biennium budgets for 2000–2001 from the 1998–1999 budget levels.[89]
9. The assessed share of the budget of UN specialized agencies must not exceed 22 percent for any single member state.[90]

Authorization for and payment of the $244 million covered by tranche three was not initially forthcoming because of a strong reaction in the House of Representatives to the UN Human Rights Commission's failure to reelect the United States to the Commission on May 3, 2001.[91] But again the change in the political atmosphere after September 11 resulted in a change of heart, and the United States has now completed payment of its arrears to international organizations under the 1999 Helms-Biden agreement. Moreover, it appears that another US–UN dues problem may be close to resolution. The United States, along with many other member governments, has compounded the problems created by its withholding of dues by failing to pay its annual assessed contributions to the regular budget within 30 days of notification of assessments or as of the first day of the calendar year to which they relate, whichever is later, as required by UN Financial Regulations.[92] The US practice has been to pay its dues on October 1 of the fiscal year to which they relate, which especially exacerbates the United Nations' fiscal difficulties. Under legislation enacted into law in September 2002,[93] Congress called on the administration to "initiate a process to synchronize the payments of its assessment to the

United Nations and other international organizations over a multiyear period so the US can resume paying its dues to such international organizations at the beginning of each calendar year." At this writing, the State Department has not yet submitted such a plan to Congress.

One of the major contributors to the US dues deficit was the 1994 US law that limited the US share of peacekeeping to 25 percent at a time when the US share was just over 30 percent, and "the resulting differential caused the United States to accrue some $500 million in arrears."[94] In late 2000 the UN General Assembly reduced the US assessment over several years to a new level of 27 percent. Congress then agreed to suspend the cap until fiscal year 2004, by which time it is hoped that the General Assembly will have agreed to reduce further the US assessed share. To avoid the accumulation of new arrears, at this writing President George W. Bush is asking Congress to lift its ceiling on peacekeeping permanently.

The United States and the United Nations still disagree on precisely how much arrears the United States still owes, but negotiations are under way to resolve this discrepancy.[95]

There therefore currently appears to be little inclination on the part of the United States to withhold, for political purposes, dues owed to the United Nations. Also, Senator Helms, the most fervent opponent of the United Nations, has retired from the Senate, and has been replaced as chairman of the Senate Committee on Foreign Relations by the moderate Richard Lugar. One may well ask, then, whether the UN dues issue is purely of historical interest with no current significance. In my view the answer is definitely not. The United States and the United Nations still differ on how much the United States is in arrears, based in part on the UN including as arrears money owed for projects of which the United States disapproved and therefore refused to pay. Moreover, there is no indication that the recent payment by the US Congress was based on its recognition of an international obligation to pay rather than the political vagaries of the moment. Hence we turn in the next section of this chapter to an examination of the compatibility (or lack thereof) of the US withholding of dues with the rule of law in international affairs.

US withholding and the rule of law

At the outset of this discussion of the compatibility of US withholding of its UN dues with the rule of law in international affairs, it is worth noting how little effort the United States has made to defend or even consider the international legality of its withholding. In early debates on the Kassebaum amendment, some concern was expressed that withholding pursuant to the amendment might cause the United States to lose its vote in the General Assembly or in such specialized agencies as the World Health Organization or the United Nations Educational, Scientific and Cultural Organization or that the withholding would violate US obligations under international law.[96] By 1985, the year the amendment was adopted, such concerns had apparently disappeared. Moreover, as noted by Alvarez:

To the extent legalities were raised, US officials characterized many US withholdings as appropriate responses to "*ultra vires*" acts by the UN. US officials condemned expenditures on behalf of the PLO, SWAPO, or the Decade of Racism or GA Resolution 33/79 as violations of the Charter or contrary to international law. Similarly, expenses for the Law of the Sea Preparatory Commission were branded as "illegal" because the Commission was not a "subsidiary organ" answerable to the UN. Alleged "kickbacks" by seconded UN officials allegedly violated Articles 100–101 of the Charter providing for independent international civil servants.

With the possible exception of US withholdings regarding the Law of the Sea Preparatory Commission, scholars have not found the threadbare US legal justifications for these withholdings convincing. Thus, commentators found at most political, not legal, justifications for those withholdings designed to effect budgetary reforms such as Kassebaum, withholdings for the Ethiopian Conference Center, and other across-the-board cuts. Frederic Kirgis found US threats growing out of the possibility of a change in status of the PLO not justified under treaty law and "disproportionate" as a legitimate reprisal.[97] Further, the factual or legal premises underlying other US withholdings have been or remain questionable. Finally, there are difficulties squaring withholdings with the UN's internal law since nothing in the UN's Financial Regulations authorizes the organization to accept "earmarked" contributions; as the US Government repeatedly argued prior to 1980, the Secretary-General is "not authorized to finance some programs in the regular budget and not finance others." Thus, shortfalls in members' contributions to the regular budget, however intended to "target" allegedly *ultra vires* activities, affect all UN programs equally, and not solely the targeted activity. Similar objections have been raised in connection with US withholdings to other UN system organizations.[98]

Alvarez then goes on to examine "more general arguments concerning the legality of unilateral withholding of assessed contributions to international organizations in response to allegedly *ultra vires* acts."[99] Three approaches identified by Alvarez include: (i) the law of treaties; (ii) doctrines of state responsibility, including reprisals; and (iii) international institutional law.[100] In a careful exegesis, Alvarez finds each of these justifications unconvincing.[101] Especially noteworthy is his conclusion that "[w]hether any of the challenged actions to date [as of 1995] rise to the level of violations of essential provisions of the UN Charter is questionable."[102] Equally worthy of note is his refutation of the view of Zoller[103] and some other commentators[104] that "international institutional law within the context of the UN Charter scheme sanctions unilateral withholding by UN members where, in the views of member states, such withholdings are 'compelling' and necessary to protect members from the 'tyranny of the majority' since such withholdings are 'necessitated through the need' to keep the organization from turning into 'a super-State.'"[105]

In his refutation of the view of Zoller et al., Alvarez invokes the majority and concurring opinions in the *Certain Expenses* case. Specifically, he cites the Court's presumption of validity of UN assessments in the *Certain Expenses* case and its view that the Organization has "no alternative but to honor" commitments made to third parties.[106] In his view the Court's approach leads to "the requirements that at a minimum, prior to withholding, a member state must establish a prima facie case for invalidity and seek judicial or third party resolution of the question. If the majority opinion in the *Expenses* case is taken seriously, unilateral withholding in response to *ultra vires* action is, at most, an option of last resort, to be taken only after the complaining member has given the organization the opportunity to correct any error."[107]

Regardless of how "threadbare" US legal justifications for withholding of UN dues may have been prior to the Helms-Biden legislation, they compare favorably to those advanced to justify the Helms-Biden withholdings. Indeed, there has been no attempt to justify the Helms-Biden withholdings under international institutional law or general international law. Rather, the attitude of the sponsors of the legislation has been that of John Bolton, that is, that there is no international legal obligation to pay UN dues. In the words of Senator Jesse Helms:

> The United States Constitution places the authority to tax United States citizens and to authorize and appropriate those funds solely in the power of the United States Congress. The requirement in Article 17 of the United Nations Charter that member states approve a budget to be borne by the members of the United Nations in no way creates a "legal obligation" on the United States Congress to authorize and appropriate the amounts requested by United Nations [sic] of the United States to meet the United Nations annual budget.[108]

Few other members of Congress made any reference to the question of a legal obligation to pay UN dues, and those who did, did so only in passing.[109] Perhaps more surprisingly, US executive branch representatives testifying at hearings on the Helms-Biden legislation made no reference to any such legal obligation. Rather, they argued that the United Nations serves US national interests at a comparatively low cost to US taxpayers. For example, Richard Holbrooke, then the US permanent representative at the United Nations, stated: "this is not a vote to give money to the bureaucratic fat cats . . . this is money for our national security interests."[110] To support this argument, Holbrooke pointed out that but for UN peacekeeping troops, thousands more US soldiers would need to be employed to keep the peace.[111]

All of this stands in sharp contrast to US actions in response to Soviet and French withholdings of assessed dues for the UNEF and ONUC expenses during the 1960s. This time around the United States has made no effort to establish a prima facie case for the alleged *ultra vires* nature of UN assessed dues or to seek judicial or third-party resolution of the issue. Indeed, the various criteria set forth in the Helms-Biden legislation that must be met before the United States will pay its assessed dues are not based on alleged *ultra vires* actions of the United Nations. Rather, they constitute non-negotiable policy preferences that the United States is unilaterally imposing on the Organization. A sharper deviation from the rule of law paradigm is hard to imagine.

In a recent article John Bolton provides some insight into the thinking behind the anti-rule-of-law position in keeping with themes already explored in this study. After an introductory section setting forth his view that treaties create only "moral" or "political" but not "legal" obligations for the United States, Bolton states:

> Why does any of this matter? In the United States, until now, "international law" has hardly touched us. We have not thought it terribly important. Before World War II, the "law of nations" dealt with fishing rights, rights of passage through international waters, the return of prisoners of war, and very little else. Since World War II, however, "international law" has grown enormously, and it is *accumulating force that will even more dramatically impede us in the future. In the rest of the world, international law and its "binding" obligations are taken for granted.* Even here, many believe that international problems can be solved through legal devices, that nations can, for example, sign a treaty that renounces aggressive war. Once we have signed such a treaty, then that law is binding on us, is it not? We will abjure aggression, and, of course, the other signatories will do so as well. And if they do not, why that's just illegal! Unfortunately, this enthusiasm has never troubled even slightly those inclined to use force, but it does impair our ability to understand real events in the real world.[112]

In other words, the development of international law, and the acceptance by "the rest of the world" of its legally binding nature, is a grave threat to the vital interests of the United States. Bolton's sarcastic dismissal of efforts before, during, and after World War II to put in place legal limitations on the use of armed force is examined in chapter 4 of this study.

In a nuanced commentary on reasons for the US failure to pay its dues, José Alvarez has suggested that national political considerations loom large and sounds a warning to international lawyers:

> In the end, the battle over who pays for the United Nations is a fight over who controls it. This results in tensions between major and small contributors *but also* among members' executive branches that set the UN agenda and legislative branches that typically pay for it. In the United States, the battle over who "controls" – legislature or executive – has increasingly become part of the perennial interbranch struggle over who "controls" US foreign policy. For some of the participants in recent congressional/executive squabbles over peacekeeping budgets, those confrontations are an essential element of constitutionally mandated "checks and balances" on the waging of war.
>
> As all this suggests, we international lawyers should not be so confident that we occupy the "high ground" on this issue. We will continue to lose the argument over UN financing so long as many on the Hill sincerely believe that they are exercising a constitutional prerogative that is the equal of the Supremacy Clause, if not its moral superior: the duty of a legislature in a democracy to keep lawmaking institutions, whether national or international, accountable to the taxpayers who ultimately pay the bills. We will lose if keeping the United Nations one step away from bankruptcy continues to be seen as the necessary price of the US separation of powers.[113]

Whatever the reasons for it, the US rejection of the rule of law approach to UN dues sets, as Michael Scharf has suggested, "a dangerous precedent, whereby other countries will be encouraged to withhold dues in order to coerce the members of the UN to reduce their assessed share of the budget and forgive their arrears."[114]

To be sure, a realpolitik response to this criticism might be that advanced by Senator Kassebaum: only the threat of US withholding of dues has been successful in inducing the United Nations to undertake real reform. There is a substantial measure of truth in this position. But we should keep in mind some "caveats" advanced by Edward Luck in a commentary on the Helms-Biden legislative approach. Luck suggests, for example, that "down the road other member states could well follow our lead and begin to condition their UN payments on various benchmarks that we find obnoxious. Now that America's traditional adherence to the legal standard that assessed contributions should be paid on time, in full, and without conditions has been abandoned, what will be the long-term consequences for the integrity of the principle of collective responsibility and for the viability of international institutions?"[115] Luck goes on to warn, "what lesson will future Congresses learn from this episode: that the more they impose unilateral withholdings, the more concessions the other UN member states will make? Based on the current precedent, will there be further rounds of withholdings and acrimony in the years ahead, diverting attention from the urgent task of finding a common platform for building a stronger and more effective UN system?"[116] He concludes:

Over the past decade, while surface-level reforms absorbed our attention, both the UN and the conditions in which it operates were undergoing some fundamental changes without the guidance of any blueprint or plan. Multilateral cooperation is burgeoning in field after field, spurring the creation of countless organizations and arrangements. Yet many of the most consequential, such as the WTO, have been placed outside of the UN system. We have insisted that the central UN contract year after year in terms of staff, of real spending, and of authority. Those who prefer voluntary to assessed contributions – even for peacekeeping – have largely won the day. The regular budget now covers less than one-fifth of UN system-wide spending and extra-budgetary outlays far exceed those that are assessed. More and more, the wealthier countries – and even private donors such as Ted Turner – are bypassing the regular budget process to fund unilaterally selected program initiatives. As a result, ad hoc priority setting is coming to replace coherent planning and truly multilateral decision-making. Consequently, the pieces are prospering and the center is fading.

Perhaps this is as it should be: change without reform, adaptation without planning. For a dominant power, like our country, it may be just as well to let the pieces fall where they may, to bend or ignore the old rules as circumstances dictate, and to champion the virtues of ad hocism and expediency in the name of realism and pragmatism. But the price, at some unknown future juncture, may be greater than we can imagine at this time of exceptional power and wealth. Half a century from now, our children may well regret our lack of foresight, our reluctance to try to consciously reshape the system when we have the power, when we are in the driver's seat. If not now, when will the time be ripe?[117]

Perhaps it is appropriate to conclude this chapter with a commentary on Helms-Biden from a non-American voice, the voice of a representative of a country that has long been a foremost proponent of the rule of law in international affairs, the Netherlands. Arnold Peter van Walsum, permanent representative of the Netherlands at the United Nations, participated in the historic visit of the UN Security Council to the US Senate on March 30, 2000. When his turn came to speak, Ambassador Walsum was frank in his comments on Helms-Biden:

What disturbs us about the Helms-Biden legislation is the conditionality . . . The element we do not like is the concept of withholding money, money that is due under a treaty obligation, to enhance one's influence on a given process.

The reason we are so sensitive about that is that my country is in relative terms pouring money into the United Nations and getting very little in return. The Netherlands is a country with fewer than 16 million inhabitants and last year it spent over 40 million US dollars on assessed contributions and over $365 million on voluntary contributions to the United Nations.

In the scale of assessments for the regular budget, the Netherlands ranks among the top ten contributors. Moreover, with a percentage of .81 of GNP, it belongs to the top seven country contributors of net official development assistance.

For all this, it obtains very little influence in return. It does currently sit on the Security Council, but that is only for a term of 2 years and it enjoys that privilege on average only once in a generation.

If our parliament should approach this situation even remotely along the same lines as the Senate Foreign Relations Committee, the Netherlands would seriously consider leaving the United Nations. If we did, some people might be sorry, but the United Nations would continue to exist. And that is the crucial difference between our two countries. The United Nations cannot survive without the United States, and this is why we cooperate and why we agree that a solution has to be found.

But it should be clear that we are not cooperating because we think your arguments are valid, but simply because we feel that the United States has to not only stay in the United Nations, but has to be a committed, influential member. So we are not – I just want to make that clear. We are not persuaded by your arguments, but by our enlightened self-interest.[118]

Notes

1. See *supra* ch. 1, at 11.
2. John R. Bolton, *US Isn't Obligated to Pay the UN*, WALL ST. J. Nov. 17, 1997, at A27, col. 3.
3. José E. Alvarez, *Legal Remedies and the United Nations A La Carte Problem*, 12 MICH. J. INT'L L. 229, 255–56 (1991).
4. Art. 18(2) of the UN Charter provides in pertinent part: "Decisions of the General Assembly on important questions shall be made by a two-thirds majority of the members present and voting. These questions shall include: ... budgetary questions."
5. José E. Alvarez, *Financial Responsibility*, *in* 2 UNITED NATIONS LEGAL ORDER 1091 (Oscar Schachter & Christopher C. Joyner eds., 1995).
6. See Richard W. Nelson, *International Law and US Withholding of Payments to International Organizations*, 80 AM. J. INT'L L. 973, 978 (1986).
7. *Id.* As noted by Michael Scharf, in 2000, when the US share of the UN's budget was assessed at 25 percent, the US share of the world's gross domestic product was 27 percent. In comparison, the fifteen countries of the European Union together paid 36 percent of the UN budget, although the EU's share of the world's gross domestic product was virtually the same as that of the United States (27 percent). See Michael P. Scharf, *Dead Beat Dead End: A Critique of the New US Plan for Payment of UN Arrears*, 6 NEW ENG. INT'L & COMP. L. ANN. 5 (2000).
8. Nov. 3, 1950, UNGA Res. 377A(V), 5 UN GAOR, Supp. (No. 20) 10, UN Doc. A/1775 (1951).
9. The Soviet delegate had been absent since Jan. 1950 because of a dispute over the representation of China.
10. Section A(1) of the resolution.
11. Much of the discussion of the background to the crisis over UNEF and ONUC is taken from JOHN F. MURPHY, THE UNITED NATIONS AND THE CONTROL OF INTERNATIONAL VIOLENCE (1982).

12. Art. 27(2) of the UN Charter provides that "[d]ecisions of the Security Council on procedural matters shall be made by an affirmative vote of nine members."
13. General Assembly Res. 1000(ES-1), Nov. 5, 1956.
14. Art. 11(2) of the UN Charter provides: "The General Assembly may discuss any questions relating to the maintenance of international peace and security brought before it by any Member of the United Nations, or by the Security Council, or by a state which is not a Member of the United Nations in accordance with Article 35, paragraph 2, and, except as provided in Article 12, may make recommendations with regard to any such questions to the state or states concerned or to the Security Council or to both. Any such question on which action is necessary shall be referred to the Security Council by the General Assembly either before or after discussion."
15. For discussion of this backdrop see MURPHY, *supra* note 11, at 148–56.
16. See FREDERIC L. KIRGIS JR., INTERNATIONAL ORGANIZATIONS IN THEIR LEGAL SETTING 248 (2d ed., 1993).
17. Alvarez, *supra* note 5, at 1098.
18. *Id.*; Nelson, *supra* note 6, at 978. Art. 43(1) of the UN Charter provides that "[a]ll Members of the United Nations, in order to contribute to the maintenance of international peace and security, undertake to make available to the Security Council, on its call and in accordance with a special agreement or agreements, armed forces, assistance, and facilities, including rights of passage, necessary for the purpose of maintaining international peace and security."
19. 1962 ICJ Pleadings (Certain Expenses of the United Nations) (UN Charter Art. 17, para 2), 424 (Oral Statement of Mr. Chayes), quoted in Alvarez, *supra* note 3, at 280.
20. Certain Expenses of the United Nations (Article 17, paragraph 2 of the Charter), 1962 ICJ Rep. 151 (Advisory Opinion of July 20).
21. *Id.* at 167.
22. *Id.* at 168.
23. E.g., see *id.* at 239 (Moreno Quintana, J., dissenting), and Nelson, *supra* note 6, at 979.
24. 1962 ICJ Rep. at 168.
25. See, e.g., Louis B. Sohn, *The UN System as Authoritative Interpreter of its Law*, *in* 1 UNITED NATIONS LEGAL ORDER 169, 198 (Oscar Schachter & Christopher C. Joyner eds., 1995); MURPHY, *supra* note 11, at 80–81; Leo Gross, *Expenses of the United Nations for Peace-Keeping Operations: The Advisory Opinion of the International Court of Justice*, 17 INT'L ORG. 1 (1963).
26. Gross, *supra* note 25, at 26.
27. See MURPHY, *supra* note 11, at 82.
28. GA Res. 1854A(XVII), 17 UN GAOR 1199, UN Doc. A/PV. 1199 (1962).
29. 22 USC Section 287k (1982) (Pub.L. No. 87–731, sec. 5, 76 Stat. 696, approved Oct. 2, 1962), noted in Nelson, *supra* note 6, at 979.
30. This discussion of the Art. 19 crisis is taken primarily from MURPHY, *supra* note 11, at 82–83.
31. It is worth noting that the Charter provisions on voting in the General Assembly, Arts. 18 and 19, make no distinction between votes on substantive matters and those on procedural matters. In contrast, Art. 27 makes such a distinction for voting in the Security Council, limiting the veto of permanent members to matters of substance.
32. UN Doc. A/5916/Add.1(1965), *reprinted in* 53 Dep't State Bull. 454–57(1965).
33. Elisabeth Zoller, *The "Corporate Will" of the United Nations and the Rights of the Minority*, 81 AM. J. INT'L L. 610, 617(1987).
34. See THOMAS M. FRANCK, NATION AGAINST NATION 259 (1985); HENRY G. SCHERMERS, INTERNATIONAL INSTITUTIONAL LAW 88, Section 133 (1980).

35. Zoller, *supra* note 33, at 620.
36. Alvarez, *supra* note 5, at 1101.
37. For reference to the United States as "Uncle Deadbeat," see Alvarez, *supra* note 3, at 232. See also Scharf, *supra* note 7.
38. See Alvarez, *supra* note 3, at 234.
39. Herbert J. Hansell, Memorandum of Aug. 7, 1978, 1979 Digest of United States Practice in International Law 225,226, *quoted in* Zoller, *supra* note 33, at 610.
40. Alvarez, *supra* note 3, at 235.
41. GA Res. 3379(XXX), 30 UN GAOR Supp. (No. 34) at 83, 84, UN Doc. A/10034 (1975).
42. Alvarez, *supra* note 3, at 235–36.
43. *Id.* at 236.
44. Pub. L. No. 99–93, s. 143, 99 Stat. 405 (1985).
45. Alvarez, *supra* note 3, at 237.
46. 131 Cong. Rec. S7736 (June 7, 1985) (statement of Sen. Kassebaum).
47. *Id.*
48. *Id.* (statement of Sen. Ford).
49. GA Res. 41/213 (1986), 26 INT'L LEG. MATERIALS 145 (1987).
50. Zoller, *supra* note 33, at 634.
51. See Alvarez, *supra* note 3, at 238.
52. *Id.* at 239.
53. *Id.* at 242.
54. Secretary's Statement, May 1,1989, Press Release 75, reported in 89 Dep't St. Bull. 65 (July 1989) and quoted in Alvarez, *supra* note 3, at 242.
55. Zoller, *supra* note 33, at 612.
56. Balanced Budget and Emergency Deficit Control Act of 1985, Pub. L. No. 99–177, 99 Stat. 1037 (1985).
57. Foreign Relations Authorization Act, Fiscal Years 1986–1987, Pub. L. No. 99–93, s. 151, 99 Stat. 405, 428 (1985).
58. See John Quigley, *The New World Order and the Rule of Law*, 18 SYRACUSE J. INT'L L. & COM. 75, 84 (1992).
59. Pub. L. No. 101–246, s. 405, 104 Stat. 15 (1990).
60. Alvarez, *supra* note 5, at 1097.
61. *Id.*
62. Pub. L. No. 105–236, tit. IV,108 Stat. 382 (1994).
63. David Stout, *Clinton Vetoes Measure to Pay $1 Billion in Late U.N. Dues*, NY TIMES, Oct. 22, 1998, at A3.
64. Barbara Crossette, *Holbrooke Accuses House of Hurting US Role in the World*, NY TIMES, Oct 27, 1999, at A12.
65. The Admiral James W. Nance and Meg Donovan Foreign Relations Authorization Act, FY 2000-FY2001, Pub. L. No. 106–113, ss. 901–952, 113 Stat. 1501 (1999).
66. Pub. L. No. 106–113, s. 921(a)(1),(2), and (6), 113 Stat. 1501 (1999).
67. *Id.* at s. 921(a)(3).
68. *Id.* at s. 921(a)(4).
69. *Id.* at s. 921(a)(5).
70. *Id.* at s. 921(a)(7).
71. See, *US Pays UN $151 Million, Saves its Vote*, WASH. POST, Dec. 22, 1999, at A2. In the words of the newspaper account, "The United States has paid $151 million to the United Nations since Thursday, enough to save its vote in the General Assembly, the State Department said yesterday. The two payments, $100 million Thursday and

$51 million Monday, include all of the $100 million first portion of arrears payments authorized by Congress in November."

72. Pub. L. No. 106–113, s. 931(b)(1).
73. *Id.* at s. 931(b)(2).
74. *Id.* at s. 931(b)(3).
75. *Press Release: Assembly Approves new Scale of Assessments, as it Concludes main Part of its Millennium Session*, UN Doc. GA/9850 (Dec. 23, 2000). The Assembly adopted the new scale of assessments through the passage of Res. 55/235 (2001).
76. *Id.*
77. 147 Cong. Rec. S1110, S1111 (Feb. 7, 2001) (statement of Sen. Helms).
78. *Id.*
79. At this writing, it is unclear precisely when or whether the United States will reach 25 percent. For the year 2003, the rate will be 26.5 percent. Beyond 2003 the picture becomes murky. In hearings before the Senate Foreign Relations Committee, Senator Helms asked Ambassador Holbrooke to predict when the United States would reach 25 percent. In response Holbrooke said that it was difficult to predict what would happen, but the prospect of having a rate lower than 26.5 percent in 2004 was "substantially better than 50–50." See Senator Joseph Biden (D-DE) Holds Hearing on US Payment of Back UN Dues, Senate Foreign Relations Committee (Jan. 9, 2001) (testimony of Richard Holbrooke, US Ambassador to the United Nations), available at Lexis-Nexis Congressional Universe.

    According to Holbrooke, several factors are likely to determine the US percentage after 2003: (i) whether Switzerland joins the United Nations, as it has indicated it will; (ii) the attention the Bush administration gives UN reforms. If its representatives at the United Nations lobby effectively among member states, the rate will drop to 25 percent; (iii) the economic stability of member states' economies. If they decline, the US share of the world economy will go up, and with it, the US assessments. *Id.*
80. Christopher Marquis, *Satisfied with UN Reforms, Helms Relents on Back Dues*, NY TIMES, Jan 10, 2001, at A8.
81. See Lizette Alvarez, *House Approves $582 Million for Back Dues Owed to UN*, NY TIMES, Sept. 25, 2001, at A8, col. 1.
82. Pub. L. No. 106–113, s. 941(b)(1), 113 Stat. 1501 (1999).
83. *Id.* at s. 941(b)(2).
84. *Id.* at s. 941(b)(3) and (9).
85. *Id.* at s. 941(b)(4).
86. *Id.* at s. 941(b)(5).
87. *Id.* at s. 941(b)(6).
88. *Id.* at s. 941(b)(7).
89. *Id.* at s. 941(b)(8).
90. *Id.* at s. 941(b)(10).
91. See David E. Sanger, *House Threatens to Hold UN Dues in Loss of a Seat*, NY TIMES, May 9, 2001, at A1. See also *The UN Commission on Human Rights: A Review of its Mission, Operations, and Structure*, House International Relations Subcommittee on International Operations and Human Rights, 107th Cong. (June 6, 2001), available *at* http://www.state.gov/g/drl/rls/rm/2002/3300.htm.
92. See Alvarez, *supra* note 5, at 1097.
93. Foreign Relations Authorization Act, Fiscal Year 2003, Pub. L. No. 107–228, Sept. 30, 2002, 116 Stat. 1350.

94. See *A UNA-USA Advocacy Agenda 2003 Fact Sheet: Status of US Financial Obligations to the United Nations*, June 2003, at 2, available *at* http://www.unavsa.org/newsactionalerts/advocacy/usunfin.asp.
95. *Id.* at 2–3. According to the UNA-USA Fact Sheet:

> Over the course of its dispute with the United Nations over the issue of arrears, the United States and the UN did not agree on a single figure for outstanding arrears owed by the US to the world organization. The discrepancy is due to several factors, including: 1) congressional and executive branch actions that required the withholding of specific funds, i.e., for the construction of a UN conference center in Ethiopia in the 1980s, among others; 2) a long standing dispute between the US and the UN over the methodology used by the United Nations to deduct federal income taxes from the salaries of American citizens employed in the UN Secretariat (now resolved); and 3) the existence of the 25 percent cap on US assessed contributions to UN peacekeeping that prevented the US from meeting its obligations fully over a half-decade – the single largest reason for the discrepancy. Based on UN figures, as of 28 February 2003, the United States owed $1.327 billion in both past and current (2003) obligations to the United Nations regular budget, international tribunals, and peacekeeping. Of this amount, arrears owed prior to 1 January 2003 total $738 million. Payment of arrears owed prior to 2003 would require legislative action that either repeals or rescinds the legislation that prompted the withholding in the first place.

96. See e.g., The US Role in the United Nations: Hearing Before the Subcomm. on Human Rights and International Organizations of the House Committee on Foreign Affairs, 98th Cong., 1st Sess. 10, 17 (1983) (Testimony of Rep. Leach).
97. Here Alvarez is referring to Frederic L. Kirgis, *Admission of "Palestine" as a Member of a Specialized Agency and Withholding the Payment of Assessments in Response*, 84 Am. J. Int'l L. 218 (1990).
98. Alvarez, *supra* note 5, at 1101–3.
99. *Id.* at 1103.
100. *Id.*
101. *Id.* at 1103–18.
102. *Id.* 1105.
103. See Zoller, *supra* note 33, at 631–32.
104. For a listing of these commentators, see Alvarez, *supra* note 5, at 1108, n. 95.
105. *Id.* at 1107–8.
106. See Certain Expenses of the United Nations, *supra* note 20, at 204 (Fitzmaurice), 182–7(Spender), 216–26(Morelli). Alvarez, *supra* note 5, at 1108, n. 99.
107. Alvarez, *supra* note 5, at 1108.
108. S. Rep. No. 105–28, at 7 (1997). For a recent, elaborate expression of Bolton's views, see John R. Bolton, *Is There Really "Law" in International Affairs?*,10 Transnat'l L. & Contemp. Probs. 1 (2000).
109. Senator Feingold said, for example, that he was "very concerned that the United States is not honoring its financial commitments to the United Nations." The United Nations: Progress in Promoting US Interests, Senate Hearing Before the Subcommittee on International Operations of the Committee on Foreign Relations, 106th Cong., at 7 (1999). Congressman Serrano was similarly "concerned about our country's failure to meet its legal obligations to the UN." Fiscal Year 2000 State Department Appropriations, Hearing of the Commerce, Justice, State and Judiciary Subcommittees of the House Appropriations Committee, 106th Cong., 1 (1999), available on

Lexis-Nexis Congressional Universe. Neither member of Congress pursued further the legal implications of US withholding of UN dues.

110. The United Nations: Progress in Promoting US Interests, Hearing Before the Subcommittee on International Operations of the Senate Committee on Foreign Relations, 106th Cong. 8 (1999).
111. *Id.* at 17.
112. Bolton, *supra* note 108, at 8 (emphasis added).
113. José E. Alvarez, *The United States Financial Veto*, 90 AM. SOC'Y INT'L. PROC. 319, 324 (1996).
114. Scharf, *supra* note 7, at 8.
115. See *Prepared Statement of Edward C. Luck, in* THE FUTURE OF US–UN RELATIONS: A DIALOGUE BETWEEN THE SENATE FOREIGN RELATIONS COMMITTEE AND THE UNITED NATIONS SECURITY COUNCIL 53–54 (2000).
116. *Id.* at 54.
117. *Id.* at 54–55.
118. *Statement of His Excellency Arnold Peter Van Walsum, Permanent Representative of The Netherlands*, *id.* at 127–28 (2000).

4 Use of force

Use of force: a brief background

As Article 1(1) and (2) of the UN Charter state, the primary purposes of the United Nations are:

1. To maintain international peace and security, and to that end: to take effective collective measures for the prevention and removal of threats to the peace, and for the suppression of acts of aggression or other breaches of the peace, and to bring about by peaceful means, and in conformity with the principles of justice and international law, adjustment or settlement of international disputes or situations which might lead to a breach of the peace;

and

2. To develop friendly relations among nations based on respect for the principle of equal rights and self-determination of peoples, and to take other appropriate measures to strengthen universal peace.

Moreover, as I have noted elsewhere, "[t]he 'law' on the use of force that has developed through the United Nations is substantial indeed."[1] The focus in this chapter is on the *jus ad bellum* (the recourse to force) rather than on the *jus in bello* (the conduct of combatants in armed conflict). Aside from a parenthetical reference or two, this chapter does not discuss *jus in bello* issues.

Elsewhere, also, I have discussed the *jus ad bellum* in considerable detail.[2] There will be no effort to reprise this discussion in this chapter. Rather, for present purposes, it suffices to state my agreement with the basic proposition that, under the UN Charter, the use of military force is permitted in only two instances: in individual or collective self-defense under Article 51 of the Charter[3] or pursuant to a Security Council resolution adopted by the Council under Chapter VII of the Charter.[4] Challenges to this basic proposition, however, will be addressed throughout this chapter.

Under the Charter paradigm member states of the United Nations agree to settle all disputes peaceably[5] and to refrain from the use of force in their international relations. The key provision barring the use of force is Article 2(4), which provides that "all Members shall refrain in their international relations from the threat or use of force against the territorial integrity or political independence of any state, or in any other manner inconsistent with the Purposes of the United Nations." Some commentators who favor limited constraints on the right of states to use force have relied on textual analysis to interpret Article 2(4) as authorizing a number of exceptions to that article's prohibition against the "threat or use of force." But by and large these arguments have not been accepted by governments which "tend to hold to the sweeping Article 2(4) prohibition against the use or threat of force, except where self-defense or Security Council enforcement action is involved."[6]

As an express exception to Article 2(4)'s prohibition, Article 51 provides:

> Nothing in the present Charter shall impair the inherent right of individual or collective self-defence if an armed attack occurs against a Member of the United Nations, until the Security Council has taken measures necessary to maintain or restore international peace and security. Measures taken by Members in the exercise of this right of self-defence shall be immediately reported to the Security Council and shall not in any way affect the authority and responsibility of the Security Council under the present Charter to take at any time such action as it deems necessary in order to maintain or restore international peace and security.

Chapter VII of the UN Charter contains a number of provisions relevant to the Security Council's authority to authorize member states to use force. Many of them will be discussed in various places in this chapter. For present purposes, a keystone provision is Article 39, which provides:

> The Security Council shall determine the existence of any threat to the peace, breach of the peace, or act of aggression and shall make recommendations, or decide what measures shall be taken in accordance with Articles 41 and 42, to maintain or restore international peace and security.

Article 41 authorizes the Council to impose mandatory economic sanctions, and under Article 42, should the Council decide that economic sanctions are not equal to the task, it "may take such action by air, sea, or land forces as may be necessary to maintain or restore international peace and security. Such action may include demonstrations, blockade, and other operations by air, sea, or land forces of Members of the United Nations." Any such decision of the Council is binding on member states under Articles 25 and 48 of the Charter.

Article 43 of the Charter envisages that member states shall "undertake to make available to the Security Council, on its call and in accordance with a special agreement or agreements, armed forces, assistance, and facilities, including rights of passage, necessary for the purpose of maintaining international peace and security." Such Article 43 agreements have never been concluded, however, and as a result it seems clear that the Council has no authority to command member states to commit their armed forces to a UN military enforcement action. But this does not preclude the Council from authorizing a member state or states to use armed force to maintain international peace and security.

Article 52 of the Charter expressly recognizes the right of member states to establish regional arrangements or agencies for dealing with matters relating to the maintenance of international peace and security, subject to the limitations that the matters dealt with must be "appropriate for regional action," and that the arrangements and agencies and their activities must be "consistent with the Purposes and Principles of the United Nations." Under Article 53, however, with the exception of measures against the enemy states of World War II, "no enforcement action shall be taken under regional arrangements or by regional agencies without the authorization of the Security Council."

The United States was highly instrumental in creating this Charter arrangement and in supporting it during the debates on the drafting of the Charter at Dumbarton Oaks and San Francisco.[7] Moreover, as noted by Louis Henkin, during the first decades of the United Nations:

> the United States was, and was generally recognized to be, a principal champion of the law of the Charter, insisting on its validity and on its interpretation to limit strictly the permissible uses of force. The United States condemned the use of force wherever it appeared and whatever state resorted to it. In 1948, and later, it condemned the use of force by Arab states against Israel. In 1950, the United States led the United Nations into war against aggression by North Korea. At Suez, in 1956, the United States condemned the use of force by its principal allies. It inveighed against "indirect aggression" in Czechoslovakia in 1948, in Hungary in 1956, and again in Czechoslovakia in 1968. The United States flatly rejected the Brezhnev Doctrine as a clear violation of the Charter. In 1980, it led the condemnation of the Soviet invasion of Afghanistan. For decades the United States was a voice for self-restraint against uses of force and for law and international order.
>
> For its own part, the United States had a good record of compliance with the law of the Charter. In general, it refrained from the use of force even in circumstances in which, in earlier times, that might have been a serious option. Nevertheless, the United States committed violations of the Charter. Other states, and many lawyers (including some in the United States), condemned it for the Bay of Pigs (1961), for sending troops to the Dominican Republic (1965), for its believed role in toppling governments in Guatemala (1957) and Chile (1973), and for its intervention in Vietnam. Like other states, the United States has not pleaded guilty to any violations, and it has not been as adept as, say, the USSR in concealing or distorting facts. However, in order to justify its actions it has

sometimes characterized complex situations in ways that the community has not accepted. But the United States did not preach what it may have practiced; it did not seek to reinterpret the law of the Charter so as to weaken its restraints. In sum, there were no compelling grounds for questioning the commitment of the United States to the law forbidding the use of force.[8]

Henkin then goes on to suggest, however, that there were compelling grounds to question the commitment of the United States to the law forbidding the use of force during the 1980s, especially during the time of the Reagan administration:

In recent years, the US commitment to the law of the Charter has come into serious question, principally because of an array of actions the United States has taken and of the justifications it has claimed for them. In a number of cases the justifications depended on assertions that the United States has not sought to prove and that have not been widely accepted. In some respects the United States also has reconstrued the law of the Charter in ways that the world – and lawyers, including most lawyers in the United States – have rejected.

The United States has recently claimed the right to use force against the territorial integrity and political independence of another state on a number of grounds and in various circumstances.

- In 1983, the United States invaded Grenada. The invasion was variously justified – as necessary to save lives of US nationals; as responding to an invitation by the governor-general; as urged by Grenada's small neighbors; as required to restore to the people the right of self-determination and democracy. The alleged grounds have been widely challenged as spurious or as not justifying the action.
- The United States bombed Libya, which it held responsible for acts of terrorism, one of which had led to the death of a number of US servicemen. Libya's responsibility for the particular terrorist attack was later questioned; the legal justification – self-defense against "armed attack" in addition to "preemption" – was widely rejected.
- The United States mined Nicaraguan harbors and supported rebellion by the contras. It claimed that its actions were legally justified on the ground that Nicaragua was guilty of aggression against El Salvador and that the United States was acting in collective self-defense with El Salvador. Many, including numerous members of Congress, questioned the US version, interpretation, and characterization of the facts. The International Court of Justice, several governments, and most lawyers (including, it appeared, most American lawyers) rejected justifications claimed by the United States.[9]

It should be noted that all of the US actions referred to above by Henkin have their defenders and that there has been considerable debate over both the law and the facts in each of the three cases.[10] For present purposes, however, the issue is not whether the United States did or did not act in conformity with its international legal obligations in resorting to the use of force in these instances. Rather, the issue is the willingness or ability (or lack thereof) of the United States to adhere to a rule of law model, such as that established by the UN Charter, in deciding whether to resort to the use of armed force. Even as of 1989, when Henkin was writing, it was becoming clear that the United States was having difficulty in adhering to a rule of law model.

As we saw previously, in the introductory chapter to this study, under a rule of law model, "[i]mpartial instrumentalities of justice, including courts, should be available to enforce the law and should employ fair procedures."[11] But, as Oscar Schachter has noted, "[i]t is true that the absence of compulsory jurisdiction means that the International Court of Justice (or any other non-political tribunal) is not available in most cases to decide the legality of the use of force."[12] In the *Nicaragua* case, however, the United States was subjected, first, to a highly controversial decision by the Court that it had jurisdiction[13] and then to an equally controversial decision on the merits.[14] As we shall see in more detail in chapter 7 of this study, the reaction of the United States was to withdraw from the Court's proceedings after the decision against it on jurisdiction and then, one year after the decision on jurisdiction, to terminate its acceptance of the compulsory jurisdiction of the Court.

Schachter has further pointed out that, under Article 39 of the Charter,[15] the Security Council is competent to render a decision on whether a use of force contrary to the Charter has occurred.[16] Decisions of the Council apply to all states, whether or not they consent to them or participate in the proceedings adopting them. In that sense, then, the Council has compulsory jurisdiction. As a permanent member of the Council, however, the United States can prevent the Council from taking such a decision against it.[17] The United States cast such a veto to block the Council from adopting a resolution condemning its 1986 raid on Libya.[18]

The United States has no such veto power in the UN General Assembly,[19] and the Assembly adopted a resolution condemning the United States for the attack on Libya by a vote of seventy-nine to twenty-eight with thirty-three abstentions.[20] This decision was not binding under the Charter, and its status as "persuasive authority" is problematical at best.[21] Earlier, by a substantially greater margin (108 for, 9 against, and 27 abstentions), the General Assembly had characterized the US armed intervention in Grenada as a gross violation of international law and of the independence, sovereignty, and territorial integrity of that state.[22]

In the waning days of 1989, on December 20, the United States invaded Panama with 11,000 troops, which joined with 13,000 US forces already present. The background to this invasion included "a declaration by the Panamanian National Assembly on December 15, 1989, that a state of war existed between Panama and the United States; an inflammatory anti-American speech given by Manuel Noriega (Panama's de facto president, who had refused to relinquish power after losing an election earlier in the year); and a series of violent attacks by Panama Defense Forces on US military personnel and dependents in Panama, including the killing of a US Marine officer and the beating of a US naval officer on December 16, 1989."[23]

In his report to Congress, President George H. W. Bush stated that the "deployment of US forces is an exercise of the right of self-defense recognized in Article 51 of the United Nations Charter and was necessary to protect American lives in imminent danger and to fulfill our responsibilities under the Panama Canal Treaties. It was welcomed by the democratically elected government of Panama."[24] Later, the then Legal Adviser to the US Department of State expanded on the President's remarks and added other arguments in defense of the international legality of the US action.[25] Not surprisingly, Henkin and others[26] strongly disagreed. Both the UN General Assembly and the Organization of American States adopted, by substantial majorities, resolutions condemning the invasion.[27]

The United States, then, ended the 1980s with a highly controversial use of armed force, thus exacerbating, in Henkin's view, the "serious question" of its commitment to the law of the Charter on the use of force. US actions in the 1990s and the new millennium, however, have raised even more serious (and complex) questions about the US commitment to the rule of law regarding the use of force in international relations, and have called into question the continuing viability of that law.

Brave new world: the 1990s and the new millennium

The 1990s were, by any measure, an extraordinary decade. The breakup of the Soviet Union, and the emergence of the countries in central and eastern Europe from under the Soviet yoke, the demise of apartheid in South Africa, and the emergence of a less confrontational atmosphere in the UN General Assembly all contributed to a lessening of support for wars of national liberation (with the important exception of Arab attitudes towards Israel) and promised to usher in a new era of international cooperation, inside and outside the United Nations, in maintaining international peace and security. The first major test of this promise came on August 2, 1990, when Iraq invaded Kuwait.

The newly revitalized Security Council immediately responded to the challenge by unanimously adopting a resolution that condemned the invasion and demanded that Iraq "withdraw immediately and unconditionally all its armed forces."[28] When Iraq failed to do so, on August 6, 1990, the Council, acting under Chapter VII of the Charter, imposed mandatory economic sanctions against Iraq.[29] On August 9, in response to Iraq's declaration of a "comprehensive and internal merger" with Kuwait, the Council adopted a resolution[30] by which it decided that annexation of Kuwait by Iraq had no legal validity and was considered null and void, called on states and international organizations not to recognize the annexation, and demanded that Iraq rescind its annexation. With respect to all three resolutions, the United States played a lead role in their development and their adoption.[31]

On August 12, however, US Secretary of State James Baker announced that the United States had decided to employ an "interdiction" at sea of Iraqi commerce.[32] It made this decision without consulting its allies or other UN member states. As legal justification, Secretary Baker cited a request from the Kuwaiti government as the basis for individual or collective self-defense under Article 51 of the Charter. Other member states of the Security Council, as well as the Secretary-General, reportedly argued that such a "blockade" could only be authorized by the Security Council under Article 42 after determining that the sanctions were not being enforced.

The US reliance on Article 51 as justification for its "interdiction" at sea of Iraqi commerce raises the complex issue of the relationship between self-defense and collective security, an issue to which we shall return later in this chapter. In the case of Iraqi commerce the issue became moot when, on August 25, the Security Council adopted a resolution that, in pertinent part, called upon "those Member States co-operating with the Government of Kuwait which are deploying maritime forces to the area to use such measures commensurate to the specific circumstances as may be necessary under the authority of the Security Council to halt all inward and outward maritime shipping, in order to inspect and verify their cargoes and destinations and to ensure strict implementation of the provisions related to such shipping laid down in resolution 661 (1990)."[33]

Later, on September 25, the Council adopted a resolution[34] that further tightened the embargo against Iraq by extending the sanctions to cover all means of transport, including aircraft. Although the resolution contained detailed requirements for enforcing the sanctions against air traffic to and from Iraq and occupied Kuwait, it did not authorize the use of military force against aircraft.

The Security Council continued to adopt resolutions on various aspects of the Gulf crisis. At the same time there was a major military buildup in the Persian gulf of US and other states' military troops.[35] Neither this military buildup nor the adoption of further resolutions by the Security Council, however, succeeded in inducing Iraq to withdraw from Kuwait, and, on November 29, the Security Council adopted Resolution 678 that authorized the use of military force to drive Iraq out of Kuwait.[36]

Resolution 678 was adopted by a twelve–two (Yemen, Cuba)–one (China) vote. In it the Security Council demanded that Iraq comply fully with all of the Council's previous resolutions and allowed Iraq "one final opportunity, as a pause of goodwill, to do so." Unless Iraq did so, "on or before January 15, 1991," member states were authorized, in cooperation with Kuwait, "to use all necessary means to uphold and implement [the previous Council resolutions] and to restore international peace and security in the area." Iraq did not withdraw from Kuwait by the January 15 deadline, and the military coalition supporting Kuwait began air strikes at that time. After the air strikes, which lasted several weeks, a ground war began that lasted until February 27, 1991, when President Bush went on television to announce his intention to suspend offensive combat operations at midnight and set forth the procedures for reaching a formal cease-fire. Iraq accepted this offer to suspend offensive combat operations and stated that it was willing to abide by all UN resolutions.

Resolution 678 refers only to Chapter VII of the Charter and does not otherwise specify the provisions of the Charter that authorize its issuance. Although there have been discussions in various forums about possible Charter bases for this resolution,[37] it is possible, indeed probable, that the Council deliberately refrained from specifying any Charter articles in Resolution 678 in order to afford the coalition forces maximum flexibility in dealing with Iraq's aggression. Moreover, the International Court of Justice's Advisory Opinion on Namibia suggests that the "Members of the United Nations have conferred upon the Security Council powers commensurate with its responsibility for the maintenance of peace and security. The only limitations are the fundamental principles and purposes found in Chapter I of the Charter."[38] One issue raised in public debates on the Gulf crisis was whether it would be compatible with the principles and purposes of the United Nations for the coalition forces to eliminate the military capability of Iraq and remove its leadership.

Carl-August Fleischhauer, then Under-Secretary-General and Legal Counsel of the United Nations, expressed the view that Resolution 678 would not permit such an action. In support of his position, Fleischhauer emphasized that Resolution 678 authorized the use of force to implement the Security Council's Resolution 660, which demands only that Iraq withdraw immediately and unconditionally its forces from Kuwait. Under this view once the liberation of Kuwait was assured, the Council's authorization to use force ceased to be in effect.

This view is debatable. Resolution 678 authorized member states to use "all necessary means" not only to implement Resolution 660 but also "all subsequent relevant resolutions and to restore international peace and security." One of these subsequent resolutions, Resolution 670, reaffirms that the Fourth Geneva Convention applies to Kuwait and that Iraq "is liable under the Convention in respect of the grave breaches committed by it, as are individuals who commit or order the commission of grave breaches." Arguably, a "March on Bagdad" or at least the continuance of the fighting would have been justified as action required to ensure that Saddam Hussein, the Iraqi leader, would be brought to trial for his ordering of grave breaches of the Convention. Moreover, the terms "all necessary means . . . to restore international peace and security" also arguably would justify such action, as long as the people of Iraq would have the opportunity to choose their new leaders and to enjoy basic human rights.

The political decision, as we know, was to stop the attack in Iraq well short of occupying of Baghdad. The issue of the scope of authority conferred by Resolution 678 is not just an academic question, however, as we shall see later in this chapter, when we turn to the 2003 attack on Iraq that removed Saddam Hussein from power.

Although, as always when the use of force is involved, not all would agree,[39] most states and commentators would support the proposition that the US and the coalition's use of force in Kuwait and Iraq was in full accord with international law, either as an act of collective self-defense or as a UN-authorized collective security action.[40] Some, moreover, including President Bush, envisaged a "new world order" in which the UN Security Council would finally be able to perform its collective security function along the lines of the Charter paradigm. A harsher reality, however, soon intruded itself.

In a sense, this harsher reality began for the United States on April 3, 1991, when the Security Council unanimously adopted Resolution 687, which, among many other things, decided that Iraq must unconditionally accept the destruction, under international supervision, of all its chemical and biological weapons and all its ballistic missiles with a range greater than 150 kilometers and must unconditionally agree not to acquire or develop nuclear weapons or nuclear-weapons-usable material and to place all such materials under the exclusive control, for custody and removal, of the International Atomic Energy Agency (IAEA). It also constituted a formal cease-fire to the Gulf conflict.[41] Shortly after the de facto cease-fire, however, in March 1991[42] there were reports of widespread attacks by Iraqi forces against Iraq's Kurdish and Shiite populations, causing nearly two million refugees to flee toward the Turkish and Iranian borders. On April 5, 1991, "Recalling Article 2, paragraph 7, of the

Charter of the United Nations," the Council adopted Resolution 688,[43] which condemned Iraq's repression of its civilian population and noted that this repression led to "a massive flow of refugees towards and across international frontiers and to cross-border incursions, which threaten international peace and security in the region." Resolution 688 further demanded that Iraq, "as a contribution to removing the threat to international peace and security in the region," immediately cease this repression, insisted that Iraq allow immediate access by international humanitarian organizations to all those in need of assistance in all parts of Iraq, requested the Secretary-General to pursue his humanitarian efforts in Iraq and to use all the resources at his disposal to address the critical need of the refugees, and appealed to all member states and to all humanitarian organizations to contribute to these humanitarian relief efforts. The United States, the United Kingdom, and France cited this resolution as support for the establishment by force of refugee camps in northern Iraq, and later of no-fly zones in northern Iraq (to protect the Kurds) and in southern Iraq (to protect the Shiites), but the Secretary-General disagreed and suggested the need for Iraq's consent or further Security Council action.

The Secretary-General's position is not easily dismissed. As a preliminary matter one should note that Resolution 688 does *not* invoke Chapter VII of the Charter; rather, it recalls Article 2(7), which precludes the United Nations from intervening in matters which are "essentially within the domestic jurisdiction of any state," unless the "application of enforcement measures under Chapter VII" is involved. By adopting Resolution 688, the Council thus decided that Iraq's repression of its civilian population was not a matter essentially within its domestic jurisdiction. But it does not follow that the resolution therefore authorized the use of armed force to prevent that repression by setting up enclaves in northern and southern Iraq. On the contrary, nothing in the language or negotiating history of Resolution 688 suggests the right of any member state to deploy troops to that end. Unlike the Council's earlier resolutions authorizing the trade embargo or the armed attack against Iraq, nothing in Resolution 688 even hints at the use of armed force to protect the civilian population of Iraq.

To be sure, as Sean Murphy has noted, Britain and France may have relied on the doctrine of "humanitarian intervention" as an additional justification for their actions in northern Iraq, although the record is somewhat unclear in this regard.[44] It is debatable whether "humanitarian intervention" constitutes an exception to Article 2(4)'s prohibition on the use of force, and we shall consider this issue when later in this chapter we turn to US and NATO use of force in Kosovo. In any event, the United

States did not rely on the doctrine in support of its actions in northern Iraq, and indeed has never expressly endorsed a right of humanitarian intervention under the UN Charter, although various US officials have from time to time cited humanitarian concerns as a *policy* justification for the use of force.[45] Also, the UN General Assembly never adopted a resolution condemning the interventions in either northern or southern Iraq. This inaction, plus various statements made by governments and non-governmental entities over an extended period of time, arguably "leads to a conclusion that, while many governments and others expressed serious reservations, ultimately the interventions in Iraq were regarded by the world community as *somehow* emanating from authority granted by the Security Council.[46] One is reminded by this argument of the practice of "jury nullification" that one finds in domestic legal orders, especially that of the United States.

Throughout the rest of the 1990s and into the 2000s the United States and other states employed the use of armed force in and over Iraqi territory. The no-fly zones were enforced by coalition aircraft from a base in Turkey or from aircraft carriers in the Persian Gulf. The US and other states have mounted air strikes or other military actions when Iraq has violated the terms of the cease-fire resolution, trespassed into Kuwait, renewed attacks on its Kurdish or Shiite populations, or otherwise acted in a hostile manner. In January 1993, US, British, and French forces carried out air strikes in response to cease-fire violations, including unauthorized incursions into Kuwaiti territory and the refusal to guarantee the safety and free movement of the Special Commission (of weapons inspectors) established under Resolution 687 (UNSCOM).[47]

Iraq's interference with the free movement of UNSCOM intensified over the 1990s and resulted in the departure of the UNSCOM inspectors in 1998 and Iraq's refusal to permit them or a successor team to resume their functions. The response of the United States and the United Kingdom, and the legal authority cited for their actions, have been aptly summarized by Christine Gray:

> Thus in December 1998 the USA and UK undertook *Operation Desert Fox* in response to the withdrawal by Iraq of co-operation with the UN weapons inspectors; this was a major operation lasting four days and nights and involving more missiles than used in the entire 1991 conflict. The USA and UK referred to Security Council Resolutions 1154 and 1205 as providing the legal basis for their use of force; these resolutions had been passed under Chapter VII, but had not made express provision for the use of force. The first said that Iraq must, under Resolution 687, accord immediate and unrestricted access to UNSCOM and IAEA inspectors and that any violation would have "the severest consequences for Iraq." The second resolution condemned the decision by Iraq to stop cooperation with UNSCOM

> and demanded that Iraq rescind its decision. Although these resolutions did not explicitly authorise force, the UK argued that they provided a clear basis for military action; by Resolution 1205 the Security Council had implicitly revived the authority to use force given by Resolution 678. The USA also said that its forces were acting under the authority provided in the Security Council resolutions. But this argument of implied authorisation was not accepted by other states; in the Security Council debate following the operation only Japan spoke out clearly in its favour... The argument of implied authorisation was not used on its own by the USA and the UK; this justification was supplemented by the claim that the use of force was a lawful response to a breach by Iraq of the ceasefire. Thus the USA argued that Iraq had repeatedly taken actions which constituted flagrant, material breaches of its obligations; following these breaches of its obligations... the "coalition" had exercised the authority given by Security Council Resolution 678 for Member States to employ all necessary means to secure compliance with the Council's resolutions and restore international peace and security in the area. The UK, in the Security Council debate, said that Resolution 687 made it a condition of the ceasefire that Iraq destroy its weapons of mass destruction and agree to the monitoring of its obligations to destroy such weapons. By Iraq's flagrant violation of the ceasefire resolution the Security Council implicitly revived the authority to use force given in Resolution 678 (1990).[48]

One may question whether it ever is justifiable to rely on a Security Council resolution *implicitly* authorizing the use of force. In light of the emphasis the UN Charter places on member states refraining from the use of force to settle disputes, arguably Security Council authorization of the use of force must be *explicit* and the focus of debate and discussion in the Council's deliberations before adoption of the resolution in question.[49] Moreover, in my view, Gray has convincingly responded to the US and UK arguments:

> the argument of material breach has been criticised by commentators because it arrogates to individual states power that properly resides with the Security Council. It is for the Security Council to determine not only the existence of a breach of the ceasefire, but also the consequences of such a breach in cases where there is a binding ceasefire imposed by the Security Council. Moreover, it seems doubtful whether any breach of Resolution 687 not itself involving the use of force can justify the USA and UK in turning to force in response. Those who support this doctrine of material breach seem impatient of disagreement in the Security Council; they revive Cold War arguments that when the Security Council is unable to act because of a permanent member then the USA and the UK can go ahead to use force, if there has been a breach of a prior resolution passed under Charter VII, even in the absence of express authorisation. But this has dangers for the Security Council; it discounts the words of the resolutions reserving the Security Council's right to consider further action; it also discounts statements in debates that it is for the Security Council to take further action. This undermines the authority of the Security Council and ignores the careful negotiations between states attempting to reach agreement on controversial issues.[50]

It might also be noted that the approach adopted by the United States and the United Kingdom seems incompatible with a rule of law paradigm. Surely the Security Council has the authority and the responsibility under the Charter to interpret its resolutions and to decide on the consequences if a state violates obligations imposed on it by the resolution. We shall return to this issue later in this chapter when we consider the Bush administration's "change of regime" in Iraq.

Before we do so, however, we turn to the US (and NATO) use of force that some have alleged has strained the UN Charter's rule of law paradigm to the breaking point.

Kosovo and the Charter paradigm

The debate over the legality and morality of US and NATO actions with respect to Kosovo has been fierce. Moreover, the writings on this subject have been legion.[51] Drawing on some of these writings, as well as on other sources, this contribution to the debate focuses on the legal dimensions of the Kosovo crisis, although it also explores moral and policy considerations as well. It does not examine contentions that NATO's bombing campaign against the Federal Republic of Yugoslavia violated international humanitarian law; I have examined some of these issues elsewhere.[52] This contribution does set forth several propositions and attempts to defend them. They are as follows:

1. The use of force by NATO in Kosovo could have been avoided.
2. Assuming for the sake of argument that it could not, the use of force actually employed in Kosovo should have been different from that which was employed.
3. However employed, NATO's use of force in Kosovo could not be justified under existing international law. It might have been justified as a moral matter, but not as it was actually employed.
4. The doctrine of humanitarian intervention, which is most often, at least in the academic literature, advanced as a legal justification of the use of force in Kosovo, is not now and should not become part of international law.
5. Under the UN Charter paradigm, the Security Council can and should use humanitarian considerations as a basis for authorizing the use of force under Chapter VII of the UN Charter.

Avoiding the use of force in Kosovo

Misuse of the negotiation process There is considerable disagreement in the literature over whether it would have been possible for NATO to avoid the use of force in Kosovo through more adept use of the negotiation process.[53] This chapter does not get into this debate in any detail. It should be noted, however, that by the time the proceedings had progressed to Rambouillet, negotiations with Yugoslavia had broken down and been replaced by non-negotiable demands. There is some evidence that Yugoslavia would have been willing to withdraw most of its forces from Kosovo, to accept the stationing of a UN force there, and to grant the Kosovar Albanians autonomy.[54] Instead, NATO demanded that Yugoslavia permit a NATO force, with no UN representation, to have free access to Serbia as well as to Kosovo, and, in effect, to agree to Kosovar independence after a three-year transition period.[55] However, as noted by Richard Bilder:

> in the Petersberg agreement which ended the bombing, NATO seems to have accepted something close to the terms Yugoslavia might have been willing to accept at Rambouillet. Thus, Petersberg provides for continued Yugoslav formal sovereignty over Kosovo, albeit with Kosovar autonomy; UN authorization of and participation in the military presence and administration in Kosovo; restriction of the UN and NATO forces to Kosovo itself, with no right of NATO or UN forces to enter Serbia; and even eventual reentry of at least limited Serb forces to protect Serb historical and religious sites in Kosovo. This raises the question, if NATO could have gotten at Rambouillet much of what it finally agreed to at Petersberg, what then was accomplished by the terrible loss of life, destruction, and suffering caused by the bombing?[56]

This also raises the question whether the presentation of non-negotiable demands at Rambouillet was consistent with US and other NATO member states' obligations under Article 33 of the UN Charter, which provides, in paragraph 1, that "[t]he parties to any dispute, the continuance of which is likely to endanger the maintenance of international peace and security, shall, first of all, seek a solution by negotiation, enquiry, mediation, conciliation, arbitration, judicial settlement, resort to regional agencies or arrangements, or other peaceful means of their own choice." At a minimum, it is clear that NATO member states violated the Charter by failing to return to the Security Council when the talks at Rambouillet broke down. Article 37(1) of the Charter provides that "[s]hould the parties to a dispute of the nature referred to in Article 33 fail to settle it by the means indicated in that Article, they shall refer it to the Security Council." Although the Security Council had been involved in the Kosovo issue for some time, and had adopted three resolutions under Chapter VII of the Charter prior to the NATO bombing campaign,[57] the NATO member states declined to go back to the Security Council for strategic reasons, especially the desire to avoid the threat of a Russian or Chinese veto. The language of Article 37(1), however, uses the mandatory "shall" rather than the precatory "should." In this case strategic considerations "trumped" UN obligations.

Misuse of the military option Javier Solana, who was Secretary-General of NATO at the time of the bombing of Yugoslavia, has argued that resort to military action "came about only after all diplomatic means had been exhausted."[58] Assuming *arguendo* this was the case, arguably NATO might have avoided the use of force if, instead of announcing that it would not employ ground troops, it had amassed significant ground forces along the Kosovo border and threatened to use them in conjunction with a bombing campaign to force the withdrawal of Serb forces. To be sure, such a threat of the use of force might itself have been a violation of Article 2(4) of the Charter's prohibition of the "threat or use of force against the territorial integrity or political independence of any state . . ." In practice, however, Article 2(4) has seldom been invoked to challenge diplomatic threats of the use of armed force,[59] and, in the case of Kosovo, such a threat by NATO might have served in effect as an exercise in collective security by three of the five permanent members of the Security Council and thereby avoided the carnage that followed the bombing. In the event political considerations persuaded NATO member states to refrain from the use of ground troops. It is noteworthy, however, that renewed consideration of the use of ground troops after the bombing failed to drive the Serbian troops out of Kosovo apparently was the primary factor in Milosovic's decision to withdraw.

The bombing and international law

As we have seen, the two generally accepted exceptions to Article 2(4) of the Charter's prohibition on the use of force are actions taken in individual or collective self-defense or actions authorized by the UN Security Council under Chapter VII of the Charter. In the case of Kosovo the doctrine of humanitarian intervention has also been advanced as a justification of the bombing. We consider each of these possible justifications in turn.

Self-defense

There has been considerable debate over the scope and impact on pre-Charter law of Article 51.[60] There is little evidence, however, that self-defense would pass the straight (or red) face test as an argument in support of the NATO bombing. Under even the most expansive interpretation of "armed attack against a member of the United Nations,"

Yugoslavia's military action within Kosovo against the Kosovo Liberation Army did not qualify. Although some have suggested that massive flows of refugees across a state's borders may be the functional equivalent of an "armed attack" – the huge flow of refugees into India during the 1971 East Pakistan war of independence is the example most cited – this proposition has not been generally accepted.[61] In any event, as we shall see below, it is debatable whether the flow of refugees from Kosovo before the bombing began could be characterized as "massive."

Security Council authorization

The drafters of the UN Charter envisaged that severe limitations on the use of force by states would be offset by the United Nations playing an active role in the maintenance of international peace and security.[62] The Security Council was actively involved with Kosovo, both before and after the bombing, and some have argued that resolutions adopted by the Council constitute an authorization for NATO's actions. On examination, however, this proposition has little merit.

In more cautious terms Ruth Wedgwood has suggested that "the United States is not amiss in claiming some measure of legitimacy from Security Council resolutions, even in the absence of immediate authorization of the NATO campaign."[63] But the Charter requires that Security Council resolutions afford more than "some measure of legitimacy" for the use of force by states to be legally justified. They must authorize the use of force, and none of the Council's resolutions adopted before the bombing began provides such authorization.[64]

Some commentators have ascribed substantial significance to a decision of the Security Council not to act.[65] Specifically, three days after the bombing began, Belarus, India, and Russia introduced a draft resolution in the Security Council that would have condemned the NATO bombing as a violation of Articles 2(4), 24, and 53 of the Charter.[66] It failed to be adopted by a vote of twelve to three, with only China, Russia, and Namibia voting in favor. The issue is whether this rejection of the condemnatory draft resolution constituted, in effect, an *implicit* authorization of NATO's bombing, even if it was done three days after the bombing started.

In considering whether the Security Council, through its actions or inactions, authorized the NATO bombing in Kosovo, we should be mindful of our earlier consideration of US and UK arguments that Security Council resolutions have implicitly authorized their use of force in Iraq. Moreover, as Michael Glennon has pointed out, "[i]n the past, the Security Council has left no doubt concerning its intent whether use of force was authorized. In Korea, the Gulf War, and Bosnia, it adopted resolutions that made clear that states were allowed to use force."[67]

Ruth Wedgwood has noted that "[d]ecisions not to act are a part of state practice and *opinio juris.*"[68] But here we are not dealing with an issue of whether a norm of customary international law has been created. Rather the issue is the proper interpretation and application of UN Charter provisions. Also, the Charter provision in question, Article 2(4), contains a prohibition on the use of force that the International Court of Justice, in *Nicaragua v. United States*, stated was "a conspicuous example in a rule of international law having the character of *jus cogens*."[69] As Charney has pointed out, "Charter law may very well not be subject to change by new general international law. By its terms [Article 103] the UN Charter overrides all inconsistent treaties, regardless of the date of their entry into force. One would expect the same rule to apply to developments in general international law, especially since treaties supersede all but *jus cogens* norms."[70]

With respect, the proposition that the Council's rejection of the draft resolution condemning the bombing constitutes an authorization of the bombing is topsy-turvy reasoning. The intent of the drafters of the UN Charter was clearly that decisions to authorize the use of force by member states would be taken by a majority of the members of the Security Council, including, most importantly, all five permanent members of the Council.[71] In this case, two of the permanent members of the Council – China and Russia – voted in favor of a draft resolution that would have condemned the NATO bombing as a "flagrant violation of the UN Charter."

Lastly, Wedgwood has suggested that the "Council endorsement of 'an international armed presence' in Kosovo after the conflict, with the forced withdrawal of Yugoslav troops, is also of some significance, for it is implausible that the Council would ratify the results of an allied military campaign if it considered the means wholly illicit or tantamount to aggression."[72] But, as Charney has pointed out, "[t]o avoid a veto, the Council resolution[73] adopted subsequent to the bombing did not retroactively legalize NATO's actions but only prospectively authorized foreign states to intervene in the FRY to maintain the peace."[74]

To be sure, this is not to suggest that the Security Council resolutions, as well as the Council's rejection of the draft Russian resolution, discussed by Wedgwood are of no legal significance. We should, however, as Thomas Franck has suggested, "distinguish between mitigation and justification."[75] This is also a distinction we should keep in mind as we turn to the ground most often advanced in defense of the legality of the NATO bombing: the doctrine of humanitarian intervention.

Humanitarian intervention

The debate over whether there is a doctrine of humanitarian intervention that is an exception to the Charter provisions on the use of force is long-standing. Especially during the 1970s there was substantial debate in academic circles on this issue.[76] Those who support the doctrine argue that a proper interpretation of the language of Article 2(4) of the Charter permits the use of force for humanitarian purposes. In particular, they suggest that the article requires states to refrain from the threat or use of force only when it is "against the territorial integrity or political independence of any state" or "inconsistent with the purposes of the United Nations." Since, the argument continues, the use of force for humanitarian purposes is not directed against the territorial integrity or political independence of the state, and, far from being inconsistent with the purposes of the United Nations, is supportive of the Organization's purpose set forth in Article 1(3) of the Charter, namely to promote and encourage "respect for human rights and for fundamental freedoms," it is permitted by Article 2(4).

The problem with this interpretation of Article 2(4) is that it is contradicted both by the drafting history of the UN Charter and by subsequent state practice. As Charney (among others) has noted, the *travaux préparatoires* of the Charter establish that the phrases "territorial integrity" and "inconsistent with the purposes of the Charter" were added to Article 2(4) to "close all potential loopholes in its prohibition on the use of force, rather than to open new ones."[77] Moreover, in a scholarly and exhaustive study of humanitarian intervention, Sean Murphy has examined state practice since the enactment of the Charter (up to 1996), and has found little or no support for the doctrine.[78] Most significantly, perhaps, the International Court of Justice appears to have rejected the doctrine in its judgment in *Nicaragua v. United States*.[79]

Even in the context of Yugoslavia's suit against various member states of NATO challenging the legality of the bombing,[80] the respondent states were reluctant to offer a legal justification of the bombing. Rather, the focus of the responses has been on challenging the jurisdiction of the Court. Reportedly, at first only Belgium mentioned humanitarian intervention and then guardedly as a possible legal justification.[81] Since then the statements of governments of member states of the United Nations, including those of the US government, have given at best weak support to the doctrine of humanitarian intervention.[82]

Assuming *arguendo* that there is a doctrine of humanitarian intervention, it is highly questionable whether the NATO bombing in Yugoslavia and Kosovo qualified as an exercise of it. There is first the issue whether the human rights violations in Kosovo immediately prior to the time the intervention began were sufficiently massive and widespread to justify intervention or rather were, as suggested by Charney, only such as to render the NATO intervention an "anticipatory humanitarian intervention."[83] Prior to the bombing, the Security Council had authorized the deployment of an Organization of Security and Co-operation in Europe (OSCE) observer mission to monitor a cease-fire in Kosovo and, according to Charney, this force had effectively prevented the commission of widespread atrocities. Charney further notes that the indictment of President Milosovic on May 22, 1999, by the Prosecutor of the International Criminal Tribunal for the former Yugoslavia contains only one charge relating to actions taken before the start of the bombing campaign on March 24, 1999: the killing of forty-five civilians at Racak on January 15, 1999. All of the other counts related to events occurring after the withdrawal of the OSCE observer mission and the beginning of the bombing.

Reasonable persons can, and have differed on this issue, however. James Steinberg, for example, has pointed out that, after the Security Council had authorized the OSCE observer mission of over 1,000 persons to monitor the cease-fire in October 1998, the "Serbian forces repeatedly violated the ceasefire, exceeded the troop levels to which their leader had agreed in October, and steadily increased their harassment of the international observers until it was impossible for them to do their jobs."[84] Steinberg also reminds us that "there is already a historical record of Milosovic's aims and methods; the record of his brutal campaigns against Croatia and Bosnia . . . The same paramilitary warlords who did the dirty work in those campaigns led the charge again in Kosovo."[85]

Let us assume that Steinberg has the best of this argument and that military intervention was urgently needed to prevent Serbian ethnic cleansing in Kosovo. The doctrine of humanitarian intervention would seem to require that the military action undertaken be designed to prevent or bring to an end the humanitarian catastrophe unfolding. To be sure, the NATO leaders apparently thought that the bombing of Yugoslavia would force Milosovic to withdraw his troops from Kosovo within a brief period of time, since the US Secretary of State, Madeleine Albright, reportedly said,"I think this is . . . achievable within a relatively short period of time."[86] But when this expectation proved to be ill-founded, then NATO, if it intended to justify, at least from a moral perspective, its military action, was required to take further steps to stop the slaughter and displacement of Kosovo civilians by Serbian troops, such as the threat and, if necessary, the use of ground troops or action by air forces below 15,000 feet.

But no such steps were taken. On the contrary, NATO's decision to avoid the risk of NATO military casualties by resorting only to very high bombing and remote missile strikes was singularly ineffective in bringing to an end the actions of the Serbian troops in Kosovo. One can understand and sympathize with the desire of NATO leaders to avoid casualties, but it appears that the effect of this decision was not only to fail to protect the Kosovars, but also to enrage and increase atrocities by the Serbs against the Kosovars.[87] As noted by Michael Mandelbaum, before the NATO bombing began, approximately 2,500 people had died in Kosovo as a result of the battle between Serb forces and the Kosovo Liberation Army and 230,000 persons were estimated to have left their homes. During the eleven weeks of the bombing an estimated 10,000 people died in Kosovo, most of them Albanian civilians murdered by Serbs, and 1.4 million were displaced, 860,000 becoming refugees located outside of Kosovo.[88]

Sadly, there is a substantial measure of truth in the biting critique of Zbigniew Brzezinski, former US National Security Adviser:

> the painful reality is that the bombing campaign has been conducted as if the human lives at stake should be priced at three different levels: The most precious lives are those of the NATO pilots, with military tactics explicitly designed to minimize their loss; next are those of Milosevic's officials, whose headquarters have been targeted only when empty; least valuable are the lives of the Kosovars themselves, on whose behalf no risks have been taken.
>
> ... [T]o consider a war in which no effort is made – even at some risk to one's own professional warriors – to protect the most defenseless is to deprive the undertaking itself of its higher moral purpose.[89]

Should international law be revised to permit humanitarian intervention?

In the wake of the debate over Kosovo some commentators have proposed that international law be revised so as to provide for an express recognition of the doctrine of humanitarian intervention. Most particularly, Michael Glennon has contended that "[e]vents since the end of the Cold War starkly show that the anti-interventionist regime has fallen out of sync with modern notions of justice. The crisis in Kosovo illustrates this disjunction and America's new willingness to do what it thinks right – international law notwithstanding."[90] Glennon further suggests that the UN Charter is dysfunctional since it regards internal violence as a matter of domestic jurisdiction beyond the jurisdiction of the United Nations. In his view the current legal regime should be abandoned in favor of one that enhances justice. If necessary, the United States and other Western powers should strive toward the ideal of justice backed by power on their own. Revising international law to reflect the achievement of justice can come later.

More radically, Glennon has recently contended that "international 'rules' concerning use of force are no longer considered obligatory by states."[91] We shall examine this highly questionable proposition, as well as his contention that internal violence is a matter of domestic jurisdiction beyond the jurisdiction of the United Nations under the Charter, later in this chapter. For now let us consider Glennon's clarion call in favor of humanitarian intervention as a legal regime that would enhance "modern notions of justice."

As an initial matter, as we saw earlier, one may question whether NATO's actions in Kosovo reflect the ideal of justice. One should hesitate, moreover, to accept at face value Glennon's thesis that the "anti-interventionist regime has fallen out of sync with modern notions of justice." The doctrine of humanitarian intervention has a long and disreputable history.[92] When one thinks of the doctrine of humanitarian intervention, one is reminded of Mohandas Gandhi's reaction when asked what he thought of Western civilization: he said he thought it would be a good idea. As Richard Bilder has pointed out, "historically, claims of humanitarian intervention have typically served simply as a pretext for what are, in fact, selfish assertions of national interest, power, and greed – witness Nazi Germany's invocation of the supposed Czech abuse of Sudetan [sic] Germans as a excuse for occupying the Sudetan land [sic] and ultimately Czechoslovakia itself."[93] Similarly, Schachter has concluded: "[t]he reluctance of governments to legitimize foreign invasion in the interest of humanitarianism is understandable in the light of past abuses by powerful States. States strong enough to intervene and sufficiently interested in doing so tend to have political motives. They have a strong temptation to impose a political solution in their own national interest."[94] Interestingly, as previously noted, the United States, the sole "superpower," has so far declined to support the doctrine of humanitarian intervention.

A number of commentators have made a number of proposals[95] for developing the law to permit humanitarian intervention subject to complying with a number of conditions other than Security Council authorization that could be blocked by a veto. Relatively few governments have come out in favor of the doctrine, with the notable exception of the British government.[96] At first blush the thought of developing *legal* criteria for a doctrine of humanitarian intervention seems attractive. On deeper analysis, however, this would be a highly problematic exercise.

Most of the proposals would be politically infeasible. More important, most of them would require amendments to the UN Charter that would have the undesirable effect of providing states with more opportunities to resort to the use of armed force than they have under the current Charter regime. Almost any criteria that one could think of would be subject to manipulation by states, and in the accentuated decentralized legal order that would result from such an approach, it would be difficult if not impossible to hold states acting in violation of the criteria accountable.

It has long been the conventional wisdom that, although member states violate Article 2(4) of the Charter if they decide to intervene within a state under a doctrine of humanitarian intervention, the Security Council can authorize member states to intervene on the basis of humanitarian considerations pursuant to its Chapter VII powers. Glennon, however, has challenged this conventional wisdom by claiming that, under the Charter, internal violence is a matter of domestic jurisdiction beyond the jurisdiction of the United Nations. It is to this challenge that we next turn.

Can the Security Council authorize the use of force based on humanitarian considerations?

According to Glennon, Article 2(7) of the UN Charter bars the Organization from authorizing the use of force by member states to halt such egregious violations of human rights as genocide and mass killings within a single state. Article 2(7) provides that nothing in the Charter "shall authorize the United Nations to intervene in matters which are essentially within the domestic jurisdiction of any state," subject to the exception that this principle shall not prejudice the application of enforcement measures under Chapter VII. Leaving aside the issue of enforcement measures under Chapter VII for the moment, Article 2(7) has not constituted a barrier to the United Nations dealing with internal violence for several reasons. First and foremost, the internal conflicts that have resulted in UN action were not essentially domestic. On the contrary, they have involved the threat of, or actual intervention by, outside states; the danger of or the actual spread of violence beyond the territorial boundaries of the state in which the internal conflict is taking place; wars of national liberation against colonial powers; or the violation of treaty or customary international law (the *jus in bello*) – all matters not essentially within the domestic jurisdiction of states. The Security Council's willingness to establish a peacekeeping force in the former Yugoslavia is a recent rejection of the argument that a civil war is necessarily "essentially within the domestic jurisdiction" of states.[97]

Nor, as contended by Glennon in a response to critical commentary on his article,[98] as well as in his book,[99] does Security Council enforcement action require the presence of cross-border violence. Unlike Article 51 of the Charter, Article 39 does not require an "armed attack" across international borders for the Security Council to take a decision to employ enforcement measures. Rather, it requires that the Council make a finding of a "threat to the peace, breach of the peace, or act of aggression." As far back as 1966 the Security Council determined that the then Southern Rhodesia's unilateral declaration of independence (UDI) constituted a threat to international peace and security and imposed mandatory economic sanctions.[100] No less a personage than former US Secretary of State Dean Acheson sharply criticized the Council's action on the ground that actions taken by the Ian Smith regime entirely within its own territory could not constitute a threat to international peace and security. Rather, the threat to international peace and security, if any, came from black African states and not from Southern Rhodesia. The critics also argued strenuously that the Security Council's action constituted a clear violation of Article 2(7).[101]

The response to the critics by the defenders of the Council's sanctions had the better arguments. In their view, under Chapter VII of the Charter, a threat to the peace could consist of a situation, as well as "the threat or use of force against the territorial integrity or political independence" prohibited by Article 2(4).[102] The situation in Southern Rhodesia, the argument continued, threatened the peace in two ways. First, the threat of internal violence in Southern Rhodesia was so great that any outbreak of violence was likely to be of such intensity and magnitude that it would spill over onto the territory of adjoining states. Second, the "racist" actions of the white minority in Southern Rhodesia had so inflamed passions in neighboring black African states that indirect outside support of guerrillas and even direct military intervention was likely. It was also argued that UDI represented an illegal rebellion against British authority and that nearly all member states of the United Nations regarded the regime as illegal and in flagrant violation of fundamental human rights norms. Finally, the defenders of the sanctions pointed out that Southern Rhodesia was not a state but a territory and thus Article 2(7) was inapplicable by its terms.

Moreover, as noted by Franck in his response to the Glennon article, more recently, "the council has authorized forceful tactics in numerous civil wars and against various regimes that oppress their own citizens: in Bosnia, Somalia . . . South Africa, Haiti and Iraq. And in December 1998, the Security Council used a Chapter VII resolution to demand that the Taliban end its oppression of women in Afghanistan, opening the door to future collective enforcement should they refuse."[103] To be sure, as several commentators have noted, the Council's determination that the situation in Haiti constituted a threat to the peace was dubious, since it apparently was based solely on an outflow of refugees.[104] There have also been increasingly strident complaints that the Security Council is dominated by the United States and other developed countries[105] and debate over whether the International Court of Justice has the authority to review Security Council decisions and rule that they are *ultra vires* and therefore null and void.[106]

The issue of how well (or badly) the United Nations has done in its responses to internal violence is not so easily resolved as Glennon's dismissive tone would indicate. The reality is that the United Nations has had both its successes (South Africa, Namibia, Mozambique, El Salvador) and its failures (Somalia and Rwanda). One should also consider the appropriate standard to employ. If one adopts an ideal standard, there is no question that the United Nations has failed to cope satisfactorily with internal violence. On the other hand, if the standard is the best that could be expected of the United Nations considering the difficult economic, political, and social milieu in which it has had to operate since World War II, the evaluative process becomes more complex. It should not be forgotten, moreover, that the difficulties the United Nations has faced in fulfilling its primary responsibility for maintaining international peace and security have been due, in no small measure, to roadblocks placed in its way by member states, especially the permanent members of the Security Council. The US contribution to such difficulties is examined later in this chapter.

First, however, we need to address the "trump card" argument raised by advocates of a doctrine of humanitarian intervention: If genocide or crimes against humanity are being committed on a large scale within a state, and the Security Council is unwilling or unable to act, must member states of the United Nations refrain from intervening militarily to bring such horrific acts to an end?

Perhaps the first response to be made to this rhetorical question is that one must be careful not to assume on an a priori basis that the Security Council will not act. Considering the Council's abject failure to prevent the horrendous genocide in Rwanda,[107] and the considerable recriminations that have been forthcoming in the wake of that failure,[108] there would be intensive pressure from various sources for the Council not to stand by in the face of a similar situation in the future. Assuming a worst-case scenario, however, the answer to the question of whether states should stand idly by under such circumstances is, definitely not. From a moral perspective there can be no other choice. But it does not necessarily follow that a doctrine of humanitarian intervention should become part of international law, for the reasons we have considered above. In this situation the suggestion of Thomas Franck and Nigel Rodley, writing in 1973 in reference to India's invasion of East Pakistan and the subsequent creation of Bangladesh, remains apt. After concluding that the doctrine of humanitarian intervention was incompatible with principles of public international law, and that this law should not be changed to incorporate the doctrine, the authors stated:

Yet we freely admit that we can imagine situations in which a humanitarian rescue would be highly desirable. With Churchill, we can visualize wanting our country to "fight the menace of tyranny for years, and if necessary, alone". Undeniably, there are circumstances in which the unilateral use of force to overthrow injustice begins to seem less wrong than to turn aside. Like civil disobedience, however, this sense of superior "necessity" belongs in the realm not of law but of moral choice, which nations, like individuals, must sometimes make, weighing the costs and benefits to their cause, to the social fabric, and to themselves.[109]

More recently, Franck has further developed this line of thought in reference to NATO's actions in Kosovo:

What does a nation like the United States – one with the power and the will to ameliorate a human catastrophe – do when, to act, it must violate general rules of the game? India faced that choice before invading East Pakistan to stop the slaughter of Bengalis in 1971. People stranded on mountains or in lifeboats face a comparable personal choice when, to save many, they contemplate cannibalizing one of their number. NATO's action in Kosovo is not the first time illegal steps have been taken to prevent something palpably worse.

Law gives those taking such illegal but necessary action several well-established defensive strategies. They may deny having been authors of the illegal act, or argue that the act is not actually illegal. They may call for a change in the law to make their action legal. Or they may argue mitigation, by showing that their illegal conduct was still the least-unacceptable possible outcome. Every law student knows that even cannibalism, if demonstrably the least-gruesome alternative in the circumstances, is treated leniently by the law.

But they also know that it would be no advance for civilized society if the legal impediments to cannibalism were dismantled. Laws, including the UN Charter, are written to govern the general conduct of states in light of historic experience and the requisites of good order. If, in a particular instance, a general law inhibits doing justice, then it is up to each member of the community to decide whether to disobey that law. If some so choose, however, their best strategy is not to ridicule, let alone change the law: It is to proffer the most expiating explanation of the special circumstances that ordained their moral choice.[110]

Glennon responds to Franck's remarks by suggesting that "[a]rguing mitigation makes sense if one opposes changing the law; the objective then is to prevent the precedent, such as it is, from taking on life in justifying future violations."[111] As we have already noted, however, Glennon believes that the law should be changed, indeed that the current international rules on the use of force (not just the rule prohibiting humanitarian intervention by states absent Security Council authorization) are no longer considered obligatory by states. We will consider the validity of this thesis as we struggle to make sense of the "brave new world" of post-September 11 and its impact on US adherence to the rule of law paradigm.

The impact of September 11

September 11 and use of force in Afghanistan

The facts of September 11 are well known. In brief summary they are as follows. On September 11, 2001, terrorists seized control of four passenger aircraft in the United States. Two were flown into the Twin Towers of the World Trade Center in New York City, a third targeted the Pentagon (Defense Department) in Washington, DC, and the fourth crashed in Pennsylvania when passengers fought the terrorists for control of the plane. Over 3,000 people of more than eighty nationalities perished in the attacks.

The international reaction to the attacks was swift and almost universally one of outrage and support for the United States.[112] For its part, on September 12, the Security Council adopted a resolution that condemned the attacks as "horrifying," labeled them a threat to international peace and security, and reaffirmed the "inherent right of individual or collective self-defence as recognized by the Charter of the United Nations."[113] Similarly, on September 28, the Council adopted its wide-ranging Resolution 1373, which among other things, again cited the right to self-defense and specified steps to combat terrorism, including suppressing the financing of terrorism, denying safe haven to terrorists, and cooperating in law enforcement efforts.[114] Unlike the case of Iraq, in neither of these resolutions, nor in any of the resolutions adopted after the start of the military campaign, did the Security Council explicitly authorize the United States or any coalition of forces to use force. Nonetheless, the Security Council twice referred to the inherent right to individual and collective self-defense before commencement of combat operations, no effort was made to condemn the use of force once it began, and the Council repeatedly reaffirmed the right to self-defense as that use of force was ongoing, lending a significant amount of support to the legality of the combat operations in Afghanistan under Article 51 of the Charter.

Special note should also be taken of NATO's invocation, for the first time in its history, of Article 5 of the North Atlantic Treaty, which provides for collective self-defense if any of the member states suffers an armed attack.[115] After US officials presented evidence that the attacks were not the work of domestic terrorists, on October 2, the North Atlantic Council made the finding that there had been an armed attack against a NATO member and invoked Article 5 of the treaty.[116] Also for the first time, at a special meeting of the Organization of American States (OAS), the foreign ministers of the twenty-two states parties to the Inter-American Treaty of Reciprocal Assistance (Rio Treaty) invoked Article 3 of the Rio Treaty that specifically refers to an "armed attack by any State against an American State."[117]

After verifying evidence linking the aircraft hijackers to Al Qaeda, a terrorist group based in Afghanistan and headed by Osama bin Laden, a Saudi expatriate, the United States demanded that the Taliban, the de facto government of Afghanistan, turn over the leaders of Al Qaeda to the United States, close all terrorist training camps in Afghanistan, and provide the United States with full access to the camps to confirm their closure.[118] After the Taliban refused to do so, the United States on October 7, informed the Security Council that it was exercising its "inherent right of individual and collective self-defense" by actions "against Al Qaeda terrorist training camps and military installations of the Taliban regime in Afghanistan."[119] A similar notification was sent by the United Kingdom. On the same day, the United States and the United Kingdom launched heavy air attacks against Al Qaeda and Taliban targets in Afghanistan.

Unlike their use of force in Iraq after the cease-fire, neither the United States nor the United Kingdom has claimed an explicit or implicit authorization of their use of force in Afghanistan by the Security Council. Rather their sole basis for conducting these military operations has been self-defense, which does not require advance Council authorization.[120] In this case the United States and the United Kingdom appear to be on solid ground. Although arguments have been made that the events of September 11 should be regarded as criminal acts rather than an "armed attack" within the meaning of Article 51, or that under Article 51 an "armed attack" can only be engaged in by a state not a private entity like Al Qaeda, these and similar arguments are not persuasive, have enjoyed little support from states, and have been convincingly refuted in the scholarly literature.[121]

It appears therefore that the United States adhered closely to the rule of law paradigm in the *jus ad bellum* aspects of its use of force in Afghanistan. It is much less clear, however, that the same may be said of the recent "regime change" in Iraq.

Iraq: the sequel

After sometimes heated debate, the US Congress adopted, on October 11, 2002, a resolution authorizing President George W. Bush to "use the armed forces of the United States as he determines to be necessary and appropriate in order to . . . defend the national security of the United States against the continuing threat posed by Iraq; and . . . enforce all relevant United Nations Security resolutions regarding Iraq."[122] Thereafter, the United States and the United Kingdom lobbied hard in the Security Council to have the Council adopt a resolution that would authorize the use of force against Iraq if it failed fully to destroy its weapons of mass destruction under UN supervision. The result was that, on November 8, 2002, the Security Council adopted Resolution 1441.[123]

In Resolution 1441, the Council recalls all of its previous resolutions on Iraq, most particularly Resolution 678, which authorized member states to use "all necessary means" (i.e., the use of armed force) to implement its previous resolutions and to restore international peace and security in the area, and Resolution 687, which imposed a series of obligations on Iraq, including that it destroy its weapons of mass destruction and refrain from acts of terrorism, and declare a cease-fire based on acceptance by Iraq of the obligations contained in Resolution 687. Then, acting under Chapter VII of the United Nations Charter, the Council decides "that Iraq has been and remains in material breach of its obligations under relevant resolutions, including resolution 687 . . . , to afford Iraq . . . a final opportunity to comply with its disarmament obligations . . . to convene immediately upon receipt of a report [from UN inspectors that Iraq has committed further material breaches by false statements or omissions in its declarations or by interfering with inspection activities or by failing to comply with its disarmament obligations] to consider the situation and the need for full compliance with all of the relevant Council resolutions in order to secure international peace and security." Lastly, the Council recalls that it "has repeatedly warned Iraq that it will face serious consequences as a result of its continued violations of its obligations."

Resolution 1441 was adopted unanimously by the Security Council. It was, however, a masterpiece of diplomatic ambiguity that masked real differences of view between the United States and the United Kingdom, on the one hand, and France, Germany, and Russia, on the other, in how Iraq's failure to fulfill its obligations under Resolution 687 should be handled. To the United States, for example, the words "serious consequences" were code words for the use of armed force, but this was not the interpretation favored by France, Germany and Russia.[124] These differences of view came strikingly to the surface in the days and months following the adoption of Resolution 1441.

In mid-September, 2002, when Iraq acceded to the Council's demand that it allow UN inspectors back into its territory, France was reportedly elated but the United States saw it as a setback.[125] On December 7, when Iraq's declaration of its weapons fell far short of the full disclosure demanded by Resolution 1441, the United States government reportedly debated within itself whether to go back immediately to the Security Council and demand a new declaration that Iraq was in "material breach" of its obligations, but decided not to do so because of concern that "such a move would be seen as too provocative and too much evidence of American desire for war."[126] On February 5, 2003, however, US Secretary of State Colin Powell made a presentation to the Security Council that employed photographs, intercepts, and assertions from informants about Iraq's weapons program and that was designed to show that Iraq was not fulfilling its obligation under Resolution 687 to disarm. It was also designed to demonstrate, although this point was not emphasized, that Iraq had been evading the UN inspectors' efforts to find weapons of mass destruction. Later, however, Powell directly clashed with Hans Blix, the chief UN inspector for chemical and biological weapons, contending that the inspection process had been a diversion from the real issue – whether Saddam Hussein had been cooperating with the inspectors and revealing all of his weapons programs.[127] In Powell's view, he had not.

For his part, Blix gave a substantial measure of support to the French, German, and Russian position that the inspection process was working and should be given more time – four months was the period requested by Blix. France, Germany, and Russia all explicitly stated that they would oppose any Security Council resolution that authorized the use of force in Iraq. According to news reports, the United States and the United Kingdom attempted to round up a majority of nine votes in the Security Council on the ground that a majority vote in favor of the use of force, even with blocking vetoes by France or Russia, would lend a measure of moral if not legal support to the use of force in Iraq.[128] This effort was abandoned when it became clear that nine firm commitments to a favorable vote were not available. On March 17, 2003, US President George W. Bush announced in a speech that he was giving Saddam Hussein and his sons forty-eight hours to leave Iraq. Their refusal to do so would "result in military conflict, commenced at a time of our choosing."[129] After Saddam and his sons failed to leave Iraq, US, British, and other forces of a "coalition of the willing" attacked Iraq on March 20, 2003.

As of this writing, the US government has not issued any official statement regarding the legal justification for the coalition's attack on Iraq.[130]

On March 17, 2003, however, British Attorney General Lord Goldsmith issued a terse justification in response to a parliamentary question regarding the legal basis for the use of force against Iraq. It is worth quoting in full:

Authority to use force against Iraq exists from the combined effect of Resolutions 678, 687 and 1441. All of these resolutions were adopted under Chapter VII of the UN Charter which allows the use of force for the express purpose of restoring international peace and security:

1. In Resolution 678 the Security Council authorised force against Iraq, to eject it from Kuwait and restore peace and security in the area.
2. In Resolution 687, which set out the cease-fire conditions after Operation Desert Storm, the Security Council imposed continuing obligations on Iraq to eliminate its weapons of mass destruction in order to restore international peace and security in the area. Resolution 687 suspended but did not terminate the authority to use force under Resolution 678.
3. A material breach of Resolution 687 revives the authority to use force under Resolution 678.
4. In Resolution 1441 the Security Council determined that Iraq has been and remains in material breach of 687.
5. The Security Council in Resolution 1441 gave Iraq "a final opportunity to comply with its disarmament obligations" and warned Iraq of "the serious consequences".
6. The Security Council also decided in Resolution 1441 that, if Iraq failed to comply with and cooperate fully in the implementation of Resolution 1441, that would constitute a further material breach.
7. It is plain that Iraq has failed so to comply and therefore Iraq was at the time of Resolution 1441 and continues to be in material breach.
8. Thus, the authority to use force under resolution 678 has revived and so continues today.
9. All that 1441 requires is reporting to and discussion by the Security Council of Iraq's failures, but not an express further decision to authorise force.[131]

Lord Goldsmith's justification was challenged in a letter to the editor of the *Guardian* by a number of eminent international law scholars, who, among other things, asserted that "[b]efore military action can lawfully be undertaken against Iraq, the Security Council must have indicated its clearly expressed assent."[132]

In connection with our discussion of the US and British use of force against Iraq after Iraq expelled the UN weapons inspectors in 1998, we have had occasion to examine critically most of the arguments advanced by Lord Goldsmith in defense of the use of force against Iraq in 2003. The key issue raised by Lord Goldsmith's statement, however, is whether Resolution 1441 adds an additional and convincing legal justification for the regime change in Iraq.

In paragraph 9 of his statement Lord Goldsmith argues that the absence of an explicit requirement in Resolution 1441 of a further decision of the Security Council before resort to force may take place shows that no such requirement was intended by the Council. It is clear that the United States and the United Kingdom, in their vote for the resolution, intended that it not require a further vote of the Security Council before resort to force could take place. But as we have seen, the drafting history of Resolution 1441 demonstrates that France, Russia, and Germany viewed the absence of an explicit authorization in the resolution as precluding the use of armed force without a further decision of the Security Council.[133] As suggested before, Resolution 1441 is an exercise in deliberate diplomatic ambiguity.

There is, then, an issue regarding the proper interpretation to be given to Resolution 1441. Under a rule of law paradigm this issue should be decided by a third-party decision maker – in this case the Security Council or the International Court of Justice. For reasons fully examined earlier in this study, however, this was not an acceptable option, especially for the United States.

Moreover, the US/UK argument based on Resolution 1441 suffers from some of the same defects of the arguments based on earlier Security Council resolutions. In particular, it is doubtful whether an authorization of the use of force may ever be implicit in a Security Council resolution, and Resolution 1441 contains no explicit authorization. Nor is there any language in Resolution 1441 that suggests, implicitly or explicitly, that the cease-fire imposed by Resolution 687 has terminated because of Iraq's material breaches of the latter resolution. In paragraph 12 of Resolution 1441 the Security Council decides that it will convene immediately on receipt of a report that indicates a failure of Iraq to comply with its obligations under all relevant Council resolutions and "*Recalls*" in paragraph 13, that it has repeatedly warned Iraq of "serious consequences" if it continues to violate its obligations. Assuming that it is reasonable to interpret "serious consequences" as referring to the use of armed force, reading paragraphs 12 and 13 of Resolution 1441 together, it would appear that the purpose of the meeting envisaged in paragraph 12 would be for the Council to decide whether it should authorize the serious consequences referred to in paragraph 13, not merely to discuss Iraq's failures to fulfill its obligations, with member states of the United Nations then free to decide on an individual basis whether to use armed force against Iraq.

Even if one assumes, as I do, that, on balance, existing Security Council resolutions, including Resolution 1441, do not authorize the use of force against Iraq because of its failure to eliminate its weapons of mass destruction as required by Resolution 687, this should not be the end of the analysis. There is considerable evidence, and more is likely to be disclosed, that, far from helping to enforce Resolution 687, France and Russia have engaged in deals with the Saddam Hussein government that undermined its enforcement.[134] Moreover, in refusing to accept the US and UK proposal that the Security Council adopt a resolution explicitly authorizing the use of force if Iraq failed to carry out its obligation to disarm – for reasons that had little to do with the merits of the matter[135] – France, Germany, and Russia arguably failed to fulfill their obligation as members of the Council to allow the Council to perform its collective security functions to maintain international peace and security. As Edward Luck, a longtime observer of and commentator on the United Nations, recently noted: "The United Nations, sadly, has drifted far from its founding vision. Its Charter neither calls for a democratic council nor relegates the collective use of force to a last resort. It was a wartime document of a military alliance, not a universal peace platform."[136]

Further, as Jacques de Lisle has recently suggested, there may be a virtue in acting in an "almost legal" manner and, if so, the United States and other members of the coalition cannot justly be accused of engaging in lawless behavior.[137] De Lisle also suggests that, if after the armed conflict in Iraq is over, there is substantial evidence uncovered of weapons of mass destruction and plans to use them as well as of the heinous nature of the Iraq regime, this would "greatly strengthen the US and its partners' arguments for the near-legality and, thus, the legitimacy of their war in Iraq."[138] At this writing, there has been substantial evidence uncovered of the heinous nature of the Iraq regime, but not yet of weapons of mass destruction, although the search continues.

A full discussion of the *policy* arguments in favor of and against the invasion of Iraq is beyond the scope of this chapter. Suffice it for present purposes to say that in my view the policy arguments in favor of invading Iraq are much the stronger,[139] and would have fully supported the Security Council authorizing the use of armed force against Iraq – in which case there would have been no reasonable doubt about the legality of the invasion. But I do believe that it is necessary to respond to some arguments set forth by Harold Koh, an eminent international law scholar, in a valuable and provocative article addressing many of the themes of this study.[140] In his article Koh critically examines the UK/US legal justification based on Resolution 1441 and previous Security Council resolutions, especially a "revived force" under Resolution 678, and concludes, as I have, that the justification does not withstand close analysis.[141] He also argues, however, that failures on the part of the Bush administration prevented use of a "third way" that could have resulted in disarming Iraq and a regime change:

> But much of the blame [for the failure to reach agreement in the Security Council on how to deal with Iraq] must also go to the Bush Administration's decision to frame the issue in bipolar terms – either attack, or accept a status quo in which Saddam builds unconventional weapons and brutalizes his own citizens without sanction. By flattening the issue in this way, the Bush Administration discouraged examination of a meaningful third way: to disarm Iraq without attack through a multilateral strategy of disarmament plus enhanced containment plus more aggressive human rights intervention. That strategy would have supported continuation of the initial Bush approach of diplomacy backed by threat of force: restoring effective UN weapons inspections, disarming and destroying Iraqi weapons of mass destruction, and cutting off the flow of weapons and weapons-related goods into Iraq. At the same time, however, this strategy would have also pressed more aggressively for the insertion of human rights monitors, supporting the forces of peaceful democratic opposition in Iraq, as well as developing the "Milosevic-type" possibility of diplomatically driving Saddam and his top lieutenants into exile and bringing them to justice before an appropriate international tribunal. That strategy would have pursued disarmament and regime change not simply through coercion, but rather, through a transnational legal process solution, whereby the United States would have used the threat of UN-authorized force to demand that Saddam and his sons leave Iraq to face prosecution before either the International Criminal Court or an ad hoc tribunal. Although the Bush Administration ultimately offered this option on the eve of war, it was not a credible one, because the United States had rejected the International Criminal Court and had not invested enough in an alternative legal process solution to make coerced departure plus prosecution a realistic means of regime change.
>
> Such a strategy would have had obvious advantages: It would have avoided a bloody war, the financial and symbolic costs of that war, and the thousands of combatant and civilian deaths that war has entailed. More fundamentally, it would have secured Iraq's compliance with international law at no cost to the United States' own appearance of compliance. It would have strengthened the United States' capacity to return to the UN Security Council for the lifting of Iraqi sanctions, to secure the support of the United Nations in identifying and destroying any unconventional weapons still in Iraq, to secure a United Nations-supervised civilian reconstruction mission in Iraq, and to create an ad hoc criminal tribunal to prosecute apprehended Iraqi war criminals. But that strategy would have required genuine strategic multilateralism. It would have required the United States to work with other global democracies to fight global terrorism. Instead, the United States chose to ignore the very global partners who had helped it create the postwar system of international law and institutions precisely to provide nonmilitary multilateral options that did not exist during World War II.[142]

With respect, I believe that Koh is profoundly mistaken when he suggests there was a "meaningful third way" available to disarm Iraq and effect a regime change without the use of armed force. As Kenneth Pollack has convincingly pointed out, UN weapons inspectors during the 1990s – before they were kicked out of Iraq in 1998 – were largely unsuccessful in discovering Iraq's weapons of mass destruction (WMD), except when they were aided by Iraqi defectors, and consistently underestimated the extent of Iraqi WMD programs.[143] Nor was the Iraqi regime any more forthcoming or cooperative with respect to the UN inspectors after it was forced to readmit them in 2002 through the immediate threat of US force. It is also worth noting that the UN-imposed embargo during and after the Gulf War had been singularly ineffective in cutting off the flow of weapons and weapons-related goods into Iraq, because of widespread smuggling.

Koh's further suggestion that there be an "insertion of human rights monitors, supporting the forces of peaceful democratic opposition in Iraq" strikes me as exceedingly unrealistic. Human rights monitors would have prevented Saddam from employing the torture chambers and other horrendous violations of human rights that he had applied so adroitly to maintain himself and his regime in power for many years. No threat of force could have induced him to accept such an arrangement.

Lastly, Koh's invocation of a "Milosevic-type" possibility is inapposite. Lest we forget, Milosevic lost power in Serbia through an election on September 24, 2000, when he was defeated at the polls by the opposition candidate, Vojislav Kostunica. Much to Milosevic's shock and surprise, his successor in power had him arrested in April 2002 and turned him over to the prosecutorial authorities of the Yugoslav tribunal. By contrast, Saddam ran a Stalinist regime, with no pretense of free elections or a change of government as a result of free elections. There was every indication that only the use (not the threat) of force would remove him from power. Koh acknowledges that President Bush offered exile to Saddam and his sons as an alternative to the use of force against Iraq, but faults the President for not investing "enough in an alternative legal process solution to make coerced departure a realistic means of regime change." But the deal Bush offered Saddam was, from Saddam's perspective, more favorable than the deal proposed by Koh. He and his sons could leave with no condition attached that they submit to criminal prosecution. Criminal prosecution – whether before an international tribunal or a national court – is not an attractive prospect. It was not one that Milosevic welcomed or even expected.

It is noteworthy that neither Lord Goldsmith's statement nor the US letter to the president of the Security Council reporting the attack on Iraq make any attempt to justify the attack on Iraq as an exercise of individual or collective self-defense under Article 51 of the UN Charter. In a speech, however, the Legal Adviser of the US Department of State reportedly suggested that the president "may also, of course, always use force under international law in self-defense," without further elaboration.[144] Similarly, a staff member of the US National Security Council published a short paper contending that the United States has "clear authority" to use armed force against Iraq as an exercise of self-defense because "in the modern age in which terrorism and the proliferation of WMD pose grave risks to global security, states cannot be required to wait for an attack before they can lawfully use force to defend themselves against forces that present a clear and present danger of attack."[145]

These statements constitute part of an advocate's brief, because it is by no means clear or self-evident that the attack against Iraq can be justified as an act of self-defense. They reflect a doctrine of preemptive action against states and terrorist groups trying to develop weapons of mass destruction that the Bush administration has been promoting. According to the position paper on US national security strategy, issued by the White House in September 2002:

> We must adapt the concept of imminent threat to the capabilities and objectives of today's adversaries. Rogue states and terrorists do not seek to attack us using conventional means. They know such attacks would fail. Instead, they rely on acts of terror and, potentially, the use of weapons of mass destruction – weapons that can be easily concealed, delivered covertly, and used without warning.[146]

In pertinent part, Article 51 provides: "Nothing in the present Charter shall impair the inherent right of individual or collective self-defense if an armed attack occurs against a member of the United Nations." By its terms Article 51 seems to require the presence of an "armed attack" as a condition precedent for the use of force in individual or collective self-defense. There is no evidence that Iraq was part of an armed attack against the United States, that is, that it was involved in the September 11 attack. But many have argued, focusing on the term "inherent" in Article 51 and citing an ambiguous drafting history of that article, that Article 51 is a saving clause, preserving the right to self-defense under customary international law as it existed prior to the adoption of the UN Charter.[147] Assuming *arguendo* that Article 51 permits an exercise of anticipatory self-defense, the issue becomes whether Iraq or other so-called "rogue states" are likely, unlike the Soviet Union, to use weapons of mass destruction against the United States or alternatively to make them available to terrorist groups for their use against the United States. There is little evidence to support the likelihood of such action.

As applied to terrorist groups, however, the arguments in favor of the legality of the doctrine of preemptive action have greater cogency. There is substantial evidence that Al Qaeda, for example, has been making strenuous efforts to obtain or develop weapons of mass destruction. Moreover, as US Vice President Richard Cheney has reportedly said: "In terror, we have enemies with nothing to defend. A group like Al Qaeda cannot be deterred or placated or reasoned with. This struggle will not end in a treaty of accommodation with terrorists – it can only end in their complete and utter destruction."[148] Presumably, most armed attacks against terrorist groups will be taken only with the consent of the government of the country in which they are located. Absent such consent the legality of such attacks becomes much murkier.

One need not worry, of course, whether the use of force is compatible with UN Charter provisions and other norms of international law if one accepts Michael Glennon's thesis that the norms of the UN Charter, and indeed of international law in general, on the use of force are no longer operative. We turn to this issue in the next section of this chapter.

Are UN Charter rules on the use of force no longer operative?

The issue of the alleged demise of Article 2(4) and other international law norms on the use of force is not new. But the case in favor of the "death of Article 2(4)" was stronger in 1970, when Tom Franck first raised the issue,[149] and even then it was met with a strong challenge.[150] The 1970s was a decade when "the trend toward anarchy in the United Nations"[151] became especially intense, to the point where Daniel Patrick Moynihan, then US permanent representative at the United Nations, described the United Nations as a "dangerous place."[152] The situation in the United Nations, especially in the General Assembly, was so anarchic in large part because the Soviet Union and radical member states in the third world were strongly supporting "wars of national liberation" as an exception to the limitations of Article 2(4) on the use of force, with particular reference to Southern Africa and Israel. Franck also identified two other primary reasons for his then view that "[t]he prohibition against the use of force in relations between states has been eroded beyond recognition: [by] . . . 2, the rising threat of wars of total destruction; 3, the increasing authoritarianism of regional systems dominated by a super-Power."[153] This statement reflects the reality that the United States and the Soviet Union were extensively involved in fighting their so-called "surrogate wars." Under circumstances where two superpowers were of the view that their vital interests required sponsorship of the use of force by client states and occasionally their use of force in their areas of influence, the strain on the Charter paradigm was bound to be severe.

Even during the 1970s, however, there were counter-indications of support for Article 2(4). In particular, in 1970, the UN General Assembly adopted by consensus the Declaration on Principles of International Law Concerning Friendly Relations and Co-operation Among States (Friendly Relations Declaration).[154] Although there is some disagreement as to the precise legal status of the Declaration, it is generally regarded as an authoritative interpretation of broad principles of international law expressed in the Charter.[155] The first principle of the Declaration is that "States shall refrain in their international relations from the threat or use of force against the territorial integrity or political independence of any State, or in any other manner inconsistent with the purposes of the United Nations." The first paragraph developing this principle essentially restates Article 2(3) and (4) of the UN Charter, but addresses the rule to "Every State" rather than to "all Members." This reflects the perception that the rules of the Charter have become part of customary international law and are therefore binding on all states, even if they are not members of the United Nations. In further support of this perception, in 1987, the General Assembly adopted, again by consensus, the Declaration on the Enhancement of the Effectiveness of the Principle of Refraining from the Threat or Use of Force in International Relations.[156]

As we have already noted, beginning with the 1980s and accelerating in the 1990s and into the new millennium, the anarchic, confrontational atmosphere in the United Nations began to change. This led to a more harmonious atmosphere in the United Nations and a sharp decline in support of "wars of national liberation." To be sure, the continuing crisis between Israel and the Palestinians has stood in the way of elimination of support for armed conflict with the goal of "self-determination," but on the whole the atmosphere in the United Nations has improved immeasurably with respect to constraints on the use of armed force undertaken not in self-defense or with Security Council authorization.

As we have briefly seen previously, two of the major uses of force during the 1990s and 2000s were undertaken in accordance with the law of the Charter paradigm. The Gulf War against Iraq was authorized by the Security Council, and the coalition's use of force in Afghanistan was an exercise of collective self-defense. In contrast, Glennon notes that since 1945 and continuing until the present day there have been multiple violations of Article 2(4) and many, indeed most, have gone unredressed.[157] To Glennon, however, the coup de grace for Article 2(4), and indeed for all international law constraints on the use of force, was NATO's actions in Kosovo.[158]

As the earlier discussion in this chapter dictates, and as Glennon's analysis convincingly demonstrates,[159] there is a strong case to be made that NATO's use of force in Kosovo violated international law norms on the use of force. It does not follow, however, that this was the final blow sounding the death knell of these norms.

There is no question, of course, that there have been numerous violations of international law norms on the use of force, or that on the whole the United Nations, especially the Security Council, has not been able to fulfill its primary obligation under the UN Charter to maintain international peace and security.[160] As we have seen, the Security Council failed to perform this function with respect to Iraq. Nonetheless, writing before the collapse of the Soviet Union and other developments during the 1990s and 2000s, Oscar Schachter has reminded us:

> It is no wonder that the obligations of the Charter are widely seen as mere rhetoric, at best idealistic aspirations, or worse as providing a pretext, a cover for aggression. This evaluation, devastating as it may appear for international law, cannot be dismissed or minimized. But there is the other aspect of reality. Never before in history has there been so widespread and well-founded recognition of the costs and horrors of war. That awareness and its objective basis are powerful factors in strengthening the conscious self-interest in avoiding armed conflict.[161]

After September 11, the "well-founded recognition of the costs and horrors of war" identified by Schachter is stronger than ever. It is perhaps because of this recognition that no government, as compared with scholars, has ever contended that Article 2(4) and other Charter norms on the use of force are dead. On the contrary, in most cases where governments resort to the use of force, they attempt to defend their doing so in both legal and political terms. As we have seen, this was the case with NATO's actions in Kosovo.

The significance of states continuing to defend their actions under international law norms on the use of force has been highlighted by the International Court of Justice in the *Nicaragua* case:

> It is not to be expected that in the practice of States the application of the rules in question should have been perfect, in the sense that States should have refrained, with complete consistency, from the use of force... The Court does not consider that, for a rule to be established as customary, the corresponding practice must be in absolutely rigorous conformity with the rule. In order to deduce the existence of customary rules, the Court deems it sufficient that the conduct of States should, in general, be consistent with such rules, and that instances of State conduct inconsistent with a given rule should generally have been treated as breaches of that rule, not as indications of the recognition of a new rule. If a State acts in a way prima facie incompatible with a recognized rule, but defends its conduct by appealing to exceptions or justifications contained within the rule itself, then whether or not the State's conduct is in fact justifiable on that basis, the significance of that attitude is to confirm rather than to weaken the rule.[162]

There may be another, often overlooked, reason why governments are loath to proclaim the death of Article 2(4). Some, although not all, violations of Article 2(4) may amount to a war of aggression or a crime against peace under the Nuremberg definition. Article 6(a) of the London Charter of the International Military Tribunal[163] defined "crimes against peace" in pertinent part as the "planning, preparation, initiation or waging of a war of aggression, or a war in violation of international treaties, agreements, or assurances, or participation in a common plan or conspiracy for the accomplishment of any of the foregoing."[164] Moreover, although there have been no indictments for crimes against peace in the post-World War II era,[165] "[i]t is virtually irrefutable that present-day positive international law reflects the Judgment [of Nuremberg]. War of aggression currently constitutes a crime against peace. Not just a crime, but the supreme crime under international law."[166]

In my view Glennon's reliance on NATO's actions in Kosovo as final proof of the demise of international law's limitations on the use of force is misplaced. As Glennon himself notes, the United States has never released a formal legal justification of its actions in Kosovo.[167] The reason for this failure, however, is not that the United States believes that UN Charter rules on the use of force have fallen into "desuetude."[168] On the contrary, the United States knew that its case was weak under Charter norms and did not want NATO's actions in Kosovo to be viewed as a precedent. As suggested by the report of an independent international commission on Kosovo, co-chaired by Richard Goldstone and Carl Tham, "NATO and its supporters have wisely avoided staking out any doctrinal claims for its action either prior to or after the war. Rather than defining the Kosovo intervention as a precedent, most NATO supporters among international jurists presented the intervention as an unfortunate but necessary and reasonable exception."[169] As can be seen from my earlier discussion of Kosovo in this chapter, I would disagree with the commission's conclusion that the intervention was "necessary" or "reasonable." But I would strongly agree that Kosovo should not serve as a precedent, and am also of the view that it will not. Rather, it is likely that Kosovo will increasingly be viewed as an aberration that came about because of the extraordinary circumstances existing at the time. After September 11, as suggested by Charles Tiefer in a thoughtful review of Glennon's book,[170] there appears to be at least a temporary recognition on the part of the great powers of a common interest in cooperating to protect vital security interests. It is this unprecedented cooperation in dealing with a grave breach of the peace that should set the precedent.

Finally, there is the issue raised by Glennon of what happens when there is a collision between what states say and what they do.[171] Yoram Dinstein has effectively resolved this issue, in my view:

The discrepancy between what States say and what they do may be due to pragmatic reasons, militating in favour of a choice of the line of least exposure to censure. Even so, a disinclination to challenge the validity of a legal norm has a salutary effect in that it shows that the norm is accepted, if only reluctantly, as the rule. There is a common denominator between those who try (even disingenuously) to take advantage of the refinements of the law, and those who rigorously abide by its letter and spirit. They all share a belief in the authority of the law.[172]

The United Nations and the maintenance of international peace and security: the US role

As we have previously seen, the UN Charter envisages that the primary purpose of the United Nations is to maintain international peace and security, if necessary by the use of collective force against an aggressor. Under Article 24 of the Charter, "primary responsibility" for fulfilling this purpose is given to the Security Council and, with the Council, to the permanent members, since all five must consent, or at least acquiesce, in any decision on a non-procedural matter.[173] As a consequence, enforcement action under Chapter VII of the Charter cannot be taken against a permanent member or contrary to the wishes of a permanent member.

This special authority of the permanent members of the Security Council stands in sharp contrast to the first principle of the United Nations, which states that "[t]he Organization is based on the principle of the sovereign equality of all of its Members."[174] Glennon suggests that, "[i]n the veto, the Charter institutionalizes a form of self-dealing that is, indeed, antithetical to the very notion of the rule of law."[175] But there seems nothing incompatible with the concept of the rule of law in an institutional arrangement that gives some members more authority than others, especially under circumstances where, as in an enforcement action, some members are expected to bear a greater responsibility than other members in carrying out a primary responsibility of the institution. To use Ronald Dworkin's terminology, in the case of a non-procedural decision by the Security Council, the legal rule of the Charter giving permanent members of the Council a veto power "trumps" the otherwise applicable first principle of the Organization of the sovereign equality of member states.[176]

By 1947 it had become apparent that ideological differences had split the wartime allies into so-called East–West blocs and prevented the collective security system based on the unified action of the world's five leading powers from becoming operational. As a consequence, until Iraq invaded Kuwait, the Security Council made relatively little use of its authority under Chapter VII. Only in 1950, when North Korea invaded South Korea, did the Council take action to meet an act of aggression, and it was able to act in this case only because the Soviet delegate had previously walked out in protest at the Council's decision to seat the Nationalist Chinese as the lawful representative of China. Rather than taking a decision to use armed force pursuant to Articles 42 and 43 of the Charter, the Council merely issued in June 1950 a recommendation that members of the United Nations repel the armed attack by providing military or other assistance to a unified command under the United States, requested the United States to designate the commander of these forces, and authorized the unified command at its discretion to use the UN flag concurrently with the flags of the various participating countries.[177] On August 1, 1950, the Soviet delegate returned to the Council and blocked it from taking any further action.[178]

Thus stymied in its efforts to enforce the peace, the United Nations began to employ other methods to maintain international peace and security. The most important of these came to be known as "peacekeeping." As defined by a former Legal Counsel of the United Nations, peacekeeping operations are "actions involving the use of military personnel in international conflict situations on the basis of the consent of all parties concerned and without resorting to armed force except in cases of self-defence."[179] The term "peacekeeping" was first applied in a UN context to the UN Emergency Force (UNEF) established by the General Assembly during the 1956 Suez war to oversee the withdrawal of Anglo-French and Israeli forces from Egyptian territory. Interestingly, the word "peacekeeping" does not appear in the UN Charter, and the constitutional basis for it has been hotly debated.[180] The contrast between peacekeeping and collective security operations under Chapter VII is sharp. Peacekeeping operations were made up largely of units from smaller states rather than the forces of the permanent members and they operated with the consent of the member states concerned. Their function initially and to this day has been to discourage hostilities, not to restore or enforce peace.

This neat division between peacekeeping and peace enforcement, however, did not always work out well in practice. The most salient early example was the UN operation in the Congo in the early 1960s. There, amid great controversy, UN forces went way beyond the use of force in self-defense and, ultimately with the express sanction of the Security Council, brought to an end the armed resistance of the Katanga forces and put to an end the attempted secession of Katanga province.[181] The situation in the Congo involved internal rather than international armed conflict, although there were threatened and actual (in the case of Belgium) interventions on the part of outside states. During the 1990s and 2000s, internal armed conflicts have posed major challenges to the whole concept of peacekeeping and have raised in sharp relief the issue of the extent to which, if at all, UN forces should be authorized to use force for purposes other than self-defense.

In the aftermath of the Congo crisis, some commentators suggested that the UN operation there might serve as a model for the future.[182] It did not. As of the early 1980s the closest analogies to the UN operations in the Congo had been the UN peacekeeping forces in Cyprus and Lebanon. Although arguably UN forces performed well in these two situations under the most difficult of conditions,[183] in neither case was there any question of UN forces moving to defeat one party to a conflict as they did with respect to Katanga. Moreover, as previously noted, the 1960s and 1970s were a chaotic period in the United Nations when, with the explosive increase in UN membership of former colonial and dependent territories, and the concomitant influence of the Soviet Union and radical third world states, the United States lost its "automatic two-thirds majority" in the General Assembly that it had enjoyed in the 1950s. Ironically, in light of the US sponsorship of the Uniting for Peace resolution in 1950, it was the Soviet Union that invoked the resolution in the aftermath of the 1967 Arab–Israeli war when the Security Council failed to pass a resolution condemning Israel as the aggressor, and it was the United States that opposed the convocation of the Assembly. In the General Assembly it proved impossible for either side to the controversy to obtain the two-thirds majority required to adopt a resolution on the conflict.[184]

During the chaotic 1960s and 1970s and into the 1980s the United Nations was unable to carry out its responsibility for maintaining international peace and security with any degree of effectiveness. As the Cold War began to cool in the mid- and late 1980s, and the confrontational atmosphere in the United Nations to dissipate, new hope arose that the Organization might finally be able to fulfill its responsibility for the maintenance of international peace and security. This hope reached its apogee after the Gulf War and the talk of a "new world order." The Gulf War, however, involved a classic case of cross-border aggression by one state (Iraq) against another state (Kuwait), precisely the kind of conflict the United Nations was established to prevent or at least suppress. Most conflicts following the Gulf War have not been of the classic interstate variety. Rather, they have been internal conflicts, often in the form of civil wars. The authority of the United Nations to deal with these internal conflicts has been challenged, and from a pragmatic operational standpoint they have proven to be very difficult to resolve.

We have already taken a look at the difficulties surrounding US, British, and (initially) French use of force in Iraq to protect Kurdish and Shiite populations. These difficulties pale in comparison, however, with those associated with the dissolution of the former Yugoslavia in 1991. In the wake of "the shock waves of a collapsed Soviet Union that reverberated throughout Central and Eastern Europe,"[185] on June 25, 1991, Slovenia and Croatia declared their independence. On June 27, armed forces controlled by Serbia attacked the provisional Slovenian militia, and by July had initiated hostilities in Croatia. The response of the Security Council, on September 25, was the unanimous adoption of a resolution that expressed support for the collective efforts of the European Community and the Conference on Security and Cooperation in Europe to resolve the conflict.[186] By the same resolution the Council decided under Chapter VII of the Charter to impose an embargo on all deliveries of weapons and military equipment. There was no suggestion in the resolution that an international act of aggression had taken place. By early 1992, however, most of the former Yugoslavian republics had attained international recognition, thus turning what had begun as an internal conflict into an international conflict.

In January 1992 special UN envoys had managed to secure a cease-fire in Croatia.[187] The result, however, was to shift the locus of the fighting to the republic of Bosnia-Herzegovina, which contained a majority of Muslims in its population but with substantial Serbian and Croatian minorities. In 1992 those minorities were supplied with extensive military assistance for use against the Bosnian army. Serbia in particular was actively involved in providing the Bosnian Serbs with significant firepower. Perversely, the arms embargo imposed against the former Yugoslavia as a whole greatly undermined Bosnia's ability to obtain arms to defend itself.[188] In April 1992 Serb forces launched an attack against Bosnia-Herzegovina from Serbia and commenced the "ethnic cleansing" and other atrocities that ultimately caused the Security Council to create the International Criminal Tribunal for the former Yugoslavia to prosecute the persons responsible.

In February 1992 the Security Council had authorized the creation of a UN Protection Force (UNPROFOR).[189] Initially, it was envisioned that this force would be interposed, in classic peacekeeping fashion, between the Serbian and Croatian combatants that had been fighting in Croatia, as one step toward an overall settlement. UNPROFOR's mandate was later extended to Bosnia-Herzegovina. On December 11, 1992, the Security Council approved a deployment of 700 UN personnel to Macedonia, another former Yugoslavian republic – the first time UN peacekeepers had been deployed as an exercise of "preventive diplomacy."[190]

In March 1993 the United States, in coordination with the United Nations, began supplying food and medicine by air to Muslim enclaves in Bosnia-Herzegovina that could not be reached by land.[191] In April and May 1993, the Security Council established six of these enclaves as "safe areas" for Bosnian civilians. UNPROFOR was given a mandate to use force "to enable it to deter attacks against those areas, to occupy certain key points on the ground to this end, and to reply to bombardments against the safe areas."[192] This mandate envisaged a use of force that went far beyond that traditionally utilized by UN peacekeeping forces. To carry out this mandate, the Secretary-General estimated that UNPROFOR would need an additional 34,000 troops at a cost of $250 million for the first six months and $26 million per month thereafter.[193] But no such additional troops were forthcoming. As a result, UNPROFOR was simply incapable of protecting the so-called safe areas in Bosnia. This was most tragically demonstrated on July 11, 1995, when Bosnian Serb forces overran the UN-designated safe area of Srebrenica, captured 430 Dutch members of UNPROFOR, and massacred Muslim civilians in such numbers that it was "said to be the worst atrocity in Europe since World War II."[194]

In short, the so-called UN peacekeeping operation in Bosnia-Herzegovina was a disastrous failure. In Bosnia, there was no peace to keep, and UNPROFOR was never given the numerical strength or military firepower to impose itself on all or even any of the warring parties. Nor did the Security Council have the political will to induce NATO to introduce sufficient troops to enforce a peace. It was only after NATO finally decided to bomb heavily Bosnian Serb positions, coupled with the use of Croatian ground troops, that it became possible to enforce a peaceful settlement.[195] The peacekeeping force established to implement the peace agreement for Bosnia and Herzegovina negotiated in Dayton, Ohio, and signed on December 14, 1995, in Paris operates under NATO auspices. By resolution the Security Council authorized the NATO peacekeeping force to replace UN peacekeepers in Bosnia and to take "such enforcement action . . . as may be necessary to ensure implementation" of the peace agreements.[196] This new implementation force or IFOR, unlike the hapless UNPROFOR, had the wherewithal (in the form, e.g., of 60,000 troops) to serve as an enforcement force.

This pattern of a Security Council-approved ambitious mandate, coupled with a failure to provide the resources to enable the forces in the field to carry out their mandate, was also present in Somalia, with tragic results. John Hillen of the US Commission on National Security/21st Century has placed the UN problems in Bosnia and Somalia in historical and political context and detailed the US contribution to these problems. His observations are worth quoting at some length.

Advocates of collective security were almost giddy in the months immediately following the Gulf War. As David Henrickson noted, the end of the Cold War and the Security Council's role in the Gulf War "have produced an unprecedented situation in international society. They have persuaded many observers that we stand today at a critical juncture, one at which the promise of collective security, working through the mechanism of the United Nations, might at last be realized." Think tanks, conferences, workshops, and task force reports trumpeting a proactive military role for the UN proliferated. In January 1992, the first ever Security Council summit declared that "the world now has the best chance of achieving international peace and security since the foundation of the UN." The heads-of-state asked Secretary General Boutros-Ghali to prepare a report on steps the UN could take to fulfill their expectations of a more active military role.

In Boutros-Ghali's subsequent "An Agenda for Peace," he outlined a series of proposals that could take the UN well beyond its traditional military role of classic peacekeeping. The Secretary-General called not only for combat units constituted under the long moribund Article 43 of the UN Charter, but for "peace-enforcement" units "warranted as a provisional measure under Article 40 of the Charter." Although these were largely theoretical and untested ideas, by the time they were published in July 1992, the Security Council had already implemented a similar agenda. A few months prior to "An Agenda for Peace," large and ambitious missions to the former Yugoslavia and Cambodia were already approved and under way.

This initial episode reflected a pattern that would develop over the next several years. The UN, many times reluctantly so, would be thrust into an ambitious and dangerous series of missions and operations by a Security Council that was enthusiastic about new and enlarged mandates for UN peacekeepers – but not so keen on providing the support necessary to make them a success. In 1992, while the Security Council was (at the request of the world's most powerful leaders) preparing a draft report on possible departures in peacekeeping, a series of international crises plunged the organization into what UN official Shashi Tharoor called "a dizzying series of peacekeeping operations that bore little or no resemblance in size, complexity, and function to those that had borne the peacekeeping label in the past."

In the former Yugoslavia, it soon became painfully obvious that . . . the UN was in over its head. Among American leaders, it was fashionable in both political parties to bemoan the ineffectiveness of the UN peacekeepers. This America was as responsible for what the UN was attempting to do in the former Yugoslavia as any other state or the organization itself. Between September 1991 and January 1996, the Security Council passed 89 resolutions relating to the situation in the former Yugoslavia, of which the United States sponsored one-third. While Russia vetoed one resolution and joined China in abstaining on many others, the United States voted for all 89 to include those twenty resolutions that expanded the mandate or size of the UN peacekeeping mission in the Balkans.

Far from the notion that the UN was pulling the international community into Bosnia, the US-led Security Council was pushing a reluctant UN even further into a series of missions and mandates it could not hope to accomplish. Boutros-Ghali warned the members of the Security Council that "the steady accretion of mandates from the Security Council has transformed the nature of UNPROFOR's mission to Bosnia-Herzegovina and highlighted certain implicit contradictions . . . The proliferation of resolutions and mandates has complicated the role of the Force." His Under-Secretary-General for Peacekeeping, Kofi Annan, was more direct. Attempts to further expand the challenging series of missions being given to the UN were "building on sand."

This did not seem to deter the US-led Security Council, however, which was happy to expand the mission further while volunteering few additional resources to the force in Bosnia. A June 1993 episode demonstrating this pattern is instructive. Then, the UN field commander estimated he would need some 34,000 more peacekeepers to protect both humanitarian aid convoys and safe areas in Bosnia. The Security Council, having given him these missions in previous resolutions, instead approved a "light option" of 7,600 troops, of whom only 5,000 had deployed to Bosnia some nine months later. Quitting his post in disgust, the Belgian general in command remarked,"I don't read the Security Council resolutions anymore because they don't help me."

The Clinton administration, which had shown unbounded enthusiasm for UN peacekeeping in the first months of the administration, began to sour slightly on its utility by September 1993. By then Ambassador Madeleine Albright's doctrine of "assertive multilateralism" had given way to President Clinton beseeching the UN General Assembly to know "when to say no." But it was the United States and its allies on the Security Council who kept saying yes for the United Nations. Even after that speech, Mrs. Albright voted for all five subsequent resolutions (and sponsored two) that again expanded the size or mandate of the UN peacekeeping mission to the former Yugoslavia. All the while, until the fall of 1995, the US steadfastly resisted participating in the UN mission or intervening itself with military forces through some other forum.

In Somalia, there was an even more direct pattern. There the United States pushed an unwilling UN into a hugely ambitious nation-building mission. In its waning days the Bush administration had put together a US-led coalition that intervened to ameliorate the man-made famine in Somalia. From the very beginning of the mission it had been the intention of the US to turn the operation over to a UN peacekeeping force. Conversely, Boutros-Ghali, an Egyptian well acquainted with the challenge of nation-building in Somalia, noted that in a meeting with the Secretary-General and his assistants on 1 December 1992, "the top UN officials rejected the idea that the US initiative should eventually become a UN peacekeeping operation."

The US kept up the pressure on the Secretary-General, who was powerless to resist the idea if it gained momentum in the Security Council. The debate resembled what Chester Crocker called "bargaining in a bazaar" and "raged out of public view" while the US and the UN negotiated over the follow-on mission. For his part, Boutros-Ghali wanted the US-led coalition to accomplish a series of ambitious tasks before the UN would take over. These included the establishment of a reliable cease-fire, the control of all heavy weapons, the disarming of lawless factions, and the establishment of a new Somali police force. For its part, the

United States just wanted to leave Somalia as soon as possible. It was now time to put assertive multilateralism to the test. Madeleine Albright shrugged off the challenge to the world body and wrote that the difficulties that the UN was bound to encounter in Somalia were "symptomatic of the complexity of mounting international nation-building operations that included a military component."

The debate, with Boutros-Ghali resisting up to the last, effectively ended on 26 March 1993 with the passage of Security Council resolution 814 establishing a new UN operation in Somalia. The resolution authorized, for the first time, Chapter VII enforcement authority for a UN-managed force. More importantly, the resolution greatly expanded the mandate of the UN to well beyond what the American force had accomplished. Former Ambassador T. Frank Crigler called the UN mandate a "bolder and broader operation intended to tackle underlying social, political, and economic problems and to put Somalia back on its feet as a nation." In the meantime, the US withdrew its heavily armed 25,000 troop force and turned the baton over to a lightly armed and still arriving UN force. The transition, set for early May 1993, was so rushed that on the day the UN took command its staff was at only 30 percent of its intended strength. The undermanned and under-equipped UN force was left holding a bag not even of its own making.

The travails of the UN mission in Somalia need no further elucidation here. Suffice it to say that the US, although no longer a direct player in Somalia, continued to lead the Security Council in piling new mandates on the UN mission there. The most consequential of these was the mandate to apprehend those Somali's [sic] responsible for the June 1993 killing of 24 Pakistani peacekeepers. The US further complicated this explosive new mission with an aggressive campaign of disarmament capped by the deployment of a special operations task force that was to lead the manhunt for Mohammed Farah Aideed. This task force was not under UN command in any way and when it became engaged in the tragic Mogadishu street battle of 3 October 1993 the UN commanders knew nothing of it until the shooting started. Even MG Thomas Montgomery, the American commander and deputy UN commander, was told of the operation only forty minutes before its launch. A US Military report afterward noted that the principal command problems of the UN mission in Somalia were "imposed on the US by itself."

This fact, that the UN was not involved in the deaths of eighteen American soldiers in Mogadishu, was buried by the administration. Even more cynically, several top-level administration officials charged in 1995 with selling the Dayton Peace Accords to a skeptical US public constantly noted that US soldiers in the NATO mission to Bosnia would not be in danger because the UN would not be in command, as it was in Somalia. Few single events have been as damaging to the UN's reputation with the Congress and American public as the continued perception that it was the United Nations that was responsible for the disaster in Somalia. Not only has this myth been left to fester, it was indirectly used, along with the UN's many other US initiated problems, to call for Boutros Boutros-Ghali's head during the 1996 presidential campaign. Then, for the first time in several years, the US used its veto to stand alone against the Security Council and bring down the Secretary-General who had resisted the US-led events that so discredited him and his organization.[197]

Sadly, the situation described by Hillen continued and arguably became even less satisfactory. The Secretary-General still has a great need for troops but is not even allowed to start collecting a peacekeeping force until the Security Council provides its mandate. In the absence of Article 43 agreements, in theory several countries have troops on standby for emergencies. But in reality, when they are called upon, they are almost always unavailable One result of this ad hoc approach to peacekeeping may be seen in Sierra Leone, where an undermanned, undertrained, under-equipped, and ill-led UN force proved disastrously unequal to the task assigned to it. The UN force, known as UNAMSIL, was dispatched to Sierra Leone late in 1999 to enforce a ten-months-old peace accord between the recently elected government and the Revolutionary United Front, which had gained international notoriety by hacking off the hands of men, women, and children across the countryside. This force proved so inept that about 500 of them wandered into the bush with outdated maps, got lost, and then were captured by the very guerrillas they were sent to disarm. The rebels also made off with armored personnel carriers and other military gear. The fundamental problem with the Sierra Leonean operation was identified by one commentator as "the product of wishful thinking on the part of Western countries, which have the world's best financed, armed and trained armies, but thought they could dispatch their commitment to peace in Africa by hiring underprepared third world soldiers and putting them in blue helmets."[198] Ultimately, the situation in Sierra Leone was stabilized by the intervention of British forces on the side of the elected government and the establishment of a 17,000-strong force, the largest ever UN peacekeeping force.[199]

All of this is a far cry from traditional UN peacekeeping, which requires the consent of the parties to the conflict, a position of neutrality by the United Nations, and the use of force only in self-defense. Moreover, the unwillingness of the United States and other permanent members of the Security Council to provide the personnel and resources to enforce the peace sharply deviates from the paradigm established by Chapter VII of the UN Charter. The collective security system envisaged by the drafters of Chapter VII calls for the permanent members of the Security Council to provide the forces and equipment necessary to enforce the peace. But the drafters of the Charter never envisaged a conflict as horrendous as, for example, the civil war in the Democratic Republic of the Congo, which may have cost as many as three million lives and has involved nine national armies and a shifting throng of rebel groups pillaging the country.[200]

In light of the unwillingness of the military powers to contribute their forces to UN peace-enforcement efforts, it has been suggested that it would be better to enlist regional groups to enforce the peace because they are more likely to have a national interest in ending the fighting.[201] Chapter VIII of the UN Charter envisages such a possible role for regional agencies or arrangements. Although Chapter VII imposes primary responsibility for maintaining international peace and security on the Security Council, Article 52 in Chapter VIII expressly recognizes the right of member states to establish regional agencies or arrangements for dealing with matters relating to the maintenance of international peace and security, subject to the limitations that the matters dealt with must be "appropriate for regional action," and that the arrangements and agencies and their activities must be "consistent with the Purposes and Principles of the United Nations." Moreover, under Article 53(1), with the exception of measures against the enemy states of World War II, "no enforcement action shall be taken under regional arrangements or by regional agencies without the authorization of the Security Council."

At first blush, regional peace enforcement appears attractive but it, too, poses major problems. To begin with, it is clear that regional peacekeeping is no panacea. NATO forces in Bosnia and Kosovo have faced many difficulties. Moreover, as noted by *The Economist*, "few regions, Europe apart, have either the men or the money to mount such an operation."[202] The regional agencies outside Europe have other problems as well. In Latin America, since the Organization of American States has no military force structure, any peace enforcement would basically be by US troops, as it was in Haiti. This is a prospect that many states in Latin America, as well as elsewhere, would not welcome. Similarly, in the states that formerly constituted the Soviet Union, Russia is likely to be the primary if not the sole enforcer of the peace – also a prospect that many states would not welcome. In the Middle East there is no obvious candidate, or candidates, for the job. The same is true in Asia. Finally, in Africa, the newly established African Union (the successor to the Organization of African Unity) would be the natural choice, and its Constitutive Act gives the new organization the authority to play a peacekeeping and peace-enforcing role,[203] but many of its member states fought each other in the Congo. In Sierra Leone an intervention by Nigerian troops was conducted in brutal fashion and resulted in a near defeat for Nigeria. Also, UN efforts in Sierra Leone have in significant part been stymied by outside support of the Revolutionary United Front by Liberia.[204]

Because so many of the potential regional actors who would intervene in internal conflicts might do so to pursue their own individual agendas, the Security Council, when authorizing a regional enforcement action under Article 53, would have to maintain close supervisory control over the actions of the regional actor. As a practical matter, this would likely prove a difficult task because of opposition by these strong regional actors to interference with their operations. But failure to exercise such supervision would amount to an abdication by the Security Council of its "primary responsibility for the maintenance of international peace and security."

At this writing it is unclear what the Bush administration's position on institutional arrangements to maintain international peace and security is. At least one prominent player in the administration's foreign policy elite, John Bolton, US Under Secretary of State for Arms Control and International Security, commented favorably on traditional peacekeeping by the United Nations when he was still in the private sector.[205] At the same time, however, he made quite clear his opposition to any UN peacekeeping operation that went beyond the traditional model, even commenting unfavorably on the UN peacekeeping force in the Western Sahara on the ground that it is "a classic case where we really do not have the consent of the parties."[206] Bolton also expressed his opposition to peacekeeping operations involving internal or "intra-national" conflicts, on the ground that these do not pose a "real threat" to international peace and security and therefore are beyond the jurisdiction of the United Nations.[207]

There is no doubt that the Bush administration is adamantly opposed to US soldiers participating in UN peacekeeping operations. Moreover, the United States recently demonstrated its willingness to scuttle both UN peacekeeping operations and NATO operations in Bosnia and Kosovo unless the Security Council agreed to exempt peacekeepers from the jurisdiction of the International Criminal Court (ICC), which came into existence on July 1, 2002, and which, as we shall see in chapter 8 of this study, the United States vehemently opposes. In the event an uneasy compromise was reached. On July 12, 2002, the Security Council, acting under Chapter VII of the Charter, adopted a resolution that requested the ICC not to bring a case against any personnel in a UN peacekeeping operation from a state not party to the Court's Statute for a 12-month period beginning July 1.[208] The resolution also expresses the Council's intention to renew this request each July 1 for further twelve-month periods for as long as they may be necessary. According to a newspaper report, Herta Daubler-Gmelin, the German Justice Minister, in commenting on this resolution, said: "Special rules for strong countries, particularly when the issue at stake is the global pursuit of the worst human rights violations, are inappropriate and not compatible with the principles of the rule of law."[209] It is compatible with the US view that it is the exceptional, indeed "indispensable," nation entitled to the benefit of special rules.

The United States has also been resistant to proposals that it get involved in postwar efforts at "nation building," or "peace building" to use the terminology of the Report of the Panel on United Nations Peace Operations, or the "Brahimi Report," named for its chairman, Lakhdar Brahimi.[210] According to the Brahimi Report, peace building "defines activities undertaken on the far side of conflict to reassemble the foundations of peace and provide the tools for building on those foundations something that is more than just the absence of war." So defined, peace building can include such activities as "reintegrating former combatants into civilian society; strengthening the rule of law (for example, through training and restructuring of local police, and judicial and penal reform); improving respect for human rights through the monitoring, education and investigation of past and existing abuses; providing technical assistance for democratic development (including electoral assistance and support for free media); and promoting conflict resolution and reconciliation techniques."[211] Despite the Bush administration's opposition to nation building, it has been forced to become involved in it in Afghanistan and Iraq. The stakes are simply too high in both countries to allow them to disintegrate into chaos and instability.

One may safely conclude that the current US administration is no fan of the collective security approach enshrined in the UN Charter. As Oscar Schachter has noted, the concept of collective security emphasizes "the obligations of all States to take action, including armed force, against any State guilty of aggression. The underlying image is that of an indivisible peace which all States have an interest in maintaining, an interest sufficient to entail sacrifices necessary to its defense."[212] In contrast, John Bolton would define the US interest in the threat or use of force much more narrowly. Under the Bolton approach the threat or use of US armed force would apparently be limited to situations where the United States itself had suffered an armed attack (Afghanistan after September 11), or where a state allied with or important to the United States (Kuwait) had suffered an armed attack, or where a state arguably threatened a massive attack on the United States, either directly or through the use of terrorists (Iraq) – in other words where the threat or use of force could at least arguably be justified as an exercise of individual or collective self-defense. He definitely does not believe that the United States should serve as "the World's Platonic guardians."[213] As noted previously, Bolton also believes that internal as compared with international armed conflicts are generally outside the jurisdiction of the United Nations because they fail to constitute a threat to international peace and security, at least in the absence of actual armed intervention by other states. In the same vein, Bolton suggests, "[s]ome longstanding tribal, ethnic, and religious struggles are simply not susceptible to external political fixes, and it is not only feckless but politically dangerous to pretend otherwise."[214]

Perhaps. But a number of these long-standing tribal, ethnic, and religious struggles have resulted in the deaths of thousands, indeed millions of people and constitute, by any measure, a threat to international peace and security. Moreover, at this writing, the United Nations is involved in several places in peacekeeping operations that are authorized, if necessary, to use force that far exceeds the pure self-defense model of traditional peacekeeping, as well as in nation or peace building.[215]

To be sure, all of these operations face enormous challenges and one or more may turn out badly. But it is at least debatable whether it would have been better not to set them up in the first place. Moreover, the chances of their being successful will be improved to the extent that they are conducted with the recommendations of the Brahimi Report, most of which have been adopted by the Security Council,[216] in mind. In particular, the Security Council should keep in mind the Report's admonition that "mandates should specify an operation's authority to use force. It means bigger forces, better equipped and more costly, but able to pose a credible deterrent threat, in contrast to the symbolic and non-threatening presence that characterizes traditional peacekeeping . . . The Security Council and the Secretariat also must be able to win the confidence of troop contributors that the strategy and concept of operations for a new mission are sound and that they will be sending troops or police to serve under a competent mission with effective leadership."[217] For its part the Bush administration may wish to reflect on the Brahimi Report's observation that "[h]istory has taught that peacekeepers and peacebuilders are inseparable partners in complex operations: while the peacebuilders may not be able to function without the peacekeepers' support, the peacekeepers have no exit without the peacebuilders' work."[218]

The Brahimi Report "recognizes that the United Nations does not wage war. Where enforcement action is required, it has consistently been entrusted to coalitions of willing States, with the authorization of the Security Council, acting under Chapter VII of the Charter."[219] Whether this arrangement is the most desirable, or whether an effort should eventually be made to try again to conclude Article 43 agreements according to the Charter paradigm, is debatable. Oscar Schachter has suggested:

> It might be considered desirable, in view of the constitutional controls that many countries have in regard to the use of troops abroad or in waging war, to seek to revive Article 43 so that armed forces could be provided promptly when the Security Council requests or requires such action. Such agreement would require approval by constitutional processes of the respective States as the Charter notes. It should be expected that the agreements would contain limitations considered necessary by the governments. The limitations would be especially important for all the States that lack the veto since they might be subject to UN mandatory

decisions requiring armed forces under the terms of the special agreements whether or not they agreed. The five permanent members, protected by the veto, should have less reason to fear military action imposed on them. However, some of them, notably the United States, would face the historic problems of executive versus legislative authority. This would complicate reaching an agreement that might render a legislative decision unnecessary. It would be excessively optimistic to expect that such special agreements could be negotiated in the near future but the hoped-for strengthening of collective security through the United Nations may in time make it politically feasible to seek such agreements.[220]

Notes

1. See J. F. Murphy, *Force and Arms*, *in* 1 UNITED NATIONS LEGAL ORDER 247 (Oscar Schachter & Christopher C. Joyner eds., 1995).
2. *Id.* See also J. F. MURPHY, THE UNITED NATIONS AND THE CONTROL of INTERNATIONAL VIOLENCE (1982).
3. For further support of this proposition, see Murphy, *supra* note 1.
4. For discussion of the authority of the Security Council to authorize the use of force by member states, see *id.* at 277–82.
5. Art. 2(3) of the UN Charter requires that "All Members shall settle their international disputes by peaceful means in such a manner that international peace and security, and justice, are not endangered." Under Art. 33(1) of the Charter the "peaceful means" that should be employed are given more specificity: "The parties to any dispute, the continuance of which is likely to endanger the maintenance of international peace and security, shall, first of all, seek a solution by negotiation, enquiry, mediation, conciliation, arbitration, judicial settlement, resort to regional agencies or arrangements, or other peaceful means of their own choice." The obligation is to settle such disputes peaceably. The choice of means is up to the parties. Art. 37(1) of the Charter further obligates parties to such a dispute, if they fail to settle the matter by the means specified, to refer it to the Security Council.
6. O. Schachter, *The Right of States to Use Armed Force*, 82 MICH. L. REV. 1620, 1632 (1984).
7. For the classical study of the drafting of the UN Charter, see R. B. RUSSELL & J. E. MURTHER, THE HISTORY OF THE UNITED NATIONS CHARTER (1958).
8. L. Henkin, *Use of Force: Law and US Policy*, *in* LOUIS HENKIN ET AL., RIGHT V. MIGHT 37, 52–53 (1989).
9. *Id.* at 53–54.
10. For example, for a debate over the US invasion of Grenada, compare J. N. Moore, *Grenada and the International Double Standard*, 78 AM. J. INT'L L. 145 (1984) (supporting the US action) with C. Joyner, *Reflections on the Lawfulness of Invasion*, 78 AM. J. INT'L L. 131 (1984) (contra). Although Libya denied responsibility for the 1986 bombing of a West German discotheque, and there were rumors that Syria was responsible, on November 13, 2001, four people, including one Libyan diplomat and a Libyan embassy worker, were convicted of the bombing by the Berlin chamber court after the United States permitted decoded interception transcripts to be made public and prosecutors had argued that Libya was responsible for "state-sponsored terrorism." S. Erlanger, *Four Guilty in Fatal 1986 Berlin Disco Bombing Linked to Libya*, NY TIMES, Nov. 14, 2001, at A7. For its part the International Court of Justice's decision in the Nicaragua case, Military and Paramilitary Activities In and Against Nicaragua (Nicaragua v. US)

1986 ICJ 14 (Judgment of June 27), has given rise to especially heated debate, for and against. See, e.g., Harold C. Maier, *Appraisals of the ICJ's Decision: Nicaragua v. United States*, 81 AM. J. INT'L L. 77 (1987).

11. Introductory chapter, *supra* at 2.
12. O. SCHACHTER, INTERNATIONAL LAW IN THEORY AND PRACTICE 107 (1991).
13. Case Concerning Military and Paramilitary Activities In and Against Nicaragua (Nicaragua v. United States) 1984 ICJ 392 (Jurisdiction).
14. See *supra* note 10.
15. Art. 39 provides: "The Security Council shall determine the existence of any threat to the peace, breach of the peace, or act of aggression and shall make recommendations, or decide what measures shall be taken in accordance with Articles 41 and 42, to maintain or restore international peace and security."
16. SCHACHTER, *supra* note 12.
17. See Art. 27 of the UN Charter.
18. UN SCOR, 41st Sess., 2682d mtg. at 43, UN Doc. S/PV.2682 (1986).
19. In pertinent part, Art. 18 of the UN Charter provides: "1. Each member of the General Assembly shall have one vote. 2. Decisions of the General Assembly on important questions shall be made by a two-thirds majority of the members present and voting. These questions shall include: recommendations with respect to the maintenance of international peace and security."
20. GA Res. 41/38 (1986).
21. Michael Reisman has noted the international reaction to the 1986 US bombing of Libya changed over time: "In this incident, as in others, an elongation of the time horizon yields a different picture of international responses. After the immediate reaction to the raid and the regional and national condemnations, Western European nations began to adopt economic and diplomatic sanctions against Libya." W. M. Reisman, *International Legal Responses to Terrorism*, 22 HOUS. J. INT'L L. 3, 34 (1999).
22. GA Res. 38/7 (Nov. 2, 1983).
23. L. F. DAMROSCH ET AL., INTERNATIONAL LAW 966–67 (4th ed., 2001).
24. Report on the Development Concerning the Deployment of United States Forces to Panama, House Doc. 101–127, 101st Cong., 2d Sess. (1990).
25. A. D. Sofaer, *The Legality of the United States Action in Panama*, 29 COLUM. J. TRANSNAT'L L. 281 (1991).
26. L. Henkin, *The Invasion of Panama Under International Law: A Gross Violation*, 29 COLUM. J. TRANSNAT'L L. 293 (1991); *Report, the Use of Armed Force in International Affairs: The Case of Panama*, 47 REC. ASSOC. B. CITY NY 604 (1992). For a debate setting forth both sides of the issue, see *Agora: US Forces in Panama: Defenders, Aggressors or Human Rights Activists?*, 84 AM. J. INT'L L. 494 (1990).
27. See Ved P. Nanda, *The Validity of the United States Intervention in Panama Under International Law*, 84 AM. J. INT'L L. 494, 500, n. 34 (1990).
28. SC Res. 660 (Aug. 2, 1990), repr. in 29 INT'L LEG. MATERIALS 1325 (1990).
29. SC Res. 661 (Aug. 6, 1990), repr. in *id.* In adopting this resolution, the Council did not refer to any specific article in Chapter VII as the basis for its action, although Art. 41 would appear to be the article most on point. With one exception, the Council continued this practice in the series of later resolutions it adopted on the Gulf crisis. See Murphy, *supra* note 1, at 283.
30. SC Res. 662 (Aug. 9, 1990), repr. in 29 INT'L LEG. MATERIALS 1327 (1990).
31. Resolution 660 was adopted by a vote of 14-0, with Yemen abstaining. Resolution 661 was adopted by a vote of 13-0, with Cuba and Yemen abstaining. Resolution 662 was adopted unanimously.

32. For further discussion see Murphy, *supra* note 1, at 284–85.
33. SC Res. 665 (Aug. 25, 1990), para. 1.
34. SC Res. 670 (Sept. 25, 1990), reprinted in 29 INT'L LEG. MATERIALS 1334 (Sept. 25, 1990).
35. Reportedly, "[b]y the end of November 1990 . . . the US had more than 250,000 military personnel in the region, part of a planned deployment of 400,000 troops by mid-January. Other states, including Egypt, Saudi Arabia, Britain, France, Argentina and Canada, had reportedly deployed between 200,000 and 250,000 troops." DAMROSCH ET AL., *supra* note 23, at 1014.
36. SC Res. 678 (Nov. 29, 1990), repr. in 29 INT'L LEG. MATERIALS 1565 (1990).
37. See Murphy, *supra* note 1, at 286–87.
38. Advisory Opinion of the Continued Presence of South Africa in Namibia (South West Africa), 1971 ICJ 16.
39. See, e.g., J. Quigley, *The United States and the United Nations in the Persian Gulf War: New Order or Disorder?*, 25 CORNELL INT'L LJ 1 (1992); B. Weston, *Security Council Resolution 678 and Persian Gulf Decision Making: Precarious Legitimacy*, 85 AM J. INT'L L. 516 (1991).
40. As Oscar Schachter has noted, Resolution 678 could be regarded either as an authorization of collective self-defense under Art. 51 or UN action under Art. 42. In his view, however, it is more accurate to classify the Security Council's action as an endorsement of collective self-defense than as a UN enforcement action, since the Council did not establish a UN command or call upon the Military Staff Committee for assistance and advice. O. Schachter, *United Nations Law in the Gulf Conflict*, 85 AM. J. INT'L L. 452, 458 (1991).
41. See operative para. 1 of SC Res. 687 (April 3, 1991), repr. in 30 INT'L LEG. MATERIALS 847 (1991).
42. See SC Res. 686 (March 2, 1991), reprinted in 30 INT'L LEG. MATERIALS 567 (1991), which, *inter alia*, takes note of letters from Iraq's Foreign Minister confirming Iraq's agreement to comply fully with all previous Council resolutions.
43. SC Res. 688 (April 5, 1991), reprinted in 30 INT'L LEG. MATERIALS 858 (1991).
44. See S. MURPHY, HUMANITARIAN INTERVENTION: THE UNITED NATIONS IN AN EVOLVING WORD ORDER 1887–90 (1996). For general consideration of the debate over Resolution 688, see also J. Stromseth, *Iraq's Repression of its Civilian Population: Collective Responses and Continuing Challenges*, *in* ENFORCING RESTRAINT: COLLECTIVE INTERVENTION IN INTERNAL CONFLICTS 77, 85 (L. Damrosch ed., 1993).
45. MURPHY, *supra* note 44, at 1021.
46. *Id.* at 194.
47. *Id.*
48. C. Gray, *From Unity to Polarisation: International Law and the Use of Force Against Iraq*, 13 EUR. J. INT'L L. 1, 11–12 (2002).
49. See J. Lobel & S. Ratner, *Bypassing the Security Council: Ambiguous Authorizations to Use Force, Cease-Fires and the Iraqi Inspection Regime*, 93 AM. J. INT'L L. 124 (1999).
50. Gray, *supra* note 48, at 12–13.
51. This section of the chapter draws heavily from my own contribution to the debate, J. Murphy, *Kosovo Agonistes*, *in* TRILATERAL PERSPECTIVES ON INTERNATIONAL LEGAL ISSUES 185 (C. Carmody, Y. Iwasawa & S. A. Rhodes, eds., 2002). For some other noteworthy writings, see M. Mandelbaum, *A Perfect Failure: NATO's War Against Yugoslavia*, 78 FOREIGN AFF. 2 (Sept.–Oct. 1999); J. B. Steinberg, *A Perfect Polemic: Blind to Reality on Kosovo*, 78 FOREIGN AFF. 128 (Nov.–Dec. 1999); J. Solana, *NATO's Success in Kosovo*, 78 FOREIGN AFF. 114 (Nov.–Dec. 1999); I. H. Daalder & M. O'Hanlon,

Unlearning the Lessons of Kosovo, 78 FOREIGN POL. 128 (Fall 1999); M. Weller, *The Rambouillet Conference on Kosovo*, 75 INT'L AFF. 211 (1999); L. Henkin, *Kosovo and the Law of "Humanitarian Intervention,"* 93 AM. J. INT'L L. 824 (1999); R. Wedgwood, *NATO's Campaign in Yugoslavia*, 93 AM. J. INT'L L. 828 (1999); C. Chinkin, *Kosovo: A "Good" or "Bad" War?*, 93 AM. J. INT'L L. 841 (1999); R. Falk, *Kosovo, World Order, and the Future of International Law*, 93 AM. J. INT'L L. 847 (1999); T. Franck, *Lessons of Kosovo*, 93 AM. J. INT'L L. 857 (1999); W. M. Reisman, *Kosovo's Antinomies*, 93 AM. J. INT'L L. 860 (1999); B. Simma, *NATO, the UN and the Use of Force: Legal Aspects*, 10 EUR. J. INT'L L. 1 (1999); Antonio Cassese, *Ex Iniuria Ius Oritur: Are We Moving Towards International Legitimation of Forcible Humanitarian Countermeasures in the World Community?*, 10 EUR. J. INT'L L. 23 (1999); J. Charney, *Anticipatory Humanitarian Intervention in Kosovo*, 32 VAND. J. TRANSNAT'L L. 1231 (1999); R. Bilder, *Kosovo and the "New Interventionism": Promise or Peril?*, 9 J. TRANSNAT'L L. & POL. 153 (1999); M. Glennon, *The New Interventionism: The Search for a Just International Law*, 78 FOREIGN AFF. 2 (May–June 1999); M. GLENNON, LIMITS OF LAW, PREROGATIVES OF POWER: INTERVENTIONISM AFTER KOSOVO (2001); *Kosovo: House of Commons Foreign Affairs Committee 4th Report, June 2000: Memoranda*, 49 INT'L & COMP. LQ 876 (2000).

52. See J. Murphy, *Some Legal (and a Few Ethical) Dimensions of the Collateral Damage Resulting from NATO's Kosovo Campaign*, 31 ISRAEL Y.B. HUM. RTS. 51 (2001). See also Bilder, *supra* note 51, at 167.
53. Contrast, for example, Mandelbaum, *supra* note 51, at 4, with Steinberg, *supra* note 51, at 130.
54. See Bilder, *supra* note 51, at 179.
55. *Id.* at 179–80. To be sure James Steinberg has contended that "[t]he plan the allies presented there [at the Rambouillet talks] did not call for a 'referendum after three years to decide Kosovo's ultimate status.' Instead it offered an international meeting that would determine a mechanism for defining Kosovo's future, which would take into account the will of the people concerned, the opinions of relevant authorities, the degree of compliance by the parties, and the Helsinki Final Act." See Steinberg, *supra* note 51, at 130. Nonetheless, a disinterested reading of the negotiations at Rambouillet would seem to support the conclusion that the Kosovars fully expected this international meeting to result in their independence.
56. Bilder, *supra* note 51, at 180.
57. For discussion, see Charney, *supra* note 51, at 1233.
58. Solana, *supra* note 51, at 117.
59. See SCHACHTER, *supra* note 12, at 111.
60. See e.g., Murphy, *supra* note 1, at 253–70.
61. There is no question, however, that a heavy refugee flow may be a motivating factor in armed intervention. As noted by Paul Szasz: "during the 1971 East Pakistan war of independence, which resulted in the creation of Bangladesh, so many Bengalis took refuge in India that the intervention of that country became almost inevitable." P. Szasz, *Role of the United Nations in Internal Conflicts*, 13 GA. J. INT'L & COMP. L. 345, 348 (1983).
62. For more extensive discussion, see Murphy, *supra* note 1, at 270–300.
63. Wedgwood, *supra* note 51, at 829.
64. The resolutions adopted by the Council prior to the bombing include SC Res. 1160, UN SCOR, 53d Sess., UN Doc. S/RES/1160 (1998); SC Res. 1199, UN SCOR, 53d Sess., UN Doc. S/RES/1199(1998); SC Res. 1203, UN SCOR, 53d Sess., UN Doc. S/Res/1203 (1998). Although these resolutions determined that the situation in Kosovo constituted a threat to international peace and security, imposed an arms

embargo on Yugoslavia, authorized the Organization for Security and Cooperation in Europe to place an observer force in Kosovo, called upon Yugoslavia, the Kosovo Liberation Army, and all other states and organizations to stop using force, and called for a halt to violations of human rights, they did not authorize the use of force by any outside entity. On the contrary, the preamble of Resolution 1199 reaffirmed the sovereignty and territory integrity of the Federal Republic of Yugoslavia. See Charney, *supra* note 51, at 1233.

65. See, e.g., Wedgwood, *supra* note 51, at 830.
66. See Belarus, India, and Russian Federation: Draft Resolution, UN Doc. S/1999/328 (Mar. 26, 1999), reprinted in *Security Council Rejects Demand for Cessation of Use of Force Against Federal Republic of Yugoslavia*, UN Press Release SC/6659 (Mar. 26, 1999).
67. GLENNON, LIMITS OF LAW, *supra* note 51, at 31.
68. Wedgwood, *supra* note 51, at 830.
69. Military and Paramilitary Activities (Nicaragua v. United States), 1986 ICJ 14 (Judgment on Merits).
70. Charney, *supra* note 51, at 1239–40.
71. Art. 27(3) of the UN Charter provides, in pertinent part, that "[d]ecisions of the Security Council on all other matters [other than procedural matters] shall be made by an affirmative vote of nine members including the concurring votes of the permanent members."
72. Wedgwood, *supra* note 51, at 830.
73. SC Res. 1244, UN SCOR, 54th Sess., UN Doc. S/RES/1244 (1999).
74. Charney, *supra* note 51, at 1233.
75. Franck, *supra* note 51, at 859.
76. For arguments in favor of a doctrine of humanitarian intervention published during the 1970s see, e.g., R. Lillich, *Humanitarian Intervention: A Reply to Ian Brownlie and a Plea for Constructive Alternatives*, *in* LAWS AND CIVIL WAR IN THE MODERN WORLD 229 (J. N. Moore ed., 1974); M. Reisman, *Humanitarian Intervention to Protect the Ibos*, in HUMANITARIAN INTERVENTION App. A (R. Lillich ed., 1973); I. Brownlie, *Humanitarian Intervention*, *in* LAW AND CIVIL WAR IN THE MODERN WORLD 217 (J. N. Moore ed., 1974).
77. Charney, *supra* note 51, at 1234 (citing I. BROWNLIE, INTERNATIONAL LAW AND THE USE OF FORCE BY STATES 266–68 (1991)).
78. MURPHY, *supra* note 44, at 366, 387.
79. In its decision on the merits in Nicaragua v. United States, the Court said, by way of dicta:

> The court also notes that Nicaragua is accused by the 1985 findings of the United States Congress of violating human rights . . .
>
> . . . [W]hile the United States might form its own appraisal of the situation as to respect for human rights in Nicaragua, the use of force could not be the appropriate method to monitor or ensure such respect. With regard to the steps actually taken, the protection of human rights, a strictly humanitarian objective, cannot be compatible with the mining of ports, the destruction of oil installations, or again with the training, arming and equipping of the contras. The Court concludes that the argument derived from the preservation of human rights in Nicaragua cannot afford a legal justification for the conduct of the United States, and cannot in any event be reconciled with the legal strategy of the respondent State, which is based on the right of collective self-defence. Military and Paramilitary Activities (Nicaragua v. United States), 1986 ICJ 14,134–35 (Judgment on Merits).

For support of the proposition that this language suggests that the Court, at least under the facts of the Nicaragua case, rejected the doctrine of humanitarian intervention, see N. Rodley, *Human Rights and Humanitarian Intervention: The Case Law of the World Court*, 38 INT'L & COMP. LQ 321, 332 (1989); MURPHY, *supra* note 44, at 129.

80. Case Concerning Legality of Use of Force (Yugoslavia v. Belgium), 1999 ICJ (commenced June 2, 1999). Further information available *at* www.icj-cij.org/icjwww/idocket/iybe/iybeframe.htm.
81. For discussion see Charney, *supra* note 51, at 1239 and n. 27.
82. As noted by Michael Glennon, "[i]n the United States, no argument was made that the law permitted humanitarian intervention, and official legal justifications of any sort were hard to come by. Such legal defenses of NATO's actions as were presented constantly shifted from one ground to the next, with no press notice whatsoever." Glennon, LIMITS OF LAW, *supra* note 51, at 25. As reported by Glennon, in the action against the United States brought by Yugoslavia in the International Court of Justice, the United States cited the following humanitarian considerations by way of justification of NATO's actions: (i) "the humanitarian catastrophe that has engulfed the people of Kosovo as a brutal and unlawful campaign of ethnic cleansing has forced many hundreds of thousands to flee their homes and has severely damaged their lives and well-being"; (ii) the serious violation of international humanitarian law and human rights obligations by forces under the control of the Federal Republic of Yugoslavia, including widespread murder, disappearances, rape, theft, and destruction of property. "Under these circumstances," the United States further argued, "a failure by NATO to act immediately would have been to the irreparable prejudice of the people of Kosovo. The Members of NATO refused to stand idly by to watch yet another campaign of ethnic cleansing unfold in the heart of Europe." *Id.* at 26. It should be noted, however, that the United States made no attempt to present these considerations in the framework of a legal argument that demonstrated their relevance, if any, to the law of the Charter.

    By contrast, the British government has apparently explicitly accepted the doctrine of humanitarian intervention. The then British Secretary of State for Defence, George Robertson, reportedly said: "We are in no doubt that NATO is acting within international law and our legal justification rests upon the accepted principle that force may be used in extreme circumstances to avert a humanitarian catastrophe." An earlier British note of October 1998 had stated that "as matters now stand and if action through the Security Council is not possible, military intervention by NATO is lawful on grounds of overwhelming humanitarian necessity." See DAMROSCH ET AL., *supra* note 23, at 1000, reporting quotes from Simon Duke, Hans-Georg Ehrhart & Matthias Karadi, *The Major European Allies: France, Germany and the United Kingdom*, *in* KOSOVO AND THE CHALLENGE OF HUMANITARIAN INTERVENTION 128, 137 (Albrecht Schnabel & Ramesh Thakur eds., 2000). For further discussion of the British position and other issues, see A. Roberts, *NATO's "Humanitarian War" Over Kosovo*, 41 SURVIVAL 102 (Oct. 1, 1999).
83. Charney, *supra* note 51, at 1245–47.
84. Steinberg, *supra* note 51, at 130.
85. *Id.* at 129.
86. Quoted in Mandelbaum, *supra* note 51, at 4.
87. Reportedly, on March 24, hours before the first attacks took place, UK Defense Minister George Robertson was testifying before the House of Commons Select Committee on Defence when he was asked by a member of the Select Committee: "With 50,000 Serbian soldiers either in or around Kosovo, once we attack the opportunity for them to give instant payback to the Kosovars is obviously a very great incentive on their

part. They will be able to dish out an awful lot of punishment very quickly. What is the plan to safeguard the interest of those Kosovars?" Reportedly, there was no answer. See Roberts, *supra* note 82.

88. Mandelbaum, *supra* note 51, at 2–3.
89. Z. Brzezinski, *Compromise Over Kosovo Means Defeat*, WALL ST. J. EUROPE, May 25, 1999, at 14, quoted in L. HENKIN ET AL., HUMAN RIGHTS 737 (1999).
90. Glennon, *The New Interventionism*, *supra* note 51, at 2.
91. M. Glennon, *The Fog of Law: Self-Defense, Inherence, and Incoherence in Article 51 of the United Nations Charter*, 25 HARV. J. L. & PUB. POL'Y 539, 540, and 541 (2002). For a more elaborate development of this thesis, see GLENNON, LIMITS OF LAW, *supra* note 51.
92. According to Bilder, *supra* note 51, at 160: "The so-called doctrine of humanitarian intervention has of course been around for a long time – at least since the time of Hugo Grotius some 350 years ago."
93. *Id.* at 160–61.
94. O. Schachter, *International Law in Theory and Practice: General Course in Public International Law*, 178 REC. DES COURS 9, 143–44 (1982–V), quoted in Bilder, *supra* note 51, at 161.
95. See e.g., Charney, *supra* note 51, at 1242; Cassese, *supra* note 51; V. P. Nanda, *The United States Action in the 1965 Dominican Crisis: Impact on World Order – Part I*, 43 DENV. LJ 438, 473–74 (1966); R. B. Lillich, *Forcible Self-Help by States to Protect Human Rights*, 53 IOWA L. REV. 325, 347–51 (1967).
96. After the bombing campaign in Kosovo had come to an end, the Foreign Affairs Committee of the British House of Commons, on the basis of a comprehensive inquiry, issued a lengthy report. In it, both the Foreign Secretary and the Minister of State are reported as having told the Committee that states could use force in situations of "overwhelming humanitarian necessity where, in the light of all the circumstances, a limited use of force is justified as the only way to avert a humanitarian catastrophe." Quoted in GLENNON, LIMITS OF LAW, *supra* note 51, at 24. Glennon also quotes from a speech by British Prime Minister Tony Blair in which he said:

    No one in the West who has seen what is happening in Kosovo can doubt that NATO's military action is justified. Bismarck famously said the Balkans were not worth the bones of one Pomeranian Grenadier. Anyone who has seen the tear-stained faces of the hundreds of thousands of refugees streaming across the border, heard their heart-rending tales of cruelty or contemplated the unknown fates of those left behind, knows that Bismarck was wrong. *Id.* at 161.

97. For further discussion, see Murphy, *supra* note 1, at 295–96.
98. See Michael J. Glennon, *Glennon Replies*, 79 FOREIGN AFF., July–Aug. 1999, at 120–21.
99. GLENNON, LIMITS OF LAW, *supra* note 51, at 100.
100. For further discussion, see MURPHY, *supra* note 2, at 139–40.
101. See, e.g., D. Acheson, *The Arrogance of International Lawyers*, 2 INT'L LAW. 591 (1968).
102. See in particular, M. S. McDougal & W. M. Reisman, *Rhodesia and the United Nations: The Lawfulness of International Concern*, 62 AM. J. INT'L L. 1 (1968).
103. T. M. Franck, *Break It, Don't Fake It*, 78 FOREIGN AFF. 116 (July–Aug. 1999).
104. See R. Falk, *The Haitian Intervention: A Dangerous World Order Precedent for the United Nations*, 36 HARV. INT'L LJ 341 (1995).

105. For an especially thoughtful examination of this issue, see J. E. Alvarez, *Judging the Security Council*, 90 AM. J. INT'L L. 1 (1996).
106. See, e.g., *id.* In cases arising out of the bombing of PanAm Flight 103, Libya challenged the Security Council sanctions imposed against it for failure to surrender two Libyan security agents accused of the bombing to the United States or the United Kingdom. See Libya v. United States, 1992 ICJ 114 and Libya v. United Kingdom, 1992 ICJ 3. Libya contended that it had the right under the 1971 Montreal Convention for the Suppression of Unlawful Acts against the Safety of Civil Aviation to decline to extradite the accused and instead submit them to its own prosecutorial authorities. The Security Council resolutions imposing the sanctions, it argued, violated its rights under the Convention and were beyond the authority of the Council to adopt. For their part the United States and the United Kingdom argued that any rights of Libya under the Convention were superseded by the Security Council resolutions, which under Art. 103 of the Charter take precedence over any rights under the Convention. The Court denied Libya's request for provisional measures to prevent further action by the United States and the United Kingdom to compel Libya to surrender the accused, but ruled that it has jurisdiction to consider Libya's claim under the Montreal Convention. Case Concerning Questions of Interpretation and Application of the 1971 Montreal Convention Arising from the Aerial Incident at Lockerbie (Preliminary Objections), 1998, repr. in 37 INT'L LEG. MATERIALS 587, 604–5 (1998). In his dissent to the Court's ruling that it had jurisdiction to consider Libya's claim, President Judge Schwebel argued that the Court has no power to exercise judicial review over the decisions of the Security Council and that it is especially "without power to overrule or undercut decisions of the Security Council made by it in pursuance of its authority under Articles 39, 41, and 42 of the Charter." *Id.* at 625. Others, however, have suggested that President Schwebel "went too far" and that, while there must be a prima facie presumption that the Council's resolutions are valid, this presumption may be rebutted in extraordinary circumstances. See Y. DINSTEIN, WAR, AGGRESSION AND SELF-DEFENCE, 281 (3rd ed., 2001).
107. For a blow-by-blow description, see MURPHY, *supra* note 44, at 243–60.
108. In 1999, UN Secretary-General Kofi Annan, who headed the UN Department of Peacekeeping in 1994, when the massacre in Rwanda took place, called for an independent inquiry into UN actions in Rwanda during that time. The result was a highly critical report, I. Carlsson et al., *Report of the Independent Inquiry into the Actions of the United Nations During the 1994 Genocide in Rwanda*, UN Doc. S/1999/1257, at 26 (1999). Also, on March 25, 1998, President Clinton publicly apologized for US failure to support more forceful action by the United Nations in Rwanda. See Administration of William J. Clinton, *Remarks to Genocide Survivors in Kigali, Rwanda*, 1 PUB. PAPERS 431 (Mar. 25, 1998).
109. T. M. Franck & N. Rodley, *After Bangladesh; The Law of Humanitarian Intervention by Military Force*, 67 AM. J. INT'L L. 275, 304 (1973).
110. Franck, *supra* note 103, at 118.
111. GLENNON, LIMITS OF LAW, *supra* note 51, at 188.
112. For widespread examples of this support, see J. M. Beard, *America's New War on Terror: The Case for Self-Defense Under International Law*, 25 HARV. JL & PUB. POL'Y, 559, 568–73 (2002).
113. SC Res. 1368 (Sept. 12, 2001).
114. SC Res. 1373 (Sept. 28, 2001).
115. North Atlantic Treaty, Aug. 24, 1949, Art. 5, TIAS No. 1964, 34 UNTS 243.

116. Secretary-General Lord Robertson, Statement at NATO Headquarters (Oct. 2, 2001).
117. Art. 3 of the Inter-American Treaty of Reciprocal Assistance, Sept. 2, 1947, TIAS No. 1838, provides:

 The High Contracting Parties agree that an armed attack by any State against an American State shall be considered as an attack against all the American States and, consequently, each one of the said Contracting Parties undertakes to assist in meeting the attack in the exercise of the inherent right of individual or collective self-defense recognized by Article 51 of the Charter of the United Nations.

 The resolution unanimously adopted by the OAS foreign ministers on Sept. 22, 2001, invoking the Rio Treaty, declares:

 These terrorist attacks against the United States of America are attacks against all American states, and . . . in accordance with all the relevant provisions of the [Rio Treaty] and the principle of continental solidarity, all States Parties to the Rio Treaty shall provide effective reciprocal assistance to address such attacks and the threat of any similar attacks . . . (Twenty-Fourth Meeting of Consultation of Ministers of Foreign Affairs, Terrorist Threat to the Americas, OAS Doc. RC24/Res. 1/01 (Sept. 21, 2001)).

118. For further discussion and citations, see S. D. Murphy, *Terrorism and the Concept of "Armed Attack" in Article 51 of the UN Charter*, 43 Harv. Int'l LJ 41 (2002).
119. Letter from the Permanent UN Representative of the United States to the President of the UN Security Council (Oct. 7, 2001), UN Doc. S/2001/946 (Oct. 7, 2001). Among other things, the letter noted that the United States had been the victim of "massive and brutal attacks" that were "specifically designed to maximize the loss of life" and resulted in "the death of more than 3,000 persons, including nationals of 81 countries, as well as the destruction of four civilian aircraft, the World Trade Center towers and a section of the Pentagon."
120. Jonathan Charney, however, has argued that the US use of force without Security Council authorization under Chapter VII of the Charter creates an undesirable precedent damaging to the UN system. See J. Charney, *The Use of Force Against Terrorism and International Law*, 95 Am. J. Int'l L. 835 (2001).
121. See, e.g., T. M. Franck, *Terrorism and the Right of Self-Defense*, 95 Am. J. Int'l L. 839 (2001); Beard, *supra* note 112; Murphy, *supra* note 118.
122. The US Senate voted 77 to 23, and the House 296 to 133, in favor of the resolution. The text of the resolution may be found in NY Times, Oct. 12, 2002, at A12.
123. SC Res.1441, UN SCOR, 4644th mtg., UN Doc. S/Res/1441 (2002).
124. See B. Sherwood, *Military Force: Pre-Emptive Defence or Breach of International Law?*, Financial Times, March 11, 2003, at 17, col. 2.
125. See S. R. Weisman, *A Long, Winding Road to a Diplomatic Dead End*, NY Times, March 17, 2003, at A1, col. 2.
126. *Id.*
127. See S. R. Weisman & F. Barringer, *Powell Attacks Validity of the Work by Weapons Inspectors in Iraq*, NY Times, March 6, 2003, at A17, col. 2.
128. *Id.*
129. See Bush's speech on Iraq: *Saddam Hussein and His Sons Must Leave*, NY Times, March 18, 2003, at A14, col. 1.
130. There are, however, brief arguments of legal justification in *id.* and in the US report to the Security Council of the commencement by coalition forces of military operations

in Iraq. Letter dated 20 March, 2003, from the Permanent Representative of the United States of America at the United Nations addressed to the President of the Security Council (March 21, 2003), UN Doc. S/2003/351. These arguments rely on previously adopted Security Council resolutions, including Resolution 1441.

131. The text of Lord Goldsmith's statement may be found in THE TIMES (London), March 18, 2003, at A2.
132. Letter to the Editor, *War Would be Illegal*, *Guardian*, March 7, 2003, at 13 (letter signed by sixteen professors of international law at Oxford, Cambridge, London, and Paris, asserting the illegality of a war commenced without a second Security Council resolution). For a contrary view from an eminent British international law scholar, see Christopher Greenwood, *International Law and the Pre-emptive Use of Force: Afghanistan, Al-Qaida, and Iraq*, 4 SAN DIEGO INT'L LJ 7 (2003).
133. See, e.g., Russia Hails "Optimum Solution," Nov. 8, 2002, *at* http://www.cnn.com/2002world/europe.11/08/un.reaction/index.html.
134. See especially KENNETH M. POLLACK, THE THREATENING STORM: THE CASE FOR INVADING IRAQ 100–01, 204–06 (2002); Gary Milholin and Kelly Motz, *A Vile Business*, WALL ST. J., March 24, 2003, at A16, col. 3.
135. See Michael J. Glennon, *Why the Security Council Failed*, FOREIGN AFF., May/June 2003, at 16.
136. Edward C. Luck, *Making the World Safe for Hypocrisy*, NY TIMES, March 22, 2003, at A11, col. 1.
137. Jacques de Lisle, *Illegal? Yes. Lawless? Not so Fast: The United States, International Law, and the War in Iraq*, March 28, 2003. Paper distributed by e-mail under the auspices of the Foreign Policy Research Institute. Copy on file with author.
138. *Id.* at 9.
139. See POLLACK, *supra* note 134; Kenneth M. Pollack, *A Last Chance to Stop Iraq*, NY TIMES, Feb. 21, 2003, at A27, col. 2.
140. Harold Hongju Koh, *On American Exceptionalism*, 65 STAN. L. REV. 1479 (2003).
141. *Id.* at 1521–25.
142. *Id.* at 1519–21.
143. See Pollack, *A Last Chance to Stop Iraq*, *supra* note 139.
144. See Peter Slevin, *US Says War Has Legal Basis: Reliance on Gulf War Resolutions is Questioned by Others*, WASH. POST, March 21, 2003, at A14.
145. See John Bellinger III, *Authority for Use of Force by the United States Against Iraq Under International Law* (Apr. 10, 2003), at http://www.cfr.org/publication.php?Id=5862.
146. The National Security Strategy of the United States of America 15 (Sept. 2002).
147. In the Nicaragua case, the International Court of Justice declined to pass judgment on "the issue of the lawfulness of a response to the imminent threat of armed attack." Military and Paramilitary Activities in and Against Nicaragua (Nicaragua v. US), 1986 ICJ 14, 102–06 (Judgment of June 27).
148. See L. Adetunji, *Bush to Lay Out First-Strike Policy Against Terrorism*, FINANCIAL TIMES, June 11, 2002, at 11.
149. See T. M. Franck, *Who Killed Article 2(4)? Or: Changing Norms Governing the Use of Force by States*, 64 AM. J. INT'L L. 809 (1970).
150. See L. Henkin, *The Reports of the Death of Article 2(4) Are Greatly Exaggerated*, 65 AM. J. INT'L L. 544 (1970).
151. The trend first became apparent during the 1960s. See J. F. Murphy, *The Trend Towards Anarchy in the United Nations*, 54 AM. BAR ASS'N J. 267 (1968).
152. D. P. MOYNIHAN, A DANGEROUS PLACE (1978).

153. Franck, *supra* note 149, at 835.
154. GA Res. 2625, UN GAOR, 26th Sess., Supp. No. 28, at 121, UN Doc. A/8028 (1971).
155. See R. Rosenstock, *The Declaration of Principles of International Law Concerning Friendly Relations: A Survey*, 65 AM. J. INT'L L. 713, 714 (1971).
156. GA Res. 42/22, 42(1) GAOR 287, 288 (1987).
157. GLENNON, LIMITS OF LAW, *supra* note 51, at 67–69.
158. See, e.g., *id.*, at 84–89.
159. See *id.*, at 17–35.
160. The record of the United Nations in maintaining international peace and security is, however, better than is commonly recognized, especially if one considers all the obstacles that have stood in the way of the United Nations fulfilling its responsibilities. See MURPHY, *supra* note 2.
161. See SCHACHTER, *supra* note 12, at 106.
162. Military and Paramilitary Activities in and Against Nicaragua (Nicaragua v. United States), *supra* note 147, at 998.
163. Charter of the International Military Tribunal, Annexed to the London Agreement for the Establishment of an International Military Tribunal, 1945, 9 INT'L LEGIS. 632, 637.
164. *Id.* at 639–40.
165. See J. F. Murphy, *Crimes against Peace at the Nuremberg Trial*, *in* THE NUREMBERG TRIAL AND INTERNATIONAL LAW 141, 153 (G. Ginsburgs & V. N. Kudriavtsev eds., 1990).
166. DINSTEIN, *supra* note 106, at 109.
167. GLENNON, LIMITS OF LAW, *supra* note 51, at 25.
168. *Id.* at 60.
169. For this quote from the commission's report, see DAMROSCH ET AL., *supra* note 23, at 1001, 1002.
170. See C. Tiefer, *Review of Limits of Law, Prerogatives of Power: Interventionism After Kosovo*, 96 AM. J. INT'L L. 489, 492 (2002).
171. GLENNON, LIMITS OF LAW, *supra* note 51, at 37.
172. DINSTEIN, *supra* note 106, at 89–90.
173. UN Charter, Art. 27(3).
174. UN Charter, Art. 2(1).
175. GLENNON, LIMITS OF LAW, *supra* note 51, at 151–52.
176. For the distinction between legal principles and legal rules, see R. DWORKIN, TAKING RIGHTS SERIOUSLY, 22–28 (1978).
177. For further discussion, see MURPHY, *supra* note 2, at 19–33.
178. In response, and at the initiative of the United States, the General Assembly adopted the so-called "Uniting for Peace" resolution, GA Res. 377A (Nov. 3, 1950). On Feb. 1, 1951, in response to China's armed intervention in Korea and with the Council unable to act, the Assembly, acting under the Uniting for Peace procedures, passed a resolution condemning the Chinese action as aggression, calling on them to withdraw their forces from Korea, and recommending that all states lend every assistance to the United Nations' action in Korea. GA Res. 498 (Feb. 1, 1951). Interestingly, in light of the International Court of Justice's Advisory Opinion in the Certain Expenses case, it is questionable whether the General Assembly has the authority it claims in the Uniting for Peace resolution to recommend the establishment of an armed force under its auspices to enforce the peace against an aggressor state. See MURPHY, *supra* note 2, at 81–82. The question is largely academic now, however, because

with the loss of their control of voting patterns in the General Assembly, the permanent members have tacitly agreed to the Soviet position expressed in the Certain Expenses case – that only the Security Council should authorize the use of armed force.

179. Suy, *Peace-keeping Operations*, *in* A HANDBOOK ON INTERNATIONAL ORGANIZATIONS 379 (R. Dupuy ed., 1988).
180. For further discussion, see Murphy, *supra* note 1, at 292–96.
181. For further discussion, see MURPHY, *supra* note 2, at 148–61; O. Schachter, *Authorized Uses of Force by the United Nations and Regional Organizations*, *in* LAW AND FORCE IN THE NEW INTERNATIONAL ORDER 65, 84–86 (L. F. Damrosch & D. J. Scheffer eds., 1991); G. ABI-SAAB, THE UNITED NATIONS OPERATION IN THE CONGO (1978).
182. For reference to some of these commentators see MURPHY, *supra* note 2, at 160.
183. *Id.*
184. See DAMROSCH ET AL., *supra* note 23, at 1007–8.
185. MURPHY, *supra* note 44, at 198.
186. SC Res. 713 (September 25, 1991).
187. MURPHY, *supra* note 44, at 199.
188. As noted in *id.*, at 200, Bosnia's inability to obtain these arms was later part of the suit it brought against Serbia and Montenegro before the International Court of Justice. On April 8, 1993, the Court issued a provisional order demanding that Serbia and Montenegro take measures to prevent the crime of genocide in Bosnia-Herzegovina, but did not rule on Bosnia's request to be exempted from the Security Council's arms embargo. Application of the Convention on the Prevention and Punishment of the Crime of Genocide (Bosnia and Herzegovina v. Yugoslavia (Serbia and Montenegro)), 1993 ICJ 3 (Order of April 8).
189. SC Res. 743 (Feb. 21, 1992).
190. Secretary-General Boutros-Ghali had called for such an approach in his Agenda for Peace, UN Doc. A/47/277, S/24111 (1992).
191. See MURPHY, *supra* note 44, at 206.
192. *Id.*
193. *Id.* at 207.
194. See DAMROSCH ET AL., *supra* note 23, at 1040.
195. For the sad history of failure in Bosnia, see P. C. Szasz, *Peacekeeping in Operation: A Conflict Study of Bosnia*, 28 CORNELL INT'L LJ 685 (1995); T. Varady, *The Predicament of Peacekeeping in Bosnia*, 28 CORNELL INT'L LJ 701 (1995); V. Bunce, *The Elusive Peace in the Former Yugoslavia*, 28 CORNELL INT'L LJ 709 (1995).
196. SC Res. 1031 (Dec. 5, 1995).
197. See *Hearing on United Nations Peacekeeping Missions and Their Proliferation Before the Subcommittee on International Operations of the Senate Committee on Foreign Relations*, 106th Cong., 13, 115–17 (2000) (Statement of Dr. John Hillen).
198. Michael Maren, *Outmanned, Outgunned in Sierra Leone*, NY TIMES, May 9, 2000, at A25, col. 2.
199. M. Peel, *Peacekeepers to Stay in Sierra Leone, Says the UN*, FINANCIAL TIMES, May 17, 2002.
200. M. Lacey, *Congo Tires of War, but the End is Not in Sight*," NY TIMES, July 15, 2002, at A3, col. 1.
201. See, e.g., M. Hirsh, *Calling All Regio-Cops: Peacekeeping's Hybrid Future*, FOREIGN AFF., Nov.–Dec. 2000, at 2. GLENNON, LIMITS OF LAW, *supra* note 51, at 198–201.
202. See *Peacekeeping: The UN's Missions Impossible*, THE ECONOMIST, Aug. 5–11, 2002, at 24.

203. See C. A. A. Packer & D. Rukare, *The New African Union and Its Constitutive Act*, 96 AM. J. INT'L L. 365, 372–73 (2002).
204. See *West Africa's Widening Conflict*, NY TIMES, Dec. 6, 2000, at A32.
205. See *Hearing on United Nations Peacekeeping Missions and Their Proliferation, supra* note 197, at 21 (Statement of John Bolton).
206. *Id.* at 22. It recently proved impossible to reach agreement in the Security Council on whether Western Sahara should remain part of Morocco or be granted a referendum on independence. See C. Hoyos, *Western Sahara Agreement Eludes UN*, FINANCIAL TIMES, July 31, 2002, at 6, col. 8.
207. *Id.* at 26.
208. SC Res. 1422 (July 12, 2002).
209. See J. Dempsey, *UN Balancing Act on Criminal Court Wins Scant Applause*, FINANCIAL TIMES, July 15, 2002, at 8, col. 1.
210. The formal name for the Brahimi Report is the Comprehensive Review of the Whole Question of Peacekeeping Operations in All Their Aspects, UN Doc. A/55/305S/2000/809 (Aug. 21, 2000).
211. *Id.* at 3.
212. SCHACHTER, *supra* note 12, at 389.
213. See Statement of John Bolton, *supra* note 205, at 31.
214. *Id.* at 32.
215. For a listing and brief description of international peacekeeping operations as of July 2, 2000, see FINANCIAL TIMES, July 2, 2002, at 9, col. 3.
216. See SC Res. 1327 (Nov. 13, 2000). The decisions and recommendations adopted by the Security Council are contained in an annex to the resolution.
217. See Brahimi Report, *supra* note 210, at 9–10.
218. *Id.* at 5.
219. *Id.* at 10.
220. SCHACHTER, *supra* note 12, at 396.

5 Arms control, disarmament, nonproliferation, and safeguards

In this chapter we consider the closely related subjects of arms control, disarmament, nonproliferation, and safeguards. All of these subjects are, in turn, closely related to regulation of the use of force. Indeed, as we have seen in chapter 4, Security Council Resolution 687 constitutes an unprecedented effort to force a member state of the United Nations unilaterally to disarm with respect to weapons of mass destruction.

Traditionally, all of these subjects, especially arms control and disarmament, have been subject to an extensive network of multilateral and bilateral treaties.[1] Many, indeed most, of these treaties were concluded with strong US support. It is clear, however, that, with the second Bush administration, there has been a sea change in US attitudes toward such treaties. Reflecting in large part the substantial distrust of John Bolton of arms control and multilateral treaties, the Bush administration "has pulled out of the Anti-Ballistic Missile Treaty with Russia, scuttled an important protocol to the biological-weapons ban, ousted the head of the organization that oversees the chemical weapons ban, watered down an accord on small-arms trafficking and refused to submit the nuclear test ban treaty for Senate ratification [actually Senate advice and consent to ratification]."[2]

Reportedly, the view of the Bush administration is that treaties on arms control, disarmament, and, to a lesser extent, nonproliferation at best do not work and at worst can endanger vital US interests. It appears especially skeptical of multilateral treaties that set up verification and enforcement regimes. The Bush administration's view appears to be that states that cheat and violate the treaty norms are not prevented from doing so by the treaty, while intrusive verification regimes subject countries like the United States that act in accordance with the treaty's norms to infringements of their national sovereignty and to the possible loss of proprietary information from US laboratories and businesses. In place of treaty regimes, the Bush administration would rely on military and other forms of US power to defend against weapons of mass destruction and other possible kinds of armed attack endangering US national security.

What follows is a brief survey of some recent case histories of where the United States has either rejected entirely or failed to act fully in accordance with a multilateral treaty regime. We begin with the Comprehensive Nuclear Test Ban Treaty.

The Comprehensive Nuclear Test Ban Treaty

As noted by a recent report, "[a] complete nuclear test ban has been a goal of the global movement for nuclear disarmament and the governments of many countries for half a century."[3] The Treaty Banning Nuclear Weapons Tests in the Atmosphere, in Outer Space, and Under Water,[4] commonly called the Limited Test Ban Treaty or Partial Test Ban Treaty, was the first major step toward this goal. The treaty was negotiated by the United States, the United Kingdom, and the Soviet Union largely outside the United Nations, and was concluded in Moscow. It is, however, open to all states, and the General Assembly and other UN organs have encouraged member states to become parties to it. The treaty entered into force in October 1963. The preamble of the Limited Test Ban Treaty provides that the goal of the parties is "to achieve the discontinuance of all test explosions for all time."

Toward this end, on September 24, 1996, the Comprehensive Nuclear Test Ban Treaty (CNTBT)[5] was opened for signature at the United Nations. It was quickly signed by more than 135 states, including all five permanent members of the Security Council. India and Pakistan did not sign. Article I of the CNTBT bans all nuclear explosions, for any purpose, military or peaceful.[6] Significantly, it does not ban possession of nuclear weapons, only their testing. The CNTBT would also create a comprehensive Nuclear Test Ban Treaty Organization headquartered in Vienna, which would carry out verification activities under the treaty (Article II). These verification activities include international monitoring, consultation and clarification, on-site inspections, and confidence measures (Article IV).

By its terms (Article XIV), however, the CNTBT can enter into force only after all forty-four states listed in its Annex 2 have ratified. As of March 2002 only thirty-one had ratified it, including Russia, France, and the United Kingdom. China and Israel had signed but not ratified it, and Indian, Pakistan, and North Korea had not signed it. The United States had signed but not ratified it.

Nor is the United States likely to ratify it. In October 1999, the Senate declined, by a vote of forty-eight in favor, and fifty-one against (a two-thirds vote of sixty-seven in favor being required), to give its advice and consent to ratification. Proponents of ratification, including representatives of the Clinton administration, had primarily argued that the treaty had value as a nonproliferation measure because it would make it difficult for nonnuclear countries to test to develop nuclear arsenals. A few proponents, but not representatives from the administration, argued that the treaty should be viewed as a disarmament measure as well, since it would encourage nuclear states to reduce their nuclear arsenals.[7]

The arguments of the opponents of the treaty proved more persuasive to the members of the US Senate. They contended, among other things, that (i) the treaty could not be verified, because even the Central Intelligence Agency (CIA) had admitted that it had no ability to detect low-yield tests; (ii) testing is critical to ensure the reliability and safety of US nuclear weapons as well as their modernization; (iii) testing therefore is vital to maintaining the reliability and credibility of the US nuclear deterrent; and (iv) the nuclear deterrent "has never been as important to the security of Americans as it is today with rogue states developing the capacity to attack our cities and our population. Americans and their allies are more vulnerable than we have ever been."[8]

After the vote in the Senate, President Clinton claimed that this defeat was only a temporary setback and that the treaty could be considered again at a more auspicious time.[9] President Bush, however, has announced that he is opposed to the treaty, and reportedly there is a debate within his administration as to whether the United States should remove its signature from the treaty.[10] This debate is significant because of Article 18 of the Vienna Convention on the Law of Treaties, which requires a signatory to a treaty to refrain from acts which would defeat its object and purpose. Although the United States is not a party to the Vienna Convention, it has taken the position that Article 18 is also part of customary international law. Some critics have claimed that the United States is currently engaged in activities that are contrary to the object and purpose of the CNTBT.[11]

The Nuclear Non-Proliferation Treaty (NPT)

In sharp contrast to its attitude with respect to most multilateral treaties involving national security concerns, the Bush administration apparently strongly approves of the Nuclear Non-Proliferation Treaty (NPT).[12] The regime established by the NPT,[13] however, is highly controversial. The first two articles of the NPT allocate responsibilities between nuclear weapons states and nonnuclear weapons states.[14] Article I requires the nuclear weapons states not to transfer nuclear weapons or devices, or control over them, and not to assist nonnuclear weapons states in acquiring nuclear weapons. Article II reciprocally obligates nonnuclear weapons states not to manufacture or acquire nuclear weapons. The key provision of the NPT is Article III, which requires bilateral "full scope safeguards" agreements with the International Atomic Energy Agency (IAEA) on all nuclear facilities of nonnuclear weapons states that are NPT parties, and IAEA safeguards in nuclear exports by any of its parties. Articles IV and V assure nonnuclear weapons states full access to nuclear power technology. Under Article VI the nuclear weapons states agree to seek an early end to the nuclear arms race and to pursue nuclear disarmament as well as general and complete disarmament "under strict and effective international control."

In 1968 the United States, the United Kingdom, and the Soviet Union gave, in a letter to the president of the Security Council,[15] security assurances to nonnuclear weapons states that each would seek immediate Security Council action to assist any nonnuclear weapons state party to the NPT that was the target of nuclear aggression or threats.

Criticisms of the NPT regime have primarily been along the following lines. Several nonnuclear weapons states that have the capacity to become nuclear weapons states have rejected the NPT on the ground that states would receive adequate security guarantees only in the event of nuclear disarmament and that, contrary to their obligations under Article VI of the NPT, the nuclear weapons states have been expanding their nuclear weapons capacity. In 1998, as a result of their testing of nuclear weapons, India and Pakistan joined the ranks of nuclear weapons states.[16] Neither has signed the NPT. Israel, while not yet formally a nuclear weapons state, is believed to have a nuclear weapons capacity, and has also declined to sign the NPT.

Critics of the regime also have alleged that IAEA safeguards are not adequate for the task. They have alleged, among other things, that the IAEA is underfunded and understaffed, and that it has been weakened by political questions not relevant to nonproliferation. Moreover, these critics contend, the IAEA "full scope" safeguards stipulated in Article III of the NPT are designed only to detect a diversion of nuclear material to military uses and do not prevent a clandestine nuclear program.

Critics of the IAEA safeguards system have especially pressed their arguments since the discovery by a UN and IAEA inspection team in the summer of 1991 of a secret Iraqi nuclear arms program in violation of Iraq's safeguard agreements with the IAEA. It should be noted, however, that the inspections in Iraq after the Gulf War were conducted pursuant to the extraordinary powers granted to the UN and IAEA inspectors by Resolution 687, which allowed for much more intrusive inspections than those under the IAEA safeguards program. In any event, in response, on

December 6, 1991, Hans Blix, then Director-General of the International Atomic Energy Agency, formally proposed strengthening the Agency's system of safeguarding nuclear material. At a meeting of the IAEA's Board of Governors, Blix requested the Board to back special inspections on sites where the Agency suspects that safeguards agreements are being violated. Such special inspections, which would be possible only in the eighty-eight countries that have full safeguards agreements with the Agency, would be aimed at sites that a country had not declared to the Agency, such as the dozen secret nuclear installations discovered in Iraq. On February 24–25, 1992, the IAEA Board approved most of Blix's recommendations.

Although the IAEA apparently already has the authority to undertake special inspections, it had never made them on undeclared sites before the Iraqi case. The purpose of Blix's proposal was to alert countries with which the IAEA has safeguards agreements that no site is off-limits for inspectors. If a country refuses to permit a special inspection, the Director-General could take the matter to the UN Security Council, which then would have to decide whether the country posed a threat to international peace and security.

More recently, the issue came to the fore in the case of North Korea. In 1985 that country became a party to the NPT, but for a number of years thereafter it failed to conclude a safeguards agreement with the IAEA. Finally, in January 1992, it reached agreement with the IAEA on the terms of a safeguards agreement with the IAEA, accepting six IAEA inspection visits before refusing access to two facilities near its Yongbyong nuclear reactor complex on the ground that these were conventional military facilities. Evidence began to emerge that North Korea may have used more nuclear fuel, and may have been able to separate more plutonium for possible weapons use, than it had declared. As a consequence, on April 1, 1993, the IAEA's Board of Governors ruled that North Korea had violated its safeguards agreement, and referred the issue to the UN Security Council. For its part North Korea gave formal notice of its intention to withdraw from the NPT. There then ensued a period of great tension that brought the United States and North Korea to the brink of war. The crisis was resolved diplomatically, however, when the United States and North Korea signed an agreement called the Agreed Framework on October 21, 1994. Under the agreement, North Korea agreed to shut down its nuclear reactors, freeze its nuclear activities, and put its nuclear materials under IAEA inspection. In return, the United States gave a pledge that a consortium of outside powers would build North Korea two modern nuclear reactors and provide it with large shipments of oil. "Though bedeviled by problems, implementation delays, and mutual recriminations, the Agreed Framework succeeded in freezing North Korea's plutonium program for nearly 10 years."[17]

Because of the difficulties in monitoring the safeguards agreement with North Korea, member states of the IAEA and the IAEA Secretariat turned to plans to strengthen the safeguards system. In May 1997 a "major milestone" was reached when the IAEA Board of Governors approved a model Additional Protocol to safeguards agreements.[18] The next step was for the IAEA to begin the process of negotiating with each member state to secure its adherence to an additional protocol. According to the IAEA, as of July 11, 2003, there were thirty-five contracting states which had ratified additional protocols.[19] For its part, the United States signed an additional protocol on June 12, 1998, and, on May 9, 2002, President George W. Bush transmitted it to the Senate for its advice and consent to ratification.[20] As of this writing, however, the United States is not a party to the protocol.

According to the US Department of State, the additional protocol "is designed to improve the Agency's ability to detect clandestine nuclear weapons programs in nonnuclear weapons states by providing the IAEA with increased information about and expanded access to nuclear fuel cycle activities and sites."[21] Once it becomes a party to an additional protocol, a state must provide the IAEA with "broader information covering all aspects of its nuclear fuel cycle-related activities, including research and development and uranium mining."[22] In addition, a state party must grant the IAEA "broader access rights" and the ability to employ "the most advanced verification technologies."[23] Some specific examples of additional protocol provisions cited by the IAEA include:

- information about, and access to, all aspects of states' nuclear fuel cycle, from uranium mines to nuclear waste and any other locations where nuclear material intended for nonnuclear uses is present;
- short-notice inspector access to all buildings on a nuclear site;
- information on the manufacture and export of sensitive nuclear-related technologies and inspection mechanisms for manufacturing and import locations;
- access to other nuclear-related locations; and
- collection of environmental samples beyond declared locations when deemed necessary by the IAEA.[24]

Pierre Goldschmidt, IAEA Deputy Director-General and Head of the Department of Safeguards, has neatly distinguished between the IAEA's goals with respect to a state with a comprehensive safeguards agreement, on the one hand, and a state with both a comprehensive safeguards agreement and an additional protocol, on the other. As to the former, the goal is "to enable the Agency to draw the credible conclusion that '*the nuclear material placed under safeguards remains in peaceful nuclear activities or is otherwise adequately accounted for.*'" With respect to the latter, the goal is to "draw the credible conclusion that '*all nuclear material in the State has been placed under safeguards and remains in peaceful nuclear activities or is otherwise adequately accounted for.*'"[25]

Neither comprehensive safeguards agreements nor additional protocols thereto will work, however, unless they are in place and operational. In the case of North Korea, at this writing neither is in place. To the contrary, in October 2002, during a visit to Pyongyang, officials of the US Department of State confronted North Korea with evidence of a clandestine North Korean program for the enrichment of uranium.[26] This was a second North Korean nuclear weapons program – this one based on uranium – in addition to the plutonium program frozen by the 1994 agreement, constituting a violation of both the NPT and the Agreed Framework. Far from denying these allegations, North Korea acknowledged that it had such a program and asserted its right to pursue nuclear weapons. Thereafter, the situation rapidly deteriorated:

> In rapid succession during December 2002 and January 2003, North Korea announced its intention to restart its long idle nuclear reactors, began to access materials and equipment that had been sealed and tagged by the IAEA to prevent their use, dismantled IAEA surveillance cameras at its nuclear facilities, and expelled IAEA inspectors from the country. On January 10, 2003, . . . North Korea declared its withdrawal from the NPT and hence its rejection of the commitment to remain non-nuclear. Later in January 2003, it was reported that Pyongyang had begun to move its 8,000 spent nuclear fuel rods, formerly safeguarded by the IAEA, out of storage facilities, raising concerns that it was about to begin "reprocessing" in order to extract the plutonium necessary for making nuclear weapons. These fuel rods contain enough plutonium for at least six nuclear weapons. Once reprocessing begins the clock will count down rapidly to the point where North Korea possesses a small nuclear arsenal: six weapons in six months is the common estimate. Meanwhile, with its reactors again running and its no longer clandestine (though still geographically hidden) uranium enrichment capacity developing at some unknown pace, Pyongyang will have future options for further augmenting its nuclear weapons capability.[27]

At this writing intensive negotiations are under way with a view to resolving the crisis. If the crisis is resolved peacefully, it is highly likely that a new comprehensive safeguards agreement and additional protocol for North Korea will be an integral part of it.

The United States has come under increased criticism for its alleged failure to comply with its obligations under Article VI of the NPT to seek an early end to the nuclear arms race and to pursue nuclear disarmament as well as general and complete disarmament. Until the 1995 Review and Extension Conference of the NPT, the nuclear weapons powers, especially the United States, had largely succeeded in keeping the primary focus of the five-yearly NPT review conferences on proliferation rather than disarmament. In 1995, however, in order to obtain the indefinite extension of the NPT, the nuclear weapons states agreed to "Principles and Objectives of Nuclear Non-Proliferation and Disarmament."[28] These "Principles and Objectives" included, among other things, a commitment to the negotiation of a Comprehensive Test Ban Treaty by 1996, "immediate commencement and early conclusion of negotiation" of a ban on production of fissile materials for nuclear weapons use, and "the determined pursuit by the nuclear-weapon States of systemic and progressive efforts to reduce nuclear weapons globally, with the ultimate goals of eliminating those weapons, and by all States of general and complete disarmament under strict and effective control."

As noted in the previous section of this chapter, in 1996, the United Nations adopted the Comprehensive Nuclear Test Ban Treaty, but the US Senate voted against giving its advice and consent to ratification. Also in 1996, the International Court of Justice issued its advisory opinion on the *Legality of the Threat or Use of Nuclear Weapons*,[29] in which the Court interpreted Article VI of the NPT as requiring the nuclear weapons states parties "to pursue in good faith and bring to a conclusion negotiations leading to nuclear disarmament in all its aspects under strict and effective international control."[30] In 1998, a so-called New Agenda group consisting of Brazil, Ireland, Mexico, New Zealand, South Africa, and Sweden was formed to press for disarmament commitments from the nuclear weapons states. They enjoyed a substantial measure of success at the 2000 NPT Review Conference.

At the 2000 review conference the New Agenda states first succeeded in inducing the five nuclear powers (United States, United Kingdom, France, Russia, and China) to issue a joint statement: "We remain unequivocally committed to fulfilling all of our obligations under the treaty . . . None of our nuclear weapons are targeted at any state."[31] More significantly, the New Agenda states succeeded in having the final document of the review conference include thirteen "practical steps for the systematic and progressive efforts" to achieve nuclear disarmament.[32] These thirteen practical steps, as well as the final document itself, are not legally binding. Nonetheless, adopted by consensus, they serve at a minimum as a significant political commitment and arguably give some substantive content to Article VI of the NPT. Although the thirteen practical steps were adopted by consensus, the United States, as well as the other nuclear weapons states, has had great difficulty adhering to them.

Two of the thirteen practical steps have been specifically repudiated by the United States. As we have seen, the United States has now made it clear that it does not intend to ratify the Comprehensive Nuclear Test

Ban Treaty and is contemplating removing its signature from the treaty. Practical step 7 calls for the "early entry into force and full implementation of START II and the conclusion of START III as soon as possible while preserving and strengthening the Treaty on the Limitation of Anti-Ballistic Missile Systems as a cornerstone of strategic stability and as a basis for further reductions of strategic offensive weapons, in accordance with its provisions." But on June 13, 2002, the United States formerly withdrew from the ABM treaty[33] and rather than seek the entry into force of the START II treaty or the negotiation of a START III treaty along the lines indicated by then Presidents Clinton and Yeltsin in March 1997, the United States sought (and achieved) a new agreement with Russia to reduce the number of deployed strategic nuclear warheads.[34] Moreover, the Treaty Between the United States of America and the Russian Federation on Strategic Offensive Reductions, signed at Moscow on May 24, 2002 (the Moscow Treaty),[35] has itself been criticized as "contrary to long-standing US arms control goals"[36] and as incompatible with the "criteria set forth by the 2000 Review Conference in significant respects."[37] The Moscow Treaty would require the United States and Russia to reduce the number of each country's strategic nuclear warheads from about 6,000 to between 1,700–2,200 by December 31, 2012. As pointed out by Joe Biden, then chairman of the US Senate's Committee on Foreign Relations, however, the treaty would not require the actual destruction of a single missile or warhead. Rather, each country would be able to warehouse its weapons and deploy them later. More important, unlike START II, the treaty would allow Russia to place multiple warheads on its intercontinental missiles (ICBMs). Critics have argued that this would be destabilizing, especially in light of the Bush administration's intention to develop and deploy a missile defense, "which may cause Russia to retain existing deployed multiple warhead missiles and to deploy new ones."[38]

In general, the United States has been subject to sharp criticism for its alleged failure to implement the thirteen practical steps.[39] Regardless of the validity or invalidity of these charges, however, the overriding question is whether the United States, or for that matter the other four primary nuclear weapons states, truly intends to fulfill its obligation under Article VI of the NPT to negotiate in good faith toward the ultimate elimination of nuclear weapons. At this writing the evidence is substantial, some might even say overwhelming, that the answer to this question is no. As we have already noted, the recently concluded Moscow Treaty allows the parties to store most of the warheads covered by the treaty rather than to destroy them, and the Bush administration has indicated that it plans to do so. Also, a recently completed US nuclear posture review "projects that the United States will retain nuclear weapons for the indefinite future."[40]

Finally, there are significant indications that the United States wishes to emphasize the nonproliferation aspects of the NPT while downplaying its disarmament obligations.[41]

Biological Weapons Convention and Chemical Weapons Convention

After the terrorist attacks of September 11, and subsequent anthrax attacks in the United States in September and October 2001, President Bush issued a statement[42] that, among other things, called for strengthening the Convention on the Prohibition of the Development, Production and Stockpiling of Bacteriological (Biological) and Toxin Weapons and on Their Destruction (Biological Weapons Convention).[43] The Biological Weapons Convention has been in force since 1975, but has no enforcement mechanisms and is widely regarded as an ineffective mechanism for preventing the spread of biological weapons. Accordingly, in 1994, states parties to the Biological Weapons Convention established an Ad Hoc Group, which included the United States, to work toward strengthening the convention. For six years the parties worked on a draft protocol to the convention with a view to enhancing transparency and promoting compliance. On the last day of the conference (December 7, 2001), however, to the great surprise, not to say shock, of the other parties, the United States announced its opposition to continuation of work by the Ad Hoc Group. In response the parties to the convention agreed to adjourn and meet again on November 11–22, 2002.

John Bolton has set forth the three primary US objections to the draft protocol.[44]

> The first was that, as written, if it were actually implemented, it would compromise our important biodefense preparations. That would arise from the risk of inspections by people who didn't particularly bear us the best wishes, who by inspecting our biodefense facilities would be able to develop countermeasures that could frustrate the defenses that we were preparing.
>
> The second major area of concern was the risk to our pharmaceutical and biotec industries, that inspections would compromise their intellectual property assets and risk widespread interference in their activities. And the experience of some test inspections over the 90's I think helped corroborate that, and it was a very serious issue that we did not see being addressed.
>
> The third principal concern for the United States was the undermining of our system of export controls and the multilateral framework of export controls known as the Australia Group to prevent the export both of dual-use items and others that could be used in an offensive BW program.[45]

These and other objections to the protocol have been subjected to considerable critical analysis.[46] The crucial point for present purposes, however, is not the validity or invalidity of the US objections to the draft protocol. It is that the US rejection of the draft protocol, including its creation of a compliance mechanism under an international body to investigate suspicious outbreaks of diseases, alleged use, and suspicious facilities, is another example of the Bush administration's abandonment of the rule of law approach that has characterized efforts toward arms control, disarmament, and nonproliferation since World War II. In its place the United States has proposed a series of national measures or a unilateral approach to combating the risk of the use of biological weapons of mass destruction. Such measures would include "tightened export controls, an intensified nonproliferation dialogue, increased domestic preparedness and controls, enhanced biodefense and counter-bioterrorism capabilities, and innovative measures against disease outbreaks. Strict compliance by all parties with the BWC is also critical."[47]

There seems little doubt that many of these proposed national measures, if carried out, would be positive steps. It would be desirable, for example, for states parties to the Biological Weapons Convention to enact legislation that would make it a criminal offense for any person to engage in activities prohibited by the convention and that would enhance bilateral extradition agreements with respect to biological weapons offenses. But as pointed out by one critical study, the enactment of such criminal legislation has long been encouraged by the states parties to the convention at the review conferences.[48] Apparently the same may be said for most of the other US proposals. More significantly, a prominent US criticism is that the Biological Weapons Convention has not prevented so-called rogue states from developing and deploying biological weapons. Implementation of the US proposals, however, would do little to resolve this problem.

It may be that, as alleged by the United States, the draft protocol to the Biological Weapons Convention was a "flawed text" that could not be salvaged by further discussion and negotiations. This is a debatable proposition, however.[49] It is also arguable that legally binding measures are the key to the strengthening of measures to combat biological weapons by all states parties, instead of the very spotty implementation of political measures agreed to at the review conferences.[50]

In sharp contrast to its rejection of the draft protocol to the Biological Weapons Convention, and its insistence that no further efforts to revise the protocol be undertaken, the Bush administration appears to be strongly supportive of the Convention on the Prohibition of the Development, Production, Stockpiling and Use of Chemical Weapons and on Their Destruction (Chemical Weapons Convention).[51] Here, too, however, the US approach to the convention has been sharply criticized.

The Chemical Weapons Convention prohibits states parties from using, producing, or stockpiling poison gas or lethal chemical weapons, and requires them to dispose of existing chemical weapons by the year 2010 at the latest. Significantly, the convention contains rigorous verification procedures administered by a new Organization for the Prohibition of Chemical Weapons that is located in The Hague and has been functioning since 1997. Implementation procedures include routine inspections at facilities that are declared to possess or use chemicals that may be precursors to weapons agents, and so-called "challenge inspections" to guard against cheating. When the convention was under consideration by the US Senate, some critics challenged its inspection regime, especially its system for challenging inspections, on the ground that it posed constitutional problems in view of the Fourth Amendment's requirements for searches and seizures and the Fifth Amendment's protection of private property. It was also argued that the treaty power should not be used to transfer enforcement powers to an international organization whose officials would not be held accountable through constitutional processes.[52] The Senate, however, gave its advice and consent to ratification, finding that there were no insuperable constitutional barriers.

The Chemical Weapons Convention is a non-self-executing treaty and therefore required implementing legislation by Congress. Critics have contended that the convention's implementing legislation contains limitations on verification efforts by the Organization for the Prohibition of Chemical Weapons that undermine these efforts and are incompatible with US obligations under the convention.[53] These limitations give the president the right to refuse inspection of any facility on the determination that the inspection may "pose a threat to the national security interests";[54] narrow the number of facilities that are subject to the inspection and declaration provisions of the convention; and prohibit samples to be transferred for analysis to any laboratory outside the United States. According to the critics, these limitations have had a contagion effect among other states parties to the convention.

The Landmines Convention

As briefly noted in the introduction to this study, the United States cited its responsibilities for the defense of South Korea and for maintaining the peace in refusing to become a party to the Convention on the Prohibition of the Use, Stockpiling, Production and Transfer of Anti-Personnel Mines and Their Destruction (the Landmines Convention).[55] Leaving aside for the moment the issue whether these reasons are valid, they are a striking example of the US view of its "exceptional" position with respect to use of force and disarmament matters. In no small part the refusal of other states parties to recognize an exception for the US position over Korea was due to the opposition to such an exception by nongovernmental organizations (NGOs).[56]

The convention bans the use, production, stockpiling, and sale of antipersonnel mines, and requires the destruction of stockpiles and of mines in the ground in territories under the jurisdiction of states parties on specified timetables. No reservations to the convention are permitted, and parties are required to report to the UN Secretary-General on their implementation measures. Having played such a prominent role in the negotiations on the convention, the NGOs are also closely monitoring its implementation by states parties. At this writing the United States has neither signed nor ratified the convention, joining Russia and China outside the treaty framework.

At the close of the negotiations on the convention, on September 17, 1997, President Clinton announced that, while the United States would not be signing the treaty, it would "unilaterally stop using antipersonnel mines everywhere but in Korea by 2003, and in Korea by 2006."[57] The commitment to stop using antipersonnel mines in South Korea was made conditional on the availability by 2006 of alternatives to antipersonnel mines.

At this writing the Bush administration is reportedly conducting a review of US landmine policy.[58] Therefore, it is not clear whether the Clinton administration's policy toward antipersonnel landmines remains in effect. One may speculate, however, that with President Bush having included North Korea in his "axis of evil," it is unlikely that any change that arguably would weaken the US ability to defend South Korea is imminent – despite the arguments of some eminent retired military leaders that antipersonnel mines are not necessary to the defense of South Korea.[59]

The UN Conference on the Illicit Trade in Small Arms and Light Weapons in all its aspects

As we have seen, most national and international efforts in the arms control and disarmament arena, with the notable exception of landmines, have focused on weapons of mass destruction – nuclear, chemical, and biological. Most wars are fought, however, and most people have been killed, not by weapons of mass destruction but by small arms and light weapons – such as pistols, assault rifles, and handheld grenades. It has been estimated that some six million people have been killed in armed conflicts around the world in the last decade, half of them by small arms.[60]

Most of these armed conflicts have been civil rather than cross-border wars.

This killing is greatly abetted by a thriving trade in arms trade, with between four to six billion weapons a year changing hands. The biggest-grossing producers involved in this arms trade are the United States, the United Kingdom, France, and Russia – four of the five permanent members of the UN Security Council. Together, these four countries export 83 percent of the world's arms.[61] The United States is the leading exporter of such weapons, in 1998 selling about $1.2 billion worth, according to the Small Arms Survey, a Geneva-based NGO.[62]

Perhaps not surprisingly, efforts to put constraints on this arms trade have been few and fleeting. On December 6, 1991, the UN General Assembly adopted a resolution[63] whereby it established a UN register of arms transfers and called on member states to provide information to the Secretary-General regarding their transfers of conventional arms. Initially, however, the register applied only to sales of heavy arms, for example, tanks, armored fighting vehicles, artillery pieces, combat aircraft, and attack helicopters, that can be used to seize and hold territory.

The goal of the register is to limit the international traffic in arms by publicizing transactions and identifying potential trouble spots by showing where arms stocks are increasing. The resolution also requests the Secretary-General to establish a group of experts to explore ways of extending the register to include lighter arms as well as production sites and national weapons stocks. This is to meet a concern expressed by many developing countries that the register would discriminate against poorer nations, which import their arms, by requiring them to disclose their purchases, while protecting richer nations with indigenous arms industries against revealing their military strength. At this writing, however, the register has not been expanded to include small arms and light weapons.

A potentially much more significant step was taken when the UN General Assembly decided to convene a Conference on the Illicit Trade in Small Arms and Light Weapons on July 9–20, 2001. The goal of this conference was to explore means to eliminate or at least limit the global illicit trade in small arms and light weapons. To this end the conference, as an initial matter, worked on a nonbinding Program of Action. From the very beginning of the conference, however, the United States made it clear that it did not favor measures that were favored by many of the other participants, including European Union member states. For example, the United States opposed a ban on private ownership of military weapons, including assault weapons and grenade launchers.[64] It also drew a sharp distinction between *illicit* trade in small arms and light weapons and legal trade in and legal manufacturing of such arms, refusing to support any measures that would constrain the latter.[65] In sharp contrast, others at the conference were of the view that "[t]he illicit trade cannot be tackled without involving the legal arms trade."[66] The United States was also opposed to any movement toward a legally binding instrument. Following a pattern set at other arms control conferences, the United States favored instead national measures, such as "strict export and import controls, strong brokering laws, and secure stockpiles." In its view the responsibility to eliminate illicit arms trade fell on each individual nation.[67]

From this survey of US policies and actions regarding arms control, disarmament, and nonproliferation one may safely conclude that the United States has had substantial difficulty in accepting a rule of law paradigm in these areas. This difficulty has been compounded with the coming into office of the George W. Bush administration because of its considerable distrust of any external constraints on its behavior, especially constraints imposed by international norms and institutions.

In the arms control and disarmament field the Bush administration's break with the past has been particularly pronounced. Here, the views of John Bolton have seemingly prevailed, and the bias in favor of national efforts and informal arrangements for enforcement in place of formal treaties and international verification institutions has won the day.

Even with respect to the Nuclear Non-Proliferation Treaty, which the Bush administration has strongly supported, its support has been highly selective. George Perkovich has suggested that the Bush administration "suffers from triple selectivity. It deems some states' nuclear weapons good, while others' are bad. It selects one treaty, the NPT, for enforcement while dismissing others. And it selects only some provisions of the NPT – the constraints on others – for enforcement." He further contends that "[s]uch selectivity mocks the equitable rule of law and engenders apathy and resistance from other states that makes stopping WMD proliferation even harder than it would otherwise be."[68]

Notes

1. For a listing of many of these treaties, see L. F. Damrosch et al., International Law, 1077–80 (4th ed., 2001).
2. C. A. Robbins, *Disarming America's Treaties*, Wall St. J., July 19, 2002, at A4, col. 3.
3. See Rule of Power or Rule of Law? An Assessment of US Policies and Actions Regarding Security-Related Treaties 57 (N. Deller, A. Makhijani, & J. Burroughs eds., 2002).
4. Treaty Banning Nuclear Weapons Tests in the Atmosphere, in Outer Space and Under Water, Aug. 5, 1963, 14 UST 1313, TIAS No. 5433, 480 UNTS 43 (hereinafter Limited Test Ban Treaty or Partial Test Ban Treaty).

5. For the text of the treaty, see 35 INT'L LEG. MATERIALS 1439 (1996).
6. Art. 1 of the CNTBT provides:

   1. Each State Party undertakes not to carry out any nuclear weapons test explosion or any other nuclear explosion, and to prohibit and prevent any such nuclear explosion at any place under its jurisdiction or control.
   2. Each State Party undertakes, furthermore, to refrain from causing, encouraging, or in any way participating in the carrying out of any nuclear weapon test explosion or any other nuclear explosion.

7. See RULE OF POWER, *supra* note 3, at 61–62.
8. *Id.* at 64 (quoting the testimony of Jeanne Kirkpatrick, former US permanent representative at the United Nations). See also J. Kyl, *Maintaining "Peace Through Strength": A Rejection of the Comprehensive Test Ban Treaty*, 37 HARV. J. ON LEGIS. 325 (2000).
9. See *Contemporary Practice of the United States Relating to International Law: Senate Rejection of the Comprehensive Test Ban Treaty*, 94 AM. J. INT'L. L. 102 137–39 (2000).
10. According to the *Wall Street Journal*, John Bolton has fought hard to have the United States remove its signature from the CNTBT, but so far has been overruled by US Secretary of State Colin Powell and the White House, C. A. Robbins, *Disarming America's Treaties*, WALL ST. J., July 19, 2002, at A4, col. 3.
11. See e.g., RULE OF POWER, *supra* note 3, at 65–69.
12. In remarks made to the 12th Annual International Arms Control Conference on April 19, 2002, John S. Wolf, Assistant Secretary of State for Nonproliferation, stated that "[t]he Nonproliferation Treaty (NPT) remains the bedrock of our nonproliferation policy." See J. S. Wolf, *US Approaches to Nonproliferation*, US Department of State Press Release, April 19, 2002, at 2, *at* www.state.gov/t/np/rls/rm/9635.htm.
13. Treaty on the Non-Proliferation of Nuclear Weapons, July 1, 1968, 21 UST 483, TIAS No. 6839, 729 UNTS 161.
14. For further discussion of the NPT regime, see J. F. Murphy, *Force and Arms*, *in* THE UNITED NATIONS AND INTERNATIONAL LAW 97, 122–29 (C. C. Joyner ed., 1997).
15. See Letter from the US, USSR, and UK to the President of the Security Council (June 12, 1968), 23 UN SCOR Supp. (Apr.–June 1968) at 216, UN Doc. S/8630 (1968).
16. Strictly speaking, neither is a "nuclear weapon State" under the NPT, since Article IV of the treaty requires such a state to have "manufactured and exploded a nuclear weapon or other nuclear explosive device prior to January 1967."
17. See Steven E. Miller, *The Real Crisis: North Korea's Nuclear Gambit*, HARV. INT'L REV., summer 2003, at 84.
18. See Richard Hooper, *The Changing Nature of Safeguards*, 45 IAEA BULLETIN, June 2003, at 7–8.
19. Strengthened Safeguards System: Status of Additional Protocols, IAEA, at http://www.iaea.org/ourwork/SV/safeguards/sq_protocol-html.
20. See US Department of State, *US–IAEA Additional Protocol*, Fact Sheet–Bureau of Nonproliferation, May 14, 2002, *at* http://www.state.gov/t/np/rls/fs/2002/10316.htm.
21. *Id.*
22. *IAEA Safeguards: Stemming the Spread of Nuclear Weapons*, IAEA SAFEGUARDS AND VERIFICATION, *at* http://www.iaea.org/publications/Factsheets/English/S1Safeguards.pdf (no date specified), at 3.
23. *Id.*
24. *Id.*
25. Pierre Goldschmidt, *Strengthened Safeguards: Meeting Present and Future Challenges*, 43 IAEA BULLETIN, 4 (2001), at 6–7 (italics in original).

26. See Miller, *supra* note 17.
27. *Id.* at 84-85.
28. See RULE OF POWER, *supra* note 3, at 45.
29. Legality of the Threat or Use of Nuclear Weapons (Advisory Opinion), 1996 ICJ 226.
30. *Id.*, para. 105(2)(F).
31. See RULE OF POWER, *supra* note 3, at 46.
32. See Final Document: 2000 Review Conference of the Parties to the Treaty on the Non-Proliferation of Nuclear Weapons, at 14–15 (2000), *at* www.basicint.org/nuclear/npt/2000revcon/finaldoc-advance.htm.
    The thirteen practical steps are:

    1. The importance and urgency of signatures and ratifications, without delay and without conditions and in accordance with constitutional processes, to achieve the early entry into force of the Comprehensive Nuclear-Test-Ban Treaty.
    2. A moratorium on nuclear-weapon-test-explosions or any other nuclear explosions pending entry into force of that Treaty.
    3. The necessity of negotiations in the Conference on Disarmament on a non-discriminatory, multilateral and internationally and effectively verifiable treaty banning the production of fissile material for nuclear weapons or other nuclear explosive devices in accordance with the Statement of the Special Coordinator in 1995 and the mandate contained therein, taking into consideration both nuclear disarmament and nuclear non-proliferation objectives. The Conference on Disarmament is urged to agree on a programme of work which includes the immediate establishment of such a body.
    4. The necessity of establishing in the Conference on Disarmament an appropriate subsidiary body with a mandate to deal with nuclear disarmament. The Conference on Disarmament is urged to agree on a programme of work which includes the immediate commencement of negotiations on such a treaty with a view to their conclusion within five years.
    5. The principle of irreversibility to apply to nuclear disarmament, nuclear and other related arms control and reduction measures.
    6. An unequivocal undertaking by the nuclear-weapon States to accomplish the total elimination of their nuclear arsenals leading to nuclear disarmament, to which all States Parties are committed under Article VI.
    7. The early entry into force and full implementation of START II and the conclusion of START III as soon as possible while preserving and strengthening the ABM Treaty as a cornerstone of strategic stability and as a basis for further reductions of strategic offensive weapons, in accordance with its provisions.
    8. The completion and implementation of the Trilateral Initiative between the United States of America, the Russian Federation and the International Atomic Energy Agency.
    9. Steps by all the nuclear-weapon States leading to nuclear disarmament in a way that promotes international stability, and based on the principle of undiminished security for all:
        - Further efforts by the nuclear-weapon States to reduce their nuclear arsenals unilaterally.
        - Increased transparency by the nuclear-weapon States with regard to the nuclear weapons capabilities and the implementation of agreements pursuant to Article VI and as a voluntary confidence-building measure to support further progress on nuclear disarmament.

- The further reduction of non-strategic nuclear weapons, based on unilateral initiatives and as an integral part of the nuclear arms reduction and disarmament process.
- Concrete agreed measures to further reduce the operational status of nuclear weapons systems.
- A diminishing role for nuclear weapons in security policies to minimize the risk that these weapons will ever be used and to facilitate the process of their total elimination.
- The engagement as soon as appropriate of all the nuclear-weapon States in the process leading to the total elimination of their nuclear weapons.

10. Arrangements by all nuclear-weapon States to place, as soon as practicable, fissile material designated by each of them as no longer required for military purposes under IAEA or other relevant international verification and arrangements for the disposition of such material for peaceful purposes, to ensure that such material remains permanently outside military programmes.
11. Reaffirmation that the ultimate objective of the efforts of States in the disarmament process is general and complete disarmament under effective international control.
12. Regular reports, within the framework of the NPT strengthened review process for the Non-Proliferation Treaty, by all States parties on the implementation of Article VI and paragraph 4(c) of the 1995 Decision on "Principles and Objectives for Nuclear Non-Proliferation and Disarmament," and recalling the Advisory Opinion of the International Court of Justice of 8 July 1996.
13. The further development of the verification capabilities that will be required to provide assurance of compliance with nuclear disarmament agreements for the achievement and maintenance of a nuclear-weapon-free world.

33. See D. Sanger and M. Wines, *With a Shrug, a Monument to Cold War Fades Away*, NY Times, June 14, 2002, at A11, col. 1.
34. See Arms Control Association, "Summary of US Implementation of the '13 Practical Steps on Non-Proliferation and Disarmament' Agreed to at the 2000 NPT Review Conference," April 4, 2002, at 2, *at* www.armscontrol.org/aca/npt13steps.asp.
35. See Message of President George W. Bush to the Senate of the United States transmitting the Treaty Between the United States of America and the Russian Federation on Strategic Offensive Reductions, June 20, 2002, 138, *at* weekly.comp.pres.doc.1060–61 (June 20, 2002), *at* www.whitehouse.gov/news/releses/2002/06/print/20020620–13.html.
36. See J. R. Biden, *Beyond the Moscow Treaty*, Wash. Post, May 28, 2002, at A17.
37. See Rule of Power, *supra* note 3, at 49.
38. *Id.* at 51.
39. See, e.g., *id.* at 49.
40. Arms Control Association, *supra* note 34, at 2.
41. At the Non-Proliferation Treaty Preparatory Committee Meeting held in New York on April 8–19, 2002, the US ambassador, Norman Wulf, objected to the summary of the meeting prepared by the chairman in part on the ground that "[w]e . . . would have preferred a fairer treatment of the balance between non-proliferation and disarmament. The two are mutually reinforcing. Nuclear disarmament is not, in our view, the main criteria [sic] by which to evaluate the treaty's operation." Transcript of Ambassador Wulf's remarks, in D. Roche, "The NPT: Crisis and Challenge Report and Assessment of the Nuclear Non-Proliferation Treaty Preparatory Committee Meeting, New York, April 8–19, 2002," at para. 16, *at* http://gsinstitute.org/archives/000098.shtml.

42. The White House, Statement by the President: Strengthening the International Regime Against Biological Weapons, 1 Nov. 2001, *at* www.whitehouse.gov/news/releases/2001/11print/20011101.htm.
43. 26 UST 583, TIAS No. 8062, 1015 UNTS 163, signed in Washington, London, and Moscow on April 10, 1972 and entered into force in 1975.
44. J. R. Bolton, The Biological Weapons Convention: Challenges and Opportunities, Jan. 11, 2002, speech to the Chemical and Biological Arms Control Institute, the Monterrey Institute Center for Non-proliferation Studies, and the Nuclear Threat Initiative.
45. *Id.* at 18.
46. See e.g., G. S. Pearson, M. R. Dando, & N. A. Sims, "Strengthening the Biological Weapons Convention, Review Conference Paper No. 4, the US Statement at the Fifth Review Conference: "Compounding the Error in Rejecting the Composite Protocol," Jan. 2002, *at* http://www.bradford.ac.uk/acad/sbtwc/briefing/rcp_4.pdf.
47. See J. R. Bolton, Remarks to the 5th Biological Weapons Convention RevCon Meeting, Nov. 19, 2001, *at* www.state.gov/t/us/rm/janjuly/6231.htm.
48. See Pearson et al., *supra* note 46, at 14.
49. See, e.g., *id.* at 35–37.
50. *Id.* at 36.
51. 1974 UNTS 3, A/RES/47/391. The text of the Chemical Weapons Convention may most conveniently be found in 32 INT'L LEG. MATERIALS 800 (1993).
52. See e.g., R. Rotunda, *The Chemical Weapons Convention: Political and Constitutional Issues*, 15 CONST. COMMENT. 131 (1998); J. C. Yoo, *The New Sovereignty and the Old Constitution: The Chemical Weapons Convention and the Appointments Clause*, 15 CONST. COMMENT. 87 (1998).
53. RULE OF POWER, *supra* note 3, at 81–82.
54. Public Law 105–277.
55. For the text of the convention, see 36 INT'L LEG. MATERIALS 1507 (1997).
56. For a discussion of the influence of the NGOs in bringing about the Landmines Convention, see Ramesh Thakur & William Maley, *The Ottawa Convention on Landmines: A Landmark Humanitarian Treaty in Arms Control?*, 5 GLOBAL GOVERNANCE 273 (1999).
57. See RULE OF POWER, *supra* note 3, at 101.
58. *Id.*
59. *Id.* at 103.
60. See T. C. Fishman, *Making a Killing: The Myth of Capital's Good Intentions*, HARPER'S, Aug. 2002, at 33, 39.
61. *Id.* at 38.
62. See C. L. Lynch, *US Fights UN Accord to Control Small Arms*, WASH. POST, July 10, 2002, at A1.
63. GA Res. 46.36L (Dec. 6, 1991).
64. See Lynch, *supra* note 62.
65. See J. R. Bolton, Plenary Address to the UN Conference on the Illicit Trade in Small Arms and Light Weapons, July 9, 2001, at 2, *at* www.state.gov/t/us/rm/janjuly/4038.htm.
66. Ascribed to Jozias van Aartsen, Foreign Minister of The Netherlands. See Lynch, *supra* note 62.
67. See Cunningham's UN Security Council Remarks on Small Arms, Aug. 3, 2001, *at* http://usembassy.state.gov/islamabad/wwwh01080301.html.
68. George Perkovich, *Bush's Nuclear Revolution: A Regime Change in Non-Proliferation*, FOREIGN AFF., March/April 2003, at 2, 8.

6 The law of the sea

The law of the sea is a subject of quite extraordinary breadth and depth, and this chapter makes no pretense at exhaustive coverage. It is a field of international law, however, that the United States has played a major role in developing, yet currently remains unwilling to ratify a comprehensive convention on the subject. The history of US policy on the law of the sea provides some excellent examples of its ambivalent attitude toward adhering to the rule of law in international affairs.

As noted recently by some eminent authorities, "The Law of the Sea is commonly used to describe that part of international law that deals with the relations, activities and interests of *states* involving the sea."[1] So described, the law of the sea must be distinguished from other branches of the law relating to the sea – such as admiralty or maritime law – that primarily involve the relations, activities, and interests of *private* persons participating in the transport by sea of passengers or goods. These branches are primarily though not exclusively governed by the domestic law of states.

Until the middle of the twentieth century the law of the sea was largely customary law, and constituted a relatively stable legal system. Under this legal system, "vast areas of the oceans – the high seas – [were] generally regarded as common space, not subject to the sovereignty or exclusive control of any state."[2] Gradually, however, these "vast areas" were subject to a struggle between states that claimed special rights in them, and other states that supported the freedom to navigate and fish in all the ocean spaces. The "special rights" states have prevailed in this struggle.

An early erosion of the common spaces approach to the law of the sea was the general recognition that coastal states had special interests in waters adjacent to their shores, especially a national security interest in protecting the shoreline from hostile attack. During the seventeenth and eighteenth centuries states regularly claimed sovereignty over adjacent waters. There was, however, no agreement over the scope of this authority or how the resulting "territorial sea" was to be measured. One popular method was the so-called "cannon-shot" rule, which held that a sovereign could exercise authority over the sea that fell within a cannon's range from the shore. Delimitation by this method varied, ranging from a few thousand feet to generally less than three miles. A more consistent method of delimitation involved use of the marine league, or three nautical miles, as the unit of measure. It blended well with the cannon shot rule, since three miles was considered by some as the maximum theoretical range of a cannon.

Led by Great Britain, the dominant naval power of the time, by the end of the nineteenth century there was general agreement among the major powers on a three-mile limit for the breadth of the territorial sea – but this view was not unchallenged, since the Scandinavian countries claimed four miles, and several other states claimed larger zones for specific purposes.[3] During the twentieth century, moreover, the challenge to the three-mile limit grew in intensity. As noted by Barry Carter and Phillip Trimble:

> The two World Wars and the period between undermined the three-mile limit. First, during the hostilities a number of countries declared vast "neutrality zones" in order to assure their security. For many purposes, these neutrality zones were the equivalent of territorial seas. Second, advances in technology made the three-mile limit economically and militarily too narrow for the waters of the developed states. Finally, the newly independent nations concluded that the three-mile limit was too narrow. Among other reasons, they resented the situation where developed states (and multinational corporations) exploited the resources outside the three-mile limit.[4]

These and other developments demonstrated the need for a codification and development of the law of the sea and resulted in the first United Nations Conference on the Law of the Sea in 1958. The 1958 conference adopted four conventions,[5] all of which the United States ratified and duly came into force. But a follow-up conference held in 1960 failed by one vote to agree on the breadth of the territorial sea, despite a compromise proposal advanced by the United States and Canada that would have provided for a six-mile territorial sea plus a six-mile exclusive fisheries zone.

After the failure to reach agreement at the 1960 conference, a number of states pushed for a territorial sea of considerably beyond six miles. Many, perhaps most, of these more expansive claims were based not on national security concerns but on a desire to extend a coastal state's exclusive jurisdiction over natural resources, especially fish and various minerals, including oil. The 1945 Proclamation by US President Harry Truman of exclusive jurisdiction over the natural resources of the subsoil and seabed of the continental shelf "beneath the high seas but contiguous to the coasts of the United States"[6] had prompted many states to extend their territorial sea claims to six, twelve, or more miles, even though President Truman's Proclamation made it clear that the United States regarded the waters above its continental shelf as high seas and in no way affected by the US Proclamation.

Shortly after the conclusion of the 1960 conference on the law of the sea, and especially during the 1960s and early 1970s, it became apparent that a host of economic, political, and technological developments had created a need for a new codification of the law of the sea, including the territorial sea. The result was the Third UN Law of the Sea Conference, which reexamined virtually the whole corpus of the law of the sea. The Conference began in 1973, with the United States an active participant, and after eight years of negotiation it produced the Draft Convention on the Law of the Sea.[7] Although the Carter administration had favored the Draft Convention, the Reagan administration, which took office in 1981, objected to a number of provisions, especially the seabed mining provisions, and proposed several revisions to the Draft Convention. Most of these proposed revisions were rejected by the Conference, and, as a result, the United States was one of only four states, the other three being Israel, Turkey, and Venezuela, voting against approval of the final draft of the Convention on April 30, 1982. The draft was approved by 130 states.[8]

The United States has no problem with Article 3 of the Convention, however, which authorizes "[e]very state" to establish a territorial sea "up to a limit not exceeding 12 nautical miles, measured from baselines determined in accordance with this Convention." On the contrary, in December 1988 President Reagan formally proclaimed that the United States was extending its territorial sea to twelve nautical miles. As we shall see later in this chapter, the extension of territorial seas to twelve miles by most countries in the world raised other issues for the United States – such as passage through international straits – but the United States has nonetheless joined other states in support of the proposition that the twelve-mile limit is now part of customary international law.

As a comprehensive codification of the law of the sea, the 1982 Convention covers a quite extraordinary number of topics. The focus of this chapter, however, is limited to those provisions that have posed major problems for the United States, especially those provisions that raise rule of law issues.[9] The next section of this chapter turns to an examination of these problematical (from the US point of view) provisions. The concluding section of the chapter considers future prospects for the United States and the law of the sea.

The United States and the Law of the Sea Convention: problem areas

National security issues

Issues of national security initially prompted the United States to promote new negotiations on the law of the sea, and they remained a "make or break" concern for the United States throughout the negotiations. The claims of various states over offshore high seas areas – for example, territorial sea, fishing zones, economic zones – threatened to limit freedom of navigation and overflight to an extent the United States, as a naval and air military power, could not tolerate. The United States was especially unwilling to be subject to a regime of "innocent passage" through the waters of some 135 international straits – such as the Strait of Gibraltar and the Strait of Hormuz – that, prior to the extension of territorial seas to twelve miles by the states bordering the straits, had constituted the high seas. Even with respect to the extension of the territorial sea to twelve miles off the coasts of states not bordering on international straits, the United States insisted on clarifying the meaning of non-innocent or "prejudicial" passage and on resolving such issues as whether military ships were entitled to innocent passage type transit and the circumstances under which a coastal state might prevent passage through its territorial waters or board or arrest a ship engaged in such passage.

The United States was also concerned that it have a right of innocent passage through the archipelagic waters of such archipelagoes as the Philippines and Indonesia. As to the 200-mile exclusive economic zones to be established by the Convention, the United States was determined that the waters beyond the territorial seas retain their status as high seas, with no right of the coastal state to interfere with navigation.

In light of the high priority the United States placed during the negotiations on ensuring its rights of navigation and overflight of the seas, it is perhaps not surprising that it was largely successful in having its positions accepted at the conference. Under the 1982 Convention, there are twelve categories of activities listed as non-innocent or prejudicial and therefore not qualifying as innocent passage.[10] Any ship, including armed warships, that does not engage in these prejudicial activities is guaranteed the right of innocent passage through the territorial sea. Submarine and other underwater craft are required, however, to navigate on the surface and show their flags.

More important, the Convention establishes a new legal doctrine – transit passage – for movement through straits used for international navigation that lie within the territorial seas of the adjoining states.[11] Under this doctrine, all ships and aircraft may navigate or overfly for the purpose of continuous and expeditious transit of the strait, and submarines may transit such straits submerged, thus meeting the demand of the United States and other maritime powers that their submarines be able to transit these straits undetected. States bordering straits may designate sea lanes and prescribe traffic separation schemes to promote safe passage of ships, but may not block or otherwise interfere with transit. International straits not covered by the transit passage doctrine are governed by the innocent passage regime, which shall not be suspended.[12]

The United States and other major maritime powers also were successful in conditioning their acceptance of the concept of the archipelagic state on acceptance by the conference of the right of archipelagic sea lanes passage. Under the doctrine of archipelagic sea lanes passage, ships and aircraft enjoy the right of passage through designated archipelagic sea lanes and air routes, which must include all normal passage routes used for international navigation or overflight.[13] The sea lanes and air routes are designated by agreement between the archipelagic state and the competent international organization, principally the International Maritime Organization. Archipelagic sea lanes passage is generally governed by the same standards as transit passage through straits.[14] In archipelagic waters other than the designated sea lanes, ships have the right of innocent passage similar to the one they possess in the territorial sea, subject to exceptions for inland waters delimited by straight lines drawn across the mouths of rivers, bays, and entrances to ports, and to suspension temporarily in specified areas, if such suspension is essential for the protection of the archipelagic state's security.[15]

In addition to being a state with a strong interest in ensuring freedom of air and sea navigation on a worldwide basis, the United States is also a country with a lengthy sea coast that it wishes to protect from threats to its national security. It also is concerned with preventing and punishing infringements of its customs, fiscal, immigration, and sanitary laws and regulations within its territory or territorial sea. As early as 1799, the US Congress established a twelve-mile zone within which all foreign ships could be boarded and searched by American authorities.[16] During prohibition, in 1922, the United States established a contiguous zone of nine miles outside the three-mile limit of the territorial sea. During the nineteenth and early twentieth centuries other states established contiguous zones to the extent that this state practice created a customary norm in the international law of the sea, according to which any state had the right to establish a contiguous zone for the protection of its sanitary, customs, fiscal, immigration, and security or strategic interests.[17] This norm of customary international law was codified first in the 1958 Convention on the Territorial Sea and Contiguous Zone and then in the 1982 Convention. Article 33 of the 1982 Convention provides:

(1) In a zone contiguous to its territorial sea, described as the contiguous zone, the coastal state may exercise the control necessary to:
   (a) prevent infringement of its customs, fiscal, immigration, or sanitary laws and regulations within its territory or territorial sea;
   (b) punish infringement of the above laws and regulations committed within its territory or territorial sea.

(2) The contiguous zone may not extend beyond twenty-four nautical miles from the baselines from which the breadth of the territorial sea is measured.

On September 2, 1999, the United States extended its contiguous zone to twenty-four nautical miles, the limit permitted under Article 33 of the 1982 Convention. It is noteworthy, however, that the scope of control permitted by Article 33 to be exercised in the contiguous zone is quite limited. It covers preventing and punishing infringements of customs, fiscal, immigration, and sanitary laws and regulations of the coastal state within its territory or territorial sea. Although the question of how to protect the security of the coastal state was raised during the conference, Article 33 does not cover the protection of these interests. It is clear, moreover, that the status of waters as high seas is not affected by their inclusion within a contiguous zone.

It is not clear, however, that the list in Article 33 of purposes for which a contiguous zone may be established is exhaustive.[18] For its part the United States has on several occasions established "customs-enforcement areas" that permitted the seizure of ships intending to violate its customs laws as far out as sixty-two miles from the US coastline.[19] It has also seized or aided in the seizure of ships on the high seas on the ground that they were carrying cargo that threatened its national security.[20] Most recently, Spanish authorities, acting on intelligence provided by the United States, seized a ship sailing without a flag in the Arabian sea and discovered that it was concealing fifteen North Korean Scud missiles, warheads, and rocket propellant, hidden in the hold under sacks of cement. When the president of Yemen informed the United States that he had ordered the Scuds, the ship was allowed to proceed to Yemen under the Yemeni president's promise to keep them secure from terrorists. A US spokesman also suggested that there was "no clear authority" to seize the vessel nor any "provision under international law prohibiting Yemen from accepting delivery of missiles from North Korea." The validity of this proposition, however, is highly questionable.[21]

The United States has also used armed force to enforce its right to transit on the high seas. Perhaps the most controversial example is the US use of force in response to Libya's claim that it has sovereignty over the Gulf of Sidra off Libya's coast in the Mediterranean on the basis of historic title. In response to this claim, in 1981 US jets shot down two Libyan fighters that were challenging the presence of United States ships in Gulf waters and US jets in the airspace above. In 1986, the United States again engaged Libyan forces in the Gulf when a US fleet crossed the Libyan-set boundary to assert the right to innocent passage in waters beyond twelve miles from the Libyan shore. The Libyan claim to the Gulf of Sidra has at most a weak basis in international law.[22] But it does not necessarily follow that the United States was entitled to resort to the use of armed force to challenge it.[23]

As noted above, the United States is generally satisfied with the provisions of the 1982 Convention relating to the freedom to navigate on or under or to fly over the seas. The current position of the United States is that it will not become a party to the Convention (for reasons we shall discuss later) but will regard most of its provisions as a codification of customary international law.[24] In response, some states have argued that non-parties are not entitled to the benefits of the Convention, on the ground that the Convention is a "package deal," and a state may not enjoy the benefits of provisions it likes, while denying other states the benefits of provisions it opposes. The new transit right, for example, was regarded by many states as an essential part of the package deal. By contrast, the United States, declining to become a party to the Convention, has asserted that the right of transit has become customary international law through practice and *opinio juris*, independently of the Convention.[25] Significantly, the attitude of most coastal states with jurisdiction over international straits is that becoming a party to the Convention is a condition of transit rights through straits.[26] Disputes over transit rights could be resolved through use of dispute settlement machinery provided in the Convention. However, states that are not parties are not bound by such provisions and cannot invoke them. In theory such disputes could be resolved through reference to the International Court of Justice, but in light of current US attitudes toward the ICJ – discussed in greater detail in the next chapter – this is unlikely to happen. As noted by Oscar Schachter, "[i]t is ironic that a country like the United States, concerned over protection of its rights of navigation and therefore strongly in favour of mandatory dispute settlement, will not be able to take advantage of the convention's provisions (which responded to its aims) because of its rejection of the convention on other grounds."[27]

It might be argued that this concern is purely academic because US military might would dissuade a coastal state bordering an international strait from interfering with its right of transit. Perhaps. But as Oscar Schachter has further noted:

> Naval powers are . . . likely to use force to ensure passage through strategic straits, but coastal straits States are probably well equipped today with precision guided missiles to resist such force effectively. While bilateral arrangements may be worked out, changes in regimes (witness, the change in Iran) may render such arrangements of dubious value if the legal right of passage is not accepted. The political costs of the use of force would be much less if the naval power could rely on a clear and generally accepted treaty provision. These considerations indicate that a maritime power that does not adhere to the 1982 convention will be giving up important benefits.[28]

These considerations are also a major reason why the US Department of Defense is a strong advocate of the United States becoming a party to the Convention.

Natural resources issues

As already noted, the 1945 Proclamation by US President Harry Truman of exclusive jurisdiction over the natural resources of the subsoil and seabed of the continental shelf constituted the start of the process of territorial expansion in ocean space for the purpose of exploitation of natural resources. As for exploitation of the resources of the continental shelf, the Truman Proclamation is often cited as an example of "instant custom,"[29] since, far from being met with protests, the Proclamation stimulated similar claims by other states with continental shelves. This customary norm was codified in the 1958 Convention on the Continental Shelf, which defined the continental shelf as extending out to the 200-meter isobath (the point where the depth of the waters is 200 meters), or "beyond that limit, to where the depth of the superjacent waters admits of the exploitation of the natural resources of the said areas" (Article 1). With the development of technology raising the prospect of deep seabed mining, it became clear that the exploitability limitation to the 1958 definition of the continental shelf was no longer operative. Accordingly, the 1982 Convention qualifies the potential breadth of the continental shelf in several respects. First, it defines the continental shelf as extending out to 200 nautical miles (Article 76(1)). If certain geological conditions are present, a coastal state may be able to extend its continental shelf still further but not beyond 350 nautical miles (Sections 4–7 of Article 76). It may do so, however, only after submitting information on the limits of its continental shelf beyond 200 nautical miles to a Commission on the Limits of the Continental Shelf to be established by the states parties to the Convention and taking into account recommendations the commission is required to make. The limits the coastal state establishes "on the basis of these recommendations shall be final and binding"(Article 76(8)). Moreover, if oil and gas deposits are exploited on a state's continental shelf beyond 200 nautical miles, the Convention requires that the coastal state share a certain percentage of the proceeds with other states parties, "on the basis of equitable sharing criteria, taking into account the interests and needs of developing States, particularly the least developed and the landlocked among them" (Article 82(4)).

Although the International Court of Justice has noted that the provisions of the 1982 Convention on the continental shelf and the exclusive economic zone "were adopted without any objections," and therefore concluded that they may be "regarded as consonant at present with general international law,"[30] several issues involving the position of the United States remain unresolved. It is unclear, for example, whether a state not party to the Convention can claim that the extended definition of the continental shelf is customary international law, if it does not accept also the obligation to make payments to the international fund set up under the Convention from revenues derived from exploitation of that part of the continental shelf extending beyond 200 miles.[31]

On the whole, the claim of the United States and other states to the resources of the continental shelf has not given rise to much controversy – with the notable exception of issues regarding the delimitation of the continental shelves of states opposite or adjacent to each other[32] – but the Truman Proclamation stimulated claims by some coastal states during the 1940s and 1950s to exclusive rights to fish or to engage in whaling in a 200-mile zone off their coasts. Many of these claims were in response to extensive whaling or fishing by the fleets of long-distance fishing countries, including the United States, Japan, Norway, the United Kingdom, and France, among others. On occasion the coastal states used force to enforce their claims, resulting, for example, in the so-called "cod wars" between Iceland and the United Kingdom and the "tuna war" between Ecuador and the United States.[33]

As illustrated by the US response to Ecuador's claim to a 200-mile exclusive fishing zone off its coast, initially the United States, along with other powerful maritime states, strongly opposed claims of coastal states to preferential rights over fisheries and other resources. In a relatively short period of time, however, these claims evolved into exclusive rights over fishing zones of 200 miles and became the basis for exclusive economic zones in which coastal states exercised sovereign rights over all resources. The concept of exclusive economic zones was given its formal imprimatur by the adoption of the 1982 Convention.[34] The reasons for this change of heart by the United States and the other developed countries has been aptly noted by Oscar Schachter:

> What is striking about this process is that the powerful maritime States, originally opposed to erosion of the freedom of the seas, came to accept the exclusive zones initially proposed by a few small and weak countries. Many legal scholars strongly supportive of the freedom of the seas, and opposed to broad extensions of national authority in international waters, criticized the excessive nationalism of developing States. Some deplored the "democratization" of international law-making through United Nations Conferences in which small states could out-vote the larger "more responsible" States. They considered that international law was greatly weakened when the assertions of extended jurisdiction by coastal States were not effectively resisted by the more powerful long-distance fishing countries (such as the United States, the USSR, Japan, Great Britain and France). Why, one might ask, did these maritime powers not use force to maintain their rights? A plausible answer is that restraints on the use of force to vindicate fishing rights were influenced at least in part by the legal prohibition against force plus the political assessment that action against coastal States would provoke much opposition in "third world" countries whose support was desired in other respects. Perhaps more significant than this general political consideration was the pressure within some of the larger countries for protection of their own fisheries in near-by coastal waters. In the United States, for example, the domestic fishing industry pressed to eliminate Japanese, Russian and other long-distance, high technology fishing fleets from United States coastal waters and a 1976 United States law declared a 200-mile fishing zone. Thus it cannot be said that the developed States were out-voted or out-manoeuvred by the poorer States. In fact the triumph of the poor over the rich in regard to the exclusive zones is much less than was claimed. Major beneficiaries of the 200-mile exclusive zone include several large developed countries such as the United States, Canada, Australia and the Soviet Union. The United States, for example, added about three million square miles to areas under its jurisdiction (the largest "territorial" expansion in its history); Canada and Australia added almost as much.[35]

In 1983, President Reagan established an exclusive economic zone for the United States by proclamation, asserting rights over living and nonliving resources as set forth in the 1982 Convention.[36]

Under the 1982 Convention, the "high seas" begin where the coastal states' exclusive economic zones end – at 200 nautical miles. Issues regarding the exploitation of the mineral resources of the seabed underlying the high seas have posed the greatest problems for the United States – problems which, despite strenuous efforts to do so, remain unresolved to this day.

Up to 350 miles out, exploitation of the seabed underlying the high seas may, depending on the circumstances, be governed by the 1982

Convention's provisions on the continental shelf. Beyond the limit of the continental shelf or the exclusive economic zone, however, the seabed underlying the high seas is known as the deep seabed. The potential economic significance of the deep seabed became clear during the 1960s with the discovery of so-called "manganese nodules," which contain also nickel, copper, and cobalt, on the floor of the deep ocean beyond the continental shelves of coastal states. In 1967 Arvid Pardo, Malta's permanent representative at the United Nations, proposed that the UN General Assembly take up the subject of seabed mining and that the deep seabed be regarded as the "common heritage of mankind." There was general agreement in the Assembly that the minerals on the deep seabed are the common heritage of mankind.[37] But there was sharp disagreement over the interpretation and application of this concept. Many developing states were of the view that the minerals on the deep seabed could be exploited only by or on behalf of mankind, not by any state or person on its own account. Under this view, which is reflected in the UN General Assembly's resolution calling for a moratorium on deep seabed mining,[38] exploitation would be lawful only pursuant to the terms of a generally accepted international agreement. In sharp contrast, the US position is that deep seabed mining is one of the high seas freedoms. As such, it is permissible under international law and other states may not interfere with it. At the same time, no claim may be made of sovereign or exclusive rights over any area of the high seas or the seabed, and no seabed mining enterprise may prevent another from mining an area not yet being exploited by it. Conversely, there may be no interference with a mining activity already begun by another state's enterprise.[39]

In keeping with this view, the United States and other developed states took a minimalist view of the legal regime that would govern deep seabed mining. They envisaged an international licensing system whereby an international authority would issue licenses to governments or to their nationals and collect fees or royalties that would be used for international development purposes. The international authority would be dominated by the developed states to assure its limited function. For their part, the developing states insisted on establishing an international authority which would have the exclusive right to mine the seabed beyond national jurisdiction. To this end an International Seabed Authority (ISA) would establish an Enterprise to engage in the mining. Decisions would be taken on the basis of a one-state, one-vote majority. Some developing states also sought arrangements to ensure that the mining of deep seabed minerals would not undermine their production and sale of land-based minerals.

After long and arduous negotiations a compromise was reached, and by 1980 a draft convention had been prepared. As previously noted, the

Reagan administration refused to sign the Convention, however, largely because of its provisions on deep seabed mining. The Restatement (Third) of the Foreign Relations Law of the United States has usefully summarized the seabed regime of the 1982 Convention, as well as US objections to it, as follows:

Sea-bed regime of LOS Convention. Under the LOS Convention, any deep sea-bed mining would have to be conducted in accordance with rules, regulations, and procedures to be drafted by a Preparatory Commission, and to be adopted and from time to time revised by the International Sea-Bed Authority that will start functioning as soon as 60 states ratify the Convention... The Authority would function through: (a) an Assembly, in which all the members might participate and which would act as the "supreme organ" of the Authority with power to establish "general policies"; (b) a Council of 36 members, seats on which are guaranteed for some states, including "the largest consumer" of minerals derived from the area (the United States, as of 1986) and three Eastern European states, with power to establish "specific policies" and to approve "plans of work" for each mining project; and (c) an "Enterprise," with a separate legal personalty, which will carry out mining activities in the area, either directly or through joint ventures with national or private companies. During an interim 25-year period and within defined, strict limits, the Authority would be entitled to establish a production ceiling in order to protect the economies and export earnings of developing countries engaged in the production of certain minerals against the adverse economic effects of sea-bed production.

To facilitate the work of the Enterprise, each applicant for a mining contract would have to present to the Authority two mining sites of equal estimated mining value; the Authority would designate one of them as reserved for the Enterprise, which would be allowed to relinquish it to a developing country. The applicant would also have to arrange for the transfer to the Enterprise (or to a developing country exploiting a reserved area) on fair and reasonable terms and conditions, to be determined in case of disagreement by commercial arbitration, the technology that the contractor would be using in its sea-bed mining activities. A contractor would have a choice between two methods of payment to the Authority...

Since the activities in the deep sea-bed are to be carried out "for the benefit of mankind as a whole," taking into particular consideration the interests and needs of developing states and of peoples who have not yet attained full independence or self-government, the Authority would have the task of ensuring that such states will share equitably in the financial and other economic benefits derived from these activities. As the Enterprise is not likely to have sufficient funds at the beginning to exploit a reserved site, it was agreed... that states parties to the Convention would make available to it the necessary funds for one site, in accordance with the scale of assessments for the United Nations general budget. Such funds (estimated at more than one and a half billion dollars in 1986) would be provided half in the form of long-term interest-free loans, and half by guarantee of debts incurred by the Enterprise in raising the remainder... [40]

United States objections to Convention regime. When the Third United Nations Conference on the Law of the Sea approved the Convention, the United States cast a negative vote . . . In explaining that vote, a spokesman for the United States said that the text was unacceptable as it would deter future development of deep sea-bed mineral resources, because of lack of certainty with regard to the granting of mining contracts, the artificial limitations on sea-bed mineral production, and the imposition of burdensome financial requirements; would not give the United States an adequate role in the decision-making process; would allow amendments to the Convention to enter into force for the United States without its approval; would provide for mandatory transfer of private technology related to sea-bed mining; and would allow the transfer of a portion of funds received from the miners by the International Sea-Bed Authority to national liberation movements . . . In a later statement the White House characterized the deep sea-bed mining regime of the Convention as "hopelessly flawed," and announced that the United States would not participate in the work of the Preparatory Commission established by the Conference to draft regulations for sea-bed mining.[41]

Part XI of the 1982 Convention contains the provisions on deep seabed mining of primary concern to the United States and some other developed states. In 1994, negotiations under the auspices of the UN Secretary-General began in an effort to meet US objections. They resulted in the "Agreement Relating to the Implementation of Part XI of the United Nations Convention on the Law of the Sea of 10 December 1982."[42] By its terms, the Agreement is to be interpreted and applied together with Part XI of the 1982 Convention as a single instrument. In the event of conflict with the provisions of Part XI, the 1994 Agreement prevails. States ratifying the Convention after July 1994 are bound by the Agreement.

The Agreement and its accompanying Annex eliminate the primary US objections to Part XI. The United States is now guaranteed a seat on the Council, as well as on the Finance Committee, in perpetuity, and all substantive decisions of the Assembly shall be taken only on recommendation of the Council or of the Finance Committee. If the Assembly rejects the Council's recommendation, the issue goes back to the Council for further consideration. Most important, perhaps, the decision-making structure of the Council has been changed so that the developed countries can block proposals they reject.

Other key changes effected by the 1994 Agreement include elimination of the 1982 Convention provisions that would have allowed the entry into force for all parties of amendments after ratification by only three-fourths of the parties; elimination of the mandatory technology transfer provisions of the 1982 Convention and their replacement with a set of general principles on the issue of technology transfer; termination of the Convention's provision on production limits of seabed-based mining in order to protect land-based production; replacement of elaborate and expensive financial terms of contract with a set of principles, and reduction of the $500,000 application fee to $250,000; changes to the operational provisions of the Convention to ensure that the Enterprise would become operational only on a decision of the Council, that the Enterprise would be subject to the same obligations applicable to other miners, and that the Enterprise would conduct its initial operations through joint ventures; and elimination of the special privileges accorded to the Enterprise.[43]

The Clinton administration found the terms of the Agreement satisfactory and signed it, and on October 7, 1994, President Clinton transmitted both the 1982 Convention and the 1994 Agreement to the Senate for its advice and consent to ratification.[44] However, although the Bush administration has also expressed its support for ratification,[45] as of this writing, the Senate Committee on Foreign Relations has not yet held hearings on the Convention and the Agreement. Later in this chapter we shall explore some possible reasons for this inaction.

The Agreement entered into force on July 28, 1996. As of August 6, 2003, there are 115 parties to the 1982 Convention, including the European Union, that are bound by the Agreement.

Dispute settlement

The 1982 Convention contains elaborate, extensive, and highly complex provisions for the settlement of various disputes under the Convention.[46] At the outset the Convention emphasizes the obligation to settle disputes by peaceful means (Article 279) and informal methods of dispute settlement, such as negotiation and conciliation (Articles 280–285). If recourse to negotiation or other mechanisms fails, parties may choose among several third-party tribunals. Under Article 287, their choices include the International Tribunal for the Law of the Sea (ITLOS) established by the Convention; the International Court of Justice; an arbitral tribunal; or a special arbitral tribunal for specified categories of disputes.[47] States parties may declare their preferred type of tribunal at any time.

The reference to third-party dispute settlement is obligatory, but states have a choice. If the parties to a dispute have not accepted the same procedure for the settlement of the dispute, it shall be referred to arbitration, unless the parties otherwise agree. Similarly, if a state party to a dispute has not made a declaration as to its preferred type of tribunal, it shall be deemed to have accepted arbitration.

The Convention, however, allows a state to declare in writing that it does not accept compulsory dispute settlement procedures with respect to all or any disputes relating to the following subjects: military activities, law enforcement activities related to certain fisheries and marine scientific research, historic bays and title thereto, marine boundary delimitations, and situations over which the UN Security Council is exercising the functions assigned to it by the UN Charter (Articles 297, 298). In his message transmitting the 1982 Convention and the 1994 Agreement to the Senate, President Clinton recommended that on ratification the United States make such a declaration with respect to all the possible exceptions listed in Article 298.[48] Moreover, in his report to the President, Secretary of State Warren Christopher recommended that the United States choose special arbitration for all the categories of disputes covered and regular arbitration under the Convention for all other disputes.[49]

The choice is much more limited, however, with respect to disputes over mining of the deep seabed. Under the Convention most disputes will be heard by a distinct judicial chamber, the eleven-member Sea-Bed Disputes Chamber of the International Tribunal for the Law of the Sea (ITLOS). The Seabed Disputes Chamber has jurisdiction over disputes that arise over the interpretation or application of Part XI of the Convention, certain acts of the International Seabed Authority, mining exploration and exploitation contracts, and certain activities on the deep seabed (Article 187). States parties, the Authority, the Enterprise, states enterprises, and natural or juridical persons may appear before the Chamber in various categories of disputes.

Part XI of the Convention does provide for some flexibility. States parties may agree to submit their dispute to a special chamber of ITLOS rather than to the Seabed Chamber. Alternatively, any party to such a dispute may submit it to a different, three-member ad hoc chamber. Any party to a dispute concerning the interpretation or application of mining contracts may opt for commercial arbitration. Under the 1994 Agreement disputes relating to the subsidization of production, which are subject to the General Agreement on Tariffs and Trade and its codes and successor agreements, may be decided by World Trade Organization dispute settlement procedures.

The United States, the law of the sea, and the rule of law: prospects for the future

At this writing it is unclear whether and, if so, when, the United States will adhere to the 1982 Convention and the 1994 Agreement. Although the Bush administration has declared its support for ratification, it remains to be seen how hard it will press the Senate to give its advice and consent. Moreover, although a primary barrier to ratification – former

Senator Jesse Helms – has departed the Senate, there is still considerable opposition to ratification in that body that is not limited to the right wing of the Republican Party. It is time to turn to a consideration of some of the reasons for this opposition.

Arguments for the opposition

Perhaps the most salient argument made by those opposing ratification is that the United States already enjoys the benefits the Convention would provide while avoiding the burdens being a party would entail. Specifically, the opponents argue, the United States already benefits from the navigational and overflight provisions of the Convention because they have become part of the corpus of customary international law.[50] To support this proposition the opponents can point to the large number of parties to the Convention as a form of state practice contributing to norms of customary international law, as well as to the general acceptance of navigation and overflight rights outside the Convention context. The "package deal" limitation on these rights advanced by some developing countries, the argument continues, has not been accepted in practice.

Similarly, the opponents contend, the United States currently benefits fully from the Convention's provisions on coastal states' control over natural resources, since the declarations on its territorial sea, contiguous zone, exclusive economic zone, and continental shelf have gone unchallenged. Nor is there any likelihood of a challenge to US exercises of jurisdiction along the lines authorized by the Convention arising in the future.

In the opponents' view, the disadvantages of the United States being a party to the Convention are considerable. Most particularly, the United States and US companies would then become subject to the Convention's regulatory scheme for the mining of the deep seabed, which, even with the changes effected by the 1994 Agreement, remains unacceptable. It is not at all certain that the United States would be able to have its views prevail in the Assembly or in the Council, the two decision-making organs of the International Seabed Authority. The Enterprise is likely to be dominated by international bureaucrats with little understanding of business and may interfere with more efficient deep seabed mining by private firms. According to opponents, the 1994 Agreement does not really "fix" the deep seabed mining regime, which still represents a "giveaway" to developing countries.[51] They point to language in the Convention that, as a policy matter, activities in the deep seabed area should take into "particular" consideration the interests and needs of developing states (Article 140, paragraph 1), as well as to several other provisions in the Convention which they contend discriminate in favor of developing states to the detriment of Western states and their nationals and companies.[52]

The opponents also view with great suspicion the dispute settlement provisions of the Convention, especially their compulsory nature. As we shall see in the next chapter, the Senate has become increasingly suspicious of international adjudication as an infringement of US sovereignty, and in recent years it has routinely rejected compromissory clauses calling for reference of disputes concerning the interpretation and application of treaties to the International Court of Justice. Although the 1982 Convention would allow the United States to choose international arbitration to settle disputes, rather than the ICJ or ITLOS, the United States could still be required to submit to international adjudication against its wishes. The opponents would prefer that the United States retain complete discretion to decide on an ad hoc basis whether to agree to international adjudication and, if so, what kind.

There are, of course, numerous arguments in favor of US ratification.[53] It is not necessary for present purposes, however, to discuss these in any detail. Rather, the point is that so far they have not convinced the Senate to give its advice and consent to ratification. Because of the Senate's inaction, the United States has not become part of perhaps the single most ambitious attempt to bring the rule of law to bear on a major subject of international affairs.

The United States as "free rider"

It is ironic that the United States should so far choose not to become a party to a convention that it labored so hard to help produce, including its efforts to fix the deep seabed mining regime through the 1994 Agreement. As we have already seen before in this study, however, resistance by the Senate or both Houses of Congress has often hindered efforts by the executive branch to support the rule of law in international affairs. The US failure to become a party to the Vienna Convention on the Law of Treaties is one example we have examined. Alternatively, the executive branch may decide at a late stage in negotiations not to support a treaty it has been instrumental in developing – the Landmines Treaty, the Statute for the International Criminal Court, and the proposed protocol to the Biological Weapons Convention are examples.

In the case of the Vienna Convention on the Law of Treaties and the UN Convention on the Law of the Sea (UNCLOS), the United States has become what the economists would call a free rider, that is, "a person who receives the benefit of a good but avoids paying for it."[54] From the

Law of the Sea Convention the United States has received the benefits of those provisions of the Convention that have become norms of customary international law while avoiding the costs involved in participating in the International Seabed Authority, including helping to support its funding. It also avoids possible costs involved in participating in the mandatory dispute settlement procedures of the Convention, including the impact of an adverse judgment.

Prospects

When it signed the Agreement on July 29, 1994, the United States announced that "it intends to apply the agreement provisionally. Provisional application by the United States will allow us to advance our seabed mining interests by participating in the International Seabed Authority from the outset to ensure that the implementation of the regime is consistent with those interests."[55] On July 17, 1996, the United States notified the United Nations of "its intention . . . to continue to participate as a Member of the International Seabed Authority [ISA] on a provisional basis."[56] The United States later requested the ISA Council for an extension of its provisional membership of the Authority until November 16, 1998, the last extension permitted by the Agreement (see Agreement, Annex, Section 1, paragraph 12). On that date, its provisional membership ended and the United States became an observer state to the Authority.[57] As a result, the United States lost the seats it held on the ISA Council, the Legal and Technical Commission, the Finance Committee, and in the Assembly. When the Authority convened in August 1999, Italy replaced the United States on the Council and a national from Poland replaced the US national on the Finance Committee.

It is debatable whether the United States lost anything of value when it lost its seat in the various organs of the International Seabed Authority. At this writing the economic situation is such that there is no current interest in deep seabed mining, since there is more than an adequate supply at a modest price of the land-based minerals that constitute the manganese nodules of the deep seabed. The irony of the current situation is plain, since the debate over the deep seabed mining regime established by the 1982 Law of the Sea Convention was based in substantial measure on the expectation that the economic return from such mining would be considerable. As noted recently by one commentator, "[o]ne measure of waning expectations of a seabed mineral bonanza was the complaint by the ISA Secretary-General at the annual meeting of States Parties to the Convention that a large number of ISA members were in arrears in their assessed contributions, and it was difficult to secure a quorum at ISA meetings."[58] Another commentator has expressed his views much more emphatically:

> The most extraordinary story of the 1982 Convention's handling of high seas freedoms involves fist-sized lumps of manganese, cobalt, nickel, and copper. Known as "manganese nodules," these are found on the deep seabed, under miles of water, and far from shore. Beginning with an innocuous enough speech by Malta's delegate, Arvid Pardo, before the UN General Assembly in 1967, the international community became entranced with these nuggets. Seeing a ready source of valuable strategic minerals there for the taking, developing nations lobbied hard for the deep seabed minerals to be declared the "common heritage of mankind." What ensued at UNCLOS III were negotiations by delegates to fashion a set of international law rules to exploit this resource. And what a baroque regime it was: elaborate articles on production limits for seabed mining, complex regulatory systems including the creation of an international mining company (called "The Enterprise"), mandatory technology transfer requirements, and detailed institutional arrangements with the creation of a new, International Sea Bed Authority (ISBA).
>
> There was just one problem with all of this. No technology existed – or has been developed – to recover manganese nodules from the deep seabed. (Robots and very, very long vacuum hoses have been proposed.) More importantly, the mineral economies are such that there has been absolutely no incentive to develop such proprietary technology, especially as the LOST [Law of the Sea Treaty] required that such intellectual property be given away to the Enterprise. In short, the deep seabed mining provisions of Part XI of the LOST were a fiasco. They were, in large measure, the reason why the US refused to sign the 1982 Convention. After the most offending features of Part XI were amended in a later "Implementation Agreement," the US did sign (but has not yet ratified) the treaty...
>
> The real lesson of the deep seabed mining regime is the dangers that come with internationalizing a resource. Although the common heritage principle sounds alluring, it is often impractical, especially when private sector initiative is stifled. The negotiations of Part XI also illustrate the absurdities of lawyers and diplomats negotiating ahead of the curve of science, technology and economics. The elaborate provisions of the LOST were utterly irrelevant and fanciful, and had to be later changed. While international lawyers should take pride in developing creative legal regimes, to do so in advance of practical certainties is folly.[59]

Whether the "creative" legal regime of the 1982 Convention and the 1994 Agreement amounts to "folly" is, of course, debatable. In any event, US legislation,[60] enacted in 1980, adopts the position that, absent their becoming a party to a treaty to the contrary, states have the right to mine the seabed as an aspect of the freedom of the seas, and that national licensing of such mining is not an assertion of sovereignty over any part of the seabed. The legislation recognizes that seabed resources are the common heritage of mankind, and provides for the establishment of an international revenue-sharing fund. In adopting this legislation, Congress sought to provide "assured and nondiscriminatory access" and "security of tenure" to US nationals seeking to exploit deep seabed resources. Although the legislation was intended to be transitional pending the United States becoming party to a treaty governing deep seabed mining, it provides that any regulation issued under the legislation not inconsistent with later treaties shall remain valid. Similar interim legislation was adopted by other states, and in 1984 the United States and seven other states signed a Provisional Understanding Regarding Deep Seabed Mining, which set forth a preliminary process for resolving overlapping claims to deep seabed mining areas.

Developing countries challenged the legality of such unilateral legislation,[61] even before the adoption of the 1982 Convention and of the 1980 US legislation, and it is clearly incompatible with the approach taken by the 1982 Convention and the 1994 Agreement. Under the 1982 Convention disputes between parties involving deep seabed mining must be resolved by the International Tribunal for the Law of the Sea. The Convention, however, makes no provision for disputes with non-parties.[62]

In light of the lack of interest in undertaking deep seabed mining, such a dispute seems purely hypothetical and likely to remain so for the indefinite future.

Other disputes regarding law of the sea issues covered by the 1982 Convention, however, may well arise in the future. As long as the United States fails to become a party to the Convention, it will retain complete discretion to decide whether it wishes to use third-party adjudication to resolve such disputes. It will also have chosen to opt out of a rule of law approach in large part of its own making.

Notes

1. L. F. Damrosch et al., International Law: Cases and Materials 1384 (4th ed., 2001) (emphasis added).
2. M. W. Janis & J. E. Noyes, Cases and Commentary on International Law 639 (2d ed., 2001).
3. See B. E. Carter & P. R. Trimble, International Law: Selected Documents and New Developments 952–53 (3rd ed., 1999).
4. *Id.* at 953.
5. The Convention on the Territorial Sea and the Contiguous Zone, 15 UST 1606, TIAS No. 5639, 516 UNTS 205; the Convention on the High Seas, 13 UST 2312, TIAS No. 5200, 450 UNTS 82; the Convention on the Continental Shelf, 15 UST 471, TIAS No. 5578, 499 UNTS 311; and the Convention on Fishing and Conservation of the Living Resources of the High Seas, 17 UST 138, TIAS No. 5969, 559 UNTS 285.
6. Policy of the United States with Respect to the Natural Resources of the Subsoil and Sea Bed of the Continental Shelf, Presidential Proclamation 2667, Sept. 28, 1945, 10 Fed. Reg. 12303 (1945).

7. Draft Convention on the Law of the Sea (Informal Text), A/CONF.62/WP.10/Rev. 3 (1980).
8. The vote was 130 states in favor, 4 against, and 17 abstentions. United Nations Convention on the Law of the Sea (1982 Convention – UNCLOS), UN Doc. A/CONF 62/122, 21 INT'L LEG. MATERIALS, 1245 n. 55 UN Sales No. E.83.V. 5; 1833 UNTS 3. Done at Montego Bay, Jamaica 10 Dec. 1982; entered into force 16 Nov. 1994.
9. For a short but helpful bibliography of leading writings on the Convention, see Marjorie Ann Browne, *The Law of the Sea Convention and US Policy*, CRS Issue Brief for Congress, Feb. 14, 2001, at 11–13, *at* http://cnie.org/NLE/CRSreports/Marine/mar-16.cfm.
10. Article 19 of the 1982 Convention provides:

Meaning of Innocent Passage

1. Passage is innocent so long as it is not prejudicial to the peace, good order or security of the coastal State. Such passage shall take place in conformity with this Convention and with other rules of international law.
2. Passage of a foreign ship shall be considered to be prejudicial to the peace, good order or security of the coastal State if in the territorial sea it engages in any of the following activities:
   (a) any threat or use of force against the sovereignty, territorial integrity or political independence of the coastal State, or in any other manner in violation of the principles of international law embodied in the Charter of the United Nations;
   (b) any exercise or practice with weapons of any kind;
   (c) any act aimed at collecting information to the prejudice of the defence or security of the coastal State;
   (d) any act of propaganda aimed at affecting the defence or security of the coastal State;
   (e) the launching, landing or taking on board of any aircraft;
   (f) the launching, landing or taking on board of any military device;
   (g) the loading or unloading of any commodity, currency or person contrary to the customs, fiscal, immigration or sanitary laws and regulations of the coastal State;
   (h) any act of wilful and serious pollution contrary to this Convention;
   (i) any fishing activities;
   (j) the carrying out of research or survey activities;
   (k) any act aimed at interfering with any systems of communication or any other facilities or installations of the coastal State;
   (l) any other activity not having a direct bearing on passage.

11. See Arts. 37–44 of the 1982 Convention.
12. See Arts. 36, 38, and 45 of the 1982 Convention.
13. Art. 53 of the 1982 Convention.
14. Art. 54 of the 1982 Convention.
15. Art. 52 of the 1982 Convention.
16. See Janusz Symonides, *Origin and Legal Essence of the Contiguous Zone*, 20 OCEAN DEVELOPMENT AND INT'L L. 203 (1989).
17. *Id.*
18. See, in this connection, United States v. F/V *Taiyo Maru*, Number 28, SOI 600, 395 F. Supp. 413 (D.Me. 1975). In that case, a Japanese ship was found fishing illegally and was seized in the United States exclusive fishing zone, nine miles offshore and beyond the then three-mile territorial sea limit. The defendants argued that the seizure was not

permitted by Art. 24 of the 1958 Convention on the Territorial Sea and the Contiguous Zone, but the court held that the list in Art. 24 of purposes for which a contiguous zone may be established is not exhaustive.

19. For brief discussion, see DAMROSCH ET AL., *supra* note 1, at 1416–18.
20. One prominent incident was the US interception on the high seas of vessels bound for Cuba, on the ground that such action was necessary to meet the threat posed by the installing of Soviet missiles in Cuba in October, 1962.
21. For a contrary view see Ruth Wedgwood, *A Pirate is a Pirate*, WALL ST. J., Dec. 16, 2002, at A12, col. 2.
22. See Yehuda Z. Blum, *The Gulf of Sidra Incident*, 80 AM. J. INT'L L. 668 (1986).
23. For a view that the United States was not entitled to use armed force under these circumstances, see JOHN F. MURPHY, STATE SUPPORT OF INTERNATIONAL TERRORISM 106–08 (1989).
24. Proclamation and statement of President Reagan, March 1983. Reproduced in 22 INT'L LEGAL MAT. 462 (1983); US State Dept. Bulletin, 1983, No. 2075, at 70–71.
25. J. L. Malone (Assistant Secretary of State for Ocean Affairs) in an address to the Law of the Sea Institute, 24 Sept. 1984, State Dept. Release Current Policy No. 617 (Sep. 24, 1984).
26. For references to statements rejecting non-party rights, see Luke T. Lee, *The Law of the Sea Convention and Third States*, 77 AM. J. INT'L L. 541, 547, n. 18 (1983). For arguments against non-party rights, see Kathryn Surace-Smith, *Note, United States Activity Outside the Law of the Sea Convention,* 84 COLUM. L. REV. 1032, 1055 (1984).
27. OSCAR SCHACHTER, INTERNATIONAL LAW IN THEORY AND PRACTICE 287 (1991),
28. *Id.* at 290–91.
29. See, e.g., DAVID J. BEDERMAN, INTERNATIONAL LAW FRAMEWORKS 124 (2001).
30. See Case Concerning Delimitation of the Maritime Boundary in the Gulf of Maine (Canada/United States), [1984] ICJ Rep. 246, 294.
31. See Restatement (Third) of the Foreign Relations Law of the United States, Section 515, Reporters' Note 1.
32. Because of the inability of states to agree on maritime boundary delimitations, there have been numerous arbitrations and adjudications of these issues, including a number of cases before the International Court of Justice. For a listing and discussion of some of these cases, see DAMROSCH ET AL., *supra* note 1, at 1428–30.
33. For discussion, see SCHACHTER, *supra* note 27, at 276–77.
34. See Arts. 55–75 of the 1982 Convention.
35. SCHACHTER, *supra* note 27, at 277.
36. 19 Weekly Compilation of Presidential Documents 383 (1983), 83 Dep't. State Bull. No. 2075, at 70–71 (1983), 22 INT'L. LEG. MATERIALS 464 (1983).
37. See Declaration of Principles Governing the Sea-Bed and the Ocean Floor, and the Subsoil Thereof, Beyond the Limits of National Jurisdiction, adopted by GA Res. 2749 (XXV), 25 UN GAOR Supp. No. 28, at 24, paras. 1–4, 9 (1970).
38. Moratorium on Exploitation of Resources of the Deep Seabed, GA Res. 2574 D (XXIV) (1969).
39. See Restatement (Third) of the Foreign Relations Law of the United States, Section 523, comment b (1987).
40. Restatement (Third) of the Foreign Relations Law of the United States, Section 523, Reporters' Note 3 (1987).
41. *Id.*, Reporters' Note 4.

42. Signed July 29,1994, and endorsed as an annex to a resolution of the UN General Assembly (GA Res. 48/263, 1994) (adopted with 121 states in favor, 0 opposed, and 7 abstentions).
43. For further consideration of these changes, see Bernard H. Oxman, *The 1994 Agreement and the Convention*, 88 Am. J. Int'l L. 687, 688–695 (1994); Browne, *supra* note 9.
44. Message from the President of the United States Transmitting United Nations Convention on the Law of the Sea and the Agreement Relating to the Implementation of Part XI of the United Nations Convention on the Law of the Sea, Sen. Treaty Doc. No. 103–39, pp. vii–viii (Oct. 7, 1994).
45. See, e.g., Statement by Ambassador Mary Beth West, Deputy Assistant Secretary of State for Oceans and Fisheries, to the UN Open-Ended Informal Consultative Process on Oceans and Law of the Sea, April 8, 2002, *at* www.state.gov/gloes/ris/rm/2002/9628 htm.
46. The dispute settlement provisions are found in general in Part XV(Arts. 279–299) and Annex VI, which contains the Statute for the International Tribunal for the Law of the Sea, as well as in Annex V on conciliation, Annex VII on arbitration, and Annex VIII on special arbitration.
47. The categories of disputes that are subject to special arbitration tribunals composed of experts include fisheries, protection of the marine environment, marine scientific research, and navigation. See Annex VIII to the Convention.
48. See Message from the President of the United States, *supra* note 44, at 85–87.
49. Report of Secretary of State Warren Christopher to the President, dated Sept. 23, 1994, reproduced in part in 89 Am. J. Int'l L. 113 (1995).
50. See Browne, *supra* note 9, at 3.
51. *Id.* at 8.
52. As Marjorie Ann Browne notes:

> Article 140 of the Convention urges promoting the participation of developing States in activities in the Area. Article 150, on policies relating to activities in the Area, seeks to ensure the expansion of opportunities for participation in deep seabed mining, participation in revenues by the Authority and the transfer of technology to the Enterprise and developing States, and protection of developing countries from adverse effects on their economies (Article 150 (c),(d), (g), and (h)). Section 5, para. 1(b) of the Agreement urges contractors and their respective sponsoring States to cooperate with the ISA in facilitating access to technology by the Enterprise or its joint venture, or by the developing State. In addition, the Agreement provides for establishment of an economic assistance fund for those developing countries suffering serious adverse effects to their land-based production of minerals due to seabed mining operations (Section 7). Opponents argue that the combined effect of these provisions is to preserve a special status for developing States, at the expense of the United States and other industrialized nations and their companies. *Id.* at 8–9.

53. See, e.g., Bernard H. Oxman, *United States Interests in the Law of the Sea Convention*, 88 Am. J. Int'l L. 167 (1994); John R. Stevenson & Bernard H. Oxman, *The Future of the United States Convention on the Law of the Sea*, 88 Am. J. Int'l L. 488 (1994).
54. N. Gregory Mankiw, Principles of Economics 222 (1998).
55. As quoted in Browne, *supra* note 9, at 7. Most of the following discussion of provisional application by the United States of the 1994 Agreement is based on Browne's analysis.
56. *Id.*

57. Although recognized by Art. 25 of the Vienna Convention on the Law of Treaties, provisional application may itself be a source of controversy. As reported by Browne, *id.*, at 10, a 1993 US Senate study suggests:

    In the United States, provisional application of a treaty may be subject to question especially if it gives temporary effect to a treaty prior to its receiving the advice and consent of the Senate. An agreement to apply a treaty provisionally is in essence an executive agreement to undertake temporarily what the treaty may call for permanently. (Treaties and Other International Agreements: The Role of the United States Senate. S. Prt. 103–53, 1993, p. 84)

58. Houston Putnam Lowry, *Recent Developments in the International Law of the Sea*, 35 INT'L LAW. 787, 792 (2001).
59. BEDERMAN, *supra* note 29, at 127–28.
60. The Deep Seabed Hard Mineral Resources Act, Pub. L. No. 96–283, 94 Stat. 553 (1980).
61. See Letter dated 23 April 1979 from the Group of Legal Experts on the Question of Unilateral Legislation Addressed to the Chairman of the Group of 77, UN Doc. A/CONF. 62/77.
62. It has been suggested that the UN General Assembly might be asked in such a case to submit a question to the International Court of Justice for an advisory opinion. See Restatement (Third) of the Foreign Relations Law of the United States, Section 523, Reporters' Note 2.

7 The International Court of Justice

Earlier in this study, we have had occasion to examine US interactions with and attitudes toward the International Court of Justice.[1] In this chapter we seek to focus more precisely on the reasons for the present malaise.

From an historic perspective, the first movement toward the establishment of an international adjudicatory body came at the Hague Peace Conferences of 1899 and 1908.[2] Despite enjoying the support of a number of states, however, proposals for a permanent international court came to naught. The only institution to emerge from these conferences was the Permanent Court of Arbitration (PCA, created in 1899). But the so-called permanent court is not a true judicial institution. Rather, the PCA merely provides facilities for international arbitration, including lists of available arbitrators.

After World War I, in the wake of the extensive carnage caused by that conflict, the Permanent Court of International Justice (PCIJ) came into being as the judicial organ of the League of Nations. As is well known, the United States never joined the League of Nations or ratified the Court's Statute. As a result, in the words of Rosalyn Higgins, a British national and judge of the International Court of Justice:

> The United States – in a pattern of treaty participation that was to occur many times later in history, down to this very day – was a major player in the formulation of the Protocol and Statute, and then failed to endorse their terms because Senate approval was not forthcoming. Although refusing to approve the Paris Peace Treaties whose terms it had done so much to secure, a Judge of American nationality nonetheless served on the Bench of the PCIJ throughout its lifetime.[3]

The International Court of Justice is in every sense the direct successor of the Permanent Court of International Justice, since the Statute of the ICJ is essentially the same as that of the PCIJ. Also, the jurisprudence of the PCIJ is often cited by the ICJ and remains highly relevant to its decisions.

All members of the United Nations are parties to the ICJ Statute and therefore eligible to submit disputes to it. There are fifteen judges on the Court elected by the Security Council and the General Assembly in separate elections by majority vote. Although not required by the Court's Statute, in practice each of the permanent members of the Security Council has a national on the Court. All questions are decided by a majority vote of the judges present. In the event of a tie, the president has a casting vote. The casting vote has been used in several of the Court's most controversial cases, including the 1996 *Nuclear Weapons Advisory Opinion* when the judges were equally divided, and President Bedjaoui (Algeria) cast the deciding vote, and the 1966 South West Africa Cases,[4] when President Spender (Australia) cast the deciding vote.

The jurisdiction of the Court in contentious cases is based on the principles of consent and reciprocity. Article 36 of the Court's Statute provides:

1. The jurisdiction of the Court comprises all cases which the parties refer to it and all matters specially provided for in the Charter of the United Nations or in treaties and conventions in force.
2. The states parties to the present Statute may at any time declare that they recognize as compulsory *ipso facto* and without any special agreement, in relation to any other state accepting the same obligation, the jurisdiction of the Court in all legal disputes concerning:
   (a) the interpretation of a treaty;
   (b) any question of international law;
   (c) the existence of any fact which, if established, would constitute a breach of an international obligation;
   (d) the nature or extent of the reparation to be made for the breach of an international obligation.
3. The declarations referred to above may be made unconditionally or on condition of reciprocity on the part of several or certain states, or for a certain time.
4. Such declarations shall be deposited with the Secretary-General of the United Nations, who shall transmit copies thereof to the parties to the Statute and to the registrar of the Court.
5. Declarations made under Article 36 of the Statute of the Permanent Court of International Justice and which are still in force shall be deemed, as between the parties to the present Statute, to be acceptance of the compulsory jurisdiction of the International Court of Justice for the period which they still have to run and in accordance with their terms.
6. In the event of a dispute as to whether the Court has jurisdiction, the matter shall be settled by the decision of the Court.

Under Article 36 there are basically three ways in which a state can give its consent to the Court's jurisdiction. First, the parties to a dispute may decide on an ad hoc basis to refer it to the Court. The parties usually do so by way of a special agreement called a *compromis*. Second, the parties to a bilateral or multilateral treaty may agree in advance to submit disputes regarding the interpretation or application of the treaty to the Court, through the inclusion of a compromissory clause in the treaty. In cases involving compromissory clauses the primary jurisdictional question facing the Court is whether the dispute falls within the relevant treaty containing the clause. Third, under Article 36(2), which covers the so-called compulsory jurisdiction of the Court, states may agree in advance that the Court shall have jurisdiction over *all* legal disputes concerning the four topics listed in subparagraphs (a)–(d). This is done through a state's filing a declaration with the Court that, under Article 36(3), "may be made unconditionally or on condition of reciprocity on the part of several or certain states, or for a certain time."

It is useful to compare the consent to the Court's jurisdiction that a state gives under a compromissory clause in a treaty with the consent it gives when it files a declaration under Article 36(2). Under a compromissory clause, states consent only to the Court's jurisdiction over disputes arising over the interpretation and application of a particular treaty. By contrast, a state filing a declaration under Article 36(2) consents to the Court's jurisdiction over a broad range of future disputes that may be beyond its contemplation at the time the declaration is filed or even beyond its imagination. Clearly, for example, it was never contemplated by the United States that it would be subject to the Court's jurisdiction in a suit involving the facts of *Nicaragua v. United States*. Such a broad consent in advance of a dispute may be especially problematic in an age when the subjects covered by international law are growing at an exponential pace. In any event, of the 191 states that are parties to the Court's statute, only about 62 currently have made declarations under Article 36(2). Most significantly, the United Kingdom is the only one of the five permanent members of the Security Council which accepts the so-called compulsory jurisdiction of the Court.

As to the principle of reciprocity, this is no problem in a case where the Court's jurisdiction arises under Article 36(1) because of the mutual obligations of the parties to a *compromis* or to a treaty containing a compromissory clause. Reciprocity, or the lack thereof, may, however, be a major issue in an Article 36(2) case, where the Court must determine whether both parties, because of their unilateral declarations, have accepted the same obligation. Because of the language "in relation to any other state accepting the same obligation" in Article 36(2), the Court has decided that the respondent (defendant) may invoke, by way of reciprocity, any material conditions that the applicant (plaintiff) has placed on its own consent to jurisdiction. As we shall see, however, the US attempt to rely on the reciprocity principle in the *Nicaragua* case proved to be unavailing.

We turn now to consideration of the US experience before the International Court of Justice. It has, on the whole, not been a happy one. In part, this has been due to an unwillingness of the United States fully to accept the Court as a third-party decision maker – a primary component, of course, of the rule of law.

The United States and the Court's compulsory jurisdiction

Although the United States accepted the Court's compulsory jurisdiction, its 1946 declaration reflected a substantial distrust of the Court, through the provisos or reservations it included in the declaration. It read as follows:

I, Harry S. Truman, President of the United States of America, declare on behalf of the United States of America, under Article 36, paragraph 2, of the Statute of the International Court of Justice, and in accordance with the Resolution of 2 August 1946 of the Senate of the United States of America (two-thirds of the Senators present concurring therein), that the United States of America recognizes as compulsory *ipso facto* and without special agreement, in relation to any other State accepting the same obligation, the jurisdiction of the International Court of Justice in all legal disputes hereafter arising concerning –
(a) the interpretation of a treaty;
(b) any question of international law;
(c) the existence of any fact which, if established, would constitute a breach of an international obligation;
(d) the nature or extent of the reparation to be made for the breach of an international obligation;

Provided, that this declaration shall not apply to –
(a) disputes the solution of which the parties shall entrust to other tribunals by virtue of agreements already in existence or which may be concluded in the future; or
(b) disputes with regard to matters which are essentially within the domestic jurisdiction of the United States of America as determined by the United States of America; or
(c) disputes arising under a multilateral treaty, unless (1) all parties to the treaty affected by the decision are also parties to the case before the Court, or (2) the United States of America specially agrees to jurisdiction; and

Provided further, that this declaration shall remain in force for a period of five years and thereafter until the expiration of six months after notice may be given to terminate this declaration.

(Signed) Harry S. Truman

Done at Washington this fourteenth day of August 1946.

The most disabling proviso was (b), which excluded disputes regarding matters essentially within the domestic jurisdiction of the United States *as determined by the United States of America.* The italicized language was known as the Connally Amendment after the US senator who proposed it. The self-judging character of the Connally Amendment arrogated to the United States a decision that arguably was reserved to the Court under Article 36(6) of its Statute, which provides that if there is dispute over whether the Court has jurisdiction, "the matter shall be settled by the decision of the Court."[5] More important, from a practical perspective, the Connally Amendment disabled the United States from being an applicant (plaintiff) before the Court because under the principle of reciprocity the respondent (defendant) state could invoke the Amendment against the United States. This was done in outrageous circumstances in a case brought by the United States against Bulgaria for an attack against an El Al Israel aircraft with six American passengers on board that had been driven off course by strong winds and was flying innocently over Bulgarian territory and trying to return to its course.[6] The attack resulted in the death of all passengers on board the aircraft and the destruction of their property. In response to Bulgaria's invoking the Connally Amendment against it, the United States initially argued that Bulgaria was not entitled to determine that the dispute fell essentially within its domestic jurisdiction, because such a determination would fly in the face of the facts of the case and constitute an arbitrary determination in bad faith. The United States maintained this position up to the point where the Court scheduled open oral hearings in the case.[7] A few days prior to the date set for oral hearings, however, in a communication addressed to the Registrar of the Court on May 13, 1960, the United States reversed itself and requested the discontinuance of the proceedings and the removal of the case from the Court's docket. The Court granted the US request on May 30,1960.[8]

The reversal of the US position on the interpretation and application of the Connally Amendment was based on "further study and consideration of the history and background of reservation (b)" which led to the conclusion, contrary to the earlier US argument, that a determination under the Connally Amendment was not subject to review or approval by any tribunal. Accordingly, as stated by the Legal Adviser of the US Department of State in his letter to the Registrar of the Court, a "determination under reservation (b) that a matter is essentially domestic constitutes an absolute bar to jurisdiction irrespective of the propriety or arbitrariness of the determination."[9] It is unclear whether the "further study" cited by the Legal Adviser included consultations between the US executive branch and members of the Senate, but the possibility cannot be discounted. Whatever the motivation behind the US change of position, it is clear, as noted by David Bederman, that, since the Connally

Amendment was a major bar to the United States ever being able to pursue a case successfully under the Court's compulsory jurisdiction, it "is proof positive that the most important rule of all in international affairs is the law of unintended consequences."[10]

The same might be said of reservation (c), the second major reservation to the US declaration. Commonly called the "Vandenberg Amendment" after the US senator who proposed it, reservation (c) had as its primary purpose preventing the Court from making a ruling – on treaty interpretation in cases involving the United States and one of its treaty partners to a multilateral treaty – that would have no binding effect in disputes with other parties to the treaty because of Article 59 of the Court's Statute, which provides that a decision of the Court shall have "no binding force except between the parties and in respect of that particular case." Such a ruling might oblige the United States to take contrary positions or perform mutually contradictory actions in later cases involving other treaty parties. As we shall see below, the United States successfully invoked the Vandenberg Amendment in the *Nicaragua* case, but the result was that the Court based its rulings on the use of force on customary international law and not on the UN Charter.

Nicaragua v. United States *(Jurisdiction and Admissibility)*

The decision of the International Court of Justice in *Nicaragua v. United States*, in both its jurisdictional[11] and merits[12] phases, is perhaps the most controversial judgment ever handed down by the Court in a contentious proceeding.[13] It is noteworthy that only at the jurisdictional stage did the United States argue its case, since it withdrew from the Court's proceedings after losing on the jurisdictional and admissibility issues.

The case began in 1984 with Nicaragua charging the United States with violations of customary and treaty law by military and paramilitary activities against Nicaragua. Nicaragua accused the United States of attacks on pipelines, storage and port facilities, and Nicaraguan naval patrol boats; the mining of Nicaraguan ports; and violation of Nicaraguan air space; as well as training, arming, equipping, financing, and supplying counter-revolutionary forces (called the contras) that sought to overthrow the government of Nicaragua. Nicaragua contended that these acts constituted violations of Article 2(4) of the UN Charter and corresponding principles of international law.

At the jurisdictional stage, the United States vigorously advanced a number of arguments. Most particularly, it contended that Nicaragua had never effectively accepted the compulsory jurisdiction of the Court. Unlike the United States, Nicaragua was a member of the League of

Nations. Such membership, however, did not automatically make it a party to the Statute of the Permanent Court of International Justice. Rather, if a member state of the League desired to become a party to the Permanent Court's Statute, it was required to accede to the Protocol of Signature of the Statute of the Court. Nicaragua signed the Protocol, but the Protocol provided that it was subject to ratification and that instruments of ratification were to be sent to the Secretary-General of the League of Nations. On September 24, 1929, Nicaragua deposited with the Secretary-General of the League a declaration accepting unconditionally the jurisdiction of the Court.[14] On November 29, 1939, the Ministry of Foreign Affairs of Nicaragua sent a telegram to the Secretary-General of the League advising him of the dispatch of the instrument of ratification of the Protocol. But the files of the League contained no record of an instrument of ratification by Nicaragua ever having been received, and no evidence was adduced to show that such an instrument of ratification was ever dispatched to Geneva. After World War II Nicaragua became an original member of the United Nations.

According to the United States, therefore, Nicaragua never became a party to the Statute of the Permanent Court and its 1929 declaration was not "still in force" within the meaning of the English text of Article 36(5) of the Statute of the International Court of Justice. The majority of the Court, however, disagreed. It noted that the Nicaraguan declaration was valid at the time when the new Statute of the International Court of Justice applied, since under the PCIJ system, a declaration was valid only on condition that it had been made by a state which had signed the Protocol of Signature of the Statute, which Nicaragua had done. Since Nicaragua had not deposited its instrument of ratification, the declaration had not become binding. But it could have become binding at any time up to the time that the International Court of Justice came into existence. In any event, to the Court, the key question was whether the Nicaraguan declaration was "still in force" within the meaning of Article 36(5) of the Court's Statute.

In deciding that it was, the majority of the Court relied heavily on the French text of Article 36(5) and concluded that it indicated an intention on the part of the drafters of the Statute to give the provision a wide scope. The majority also relied heavily on Nicaragua's conduct since 1945, which in its view, demonstrated Nicaragua's consent to accepting the compulsory jurisdiction of the Court. The vote on the Court's finding that it had jurisdiction on the basis of Article 36(2) and (5) of the Statute was eleven–five, with the US, UK, German, Italian, and Japanese judges dissenting.

The five dissenting judges were of the view that Nicaragua's declaration was not an "acceptance" within the meaning of Article 36(5) of the Court's Statute because the declaration could not be "in force" unless it was ratified.[15] In later "Observations" on the Court's judgment, the Legal Adviser's Office of the US Department of State extensively attacked all bases of the Court's reasoning in contending that its finding of jurisdiction was erroneous.[16] In contrast, some eminent nongovernmental commentators applauded the Court's holding and its reasoning.[17]

The Court also rejected US claims that the Court could not exercise jurisdiction based on its declaration. When the United States sought to invoke its multilateral treaty reservation as a bar to jurisdiction, the Court held that the question of what states might be affected by the decision was not a jurisdictional problem and that, since it therefore did not possess an "exclusively preliminary character," the Court would defer a decision on the issue until the merits stage of the proceedings. In its later Observations, the reaction of the United States was sharp:

> The Court, in effect, renders the United States multilateral treaty reservation a nullity since the very purpose of the reservation was to withhold consent to adjudication in the absence of interested treaty parties. The Court's ruling requires adjudication before jurisdiction may be decided under the reservation. The multilateral treaty reservation thus can never exclude adjudication of the merits of a case such as this, even though that was the purpose of the United States in making the reservation when it accepted the Court's compulsory jurisdiction in 1946.[18]

On April 6, 1984, three days before Nicaragua instituted proceedings, the United States deposited with the Secretary-General of the United Nations a notification signed by Secretary of State George Shultz that sought to modify the US declaration so as to exclude from its scope "disputes with any Central American State or arising out of or related to events in Central America" and that sought to have the modification take place with immediate effect. In rejecting this effort the Court noted that the US declaration had a clause that required six months' notice before terminating the declaration. In response to the US argument that, under the principle of reciprocity, it could rely on the Nicaraguan declaration which, being of unlimited duration, was subject to immediate termination, the Court ruled that the principle of reciprocity was concerned only with the scope and substance of the commitments entered into, including reservations, and not with the formal conditions of their creation, duration, or extinction. The US, UK, and Japanese judges strongly dissented on this issue. In its Observations the United States argued that the Court had ignored state practice and hence customary international law, as well as its own previous opinions, and that "reciprocity is the fundamental principle underlying the Court's jurisdiction generally and was an explicit condition to the United States acceptance of the Court's compulsory jurisdiction in 1946."[19]

By a vote of fourteen to two, the Court also held that it had jurisdiction over Nicaragua's claim to the extent that it related to a dispute concerning the interpretation or application of the Treaty of Friendship, Commerce and Navigation between the United States of America and the Republic of Nicaragua of January 21, 1956. Article XXIV(2) of that treaty reads as follows:

> Any dispute between the Parties as to the interpretation or application of the present Treaty, not satisfactorily adjusted by diplomacy, shall be submitted to the International Court of Justice, unless the Parties agree to settlement by some other pacific means.

In response to Nicaragua's reliance on the treaty, the United States had contended that, since the Application had not presented any claims of violation of the treaty, there were no claims properly before the Court for adjudication, and that, since no attempt to adjust the dispute by diplomacy had been made, the compromissory clause could not operate. The majority of the Court, however, found that the failure of Nicaragua to refer to the treaty in its negotiations with the United States did not bar it from invoking the compromissory clause in that treaty. Although Nicaragua had not cited the treaty in its original pleadings, it had later alleged violations of specific provisions of the treaty, including, for example, mining of ports and territorial waters and attacks on airports that endangered traffic and trade.

In his dissenting opinion, Judge Schwebel argued that the bilateral treaty "is a purely commercial agreement whose terms do not relate to the use or misuse of force in international relations." In addition, he noted that the treaty expressly precluded its application to "traffic in arms" and to measures "necessary to protect [the] essential security interests" of a party.[20] Similar objections to the Court's holding on the compromissory clause of the bilateral treaty were raised by the US government in its Observations.[21]

The Court treated the US argument that Nicaragua's claims against it were inadmissible separately from jurisdictional issues. In advancing its arguments the United States, in effect, if not explicitly, attempted to introduce concepts found in domestic procedural and constitutional law into the jurisprudence of the International Court of Justice. Its first argument, for example, was based on the concept of "indispensable parties," since it noted that Nicaragua had failed to bring before the Court parties whose presence and participation were necessary for the rights of those parties to be protected and for the adjudication of the issues raised in Nicaragua's application. The Court rejected the US position on the grounds that neither the Court's Statute nor the practice of international tribunals supported an indispensable parties rule and that, in any event, none of the states referred to by the United States was in such a position that its presence would be indispensable to the proceedings of the Court.

The United States next attempted to convince the Court that it should adopt a variant of the "political question" doctrine developed by the US Supreme Court and discussed in chapter 2 of this study. The political question doctrine, it will be remembered, is based on a determination by the Supreme Court that the US Constitution reserves the resolution of certain issues to the political branches of government, that is, Congress and the executive branch. Similarly, the United States argued that Nicaragua was, in effect, requesting that the Court determine the existence of a threat to peace, a subject reserved under the UN Charter to the Security Council. Along the same lines the United States contended that its reliance on the inherent right of individual and collective self-defense under Article 51 of the Charter raised an issue reserved for determination by the Security Council, especially since the dispute between Nicaragua and the United States involved an ongoing armed conflict between the two states, and the Court was therefore institutionally unable to exercise the judicial function under such circumstances.

The Court rejected the US political question argument by holding that both the Security Council and the Court could consider the dispute between Nicaragua and the United States in parallel proceedings – the Council would exercise its political functions and the Court its judicial functions. These were separate but complementary functions. Moreover, the Court disagreed with the US characterization of the dispute as one involving an ongoing conflict. Rather, in the Court's view, the dispute was about a situation demanding the peaceful settlement of disputes, a matter covered by Chapter VI rather than Chapter VII of the Charter.

Lastly, the Court rejected the US argument that Nicaragua had to exhaust the established procedures for the resolution of the conflicts occurring in Central America, especially the so-called Contadora process. The Court denied the existence of any requirement of prior exhaustion of regional negotiating processes as a precondition to seising the Court, and rejected the argument that the existence of the Contadora process constituted in this case an obstacle to the examination by the Court of Nicaragua's claims.

The Court ruled unanimously that Nicaragua's application was admissible.[22]

The withdrawal of the United States

As noted earlier, on losing at the jurisdictional stage of the proceedings in the *Nicaragua* case, the United States announced, "with great reluctance," that it had "decided not to participate in further proceedings in this case."[23] There is evidence, not surprisingly, that there was substantial debate within the US government over whether this step should be taken.[24] About one year after the Court's decision on jurisdiction, the United States took the further step of terminating its acceptance of the compulsory jurisdiction of the Court.[25] In testimony before the Senate Foreign Relations Committee, Abraham Sofaer, Legal Adviser of the State Department, set forth reasons for the US withdrawal.[26]

Some of Sofaer's testimony reiterated complaints about the Court's decision on jurisdiction previously advanced by representatives of the US government. He added some new observations, however. For example, he contrasted the inability of the United States to bring another state before the Court on the basis of its acceptance of compulsory jurisdiction (because of the Connally Amendment, a self-inflicted obstacle) with the bringing of suits against the United States on three different occasions. It is worth noting, however, that of the three cases mentioned by Sofaer – *Rights of Nationals of the United States in Morocco*,[27] *Interhandel*,[28] and *Nicaragua v. United States* – only the *Nicaragua* case involved a clear defeat for the United States.

Sofaer further noted that there was nothing in the US declaration accepting the compulsory jurisdiction of the Court that "prevents another state from depositing an acceptance of compulsory jurisdiction solely for the purpose of bringing suit against the United States and, thereafter, withdrawing its acceptance to avoid being sued by anyone in any other matter."[29] In his view, this "sitting duck" or "hit-and-run" problem "places the minority of states that have accepted compulsory jurisdiction at the mercy of the majority that have not."[30]

The composition of the Court, in Sofaer's view, was a "source of institutional weakness." He pointed out that at the time he was testifying nine of the fifteen judges on the Court came from states that had not accepted compulsory jurisdiction and that most of these states had never used the Court at all. He suggested that because the judges are elected by the General Assembly and the Security Council, often after intense electioneering, "[o]ne reasonably may expect at least some judges to be sensitive to the impact of their decisions on their standing with the UN majority."[31] This implication of bias on the part of some judges was made more explicit when, commenting on these perceived weaknesses of the Court's composition, Sofaer stated: "We have hitherto endured them on the assumption that the respect states owed to the Court and the Court's own scrupulous adherence to its judicial role would insulate us from abuses of the Court's process for political or propaganda ends. The *Nicaragua* case showed that it would be unrealistic to continue to rely on that assumption."[32] As an example of the Court's "result-oriented" approach, Sofaer cited the Court's "unprecedented" action in "rejecting without a hearing El Salvador's application to intervene as of right – that betrayed a predisposition to find that it had jurisdiction and that Nicaragua's claims were justiciable, regardless of the overwhelming legal case to the contrary."[33]

"Even more disturbing," according to Sofaer,

> for the first time in its history, the Court has sought to assert jurisdiction over a controversy concerning claims related to an ongoing use of armed force. This action concerns every state. It is inconsistent with the structure of the UN system. The only prior case involving use-of-force issues – the *Corfu Channel* case – went to the Court after the disputed actions had ceased and the Security Council had determined that the matter was suitable for judicial consideration. In the *Nicaragua* case, the Court rejected without a soundly reasoned explanation our arguments that claims of the sort made by Nicaragua were intended by the UN Charter exclusively for resolution by political mechanisms – in particular, the Security Council and the Contadora process – and that claims to the exercise of the inherent right of individual and collective self-defense were excluded by Article 51 of the Charter from review by the Court.[34]

Sofaer added that the Court's decision to accept jurisdiction over claims about an ongoing use of force "made acceptance of the Court's compulsory jurisdiction an issue of strategic significance . . . For the United States to recognize that the ICJ has authority to define and adjudicate with respect to our right of self-defense . . . is effectively to surrender to that body the power to pass on our efforts to guarantee the safety and security of this nation and of its allies."[35]

Others have sharply criticized the US decision to withdraw from the *Nicaragua* case[36] and challenged Sofaer's implications of bias on the part of the Court[37] and his suggestion that the Court lacks competence to adjudicate a state's claim that its use of force was in self-defense. Oscar Schachter, in particular, has taken issue with Sofaer's contention that the Court lacked competence to evaluate the US claim that its use of force against Nicaragua was a legitimate exercise of individual and collective self-defense:

the position taken in respect to the *Nicaragua* case comes dangerously close to a rejection of the binding character of the principles on force. It does so because among the various arguments on jurisdiction and admissibility is the contention that the inherent right of a state to self-defense is a matter for determination by that state alone. Judge Sofaer, in his Senate testimony on the US withdrawal, said that for the United States to recognize that the ICJ has authority to adjudicate a US claim of self-defense is "to surrender to the Court the right to pass on efforts to protect American Security." He did not go on to make the further point that if each state is entirely free to determine for itself whether and to what extent it may use force in self-defense, the legal restraint on force virtually vanishes. A state certainly has a right to decide in the first instance that self-defense is necessary to meet an attack or an imminent threat of attack. But it makes a sham of law to allow an entity claiming a legal right to have the last word on the lawfulness of its exercise.[38]

Schachter further challenges Sofaer's argument that only the Security Council can evaluate a state's claim that it is using force in self-defense by pointing out that:

We know that a state which can exercise the veto in the Council (or is protected by another state's veto) is able to prevent any adverse decision by the Council. But does it follow that such protected states are legally entitled to use force irrespective of the Charter rules? It is astonishing that *some American international lawyers* now advance the contention that the veto in the Council – a political act to prevent Council action – should have the effect of legitimating a questionable use of force and preventing a party to a dispute from seeking a judicial determination of its rights against a state that had consented to the Court's jurisdiction.[39]

Schachter's comments implicitly suggest that the US position on the Court's rejection of its arguments on its competence to evaluate the legality of an alleged use of force in self-defense reflects an attitude of "exceptionalism," that is, that the United States bears special burdens and is entitled to special privileges, a theme that has been emphasized throughout this study.

Nicaragua v. United States *(Merits)*

Because of its withdrawal from the case after it lost on the jurisdictional and admissibility issues, the United States made no appearance in the proceedings before the Court on the merits. This nonappearance, however, did not deprive the Court of jurisdiction to hold proceedings on the merits. Under Article 53 of the Court's Statute, if one of the parties fails to appear or does not defend, the other party may call upon the Court to decide in its favor. Before doing so, however, the Court must satisfy itself that it has jurisdiction and, if so, that the Applicant's claim is well founded in fact and law. Prior to its withdrawal from the case, the United States had set forth its position that Nicaragua had supplied arms and given other support from its territory to armed opposition to the government of El Salvador, and that US actions sought to interdict this support. The United States had argued further that it had acted under Article 51 of the UN Charter in collective self-defense of El Salvador and of other Central American states threatened by Nicaraguan subversion.

The Court handed down its decision in 1986.[40] As a preliminary matter, the Court decided that it could not consider Nicaragua's claims under the UN Charter because of the multilateral treaty reservation in the US declaration accepting the Court's compulsory jurisdiction. It then proceeded to do so because of its determination that the principles on the use of force incorporated in the Charter "correspond, in essentials, to those found in customary international law." It accordingly evaluated Nicaragua's customary international law claims, in effect, under Articles 2(4) and 51 of the Charter.

By twelve votes to three (Judge Schwebel (United States), Judge Oda (Japan), and Judge Jennings (United Kingdom)) the Court decided that by its actions the United States had violated its obligations under customary international law not to use force against another state, not to intervene in the affairs of another state, and not to interrupt peaceful maritime commerce, and had breached its obligations under the Treaty of Friendship, Commerce and Navigation between the two states. The Court rejected US claims that the acts were justified as being in collective self-defense with the government of El Salvador.

Not surprisingly, the reaction of the US government to the Court's decision on the merits was highly negative and dismissive. It announced that it would not abide by the judgment, vetoed subsequent proposed Security Council resolutions seeking to enforce the judgment,[41] and appropriated additional funds for the actions in question it had taken against Nicaragua.[42]

In its ruling against the United States the majority opinion set forth a number of propositions on the law regarding the use of force and collective self-defense, as well as statements of the facts in the case, that engendered heated debate, especially in the scholarly literature.[43] In his dissenting opinion,[44] Judge Schwebel's attack on the majority's reasoning covered 128 pages, and was reinforced by a factual annex that ran to 132 pages and was intended to counteract factual claims by Nicaragua that, in Judge Schwebel's view, were based on fabrications.

The propositions of law regarding the use of force and collective self-defense are numerous and complex, and a full consideration of them is beyond the scope of this study. For present purposes it suffices to suggest that the Court's construction of the concept of an "armed attack" justifying the use of armed force in self-defense was especially troubling to the United States. The majority quoted the UN General Assembly's Definition of Aggression, itself a subject of controversy,[45] for the proposition that an armed attack could include not only action by regular armed forces across an international border, but also "[t]he sending by or on behalf of a State of armed bands, groups, irregulars or mercenaries, which carry out acts of armed force against another State of such gravity as to amount to" an actual armed attack conducted by regular forces, "or its substantial involvement therein."[46] But the Court went on to state that it did "*not* believe that the concept of 'armed attack' includes not only acts by armed bands where such acts occur on a significant scale but also assistance to rebels in the form of the provision of weapons or logistical or other support."[47] As applied to Nicaragua and El Salvador, the Court found that Nicaragua had not sent armed bands across its borders into El Salvador and its "intermittent" flow of arms to the rebels in El Salvador did not constitute an armed attack. The Court therefore concluded that the absence of a vital condition precedent precluded the United States from participating in an exercise of collective self-defense.

The Court placed other limits on the law of collective self-defense that barred the United States from its exercise. According to the majority opinion, even if there has been an armed attack, the state suffering it must "declare the view that it has been so attacked"[48] and make a specific request to other states to come to its assistance. Although El Salvador did officially declare itself to be the victim of an armed attack, and did expressly ask the United States to exercise its right of collective self-defense, the declaration and the request were made substantially later than commencement of the US activities challenged before the Court. As to this point, John Norton Moore, a special counsel for the United States in the *Nicaragua* case, had made a forceful response:

> The formalism of the Court in implying that El Salvador had made no request for assistance and had not "declared itself to have been attacked" is also incredible. Nothing in the opinion more clearly indicates how the Court is genuinely confused by a strategy of secret war. The setting of such an attack in the real world is a complex politico-military setting in which the attacked state hopes that the attack will go away and seeks diplomatically to keep the issue low-key. President Duarte, of course, has repeatedly mentioned the Nicaraguan attack against El Salvador in press conferences. But formalistic public announcements of attack and requests in such a setting are only slightly less likely than acknowledgment of its attack by the aggressor state. Moreover, how the majority of the Court could maintain this position in the face of the Salvadoran petition to the Court manifestly declaring the attack and assistance, and the Court's own denial of Salvador's request to appear, is, if possible, even harder to understand. One wonders why it was beyond

the Court's ability, if it did harbor doubts as to whether El Salvador considered itself attacked by Nicaragua, simply to ask El Salvador rather than preventing it from appearing before the Court.

Perhaps the most remarkable legal failure of the majority is its failure to condemn, even in passing, an uncontroversially illegal ongoing attack from Nicaragua against neighboring states. In this connection, the Court specifically found "that support for the armed opposition in El Salvador from Nicaraguan territory was a fact up until the early month of 1981." Even if unable to support a US defensive response, the Court could have been expected at a minimum to have condemned *all* assistance to insurgent groups, including Nicaragua's continuing assistance to the FMLN [Farabundo Martí National Liberation Front]. The Court's failure to do so is a failure that will live in infamy.[49]

John Lawrence Hargrove, former Legal Adviser to the US Mission to the United Nations, and, at the time of his writing, the Executive Director of the American Society of International Law, has pointed out some of the real-world consequences of the Court's definition of "armed attack":

Any suggestion that there are any acts of unlawful force between states that international law forbids a state from defending against by proportionate force, by the means and to the extent reasonably necessary to protect itself, degrades the concept of international law, diminishes the inducement for a responsible political leader to take its constraints seriously into account in conflict situations in the actual planning and conduct of that state's affairs.

The Court made this suggestion in several variations. Its logical effect is to require a commander in chief confronted by unlawful force, in order to determine whether or how defensive force may be used, to consult lists reflecting the Court's finely calibrated expert judgment as to what classes of acts are a priori militarily significant, or to call in the Court for such military advice on the spot. No such regime deserves or is remotely likely to command respect. The otherworldliness of such distinctions as the Court put forward (e.g., between organizing and training troops, and providing them armaments, logistical support or other support; between big attacks and little ones) is apparent when one reflects on the actual plight of a victim state: any one of the unlawful acts of force that the Court excluded or might exclude as a basis for self-defense may in fact, given the appropriate circumstances, be as critical to that state's security or even survival as any other. The way to develop a law of force or self-defense that will be taken seriously by real-world states is not to appoint the Court or any other body to such a futile function. It is to do what the Charter already does: permit real force to be resisted by force, but scrupulously require that the defense fit the conduct defended against.[50]

To be sure, there are eminent commentators who have a very different (i.e., highly favorable) view of the majority opinion.[51] For present purposes, however, the issue is not whether the supporters or the critics of the majority's opinion in the *Nicaragua* case have the better arguments. It is rather that the US government holds the view that the majority was not only wrong but egregiously so and that at least some of the judges in the majority were biased against the United States. This attitude has had far-reaching consequences. It has ruled out the United States issuing a new declaration accepting the compulsory jurisdiction of the Court for the foreseeable future and, as we have seen already in this study and shall see again, has greatly soured US views on international adjudication in general – thus undermining a pillar of the rule of law in international affairs.

Developments subsequent to the Court's judgment in the *Nicaragua* case have undoubtedly strengthened the US view that it was wise to terminate its declaration and decline to submit a new and revised one. In particular, as we saw in chapter 4, the US and other NATO states' bombing in Serbia was of dubious legality. However, when the Federal Republic of Yugoslavia brought separate cases in 1999 against ten NATO member states (including the United States) concerning the legality of their use of force during the Kosovo crisis, there was no basis for the Court assuming jurisdiction over the United States under Article 36(2) of its Statute. Yugoslavia also claimed that the Court had jurisdiction under Article 36(1) of its Statute when it invoked the compromissory clause (Article IX) of the Genocide Convention. But here too the United States was able easily to defeat Yugoslavia's claim, since it had submitted a reservation to the compromissory clause of the Genocide Convention. The Court also dismissed Yugoslavia's claim against Spain on grounds of lack of jurisdiction. As to the other eight respondents, the Court refused Yugoslavia's request for provisional measures on the ground that it lacked prima facie jurisdiction to consider the request.[52] The ruling concerning jurisdiction under Article 36(2) was based in large part on the Court's determination that the dispute had arisen before Yugoslavia had deposited its instrument of acceptance of optional clause jurisdiction. (Yugoslavia filed its declaration of acceptance of the compulsory jurisdiction on April 26, 1999, and initiated the suit three days later on April 29, 1999.) At this writing hearings against the eight remaining respondents on preliminary issues of jurisdiction and admissibility are pending, although there is some doubt whether these hearings will ever be held, since there is now a radically different government in Belgrade.[53]

The United States, compromissory clauses, and the Court

As already noted, in the *Nicaragua* case, the Court ruled that the compromissory clause of the Nicaragua–United States Treaty of Friendship,

Commerce and Navigation (FCN) served as an additional basis for its jurisdiction under Article 36(1) of its Statute. A compromissory clause is another form of so-called compulsory jurisdiction in that states parties to the treaty containing a compromissory clause consent in advance to the Court's jurisdiction over disputes arising in the future concerning its interpretation and application, and a party that would later prefer not to go to the Court is unable to object as long as the dispute involves a matter within the scope of the treaty and any condition precedents – such as negotiations – have been exhausted. In the *Nicaragua* case, the United States, as well as dissenting judges Schwebel[54] and Oda,[55] argued strenuously that the dispute between Nicaragua and the United States involved matters outside the scope of the treaty and that the negotiations required by the compromissory clause had not taken place, but to no avail.

Michael Reisman's response to the Court's ruling was to examine "the implications of the Judgment with regard to the extensive United States practice of using the Article 36(1) mode of jurisdiction"[56] and to suggest that the judgment required a reconsideration of US attitudes. He pointed out that in 1987 some thirty-five bilateral treaties to which the United States was a party contained compromissory clauses providing for reference of disputes arising thereunder to the International Court of Justice. According to Reisman, however, "the incorporation of Article 36(1) jurisdiction in American FCN treaties was premised on the assumption that such jurisdiction would be confined to the explicit terms of the treaty. Certain subject matter deemed to be of special domestic concern and, in particular, matters of military security were not, in the US view, any part of the jurisdictional bargain."[57] The Court's judgment in *Nicaragua* had, in Reisman's view, "effectively shattered key elements of the presumption of confinement."[58] As a consequence, Reisman suggested, "[t]he question the United States must urgently address is whether, all things considered, it can afford voluntarily to subject itself to the essentially new regime."[59]

Under the old regime, the United States had successfully invoked the compromissory clauses of three treaties – the Optional Protocols to the two Vienna Conventions of 1961 and 1963 on, respectively, Diplomatic and Consular Relations, and the 1955 US–Iran Treaty of Amity, Economic Relations, and Consular Rights – as the basis for the Court's jurisdiction in obtaining first an indication of provisional measures (roughly an injunction)[60] and then a judgment on the merits[61] against Iran because of its seizure of and the holding as hostages members of the US diplomatic and consular staff in Iran. The tables were turned, however, in 1996, when Iran invoked the compromissory clause in the Treaty of Amity in a suit against the United States based on incidents during the Iran–Iraq naval war of 1987–88, when the United States had destroyed certain Iranian oil platforms in the Persian Gulf which it claimed had been used by the Iranian military to mount hostile attacks on neutral merchant shipping in the Gulf. The Court held that it had jurisdiction based on the treaty, but, perhaps contemplating the strong US reaction to the *Nicaragua* decision, rejected Iran's sweeping claim that a treaty of amity should be read to reach claims involving military hostilities and limited itself to a holding that the treaty covered claims that the US conduct had interfered with freedom of navigation in violation of the treaty.[62] At this writing the proceedings on the merits are pending before the Court.

Interestingly, in the wake of the *Nicaragua* decision, the United States did not renounce US treaty obligations to third-party dispute settlement. On the contrary, although it withdrew US consent to the ICJ's Article 36(2) jurisdiction, the Reagan administration supported treaties containing provisions authorizing binding third-party dispute settlement before both the ICJ and arbitral tribunals.[63] Reportedly, however, the United States later began to avoid compromissory clauses that refer disputes to the ICJ.[64]

As illustrated by Iran's use of the compromissory clause in the US–Iran Treaty of Amity in the *Oil Platforms* case, there are a number of compromissory clauses providing for reference to the ICJ in US treaties concluded before the *Nicaragua* case. On several occasions states parties have successfully invoked these clauses as a basis for bringing suit against the United States. These suits, moreover, have proven to be quite troublesome for the United States.

Libya v. United States

On December 21, 1988, Pan Am Flight 103 was destroyed by a bomb over Lockerbie, Scotland; all 259 passengers aboard and eleven Lockerbie residents were killed. After a long investigation, the United States and the United Kingdom indicted two Libyan nationals in 1992 and demanded that they be turned over by Libya to the United States or the United Kingdom for prosecution. Libya had no extradition treaty with either the United States or the United Kingdom. All three states were parties to the Montreal Convention for the Suppression of Unlawful Acts Against the Safety of Civil Aviation, commonly referred to as the Montreal Convention. Libya argued that its only obligation under the Montreal

Convention was to investigate and, if appropriate, prosecute – extradition not being an option because of the absence of an extradition treaty and a provision in Libya's constitution prohibiting the extradition of its nationals. Libya conducted an investigation and determined that it had an inadequate basis on which to prosecute.

On Libya's refusal to surrender the two accused persons, the United States and the United Kingdom turned to the UN Security Council, which adopted a series of ever harsher economic sanctions against Libya. In response Libya instituted suit before the ICJ against the United States and the United Kingdom by invoking the compromissory clause in the Montreal Convention.[65] The United States and the United Kingdom argued that any claim that Libya might have under the Montreal Convention had been superseded by the Security Council resolutions, since, under Article 103 of the UN Charter, if there is a conflict between the obligations of member states under the Charter and their obligations under any other international agreement, their obligations under the Charter prevail. The Court denied Libya's request for provisional measures against further US and British efforts to compel Libya to surrender the accused. But it ruled that it has jurisdiction to consider Libya's claims under the Montreal Convention.[66]

After the Court's ruling, extensive discussions involving Libya, the United States, the United Kingdom, and the UN Secretary-General resulted in an agreement by Libya in April 1999 to surrender the two accused Libyans to stand trial before Scottish judges sitting as a Scottish court in the Netherlands. On January 31, 2001, one of the accused Libyans was convicted of murder and sentenced to imprisonment for life. The other was acquitted. The conviction was affirmed on appeal.

At this writing further proceedings in Libya's cases against the United States and the United Kingdom are pending. There is some question whether Libya will press these cases to judgment.[67] If it does, the Court's decision in these cases could be of great significance because Libya has challenged the sanctions imposed against it by the Security Council on the ground that they are *ultra vires.* The first issue, therefore, is whether the Court has the competence to sit in judgment of a Security Council resolution in the absence of a request from the Council that it do so. Should it determine that it has such competence, the Court would then have to decide whether the Council's resolutions against Libya exceeded its competence. A Court decision that they did would surely infuriate both the United States and the United Kingdom and call into question the precise scope of Security Council authority under Chapter VII of the Charter.

Breard, LaGrand, *and* Avena

Article 36(1)(b) of the Vienna Convention on Consular Relations (Vienna Convention)[68] provides:

> [With a view to facilitating the exercise of consular functions relating to nationals of the sending State:]
> (b) *if he so requests*, the competent authorities of the receiving State shall, without delay, inform the consular post of the sending State if, within its consular district, a national of that State is arrested or committed to prison or to custody pending trial or is detained in any other manner. Any communication addressed to the consular post by the person arrested, in prison, custody or detention shall be forwarded by the said authorities without delay. *The said authorities shall inform the person concerned without delay of his rights under this sub-paragraph* [emphasis added].

Clear and repeated failure of the United States to fulfill its obligations under the Vienna Convention has, as of the time of writing, resulted in the invocation of the compromissory clause (Article 1) of the Optional Protocol Concerning the Compulsory Settlement of Disputes to the Vienna Convention as the basis for three suits brought against the United States before the ICJ. The three cases have raised important issues of international law as well as of US law and practice. The Court's landmark decision in the *LaGrand* decision has resolved some but by no means all of these issues.

Breard

Angel Francisco Breard, a citizen of Paraguay, was convicted by a jury in Virginia on June 24, 1993, of murder and attempted rape and sentenced to death.[69] His execution was set for February 17, 1994, but was stayed pending appeals. After a series of appeals and a state petition for habeas corpus were unsuccessful in the courts of Virginia, on April 25, 1996, Breard filed a motion in the United States District Court for the Eastern District of Virginia in which he raised, along with various other new issues, his claim of a violation of Article 36(1)(b) of the Vienna Convention. Although Breard had not made a request that the Paraguayan consul be informed of his arrest, neither had the Virginian authorities informed him of his right to do so. It is not clear from the record whether state officials were aware that Breard was a dual national of Argentina and Paraguay at the time of his arrest.

Later in 1996 the Paraguayan consular officials learned of Breard's arrest and trial and raised the issue of their non-notification with the US Department of State. On July 7, 1997, the Department acknowledged that the failure to notify the consular officials was a violation of the Vienna Convention and apologized for it. The apology did not satisfy the Paraguayan authorities, however, and they raised the possibility of referring the issue to the International Court of Justice.

Meanwhile, the federal district court in Virginia rejected Breard's claim for relief. Although "Virginia's persistent refusal to abide by the Vienna Convention" troubled the court, it found that Breard's failure to raise the issue in the courts of Virginia had resulted in the claim being defaulted and federal review barred. The district court's decision was upheld on appeal.[70] Breard petitioned the Supreme Court for a writ of certiorari and a writ of habeas corpus.

In September 1996, Paraguay, its ambassador to the United States, and its consul general to the United States initiated a separate action in the United States District Court for the Eastern District of Virginia seeking a declaration of treaty violation, a *vacatur* of Breard's conviction and sentence, and an injunction against further violations of the treaty.[71] The district court found that Paraguay and its officials had standing to bring their claims, but determined that it did not have subject matter jurisdiction because the claimants were not alleging "continuous violations of federal law," which would have brought their claims within the exception to the immunity of states under the Eleventh Amendment to the US Constitution[72] permitting prospective remedies. The district court's decision was affirmed on appeal. Paraguay petitioned the Supreme Court for a writ of certiorari.

On April 3, 1998, Paraguay filed an application in the ICJ instituting proceedings against the United States. Paraguay alleged that the United States had violated the Vienna Convention, and asked the Court to declare "that Paraguay is therefore entitled to *restitutio in integrum* [i.e., a retrial of Breard], [and] . . . that the United States is under an international legal obligation not to apply the [domestic] doctrine of 'procedural default' or any other doctrine of its internal law, so as to preclude the exercise of the rights accorded under Article 36."[73]

At the same time, Paraguay filed a request for the indication of provisional measures of protection under Article 41 of the Court's Statute, which provides in pertinent part: "The Court shall have the power to indicate, if it considers that circumstances so require, any provisional measures which ought to be taken to preserve the respective rights of either party." Paraguay requested that the United States ensure that Breard would not be executed pending the disposition of the case; that the US government inform the Court of the actions it had taken to this end; and that the US government ensure that no action would be taken that might prejudice the rights of Paraguay with respect to any decision the Court might issue on the merits of the case. Lastly, Paraguay asked the Court to treat its request for provisional measures as a matter of the greatest urgency.

In response the United States argued that the Court had no prima facie jurisdiction to issue the provisional measures. It claimed, among other things, that the only remedy available under Article 36 of the Vienna Convention for a breach of that provision is an apology. In its view neither the language of the Vienna Convention, nor its drafting history, nor state practice supported a penalty of invalidation of the proceedings and return to the *status quo ante*. The Court unanimously rejected the US arguments, however, stating that the existence of the relief sought by Paraguay could only be determined at the merits stage of the proceedings, and on April 9, 1998, indicated, as provisional measures, that "[t]he United States should take all measures at its disposal to ensure that Angel Francisco Breard is not executed pending the final decision in these proceedings, and should inform the Court of all the measures which it has taken in implementation of this Order."[74]

On April 13, US Secretary of State Madeleine Albright sent a letter to the Governor of Virginia *requesting* that the Governor suspend the execution.[75] While expressing her view that the ICJ's provisional measures were nonbinding, she stated: "In light of the Court's request, the unique and difficult foreign policy issues, and other problems created by the Court's provisional measures, I therefore request that you exercise your powers as Governor and stay Mr. Breard's execution." Albright added, "I am particularly concerned about the possible negative consequences for the many US citizens who live and travel abroad . . . The immediate execution of Mr. Breard in the face of the Court's April 9 action could be seen as a denial by the United States of the significance of international law and the Court's processes in its international relations and thereby limit our ability to ensure that Americans are protected when living or traveling abroad."

In response to Breard's and Paraguay's petitions, the US Departments of State and Justice had submitted an amicus brief to the Supreme Court urging the Court to deny a writ of certiorari and a stay.[76] In its brief the United States government argued that the ICJ's provisional measures were nonbinding. But even if they were binding, the brief continued, "in any event the 'measures at [the government's] disposal' are a matter of domestic United States law, and our federal system imposes limits on the federal government's ability to interfere with the criminal justice systems of the States. The 'measures at [the United States'] disposal' under our Constitution may in some cases include only persuasion – such as the Secretary of State's request to the Governor of Virginia to stay Breard's execution – and not legal compulsion through the judicial system. That is the situation here. Accordingly, the ICJ's order does not provide an independent basis for this Court either to grant certiorari or to stay the execution."[77]

On April 14, 1998 – the day after Secretary Albright's request to the Governor of Virginia – the Supreme Court, by a vote of six to three, denied the petition for habeas corpus and the petitions for certiorari.[78] The reasons for the majority's opinion were manifold. They included, among others, a finding that Breard had "procedurally defaulted his claim, if any, under the Vienna Convention by failing to raise that claim in the state courts."[79] Also, the Court rejected the argument by both Breard and Paraguay that the Vienna Convention claim should still be heard in a federal court because the Convention is the supreme law of the land and, as such, trumps the procedural default doctrine. In the Court's view the procedural rules of the forum state govern the implementation of a treaty in that state. In any event the Court concluded that the Antiterrorism and Effective Death Penalty Act of 1996 precludes a habeas petitioner from raising alleged violations of treaties of the United States if those allegations had not been developed in state court proceedings. Under the last-in-time rule, in other words, an act of legislation adopted subsequent to a treaty trumps the latter in case of conflict. As to the effect under US law of the ICJ's indication of provisional measures, the Supreme Court stated: "Last night the Secretary of State sent a letter to the Governor of Virginia requesting that he stay Breard's execution. If the Governor wishes to wait for the decision of the ICJ, that is his prerogative. But nothing in our existing case law allows us to make that choice for him."[80]

The Governor of Virginia chose not to wait for the decision of the ICJ. Rather, he refused to issue a stay. In a statement issued on April 14, 1998, he explained his decision, in part, by saying: "The US Department of Justice, together with Virginia's Attorney General, make a compelling case that the International Court of Justice has no authority to interfere with our criminal justice system. Indeed, the safety of those residing in the Commonwealth of Virginia is not the responsibility of the International Court of Justice. It is my responsibility and the responsibility of law enforcement and judicial officials throughout the Commonwealth. I cannot cede such responsibility to the International Court of Justice."[81]

Breard's execution took place as scheduled on April 14, the same day the governor of Virginia issued his statement. The case before the ICJ never proceeded to final judgment because it was discontinued at Paraguay's request on November 10, 1998.

As we shall see below, in the *LaGrand* case, the International Court of Justice ruled, to the surprise of many and contrary to the US government's amicus curiae brief in *Breard*, that its indications of provisional measures create legally binding obligations. Even before this ruling several commentators had asked, "was there not available to the Attorney General, or to the Secretary of State, an independent proceeding in a federal court for an order to the Governor or other state officials to honor the US treaty obligation and stay the execution?"[82] After this and other rulings in *LaGrand*, issues of federalism and other issues of US law and practice arise in sharp relief.

LaGrand

In the *LaGrand* case, which involved two German nationals, the brothers Karl and Walter LaGrand, the State of Arizona failed to inform them of their right to communicate with German consular officials, either at the time they were arrested and charged with capital murder or when they were sentenced to death in 1984, although state officials admitted they were aware of their German nationality when they were arrested. Karl LaGrand was executed on February 24, 1999. Germany then filed actions in the International Court of Justice and the US Supreme Court in an attempt to prevent the execution of Walter LaGrand.[83] On March 3, 1999, the ICJ issued a provisional measures order indicating that the United States should take all measures at its disposal to ensure that, pending a final decision in the proceeding, Walter LaGrand was not executed.[84] By contrast, on the very same day, the US Supreme Court refused to exercise its original jurisdiction in the action brought by the German government against the United States and the governor of Arizona alleging violations of the Consular Relations Convention.[85] Later that evening, Walter LaGrand was executed. Unlike Paraguay in the *Breard* case, however, Germany did not withdraw its case from the ICJ. As a result, two years later, on June 27, 2001, the Court issued its judgment on the merits of Germany's case against the United States.[86] In brief summary, the Court held, among other things, that the United States had violated its obligations to Germany and to the LaGrand brothers under Article 36 of the Consular Relations Convention. It further found that the earlier provisional measures order had created a binding obligation, which the United States had also breached. Lastly, and perhaps most significantly, the Court pronounced that in future cases the United States had, by means of its own choosing, to provide for the review and reconsideration of convictions entailing severe sentences for German nationals deprived of their rights under the Consular Relations Convention.

It is noteworthy that, at the time it declined to exercise its original jurisdiction over Germany's case against the United States and the State of Arizona, the US Supreme Court was aware of the ICJ's ruling in the *LaGrand* case that its indication of provisional measures created a binding obligation for the United States. To the contrary, in a letter to the Court of March 3, 1999, the Solicitor General of the United States had stated categorically that the provisional measures were not binding and therefore could not constitute a basis for judicial relief – as compared to the earlier recognition by the US government in the *Breard* case that scholars were divided on the issue. Two justices of the Supreme Court (Souter and Ginsburg) in a concurring opinion stated that they had relied heavily on the Solicitor General's views.[87]

There has been substantial scholarly commentary on the ICJ's decision in *LaGrand*.[88] But the most significant test of the implications of the *LaGrand* decision for US adherence to the rule of law in international affairs may be afforded by the third, and most recent, case filed against the United States before the International Court of Justice for alleged violations of Article 36 of the Consular Relations Convention.

Avena

On January 9, 2003, Mexico brought a case against the United States before the International Court of Justice for failing to provide proper notification to defendants of their consular rights, alleging violations of Article 5, which provides a general list of all consular functions, and Article 36 of the Consular Relations Convention with respect to fifty-four Mexican nationals (including Avena) who have been sentenced to death in the states of California, Texas, Illinois, Arizona, Arkansas, Florida, Nevada, Ohio, Oklahoma, and Oregon.[89] On February 5, 2003, the Court unanimously granted Mexico's request for an indication of provisional measures that order the United States to take all measures necessary to prevent the execution of three Mexican nationals on death row, two in Texas and one in Oklahoma.[90] The three were the closest to execution of the fifty-four Mexican nationals sentenced to death. The Court rejected US arguments that the issuance of such an order would amount to "sweeping prohibition on capital punishment for Mexican nationals in the United States, regardless of United States law" and "would drastically interfere with United States sovereign rights and implicate important federalism interests."[91] On the merits of the case, Mexico reportedly has argued that the United States "must restore the *status quo ante* of its nationals under the Vienna Convention, that is, to their circumstances prior to their detention, convictions and sentences. Mexico contended that the US has not and must establish a meaningful remedy with its domestic law for breaches of Article 36 of Vienna Convention."[92] For its part, the United States reportedly has argued that competent authorities in the United States have taken measures providing for effective review and reconsideration in all such cases and that for the Court to accept Mexico's argument would "turn the ICJ into a general criminal court of appeals."[93]

At this writing the Bush administration has reportedly made informal approaches to state officials in Oklahoma urging them to delay the execution until the ICJ has ruled on the merits of Mexico's claim.[94] Similar approaches may be made to state officials in Texas. If these state officials refuse to delay the executions, however, the issue arises whether the United States government could or would go into federal court seeking an injunction against these state executions. Arguably, they would have the constitutional authority to do so in order to enforce the ICJ order as a treaty obligation, which, under Article VI of the US Constitution, is the "supreme law of the land." Whether the political will would be present for such an action is another question. Should the US government fail to take such action, it might be possible for the Mexican government or the individual Mexican defendant to seek relief in federal court. Although the German government was unsuccessful in the *LaGrand* case in seeking such relief, the substantial commentary on that case could conceivably cause US federal courts, including the Supreme Court, to reconsider their holdings. Also, with respect to possible relief for the individual defendants, it is noteworthy that the ICJ in *LaGrand* ruled that, contrary to the US position, rights of consular notification and access under the Consular Relations Convention are also rights of individuals, not just of states.

As to the merits of Mexico's case before the ICJ, assuming that the Court finds that the United States violated its obligations under the Consular Relations Convention with respect to the fifity-four Mexicans on death row, the crucial question will be the remedy the United States must provide for such a violation. In the *LaGrand* case, the United States argued that the only remedy that had to be provided was an apology and dissemination of information about the Consular Relations Convention. The ICJ, however, required more, and ruled that "it would be incumbent upon the United States to allow the review and reconsideration of the conviction and sentence by taking account of the violation of the rights set forth in the Convention. This obligation can be carried out in various ways. The choice of means must be left to the United States."[95]

As Joan Fitzpatrick has noted, in its *LaGrand* decision the ICJ largely left open the issue of the proper remedy for a violation of Article 36 of the Consular Relations Convention.[96] Presumably this issue will be resolved by the Court's decision on the merits in *Avena*. The United States is reportedly arguing that the only remedy available for foreign nationals whose consular rights are violated is consideration of those violations during the pardon review and clemency proceedings.[97] In sharp contrast, as noted above, Mexico is arguing that its fifty-four nationals are entitled to a new trial. It remains to be seen precisely how much discretion the Court will grant the United States in its "choice of means" of review.

It also remains to be seen whether, if it loses on the merits, the United States will abide by the ICJ's decision. A major motivation for Paraguay, Germany, and Mexico in bringing their cases before the ICJ has been their strong opposition to the death penalty. But the United States strongly defends its right to impose the death penalty and has opposed all efforts in international fora to prevent it from doing so. For the United States, moreover, this has been a major issue of federalism, because each state in the United States has the discretion to decide whether to include the death penalty among its range of possible criminal sanctions. There is a strong reluctance on the part of the US government to interfere with a state's exercise of this discretion.

The future

As we have seen, the United States has not fared well under the "compulsory" jurisdiction of the International Court of Justice – both the compulsory jurisdiction under Article 36(2) of the Court's Statute, and jurisdiction based on a compromissory clause in a treaty under Article 36(1) of the Court's Statute. With the termination of its declaration accepting the Court's jurisdiction under Article 36(2), the United States need not be concerned about the possibility of a hostile suit through that route. At this writing, however, there are several actions pending before the ICJ based on compromissory clauses in treaties – the *Lockerbie*, *Oil Platforms* and *Avena* cases – that could be embarrassing to the United States should the Court rule against it. Also, although it is not a party to Yugoslavia's action against various member states of NATO, in the unlikely event that that case should proceed to judgment against the respondents and result in a ruling that the bombing of Kosovo violated international law, the political impact on the United States would be almost as severe as that on the respondent states.

Even in the cases since the *Nicaragua* decision where the United States has agreed to the ICJ's jurisdiction on an ad hoc basis, it has not fared especially well. In the *Gulf of Maine* case,[98] for example, where the United States and Canada agreed to submit their dispute over the maritime boundary between them in the Gulf of Maine area, the delimitation by the chamber of the Court of the continental shelf and the 200-nautical-mile fisheries zones between the two countries off the east coast of North America, while it was not a clear defeat for the United States, critical US press reports on the decision suggested less than a complete victory.[99] The United States suffered a clear defeat in the *ELSI* case,[100] where it had instituted proceedings against Italy because of a dispute arising out of the requisition by the Italian government of the plant and related assets of an Italian company 100 percent owned by US corporations. There the chamber of the Court ruled four to one against the United States, with the judge of US nationality in dissent.[101]

The use of chambers to decide cases, rather than the full Court, by the United States, and other states parties to the Court's Statute, has generated considerable controversy. Critics contend that allowing parties in effect to choose the judges they wish to hear their case threatens the objectivity, neutrality, and reputation of the Court.[102] In the *Gulf of Maine* case the five judges were from Italy, Germany, France, the United States, and Canada. The judges selected for the *ELSI* case were from Italy, the United States, the United Kingdom, Japan, and India (succeeded by a judge from Argentina). Later ICJ chambers, however, have reflected a more diverse composition.[103] Other commentators have defended the practice of employing chambers on the ground that "it affords the Court the opportunity to settle international disputes in a fashion that meets the needs of the parties and the international community, and does not detract from the integrity of the Court. It has not 'fractionalized' or 'regionalized' international law in any degree."[104]

Richard Bilder has suggested that, "if most states chose only to use such specially selected panels, the World Court could become a series of ad hoc arbitral tribunals sitting at a common seat, rather than remaining a 'World Court.'"[105] Interestingly, however, after an initial heavy use of chambers, there has been no dispute submitted to a chamber since 1987 and no chamber's judgment rendered since 1992.[106]

The present posture of the United States toward international institutions, especially after the unhappy experience of the United States in the Security Council over the Iraq crisis – discussed in chapter 4 – gives little expectation that the United States is likely to make much use of the World Court in the near future. On the contrary, as US policy toward the recently created International Criminal Court, discussed in the next chapter, demonstrates, the United States is unlikely to support any international tribunal that it cannot control in large measure.

Notes

1. Most especially in ch. 1, at pages 42–49, in connection with the role of international courts and tribunals in interpreting and applying international law, and in ch. 3's discussion of the Court's advisory opinion in Certain Expenses of the United Nations at pages 117–21.

2. See David J. Bederman, International Law Frameworks 239 (2001).
3. Rosalyn Higgins, *The ICJ, the ECJ, and the Integrity of International Law*, 52 Int'l & Comp. LQ 1, 3 (2003).
4. Ethiopia v. South Africa; Liberia v. South Africa, [1966] ICJ Rep. 6.
5. The Connally Amendment has been challenged as a reservation that is incompatible with the object and purpose of an optional clause declaration. In the Case of Certain Norwegian Loans, [1957] ICJ Rep. 9, France brought a case against Norway based on the acceptance of compulsory jurisdiction by both states. The French declaration of acceptance contained a clause similar to the Connally Amendment. Judge Lauterpacht, in a separate opinion, [1957] ICJ Rep. 34, contended that a self-judging reservation was invalid and, if not separable, invalidated the acceptance of the Court's jurisdiction. The majority of the Court, however, accepted Norway's argument that it had the right to rely on the restrictions in the French declaration under the principle of reciprocity and to claim that the matter fell within its national jurisdiction. In response to Judge Lauterpacht's argument, the Court declared that it was not called upon to examine the validity of the reservation since neither party to the proceedings had raised the issue. The Court rejected the French application, a result that also would have followed had the Court accepted Judge Lauterpacht's argument. At present France does not accept the compulsory jurisdiction of the Court, having withdrawn its declaration in the aftermath of the Nuclear Tests Cases (Australia v. France) (New Zealand v. France), [1974] ICJ Rep. 253, 457. Interestingly, only four countries (Liberia, Malawi, Philippines, and Sudan) currently have declarations that contain a self-judging reservation along the lines of the Connally Amendment.
6. For an extended discussion of the Aerial Incident of 27 July 1955 case, see Leo Gross, *Bulgaria Invokes the Connally Amendment*, 56 Am. J. Int'l L. 357 (1962).
7. [1960] ICJ Rep. 146,147.
8. *Id.*, at 147.
9. See the relevant part of the letter of the Legal Adviser of the Department of State to the Registrar of the Court, quoted in Gross, *supra* note 6, at 371.
10. See Bederman, *supra* note 2, at 245.
11. Case Concerning Military and Paramilitary Activities in and against Nicaragua (Nicaragua v. United States) (Jurisdiction), [1984] ICJ Rep. 392.
12. Case Concerning Military and Paramilitary Activities in and against Nicaragua (Nicaragua v. United States) (Merits), [1986] ICJ Rep. 14.
13. The strongest competitor for this appellation would probably be South West Africa (Ethiopia v. South Africa; Liberia v. South Africa), [1966] ICJ Rep. 6.
14. Nicaragua's declaration read as follows: "On behalf of the Republic of Nicaragua I recognize as compulsory unconditionally the jurisdiction of the Permanent Court of International Justice. Geneva, 24 September 1929. (Signed) T. F. Medina." See [1984] ICJ Rep. at 399.
15. For the dissenting opinions, see [1984] ICJ Rep. 461, 471, 514, 533, 558.
16. See *Observations on the International Court of Justice's November 26, 1984 Judgment on Jurisdiction and Admissibility in the Case of* Nicaragua v. United States of America, 79 Am. J. Int'l L. 423, 423–30 (1985).
17. See especially, Herbert W. Briggs, Nicaragua v. United States: *Jurisdiction and Admissibility*, 79 Am. J. Int'l L. 373 (1985).
18. See *Observations*, *supra* note 16, at 427.
19. *Id.* at 428.
20. Schwebel, Dissenting Opinion, paras. 117–29, [1984] ICJ Rep. at 628–37.
21. See *Observations*, *supra* note 16, at 429.

22. For US criticisms of the Court's rulings on its inadmissibility arguments, see *id.* at 429–30.
23. United States: Statement on the US Withdrawal from the Proceedings Initiated by Nicaragua in the International Court of Justice, 24 Int'l Leg. Materials 246 (1985).
24. This impression is based on my discussions with persons who were involved in the proceedings before the Court. See also Thomas M. Franck, *ICY Day at the ICJ*, 79 Am. J. Int'l L. 379 (1985).
25. See 24 Int'l Leg. Materials 1742 (1985).
26. Statement of Legal Adviser of State Department, Abraham D. Sofaer, to Senate Foreign Relations Committee, Dec. 4, 1985, 86 Dept. State Bull. 67 (No. 2106, Jan. 1986).
27. Rights of Nationals of the United States in Morocco, [1952] ICJ Rep. 176 (Aug.27).
28. Interhandel Case (Switzerland v. United States of America), [1957] ICJ Rep. 105.
29. Statement of Legal Adviser of State Department, *supra* note 26, at 69.
30. *Id.*
31. *Id.*
32. *Id.*
33. *Id.* at 70.
34. *Id.*
35. *Id.*
36. See, e.g., *Remarks by Oscar Schachter*, on Panel on the World Court, [1986] Am. Soc. Int'l L. Proc. 210.
37. Edith Brown Weiss, *Judicial Independence and Impartiality: A Preliminary Inquiry*, *in* The International Court of Justice at a Crossroads 123 (L. Damrosch ed., 1987).
38. *Remarks by Oscar Schachter*, *supra* note 36, at 211.
39. *Id.* (emphasis added).
40. Case Concerning Military and Paramilitary Activities in and against Nicaragua (Nicaragua v. United States of America), [1986] ICJ Rep. 14.
41. Art. 94 of the UN Charter provides: "(1) Each member of the United Nations undertakes to comply with the decision of the International Court of Justice in any case to which it is a party. (2) If any party to a case fails to perform the obligations incumbent upon it under a judgment rendered by the Court, the other party may have recourse to the Security Council, which may, if it deems necessary, make recommendations or decide upon measures to be taken to give effect to the judgment."
42. Consequently, as suggested by Fred Morrison, the impact of the judgment "on the immediate controversy appears slight." Fred L. Morrison, *Legal Issues in the Nicaragua Opinion*, 81 Am. J. Int'l L. 160 (1987).
43. See, e.g., the series of articles in *Appraisals of the ICJ's Decision:* Nicaragua v. United States *(Merits)*, 81 Am. J. Int'l L. 77–183 (1987).
44. 1986 ICJ Rep. at 259.
45. See Julius Stone, *Hopes and Loopholes in the 1974 Definition of Aggression*, 71 Am. J. Int'l L. 224 (1977).
46. Art. 3(g), Definition of Aggression annexed to GA Resolution 3314(XXIX) (1974).
47. [1986] ICJ Rep. at 103–04, para 195.
48. *Id.*
49. John Norton Moore, *The* Nicaragua *Case and the Deterioration of World Order*, 81 Am. J. Int'l L. 151, 155 (1987). For an expanded version of Moore's views on the case, written before the Court handed down its decision on the merits, see John Norton

Moore, *The Secret War in Central America and the Future of World Order*, 80 AM. J. INT'L L. 43 (1986). For a book-length treatment, see J. N. MOORE, THE SECRET WAR IN CENTRAL AMERICA (1987).

50. John Lawrence Hargrove, *The* Nicaragua *Judgment and the Future of the Law of Force and Self-Defense*, 81 AM. J. INT'L L. 135, 139 (1987).
51. See e.g., Herbert W. Briggs, *The International Court of Justice Lives up to its Name,* 81 AM. J. INT'L L. 78 (1987); Richard Falk, *The World Court's Achievement,* 81 AM. J. INT'L L. 106 (1987).
52. Case Concerning Legality of Use of Force (Yugoslavia v. Belgium) [1999] ICJ Rep.124, 38 INT'L LEG. MATERIALS 950 (1999).
53. See John R. Crook, *Current Development: The 2001 Judicial Activity of the International Court of Justice*, 96 AM. J. INT'L L. 397 (2002).
54. [1986] ICJ Rep. at 259.
55. *Id.* at 212.
56. W. Michael Reisman, *The Other Shoe Falls: The Future of Article 36(1) Jurisdiction in the Light of* Nicaragua, 81 AM. J. INT'L L. 166, 168 (1987).
57. *Id.* at 170–71.
58. *Id.* at 171.
59. *Id.* at 172.
60. Case Concerning United States Diplomatic and Consular Staff in Tehran (United States of America v. Iran), Order of Provisional Measures, 15 Dec. 1979, 1979 ICJ 7.
61. Case Concerning United States Diplomatic and Consular Staff in Tehran (United States of America v. Iran), Judgment of May 24, 1980, [1980] ICJ Rep. 3.
62. Oil Platforms (Islamic Republic of Iran v. United States), [1996] ICJ Rep. 803.
63. See John E. Noyes, *The Functions of Compromissory Clauses in US Treaties*, 34 VA. J. INT'L L. 831, 834 (1994).
64. *Id.* at 850.
65. Libya v. United States, [1992] ICJ Rep. 114 and Libya v. United Kingdom, 1992 ICJ 3.
66. [1998] ICJ Rep. 115.
67. See Crook, *supra* note 53, at 411.
68. Vienna Convention on Consular Relations, April 24, 1963, 21 UST 77, 596 UNTS 261.
69. For a more detailed discussion of the factual background to the Breard case, see Jonathan I. Charney & W. Michael Reisman, *Agora: Breard: The Facts*, 92 AM. J. INT'L L. 666 (1998).
70. Breard v. Netherland, 949 F. Supp. 1255, 1263 (ED Va. 1996), aff'd Breard v. Pruett, 134 F. 3d 615 (4th Cir. 1998).
71. Republic of Paraguay v. Allen, 949 F. Supp. 1269 (ED Va. 1996), aff'd, 134 F. 3d 622 (4th Cir.), cert. denied *sub. nom.* Breard v. Greene, 118 S.Ct. 1352 (1998).
72. The Eleventh Amendment to the US Constitution provides: "The Judicial power of the United States shall not be construed to extend to any suit in law or equity, commenced or prosecuted against one of the United States by Citizens of another State, or by Citizens or Subjects of any Foreign State."
73. Application of the Republic of Paraguay (Para.v. US), para. 25 (Apr. 3, 1998), *at* http://www.icj-cij.org.
74. Case Concerning the Vienna Convention on Consular Relations (Paraguay v. United States), Provisional Measures (Order of Apr. 9, 1998), *at* http://www.icj-cij.org.
75. Letter from Madeleine K. Albright, US Secretary of State, to James S. Gilmore III, Governor of Virginia (Apr. 13, 1998), cited and quoted in Charney & Reisman, *supra* note 69, at 671–72.

76. Brief for the United States as Amicus Curiae, Breard v. Greene, 118 S.Ct. 1352 (1998) (Nos. 97–1390, 97–8214).
77. *Id.* at 51.
78. Breard v. Greene, 118 S.Ct. 1352 (1998).
79. *Id.* at 1354.
80. *Id.* at 1356.
81. Commonwealth of Virginia, Office of the Governor, Press Office, Statement by Governor Jim Gilmore Concerning the Execution of Angel Breard (Apr. 14, 1998), cited and quoted in Charney & Reisman, *supra* note 69, at 674–75.
82. Louis Henkin, *Provisional Measures, US Treaty Obligations, and the States*, 92 AM. J. INT'L L. 679, 681 (1998). See also Carlos Manuel Vazquez, *Breard and the Federal Power to Require Compliance with ICJ Orders of Provisional Measures*, 92 AM. J. INT'L L. 683, 691 (1998) ("If the courts lacked the authority to require the states to comply (as the administration argued), then the President had the authority").
83. This recitation of the facts in the LaGrand case is taken largely from William J. Aceves, *Case Report: Case Concerning the Vienna Convention on Consular Relations [LaGrand Case]*, 93 AM. J. INT'L L. 924 (1999).
84. LaGrand (Germany v. United States), Provisional Measures (Int'l Ct. Justice Mar. 3, 1999), *at* http://www.icj-cij.org.
85. Federal Republic of Germany v. United States, 526 US 111 (1999).
86. LaGrand (Germany v. United States) (Int'l Ct. Justice June 27, 2001), *at* http://www.icj-cij.org.
87. 526 US at 112.
88. See, e.g., Aceves, *supra* note 83, and the several articles in the Symposium on *Reflections on the ICJ's* LaGrand *Decision*, 27 YALE J. INT'L L. 423–52 (2002).
89. Case Concerning Avena and Other Mexican Nationals (Mex.v. US), [2003] ICJ Rep. (Jan. 9), *at* http://www.icj.cij.org.
90. Case Concerning Avena and Other Mexican Nationals (Mexico v. United States), Request for the Indication of Provisional Measures (Feb. 5, 2003), *at* http://www.icj.cij.org.
91. See Marcia Coyle, *A Death Penalty Duel: UN Court Orders US to Stay Executions,* NAT'L LJ, Feb. 17, 2003, at A1.
92. See Bruce Zagaris, *ICJ Grants Provisional Remedies for Mexicans on US Death Row*, 19 INT'L ENFORCEMENT L. REP., April 2003, at 148.
93. *Id.*
94. Coyle, *supra* note 91.
95. LaGrand, *supra* note 84, para. 125.
96. See Joan Fitzpatrick, *The Unreality of International Law in the United States and the LaGrand Case*, 27 YALE J. INT'L L. 427, 431 (2002).
97. See Coyle, *supra* note 91.
98. Delimitation of the Maritime Boundary in the Gulf of Maine Area (Canada v. US), 1984 ICJ Rep. 246 (Judgment of Oct. 12).
99. See Jan Schneider, *The First ICJ Chamber Experiment: The* Gulf of Maine *Case: The Nature of an Equitable Result*, 79 AM. J. INT'L L. 539, 540 (1985).
100. Case Concerning Elettronica Sicula SPA (ELSI), [1989] ICJ Rep. 15.
101. For a comment on the ELSI case by a participant on the US side, see Sean D. Murphy, *The ELSI Case: An Investment Dispute at the International Court of Justice*, 16 YALE J. INT'L L. 391 (1991).
102. See, e.g., Shigeru Oda, *Note and Comment, Further Thoughts on the Chambers Procedure of the International Court of Justice*, 82 AM. J. INT'L L. 556 (1988).

103. See MARK W. JANIS, AN INTRODUCTION TO INTERNATIONAL LAW 153–54 (4th ed., 2003).
104. Stephen M. Schwebel, *Ad Hoc Chambers of the International Court of Justice*, 81 AM. J. INT'L L. 831, 850 (1987).
105. Richard B. Bilder, *The United States and the World Court in the Post-"Cold War" Era*, 40 CATH. UL REV. 251, 256–57 (1991).
106. JANIS, *supra* note 103, at 155.

8 Prevention, prosecution, and punishment of international crimes

Introduction

"International crimes" is a concept of considerable definitional ambiguity.[1] The eminent British international law scholar Georg Schwarzenberger, writing in 1950, concluded that "international criminal law in any true sense does not exist."[2] Defining international law narrowly to cover only those rights and obligations of states and not those of individuals, Schwarzenberger was of the opinion that "an international criminal law that is meant to be applied to the world powers is a contradiction in terms. It presupposes an international authority which is superior to these States."[3]

Turning to piracy and war crimes, the examples most often "adduced as evidence *par excellence* of the existence of international criminal law,"[4] Schwarzenberger denied that these actions constitute crimes under international law. Rather, in his view:

> The rules of international law both on piracy *jure gentium* and war crimes constitute prescriptions to States to suppress piracy within their own jurisdiction and to exercise proper control over their own armed forces, and an authorisation to other States to assume an extraordinary criminal jurisdiction under their own municipal law in the cases of piracy *jure gentium* and war crimes committed prior to capture by the enemy.[5]

Most other commentators have arrived at a different conclusion. With respect to piracy the International Law Commission, a subsidiary organ of the UN General Assembly, in drafting the articles on piracy that ultimately helped constitute the 1958 Geneva Convention on the Law of the High Seas, adopted what Alfred Rubin has termed the "naturalist" model. The naturalist model views piracy as "a crime against international law seeking only a tribunal with jurisdiction to apply that law and punish the criminal." It is opposed by the "positivist" view of piracy "as solely a municipal law crime, the only question of international law being the extent of a state's jurisdiction to apply its criminal law to an accused foreigner acting outside the territorial jurisdiction of the prescribing state."[6]

As to war crimes, the decision of the International Military Tribunal at Nuremberg and subsequent action by the UN General Assembly have arguably supported the "naturalist" view.

Another dimension of "international criminal law" involves international cooperation in the enforcement of municipal criminal law. Even for those crimes arguably constituting crimes under international law as well as municipal law, it is necessary – in the absence of an international criminal court having jurisdiction – to employ national law enforcement officials and national courts for purposes of prosecuting and punishing offenders.

The United States has had difficulties in working with foreign national law enforcement officials and national courts toward the effective prosecution and punishment of those who commit international crimes. The first part of this chapter provides an overview of some of the key mechanisms for, and issues arising from, dealing with international crimes, including bases for the exercise of jurisdiction over the crimes, extradition and other methods for the rendition of persons accused of international crimes, international judicial assistance in criminal matters, and the protection of fundamental human rights. In the second part, the chapter turns to a type of international crime of particular concern to the United States: international terrorism. The third part of the chapter briefly considers various kinds of tribunals that have been established or are in the process of being established to exercise jurisdiction over international crimes, including the tribunals established by the UN Security Council for the former Yugoslavia and Rwanda, the International Criminal Court and the so-called "hybrid courts" being established for Sierra Leone and Cambodia.

Some general considerations

In 1935, a Harvard Research project[7] identified five general principles which the international community had come to recognize as bases upon which a nation might apply its criminal law to particular conduct, as follows:

- the "territorial principle" (the conduct took place in the national territory);
- the "nationality principle" (the person committing the offense was a citizen);
- the "protective principle" (the conduct was injurious to a fundamental national interest);
- the "universality principle" (the offender was in custody);
- the "passive personality principle" (the victim was a citizen).

Of these, the Harvard study concluded, the "territorial principle" is "everywhere regarded as of primary importance and of fundamental character." The "nationality principle," although universally accepted, was marked by wide differences in use. The others did not, according to the study, command wide acceptance and only when used as a basis for punishing pirates did the "universality principle" command any significant recognition at all.

This territorially centered jurisdictional approach has increasingly been subject to challenge, but a discussion of this development is beyond the scope of this chapter. For present purposes it suffices to note that "[t]he most striking challenge to international law's traditional jurisdiction scheme has been the increasing willingness of states to apply principles of universal jurisdiction."[8] The idea is that some crimes are "recognized by the community of nations" to be "of universal concern" and therefore can be prosecuted anywhere.[9] This increased willingness of states to apply principles of "universal jurisdiction" has posed major problems for the United States.

Universal jurisdiction

One of the problems of universal jurisdiction is that it is not entirely clear precisely what crimes are subject to it. The Restatement (Third) of the Foreign Relations Law of the United States, for example, lists "piracy, slave trade, attacks on or hijacking of aircraft, genocide, war crimes, and *perhaps* certain acts of terrorism" as examples.[10] The so-called antiterrorism conventions, as we shall see later in this chapter, provide for general jurisdiction over the offenses they cover, but such agreements are effective only among the parties, unless customary international law has evolved to the point where it is accepted that these offenses are subject to universal jurisdiction. The Restatement's hesitation to list terrorism as subject to universal jurisdiction is based on the inability of the world community to agree on a definition of terrorism and the failure (as of 1987, the date of the Restatement's publication) of many states to ratify the antiterrorism conventions. More recently, the number of states parties to the antiterrorism conventions has increased, and it is now generally accepted that torture and crimes against humanity, which are within the jurisdiction of the Yugoslavia and Rwanda tribunals as well as that of the International Criminal Court, are subject to universal jurisdiction.

Even if customary international law would permit the exercise of universal jurisdiction over a particular crime, in order for a court to entertain a case based on the universality principle, the state in which the court sits must have enacted legislation granting its courts universal jurisdiction over the crime in question. For its part the United States has been reluctant to grant its courts universal jurisdiction over "international crimes." For example, US courts have jurisdiction over genocide only where the crime is committed on US territory or by a US national.[11] US courts have no jurisdiction over crimes against humanity, because the crime as such is not covered by the US criminal code. They do have universal jurisdiction over torture, but this is because the United States was obligated as a party to the Convention Against Torture and Other Cruel, Inhuman or Degrading Treatment or Punishment to grant its courts universal jurisdiction over the crime.[12] Perhaps most significantly, US courts do not have universal jurisdiction over war crimes. For them to have jurisdiction, either the victim or the perpetrator must be a US national.[13] This limited approach to war crimes, it should be noted, is incompatible with the 1949 Geneva Conventions on the Law of Armed Conflict, which designate certain "grave breaches" of the conventions as universal and extraditable offenses within the criminal jurisdiction of each state party and require states parties "to enact any legislation necessary to provide effective penal sanctions for persons committing, or ordering to be committed, any of the grave breaches" defined therein.[14]

As William Burke-White has pointed out, the decision to enact legislation granting national courts universal jurisdiction may be highly controversial.[15] Nongovernmental organizations (NGOs) and victim groups normally support such legislation, while military and diplomatic authorities oppose it on the grounds that it may endanger vital military and other sovereign interests of the state. A former US Secretary of State, Henry Kissinger, has been a strenuous opponent of such legislation, suggesting that it substitutes "the tyranny of judges for that of governments."[16] In the United States, the reservations of the military and civilian government officials regarding universal jurisdiction have largely prevailed. Many other states, however, have adopted a more favorable position toward universal jurisdiction and have enacted legislation permitting their courts to exercise universal jurisdiction over the most serious international crimes, such as war crimes and crimes against humanity.[17]

Belgium had legislation[18] so wide-ranging in scope that it resulted in Belgian courts being flooded with cases based on universal jurisdiction and the Belgian government being involved in heated international controversies. One of these controversies, over a Belgian arrest warrant issued for the Foreign Minister of the Congo, resulted in a ruling by the International Court of Justice that Belgium had violated international law because the Foreign Minister enjoyed immunity from judicial process.[19] As a result of this ruling, Belgium had to drop prosecutions of officials such as Israel's Prime Minister Ariel Sharon, who had been the object of a criminal complaint for war crimes filed by the survivors of the 1982 massacres at the Sabra and Shatila refugee camps in Beirut, Lebanon. In the Sharon case, however, Belgium's highest court ruled that Sharon could be tried for war crimes after he leaves office and that his co-defendant, Amos Yaron, the former Israeli Army chief of staff, could be tried before Belgian courts.[20] Later, as the US war on Iraq was getting under way, representatives of seven Iraqi families who claimed that they had lost loved ones in the first Gulf War, filed a criminal complaint naming former US President George H. W. Bush, as well as Secretary of State Colin Powell, Vice President Dick Cheney and Norman Schwarzkopf, the general, now retired, who had been in charge of US forces during Operation Desert Storm.[21] This apparently was the last straw, and resulted in such strong political protest from the United States that Belgium modified its legislation to allow cases to be brought only if the victim or suspect is a Belgian citizen or long-term resident at the time of the alleged crime. The revised law also guarantees diplomatic immunity for world leaders and other government officials visiting Belgium.[22]

The primary benefit of universal jurisdiction is that it provides an alternate means of bringing to justice the perpetrators of major international crimes when the state where the crime is committed is unable or unwilling to prosecute. Perhaps the landmark case illustrating this point is that of Augusto Pinochet, where Chile was neither able nor willing to prosecute its former president for torture or other international crimes allegedly committed during his time as head of state of Chile. In 1998, at the request of a Spanish investigating judge for extradition, an English magistrate issued a warrant for Pinochet's arrest. The petition of the Spanish judge alleged that, while head of state of Chile, Pinochet had conspired with others to take hostage, torture, and kill numerous persons, including Spanish citizens. Pinochet was arrested in the United Kingdom.He contended in the British courts that he was immune from arrest and properly could not be extradited. The House of Lords handed down two decisions. The first decision later was vacated by the House of Lords itself on the ground that one of the law lords on the panel had failed to disclose his connection with Amnesty International, which had intervened in the case. In its second judgment the House of Lords ruled that Pinochet could not claim immunity with respect to torture that had become a universal crime because of widespread ratification of the 1987 Convention Against Torture and Other Cruel, Inhuman or Degrading Treatment or Punishment and by the criminalization of torture in national legal systems around the world. The House of Lords also ruled that Pinochet was extraditable under the double criminality requirement imposed by the UK–Spain extradition treaty, at least for any alleged acts of torture committed after 1988, the year the United Kingdom became a party to the Torture Convention. The case was remanded to the lower courts and the executive authorities for the appropriate processing of the request for extradition. The British executive authorities ultimately decided that Pinochet's bad health did not permit him to stand trial and he was permitted to return to Chile.[23]

The Pinochet case, and the precedent it sets, has been the subject of considerable commentary – both for and against.[24] William Burke-White has usefully pointed out some of the "drawbacks" of employing universal jurisdiction as a basis for prosecuting international crimes:

> First, the prosecuting court may be far removed from the locus of the crime, making investigation and community engagement with the proceedings more difficult and the potential reconciling effects of justice more elusive. Second, some individuals and groups may not recognize the right of the prosecuting state to exercise universal jurisdiction, impeding the perceived legitimacy of the process. Third, many States have not enacted the requisite domestic legislation to prosecute crimes universally, making prosecution impossible in some cases. Finally, as the Pinochet case indicates, such prosecutions are easily politicized and may cause conflict between a State's judicial and foreign affairs functions.[25]

As we shall see later in this chapter, US concerns that its military and government officials will be subject to politicized prosecutions are a major reason that the United States strongly opposes the universal jurisdiction that will be exercised by the International Criminal Court over genocide, war crimes, crimes against humanity, and, perhaps, aggression.

Extradition

Even if the United States (or any other state) has jurisdiction to try an alleged offender, it must first obtain custody of the accused before its courts can exercise such jurisdiction. When an accused person is not within the territory of the United States, this has often proved to be a difficult process. Before a suspect can be prosecuted, he or she must first be located. The failure (so far) to locate Osama bin Laden is a prominent current example.[26]

If a suspect is apprehended outside US territory, the United States has to engage in a process of rendition to get the suspect before a US court. Besides extradition, the forms of rendition include exclusion, deportation, and abduction. Subject to very limited exceptions, abduction is illegal under international law, and exclusion and deportation involve unilateral action by the state of refuge and are relatively informal measures subject to a lack of legal limitations. Extradition is generally recognized as the only process of rendition that satisfactorily protects the rights of an accused. Assuming that the United States did not wish or could not convince the state of refuge to deport the accused, it would try to extradite the suspect. The obstacles to the success of this endeavor, however, could be considerable.

Indeed, the extradition process has been described as "a creaking steam engine of an affair."[27] Former US Attorney General Benjamin R. Civiletti was of the view that extradition laws belong to "the world of the horse and buggy and the steamship, not in the world of commercial jet transportation and high-speed telecommunications."[28] Much of this negative opinion is based on the many barriers that stand in the way of successful use of the extradition process.

First, the requested country would be under no obligation to extradite absent an extradition treaty between it and the United States.[29] Although the United States is a party to more than 100 bilateral extradition treaties and to the Inter-American Convention on Extradition with thirteen parties, the absence of an extradition treaty has been a problem in some high-profile cases, such as in US efforts to induce Libya to surrender the two Libyan members of the Libyan secret service who were indicted by a US grand jury. Also, the United States will not itself extradite a person to a requesting country in the absence of an extradition treaty.

Even with an extradition treaty, the extradition process is often fraught with difficulties. Many, if not most, US extradition treaties require that, for extradition to take place, the action in question be a crime in both the requesting and requested country. This dual criminality requirement can pose major problems in, for example, computer crime cases. Another barrier to extradition may be the refusal of some countries, especially those with a civil law background, to extradite their nationals. One of the grounds advanced by Libya in refusing to surrender the two Libyan members of the Libyan secret service was that the Libyan Constitution prohibited the extradition of Libyan nationals.

On the other hand, as to certain international crimes, there is some evidence that civil law states are beginning to relax their previous practice of never extraditing their nationals, at least in their relations with common law states. For example, the 1983 extradition treaty between the United States and Italy specifically provides that extradition shall not be refused on grounds of nationality and is aimed at combating the coordinated organized crime in the two countries.[30] Further, the increasing practice of repatriating prisoners to serve their sentences in their home country has reportedly convinced some civil law countries in Europe to extradite their nationals to common law countries.

Outside Europe there has also been some movement, albeit slow and tentative. In 1979 the United States and Colombia concluded an extradition treaty that allowed for the surrender of their respective nationals.[31] The treaty was a response to the inability of the United States to secure the extradition of Colombian nationals who had imported illegal drugs, especially cocaine, into the United States and who had so corrupted Colombian law enforcement officials that trial in Colombia was not possible. The new extradition treaty was extremely unpopular in Colombia, however, and in 1988 the Colombia Supreme Court declared the treaty unconstitutional. Repeated efforts by the United States resulted in Colombia passing a new law allowing for the extradition of its nationals in 1997, and extradition of drug suspects to the United States resumed.[32]

Relations between the United States and Mexico concerning the possible extradition of Mexican nationals have been especially tortuous. Under the US–Mexican Extradition Treaty of 1980,[33] neither party is required to extradite its nationals. Rather, Article 9 of the treaty gives both parties the option to prosecute as an alternative to extradition, and from 1978 until 1996, Mexico, as a matter of policy, refused to extradite its citizens to the United States. Moreover, allegedly as a result of corruption among Mexican law enforcement officials, persons whom the United States sought to extradite, especially for drug trafficking, were often not prosecuted in Mexico. Finally, in 1996, Mexico surrendered four of its citizens to the United States for prosecution, two of them for drug trafficking. This practice resulted in court challenges to the extradition of Mexican nationals with conflicting decisions. On January 18, 2001, however, Mexico's Supreme Court of Justice ruled by a ten to one vote that the extradition of Mexican nationals is in accordance with Mexico's Constitution.[34]

In recent years, at both the state and the federal level, the United States has extended the death penalty to more and more crimes, including terrorist crimes. By contrast, since World War II, opposition outside the United States to the death penalty has resulted in many countries including clauses in extradition treaties that exclude extradition where the requesting state retains the death penalty and is unwilling or unable to provide assurances that this penalty will not be carried out if the accused is extradited. This development has greatly complicated US extradition relations with other countries.

Another important development has been the increasing importance of human rights considerations as a limitation on extradition. Opposition to the death penalty in the west European states is based in large part on the belief that it violates fundamental human rights. On the other hand, as noted by John Dugard and Christine Van den Wyngaert, "[t]oday states are irreconcilably divided over the morality and effectiveness of the death penalty,"[35] and as a result, its imposition is not prohibited by general international law. Under certain circumstances, however, according to some authorities, imposition of the death penalty may constitute cruel, inhuman, or degrading treatment or punishment, and thus violate general international law norms.

The best known of these authorities is the decision of the European Court of Human Rights in *Soering v. United Kingdom.*[36] Soering, a West German national, murdered his girlfriend's parents in the Commonwealth of Virginia and fled to the United Kingdom. In response to a US request, the United Kingdom ordered his extradition to the United States. Soering, however, petitioned the European Commission of Human Rights, which referred his case to the European Court of Human Rights. The court held that the United Kingdom had an obligation under Article 3 of the European Convention on Human Rights, which prohibits torture and inhuman or degrading treatment or punishment, not to extradite Soering to the United States, where there was a real risk that he would be subjected to inhuman or degrading treatment by being kept in Virginia on death row for a prolonged period. Eventually Soering was extradited to the United States when the United Kingdom received assurances from US officials that he would not be subjected to the death penalty.

Although it is not a judicial body with authority to hand down a decision binding on parties to a dispute, the Human Rights Committee (the body established by the International Covenant on Civil and Political Rights to supervise implementation of the covenant by states parties) found in *Ng v. Canada*[37] that California's practice of executing by gas asphyxiation resulted in prolonged suffering constituting cruel and unusual suffering within the meaning of Article 7 of the Covenant. On the basis of this finding, the committee was of the opinion that Canada, which could reasonably have foreseen that Ng would be executed in this way, had violated its obligations under the Covenant by extraditing him to the United States.

In 1980, Alona Evans identified the political offense exception, which is grounded in human rights considerations at least partially, as the "hot issue" of extradition law.[38] At that time, the political offense exception was regarded as perhaps the primary barrier to the extradition of international terrorists. But in recent years states have taken a variety of steps to limit or even to eliminate the political offense exception as a defense to extradition, and it is unclear whether the political offense exception remains a major barrier to extradition at the present time.[39]

As an alternative to or a substitute for the political offense exception, extradition treaties may permit the accused to claim that he will not receive a fair trial in the requesting country. Article 3(a) of the US–UK Supplementary Extradition Treaty of 1985,[40] for example, expressly permits a judicial inquiry into whether the extraditee will be "prejudiced at his trial or punished, detained or restricted in his personal liberty by reason of his race, religion, nationality or political opinions." This so-called "humanitarian exception" was inserted because of the concern of some US senators that the elimination of the political offense exception effected by the Supplementary Extradition Treaty would result in inadequate protection for extraditees. By giving the courts the responsibility of ruling on allegations of an unfair trial, the treaty waters down the rule of non-inquiry US courts normally apply, under which the courts defer to the executive branch to make the decision as to the validity of such allegations. In practice, however, courts in the United States have been extremely reluctant to make a finding that would reflect on the standards of justice in the United Kingdom. On the other hand, courts in both the United States and Canada have held that the rule of non-inquiry is not absolute, and that it will not be followed if the likely treatment in the requesting state would be shocking or simply unacceptable.

As a result of these many barriers to extradition, US and other countries' law enforcement officials have often turned to alternative forms of rendition in their efforts to bring alleged offenders to a forum for prosecution.

Alternatives to extradition

The methods of rendition most often utilized as alternatives to extradition are exclusion and deportation.[41] Exclusion may occur when fugitives are apprehended as they attempt to enter a country, and deportation may be an option when fugitives are arrested within a country's territory. In US practice, not surprisingly, many of these exclusions and deportations have involved Canada or Mexico and have been directed toward persons accused of drug trafficking. Exclusion and deportation are civil processes, designed for immigration control and dominated by the executive. As a consequence, exclusion and deportation proceedings utilized for rendition purposes do not apply criminal justice standards with respect to the interests of the states involved or protection of the accused. Unlike extradition, exclusion and deportation rarely involve a formal request by a state seeking a return of the alleged offender. On the contrary, exclusion and deportation are effected at the instance of the territorial state.

Perhaps the most controversial use of deportation as an alternative to extradition was the case of Joseph Doherty. Attempts to extradite Doherty, a member of the Provisional Irish Republican Army, from the United States to the United Kingdom, where he was wanted for his role in the death of a British soldier and for escape from prison, were unsuccessful because of decisions by US courts that his offenses fell within the political offense exception in the US–UK extradition treaty. The US government then tried a different approach and was ultimately successful when the US Supreme Court upheld Doherty's deportation to Northern Ireland after long and complicated legal proceedings.[42] Apparently, the deportation of Doherty was handled as a purely internal matter and not in response to a request from the United Kingdom that he be deported. Although some commentators have argued that it is improper for one state to request another to deport an individual as a means of circumventing extradition procedures, US courts have repeatedly held that the existence of an extradition treaty between the United States and another country does not bar the use of other means to obtain custody over a criminal located abroad. In contrast, complicity between the French government and another government to use deportation as an alternative to extradition may reportedly be the basis for dismissal of the prosecution in France.[43]

The most controversial alternative to extradition has, of course, been abduction or kidnapping of alleged offenders. Commentators and state practice support the general proposition that international law prohibits a state from sending its agents into another state to abduct an individual residing there without that other state's permission. Abductions would seem prima facie to violate a principal rule of international law, which states that a nation is absolutely sovereign within the boundaries of its own territory.

The most controversial of US abductions was the 1990 apprehension and deportation to the United States of Humberto Alvarez-Machain by Mexican agents paid by the US Drug Enforcement Agency (DEA). Alvarez-Machain was a prominent Mexican gynecologist who had been indicted for the kidnap and murder of Enrique Camarena, a DEA agent stationed in Guadalajara. After strong protests by the Mexican government, and a circuit court opinion holding that the abduction violated the US–Mexico extradition treaty, the US Supreme Court ruled that the abduction was not barred by the extradition treaty and that US courts could exercise jurisdiction over the case.[44] Although the majority opinion all but conceded by way of dicta that the abduction violated norms of customary international law, the Court did not address the issue of whether this might constitute a basis for US courts to decline jurisdiction. Courts in several other countries have ruled that they have discretion in such circumstances to refuse to exercise jurisdiction.[45]

The Supreme Court's decision in *Alvarez-Machain* has been subjected to sharp criticism.[46] Geoff Gilbert has suggested that, paradoxically, the Court's decision may "hasten the demise of State sponsored kidnaps of alleged international criminals, for it has brought to the fore this attempt to authorize the 'manifestly illegal.'"[47] Indeed, in the wake of *Alvarez-Machain*, the first Bush administration quickly responded with assurances that it had no intention of either increasing or institutionalizing the practice of extraterritorial abductions. In 1994, the United States and Mexico concluded a Treaty to Prohibit Transborder Abductions[48] (which, however, as of this writing has not yet been sent to the Senate for its advice and consent to ratification).

Mutual assistance in criminal matters

Regardless of how he got there, once an accused is before a US court, it is necessary to prove his guilt beyond a reasonable doubt. But if the evidence to do this is located abroad, and cannot be obtained, the successful rendition of the accused may be a pyrrhic victory.

Moreover, the legal mechanisms for obtaining evidence abroad for use in criminal proceedings are less than satisfactory. Letters rogatory, the standard mechanism, require an application to a foreign court and usually provide for advance notice and participation by opposing parties. Hence, the procedure is relatively public, as compared to the US practice of conducting criminal investigations under the veil of grand jury secrecy. It is even under the best of circumstances extremely slow, and foreign tribunals may give limited or no assistance at the pre-indictment phase of a case. In any event, the decision of foreign tribunals to respond favorably is purely discretionary, since the letters rogatory practice is based on comity considerations rather than on binding international legal norms.

Because they create binding international legal obligations for the states parties, mutual legal assistance treaties (MLATs) are of greater value. As of May 11, 2003, the United States had forty-nine MLATs in force.[49] They provide prosecutors with a channel for sending requests for assistance in obtaining evidence through a central authority in one country to a corresponding prosecutorial authority in another country, which oversees the prompt execution of the request. Under MLATs, foreign prosecutorial authorities will normally seek mandatory process under their law, when necessary, to execute the request and keep it confidential to the extent possible.

The US MLATs contain a provision that obligates a requested country to conduct searches and seizures on behalf of a requesting country if the request includes information justifying such action under the laws of the requested country. But only a few of these MLATS apply broadly to all law enforcement investigations and prosecutions rather than only to certain types of offenses such as drug trafficking and money laundering. Additionally, the political offense exception is often available in MLATs and can be a barrier to obtaining the necessary evidence.

As Michael Tigar and Austin Doyle have pointed out:

> Obtaining information from abroad in criminal cases poses many of the same problems as obtaining the defendant himself. The parallels are, with only slight exaggeration, simply stated. A treaty that imposed reciprocal obligations upon the signatories to render requested data is analogous to an extradition treaty. Deportation resembles the unilateral decision of a foreign sovereign to send data out of the country to a particular place. Defendants are sometimes kidnapped across international frontiers, and information is sometimes obtained by means beneath the law, often without the consent of the sovereign from whose territory the information is taken.[50]

The problems do not necessarily end once the information is obtained. Then the issue of admissibility at trial may arise.[51]

International terrorism[52]

As noted earlier in this study, especially in chapter 4, the United States is currently engaged in a "war on terrorism" and has utilized military force to combat it. Prior to September 11, efforts to combat international terrorism were a relatively low priority on the US national and international agendas. International terrorism was treated primarily as a criminal law matter, with emphasis placed on preventing the commission of the crime through intelligence or law enforcement means or, if prevention failed, on the apprehension, prosecution, and punishment of the perpetrators. As a consequence, the United States, and other like-minded states, promoted the adoption of so-called "antiterrorist conventions," which encouraged states parties to adopt a system of universal jurisdiction over the particular manifestations of terrorism they covered, such as aircraft hijacking or hostage taking, and which required them to extradite or submit to prosecution any alleged offender apprehended in their territories; adopted new or revised extradition treaties to improve an outmoded extradition process; entered into mutual legal assistance treaties with a view to gathering and sharing evidence of the crime; and attempted to limit or eliminate barriers to the prosecution of terrorists, such as the political offense exception to extradition.[53]

Although, after September 11, the law of armed conflict has assumed a much greater prominence than it had previously in efforts to combat terrorism, it has hardly occupied the field. On the contrary, one newly prominent issue is whether the law of armed conflict or international criminal law applies to a particular instance of US efforts. The controversy over possible US plans to use military commissions to try terrorists is a salient example. Moreover, it is important to note how, in the wake of September 11, various fields of law and methodologies for combating terrorism, some of which were not at all involved previously, or at most were applicable only occasionally, have come to the fore. These include, among others, immigration and refugee law, international human rights law, international finance, US constitutional law, private remedies (especially civil law suits), cyber law, privacy, homeland security, arms control, disarmament, and nonproliferation, intelligence gathering, and public health law.[54]

A discussion of all these fields of law, and how they apply or might apply to the US war on terrorism, is beyond the scope of this chapter. Rather, for present purposes, this section briefly considers the tortuous road the United States has taken in its efforts to create an effective regime for the prevention, prosecution, and punishment of international terrorists. As we shall see, progress has been made, but much remains to be done.

International terrorism: a definitional quagmire

It may come as a surprise to learn that there is at present no generally accepted definition of "international terrorism,"[55] as demonstrated by the cliché, "one man's terrorism is another man's heroism." Some countries believe that the causes of terrorism or the political motivation of the individual terrorists are relevant to the problem of definition. For example, the position of some governments has been that individual acts of violence can be defined as terrorism only if they are employed for personal gain or caprice; acts committed in connection with a political cause, especially against colonialism and for national liberation, fall outside the definition and constitute legitimate measures of self-defense. Under this approach, the sending of letter bombs through the mails, hijacking of aircraft, kidnappings of or attacks on diplomats and international business persons, and the indiscriminate slaughter of innocent civilians by members of revolutionary groups could *never* constitute "terrorism" if committed on behalf of a just cause.

Nevertheless, for our purposes, it is necessary to have a rough working definition of the subject. To this end, one might consider the definition of "international terrorism" that appears in the US criminal code's chapter on terrorism. According to this definition "international terrorism" means activities that:

(A) involve violent acts or acts dangerous to human life that are a violation of the criminal laws of the United States or of any State, or that would be a criminal violation if committed within the jurisdiction of the United States or of any State;
(B) appear to be intended –
  (i) to intimidate or coerce a civilian population;
  (ii) to influence the policy of a government by intimidation or coercion; or
  (iii) to affect the conduct of a government by mass destruction, assassination, or kidnapping; and
(C) occur primarily outside the territorial jurisdiction of the United States or transcend national boundaries in terms of the means by which they are accomplished, the persons they appear intended to intimidate or coerce, or the locale in which their perpetrators operate or seek asylum.[56]

As we shall see in the next section, in part because of its inability to agree on a definition of international terrorism, the world community has attempted to resolve the problem of definition by ignoring it and focusing instead on identifying particular criminal acts to be prevented and punished and on particular targets to be protected.

A brief history of efforts to combat international terrorism

The word "terrorism" was first used during the French Revolution and the reign of terror. In this manifestation it took the form of state action designed to further political repression and social control. The revolutionary anarchism that arose in the latter half of the nineteenth century presented a dramatic manifestation of individual acts of terrorism. The anarchists were regarded as the common enemy of mankind and were suppressed by harsh government action.

Terrorism played a role in the outbreak of World War I. During the early years of the twentieth century, the Balkans became a focal point for international intrigue and revolutionary violence involving bands secretly supported by Bulgaria, Serbia, and Greece. The Serbian government supported a group known as the Black Hand against the Austro-Hungarian Empire. On June 28, 1914, the Archduke Franz Ferdinand, heir to the imperial throne, was assassinated by a nineteen-year-old trained by the Black Hand. The assassination precipitated a series of actions and counteractions that led within a month to World War I.

An increase in terrorist activity following World War I led to the first concerted efforts at international control of terrorism, namely, a series of meetings in the late 1920s and early 1930s under the auspices of the

International Conference for the Unification of Penal Law. These meetings served to focus attention on the subject, and resulted in the revision of some extradition treaties to exclude certain terrorist acts from the category of "political offenses," thereby making them extraditable (especially attacks on heads of state, the so-called "attentat" clause first introduced by Belgium and France into all their extradition treaties). However, it was not until the assassination in Marseille on October 9, 1934, of King Alexander of Yugoslavia and Louis Barthou, Foreign Minister of the French Republic, that the world community began an intensive consideration at the official level of international terrorism. This concern led to the Convention for the Prevention and Punishment of Terrorism, concluded in Geneva under the auspices of the League of Nations on November 16, 1937. Under the Convention, terrorism was defined broadly to include criminal acts directed against a state and intended to create terror in the minds of a particular person, or a group of persons or the general public. Possibly because of the breadth of this definition, only one member state of the League ratified the Convention and it never came into force.

The kidnapping and killing in Munich on September 6, 1972, of eleven Israeli Olympic competitors by Arab terrorists, as well as a number of other spectacular acts of terrorism, resulted in UN General Assembly consideration of the problem of international terrorism and in the introduction by the United States on September 25, 1972, of a Draft Convention for the Prevention and Punishment of Certain Acts of International Terrorism.[57] The United States attempted to obviate the concern of some member states that the convention was directed against so-called wars of national liberation. To this end the United States pointed out that the convention was limited in its coverage to "[a]ny person who unlawfully kills, causes serious bodily harm or kidnaps another person." They noted further that, even as to these acts, four separate conditions had to be met before the terms of the convention applied. First, the act had to be committed or take effect outside the territory of a state of which an alleged offender was a national. Second, the act had to be committed or take effect outside the state against which the act was directed, unless such acts were knowingly directed against a non-national of that state. Under this provision an armed attack in the passenger lounge of an international airport would be covered. Third, the act must not be committed either by or against a member of the armed forces of a state in the course of military hostilities. And, fourth, the act had to be intended to damage the interests of or obtain concessions from a state or an international organization. Accordingly, exceedingly controversial activities arguably terrorist in nature (such as fedayeen attacks in Israel against Israeli citizens and a wide range of activities by armed forces in Indochina and in southern Africa) were deliberately excluded from the convention's coverage. A particularly broad exclusion was the requirement that the act be committed or take effect outside the country of which the alleged offender was a national. This provision would have excluded from the scope of the convention most terrorist attacks in Latin America and elsewhere against international business personnel and facilities. As to persons allegedly committing offenses covered by the convention and apprehended in their territories, states parties would have been required to establish severe penalties for covered acts and either to prosecute such persons or extradite them to another state party for prosecution. The decision whether to prosecute or extradite the alleged offender would have been left to the sole discretion of the state where he was apprehended.

Despite strenuous efforts on the part of many states to reach a compromise, the US initiative was unsuccessful. On December 18, 1972, the General Assembly adopted Resolution 3034 (XXVII) by a roll-call vote of seventy-six to thirty-five (including the United States), with seventeen abstentions. That resolution, while expressing "*deep concern* over increasing acts of violence which endanger or take innocent human lives or jeopardize human freedoms" (emphasis in original), and inviting states to become parties to existing conventions on international terrorism and to take appropriate measures at the national level to eliminate terrorism, focused its primary attention on "finding just and peaceful solutions to the underlying causes which give rise to such acts of violence." The resolution also "*reaffirms* the inalienable right to self-determination and independence of all peoples under the colonial and racist regimes and other forms of alien domination and upholds the legitimacy of their struggle" (emphasis in original). By way of implementation the resolution invited states to study the problem on an urgent basis and submit their observations to the Secretary-General by April 10, 1973, and established an ad hoc committee, to be appointed by the president of the General Assembly, to study these observations and to submit a report with recommendations for elimination of the problem to the twenty-eighth session of the Assembly. The committee was appointed. However, after meeting from July 16 to August 10, 1973, the committee reported to the General Assembly that it was unable to agree on *any* recommendations for dealing with the problem.

One of the reasons why the ad hoc committee failed to reach agreement on any recommendations for dealing with terrorism was because it got bogged down in fruitless efforts to define international terrorism. To obviate this problem, the focus in the United Nations and its specialized agencies turned to very specific criminal acts that at least most concerned parties would be able to agree should be regarded as illegitimate under *all* circumstances – no matter what the underlying cause of the act might be. This so-called "piecemeal" approach has enjoyed a measure of success. At this writing it has resulted in twelve global conventions covering a great variety of acts commonly engaged in by terrorists.[58] These conventions generally resolve the problem of defining terrorism by avoiding it. Although these treaty provisions are often loosely described as "antiterrorist," the acts they cover are criminalized regardless of whether, in a particular case, they could be described as "terrorism." All these conventions seek to maximize the probability that terrorists will be punished for their crimes by requiring that a state party which apprehends an alleged offender in its territory either extradite him or submit his case to its own authorities for purposes of prosecution. To the extent that states widely ratify these conventions, and carry out their "extradite or prosecute" requirement in good faith, terrorists are denied a safe haven to escape punishment for their crimes.

With the passage of time, gaps in the coverage of terrorist crimes by the early coventions became apparent, and new conventions covering other international crimes were concluded. For example, the Tokyo, Hague, and Montreal conventions on the hijacking of and attacks on civil aviation did not cover attacks at airports, such as those at the Rome and Vienna airports during the 1980s. As a consequence, the International Civil Aviation Organization (ICAO) adopted a Protocol to the Montreal Convention for the Suppression of Unlawful Acts of Violence at Airports Serving International Civil Aviation. Similarly, the hijacking of the Italian cruise liner the *Achille Lauro* exposed the vulnerability of maritime navigation and infrastructure to terrorist attack and led to the adoption of the Convention for the Suppression of Unlawful Acts against the Safety of Maritime Navigation and of the Protocol for the Suppression of Unlawful Acts against the Safety of Fixed Platforms Located on the Continental Shelf.

It was in the 1990s, however, that UN member states sought to fill the largest gap in coverage of terrorist crimes. Among the many extraordinary developments during this period were the collapse of the Soviet Union and the end of the Cold War, and the end of apartheid in South Africa and the coming into power of new governments in South Africa and Namibia. These and other developments led to a less confrontational atmosphere in the United Nations and a sharp decline in support for "wars of national liberation." This in turn helped to lessen the division between the Western member states, particularly the United States, and the non-aligned member states that had frustrated previous efforts to reach agreement on measures to combat terrorism. Indeed, because of the change of atmosphere, the General Assembly decided in 1997 to reincarnate the Ad Hoc Committee on Measures to Eliminate International Terrorism to prepare, among other things, a draft international convention for the suppression of terrorist bombing.

It is worthwhile to pause for a moment at this point and consider the importance, in terms of combating international terrorism, of the General Assembly's decision to mandate the preparation of a convention against terrorist bombing. In an article published in 1990, I suggested:

> A more serious deficiency is that none of the antiterrorist conventions cover those tactics most often used by terrorists, most particularly the deliberate targeting, by bombs or other weapons, of the civilian population. To understand the reason for this it is necessary to briefly return to the problem of defining terrorism.
>
> A look at the primary components of most definitions of terrorism will help us to understand why it has proved impossible to reach agreement in the United Nations and other international organizations. These definitions almost invariably include a political purpose of motivation behind the violent act and a government as a primary target, factors that serve to distinguish terrorism from violent acts classified as common crimes. The political purpose of the violent act is to influence the policy of a government by intimidation or coercion. These same factors, however, may lead some governments to be not only unwilling to criminalize such behavior but prone to actively support it.
>
> Nonetheless, there appears to be a growing recognition that even favored national liberation groups cannot be permitted to engage in certain acts of violence against certain targets. Moreover, under the law of armed conflict the deliberate targeting of the civilian population is a war crime. It should be impermissible as well when the targeting takes place under circumstances not covered by the law of armed conflict. This was the conclusion reached recently by a joint group of US and Soviet experts on international terrorism who recommended to their respective governments that they support the conclusion of an international convention that would make the deliberate targeting of a civilian population an international crime.[59]

The adoption by the General Assembly of the International Convention for the Suppression of Terrorist Bombing on December 15, 1997, vividly illustrates the sea change in the attitudes of UN member states toward terrorist acts that various developments in the 1990s brought about, including several major terrorist bombings directed against various states and some effective diplomatic initiatives on the part of the United States.

Others have written about the terrorist bombing convention in some detail,[60] and no such effort will be undertaken here. There are a few innovative aspects about the convention, however, that deserve highlighting. In keeping with the "piecemeal" approach, the convention does not define "terrorism" but identifies and defines particular conduct that is to be condemned internationally, regardless of its motivation, and subject to criminal penalties. Article 2(1) of the convention provides:

> Any person commits an offense within the meaning of the Convention if that person unlawfully and intentionally delivers, places, discharges or detonates an explosive or other lethal device in, into or against a place of public use, a State or governmental facility, a public transportation system or an infrastructure facility: (a) with the intent to cause death or serious bodily injury; or (b) with the intent to cause extensive destruction of such a place, facility or system, where such destruction results in or is likely to result in major economic loss.

To ensure that sympathy with the motivation behind the bombing will not serve as a legal justification of the act, Article 5 requires states parties to adopt any measures that may be necessary to ensure that criminal acts within the scope of the convention, especially when they are intended to create a state of terror, are "under no circumstances justifiable by considerations of a political, philosophical, ideological, racial, ethnic, religious or other similar nature and are punishable by penalties consistent with their grave nature." None of the earlier antiterrorist conventions has a similar provision. Along somewhat similar lines, Article 11 expressly eliminates, for the first time in a UN antiterrorist convention, the political offense exception for purposes of extradition and mutual legal assistance.

At the same time the bombing convention adds a protection for the accused in Article 12, which provides that nothing in the convention shall be interpreted as imposing an obligation to extradite or to afford mutual legal assistance if the requested state party has substantial grounds for believing that the request was made "for the purpose of prosecuting or punishing a person on account of that person's race, religion, nationality, ethnic origin or political opinion or that compliance with the request would cause prejudice to that person's position for any of these reasons." Such a "humanitarian" provision is normally not present in the UN antiterrorist conventions, although there is a provision along similar lines in the International Convention against the Taking of Hostages.

Only the sea change in the attitudes of the member states of the United Nations toward terrorist bombing that took place during the 1990s permitted the successful conclusion of the bombing convention. At this writing, however, there are troubling developments that could seriously undermine the success of the convention as an antiterrorist measure. Specifically, the sudden increase in suicide bombings by Palestinians against Israeli civilians risks a return to some of the divisions between Western member states and certain member states of the developing world that characterized the United Nations during the 1970s.

International Convention on the Suppression of Terrorist Financing

Hans Corell, Under-Secretary-General for Legal Affairs and Legal Counsel of the United Nations, noted in 1996 that the Secretary-General had recognized the need for an international convention dealing with terrorist fund-raising.[61] Through a series of steps, this led to the General Assembly adopting a resolution on December 9, 1999, opening for signature the International Convention for the Suppression of the Financing of Terrorism.

Like its immediate predecessor, the bombing convention, the financing convention is a "model" antiterrorist convention that incorporates what Clifton Johnson, the chief US negotiator for the convention, has called:

> increasingly standard provisions of the recent counterterrorism conventions. These include provisions: 1) limiting the Convention's application to acts with an international element; 2) obligating States Parties to criminalize the covered offenses irrespective of the motivation of the perpetrators; 3) obligating States Parties to take into custody offenders found in their territory; 4) facilitating the extradition of offenders; 5) requiring States Parties to afford one another the greatest measure of assistance in connection with the criminal investigations or proceedings relating to the covered offenses; 6) prohibiting extradition or mutual legal assistance requests relating to a covered offense from being refused on political offense grounds; and 7) providing for the transfer of prisoners in order to assist the investigation or prosecution of covered offenses.[62]

Dealing with the financing of terrorism is a delicate matter. A major problem is that terrorists often operate through "front organizations" which appear on the surface to be engaged in legitimate activities or through organizations that in fact have charitable, social, or cultural goals and engage in legitimate activities to further these goals. Moreover, in some states, such as the United States, action by the government to prevent or limit the financing of organizations with charitable or similar goals could raise serious constitutional issues. In an effort to avoid such difficulties, Article 2(1) carefully limits the scope of the convention:

> 1. Any person commits an offence within the meaning of this Convention if that person by any means, directly or indirectly, unlawfully and wilfully, provides or collects funds with the intention that they should be used or in the knowledge that they are to be used, in full or in part, in order to carry out: (a) an act which constitutes an offense within the scope of and as defined in one of the treaties listed in the annex; or (b) any other act intended to cause death or serious bodily injury to a civilian, or to any other person not taking an active part in the hostilities in a situation of armed conflict, when the purpose of such an act, by its nature or context, is to intimidate a population, or to compel a government or an international organization to do or abstain from doing any act.

Under Article 2(1)(a), the convention requires actual intention that funds should be used, or knowledge that they will be used, to carry out one of the offenses listed in an annex to the convention. Such an intention or knowledge of how the funds are to be used is also required by paragraph 1(b). The latter paragraph sets forth a definition of terrorism, although the definition is not identified as such. It therefore establishes an important precedent that may be drawn upon in future antiterrorism conventions.

As in the case of its predecessor conventions, the principal objective of the financing convention is to require states parties to criminalize and establish jurisdiction over the offenses set forth in the convention and to extradite or submit for prosecution the persons accused of the commission of such offenses. The financing convention goes further than its predecessors, however. In particular, as aptly summarized by Rohan Perera, chairman of the Ad Hoc Committee on Terrorism, the convention requires states parties to consider the following measures:

(i) Adopt regulations, prohibiting the opening of accounts, the holders or beneficiaries of which are unidentified or unidentifiable and measures to ensure that such institutions verify the real owner of such transactions.
(ii) With respect to the identification of legal entities, financial institutions when necessary are required to take measures to verify the legal existence and structure of the customer or both, proof of incorporation or other relevant information.
(iii) Obligations on financial institutions to report promptly to the competent authorities all complex, unusual large transactions and unusual patterns of transactions which have no apparent economic or obviously lawful purpose.
(iv) Measures requiring financial institutions to maintain at least for 5 years, all records on transactions, both domestic or international.[63]

More generally, the convention provides an extensive list of measures for states parties to consider in identifying, tracking, and blocking transactions involving terrorism financing.

Another innovative provision in the convention is in Article 5. It requires each state party to "take the necessary measures to enable a legal entity located in its territory organized under its laws to be held liable when a person responsible for the management or control of that legal entity" has committed an offense under the convention. Normally, the antiterrorist conventions address only the issue of criminal and not civil liability. The convention also enhances the deterrent effect of its provisions by providing for the seizure or freezing of funds and proceeds used for the commission of an offence and by prohibiting states parties from claiming privileged communication, banking secrecy, or the fiscal nature of the offence to refuse a request for mutual assistance from another state party.

As Clifton Johnson has suggested, the financing convention has the potential to have a considerable impact on efforts to combat terrorism. Johnson notes that the impact the convention has in practice will depend in no small measure on "the degree to which investigators and prosecutors can establish the necessary link between the act of financing and the terrorist intention of the contributor or collector of the funds." This may be a heavy evidentiary burden to bear, since the contributors and recipients of funds for the commission of terrorist acts are adept at using money laundering and other techniques to disguise their purpose. Moreover, relatively few member states of the United Nations currently have in place the legal infrastructure or the trained personnel to cope with the techniques of terrorist financing. One may hope, however, that the cooperative arrangements called for by the financing convention will help to remedy this situation.

For the financing convention to be effective, of course, it will have to be widely ratified and implemented. At this writing there are 132 signatories and 88 parties (including the United States). The UN Security Council itself has given an enormous boost to the convention and to the effort to combat terrorist financing. On September 28, 2001, the Security Council, acting under Chapter VII of the Charter, adopted Resolution 1373,[64] which, by any measure, constitutes a landmark step by the Council. In this extraordinary resolution, the Council sets forth a series of steps that member states are *required* to take to combat terrorism. Among the most noteworthy of these, states are to deny safe haven to terrorists, to afford one another the greatest measure of assistance in criminal investigations or proceedings relating to the financing or support of terrorist acts, including assistance in obtaining evidence necessary for such proceedings, and to prevent the movement of terrorists by effective border controls and controls on the issuance of identity papers and travel documents.

Using terms of exhortation rather than command, in Resolution 1373 the Council "[*c*]*alls* upon all States" to take a number of actions in cooperation with other states to combat terrorism, including, among others, "intensifying and accelerating the exchange of operational information," becoming parties to the relevant antiterrorist conventions, including the financing convention, and ensuring, "in conformity with international law," that refugee status is not abused by terrorists, and that "claims of political motivation are not recognized as grounds for refusing requests for the extradition of alleged terrorists."[65]

The most significant step the Council took in Resolution 1373 is to establish a committee (the Counter-Terrorism Committee) to monitor implementation of the resolution and to call upon all states to report to the committee, no later than ninety days after the date of adoption of the resolution, on the steps they have taken to implement the resolution. The Council further "[e]xpresses its determination to take all necessary steps in order to ensure the full implementation of this resolution, in accordance with its responsibilities under the Charter."[66] Failure to establish such monitoring devices to ensure that antiterrorist measures adopted by the United Nations are effective in practice has been a major deficiency of past UN efforts.

A primary example of UN antiterrorist measures that have not been effectively monitored in the past as to their implementation is the antiterrorist conventions. As we have seen, a sea change in attitudes on the part of many (though not all) member states of the United Nations has resulted in the conclusion of "model" new antiterrorist conventions, especially the bombing and financing conventions. The conclusion of new, or even the ratification of old, antiterrorist conventions, however, is not the crucial issue. The crucial issue is the extent to which the global antiterrorist conventions have been or will be vigorously *implemented*. Conclusion of antiterrorist conventions is only the first step in the process. Unfortunately, many states parties seem to regard it as the last.

Vigorous implementation, moreover, encompasses more than merely ratifying the conventions, passing implementing legislation, and adopting the necessary administrative measures, that is, creating an appropriate legal infrastructure to combat international terrorism. It requires the taking of active steps toward ensuring the primary goals of the conventions: the prevention of the crimes covered by the conventions and the prosecution and punishment of the perpetrators of the crimes. The record of the conventions in this respect is unclear.

A major part of the problem is the lack of adequate data on the extent of successful actions to prevent terrorist acts and of the successful prosecution of terrorists. Although there appear to be adequate data available on the extradition, prosecution, and punishment of aircraft hijackers,[67] information regarding other manifestations of terrorism is quite sparse. Most of the antiterrorist conventions contain provisions requiring the state party where the alleged offender is prosecuted to communicate the final outcome of the proceedings to the Secretary-General of the United Nations (or to the Director-General of the IAEA or the Council of ICAO), and the Secretary-General has issued reports on "Measures to Eliminate International Terrorism."[68] But these reports focus primarily on the terrorist events that triggered the conventions and on a summary of the most important provisions of these conventions. There appears to be little information on the extent and success of efforts to prevent the acts the conventions cover or to prosecute the perpetrators of these acts.

Sir Jeremy Greenstock, UK permanent representative at the United Nations and the first chairman of the Counter-Terrorism Committee, has emphasized the importance of implementing antiterrorist measures. According to Greenstock, "Governments were already familiar with what needed to be done. But few had done it. Resolution 1373 drew on the language negotiated by all UN members in the 12 Conventions against terrorism, but also delivered a strong operational message: get going on effective measures now."[69] Similarly, Nicholas Rostow, General Counsel to the US Mission to the United Nations and an active participant in the Counter-Terrorism Committee, has noted that the Committee's use of independent experts has been helpful in the assessment of member states' reports. For example, Rostow states, "when a country asserts, 'money laundering is illegal so no money laundering takes place,' the experts reply, 'we need to know more how this law is implemented,' or 'how do you monitor to ensure that no money laundering takes place?' "[70]

Sir Jeremy Greenstock reported that, as of May 30, 2002, 155 reports had been submitted to the Committee from member states and others.[71] A cursory review of the reports submitted by some member states with sophisticated law and order systems (the United States, the United Kingdom, Israel, Germany, and Italy) that have had major problems with international terrorism reveals that the Counter-Terrorism Committee is gathering valuable information regarding the legislative, executive, and judicial steps these countries are taking to combat international terrorism in general and the financing of international terrorism in particular. One of the questions that member states have been asked to respond to is: "What steps have been taken to establish terrorist acts as serious criminal offenses and to ensure that the punishment reflects the seriousness of such terrorist acts? Please supply examples of any convictions obtained and the sentence given." However, the examples of convictions and sentences supplied in these reports are either non-existent or very brief. The US report is the most forthcoming in this respect, noting that the United States has prosecuted cases under US laws implementing the Montreal Convention (Aircraft Sabotage), the Hague Convention (Aircraft Hijacking), the Hostages Convention, and the Internationally Protected Persons Convention, and giving, by way of footnotes, citations to cases involving the crimes covered by these conventions.[72] But even this information is skimpy, giving, for example, no information regarding how US law enforcement officials came to have custody of the accused.

This is a serious problem that should be resolved. It may be that the Counter-Terrorism Committee could request more detailed information regarding the apprehension, rendition (where applicable), prosecution, and punishment of persons who commit the crimes covered by the twelve antiterrorist conventions. Alternatively, the UN Terrorism Prevention Branch, which is part of the Centre for International Crime Prevention in Vienna, might be assigned the task of collecting such information with respect to the eleven other antiterrorist conventions.[73]

To be sure, Sir Jeremy Greenstock has indicated that the current focus of the Counter-Terrorism Committee is on the prevention of terrorism rather than pursuing and bringing to justice the perpetrators of terrorist acts.[74] This is not surprising in view of the considerable concern that terrorists are developing the capacity to use weapons of mass destruction. But in any event the establishment of the Counter-Terrorism Committee is a major step forward in the worldwide effort to combat terrorism. It is, moreover, a step in keeping with promotion of the rule of law in international affairs, and a step that the United States has from the outset strongly promoted and supported.

Alternatives to prosecution in national courts

Antiterrorist conventions expect that the crimes they cover will be prosecuted in the national courts of the states parties. In recent years, however, it has increasingly been recognized that with respect to certain crimes – war crimes, genocide, and crimes against humanity, in particular – and under certain circumstances, national courts may not be the most effective forum. Accordingly, alternative forums have been proposed, including military commissions, international criminal courts, and so-called "hybrid" courts composed of a mixture of national and foreign judges. We briefly consider each of these options in turn.

Military commissions

The United States and other countries have traditionally employed military commissions during times of war to try violations of the law of armed conflict. President George W. Bush's military Order of November 13, 2001,[75] asserting the authority to use military commissions to try members of Al Qaeda and other persons involved in acts of international terrorism against the United States, unleashed a storm of protest. Many of the protests contended that such trials should take place in US civilian courts rather than in military commissions, especially in light of the severely limited due process rights contained in the President's Order.[76] Although the US Department of Defense subsequently issued regulations substantially augmenting due process rights of an accused,[77] many critics still found the protections to be inadequate.[78] Foreign governments reportedly were unwilling to extradite terror suspects to the United States unless they received assurances that they would be tried before civilian courts rather than military tribunals.[79]

Most of the persons prosecuted before these military tribunals are expected to be members of Al Qaeda captured during the armed conflict in Afghanistan. Accordingly, a major issue has arisen regarding the applicability and interpretation of the law of armed conflict, especially the Geneva Conventions of 1949, to the suspects being detained in the US military base in Guantánamo Bay, Cuba. In particular, questions have arisen regarding US obligations under the Convention Relative to the Treatment of Prisoners of War (Third Geneva Convention).[80]

On February 7, 2002, President Bush announced the US position on this issue. He determined that: (i) the Third Geneva Convention applies to the armed conflict in Afghanistan between the Taliban and the United States; (ii) the Convention does not apply to the armed conflict in Afghanistan and elsewhere between Al Qaeda and the United States; (iii) neither captured Taliban personnel nor captured Al Qaeda personnel are entitled to the status of prisoners of war under the Convention; and (iv) nonetheless, all captured Taliban and Al Qaeda personnel are to be treated humanely and consistently with the general principles of the Convention, and delegates of the International Committee of the Red Cross may privately visit each detainee.[81] No legal defense of these decisions was published,[82] and they have been subject to sharp criticism.

The blanket decision to deny prisoner of war status to all captured Taliban and Al Qaeda detainees has especially come under fire. Ari Fleischer, the White House Press Secretary, offered the following explanation of that decision:

> Under Article 4 of the Geneva Convention . . . Taliban detainees are not entitled to POW status. To qualify as POWs under Article 4, al Qaeda and Taliban detainees would have to have satisfied four conditions: They would have to be part of a military hierarchy; they would have to have worn uniforms or other distinctive signs visible at a distance; they would have to have carried arms openly; and they would have to have conducted their military operations in accordance with the laws and customs of war.
>
> The Taliban have not effectively distinguished themselves from the civilian population of Afghanistan. Moreover, they have not conducted their operations in accordance with the laws and customs of war. Instead, they have knowingly adopted and provided support to the unlawful terrorist objectives of the al Qaeda.[83]

George Aldrich, a former Deputy Legal Adviser of the US Department of State, has pointed out some serious problems with this explanation.[84] Clearly, Fleischer was summarizing the provisions of Article 4(A)(2) of the Third Geneva Convention. However, paragraph A(2) deals only with members of militias or other volunteer corps *that are not part of the armed forces of a party to the armed conflict.* The Taliban were, of course, members of the armed force of Afghanistan, a party to the armed conflict. As to them, paragraph A(1) of Article 4 would seem apposite. Paragraph A(1) provides:

A. Prisoners of war, in the sense of the present Convention, are persons belonging to one of the following categories, who have fallen into the power of the enemy:
(1) Members of the armed forces of a Party to the conflict as well as members of militias or volunteer corps forming part of such armed forces.

The four conditions specified by Fleischer as justifying the President's decision apply only to the second category of POWs, and that category relates solely to militias and volunteer corps that do not form part of the armed forces of a party to the conflict. As suggested by Aldrich, "the protections of the Convention would be eroded if it were accepted that the armed forces of a government in effective control of a state's territory need not be accorded those protections by another state that declines to recognize that government's legitimacy."[85]

Even as to the Al Qaeda detainees, it is arguable that some may be entitled to prisoner of war status. This would appear to be the case if an individual Al Qaeda member could prove that he was a member of a militia or volunteer corps forming part of the armed forces of Afghanistan within the meaning of Article 4(A)(1) of the Third Geneva Convention.

To be sure, some commentators have argued that, contrary to the text of Article 4 of the Third Geneva Convention, the conditions cited by Fleischer apply to all claimants to prisoner of war status, including members of the armed forces of a party to the conflict.[86] According to this view, failure to fulfill these conditions results in being designated an "enemy combatant " not entitled to prisoner of war status. Two of the four conditions – wearing uniforms or other distinctive signs visible at a distance and conducting operations in accordance with the laws and customs of war – were not complied with by the armed forces of the Taliban.

At the very least there is some doubt as to whether the Taliban and some Al Qaeda detainees at Guantánamo qualify for prisoner of war status. If so, this raises another controversial issue: must the final determination of their status be made by a "competent tribunal"? Article 5(2) of the Third Geneva Convention provides that: "Should any doubt arise as to whether persons, having committed a belligerent act and having fallen into the hands of the enemy, belong to any of the categories enumerated in Article 4, such persons shall enjoy the protection of the present Convention until such time as their status has been determined by a competent tribunal." Since the Bush administration has rejected all suggestions that the status of the detainees at Guantanamo be decided by a competent tribunal, apparently it believes that there is no doubt as to what their status is under the Third Geneva Convention.

Lastly, it should be noted that, although there have been legal challenges to the detentions at Guantánamo through writs of habeas corpus filed in US courts, to date these courts have dismissed these cases on the ground that they have no jurisdiction over the detention by the military of foreigners in non-US territory abroad.[87] Hence the legality of this detention, as well as of possible trial by military tribunals, under both US constitutional law and international law, has so far been primarily addressed in the academic literature. Bills to restrict the president's use of military commissions have been introduced in the US Congress, but have not enjoyed significant support.

International criminal tribunals

At this writing there are three international criminal tribunals: the International Criminal Tribunal for the former Yugoslavia (ICTY), the International Criminal Tribunal for Rwanda (ICTR), and the International Criminal Court (ICC). The United States played a major role in the creation of all three tribunals, and, by and large, has been highly supportive of the tribunals for the former Yugoslavia and Rwanda. As we have already seen, however, the United States is adamantly opposed to the International Criminal Court and has taken strenuous steps to ensure that the Court will never exercise jurisdiction over US nationals, especially US service personnel.

The ICTY and the ICTR Various reports of atrocities in the former Yugoslavia gained the attention of the UN Security Council, which was seeking ways to respond to the violence there. Especially influential was a report by an independent commission of experts established by the Council that concluded that "ethnic cleansing " had been carried out in the former Yugoslavia "by means of murder, torture, arbitrary arrest and detention, extra-judicial executions, rape and sexual assault, confinement of civilian population in ghetto areas, forcible removal, displacement and deportation of civilian population, deliberate military attacks or threats of attacks on civilians and civilian areas, and wanton destruction of property."[88] As a result, on February 22, 1993, the Security Council adopted Resolution 808, whereby it decided that the widespread violation of the law of armed conflict and of international human rights in the former Yugoslavia constituted a threat to international peace and security and decided to establish an international tribunal for the former Yugoslavia.[89] Resolution 808 also requested the Secretary-General to submit to the Council a report "on all aspects of this matter, including specific proposals [regarding the creation of such a court]." The Secretary-General's report, submitted on May 3, 1993, discussed the legal basis for the establishment of the ICTY and included a draft statute for the ICTY with commentary.[90]

On May 25, 1993, the Security Council unanimously adopted Resolution 827, which established the ICTY and authorized it to prosecute "persons responsible for serious violations of international humanitarian law committed in the territory of the former Yugoslavia between 1 January 1991 and a date to be determined by the Security Council upon the restoration of peace." Utilizing its extraordinary powers under Chapter VII of the Charter, the Council commanded that "all States shall cooperate fully with the International Tribunal and its organs in accordance with the present resolution and the Statute of the International Tribunal." The seat of the ICTY is in The Hague, Netherlands.

The ICTY is composed of fourteen judges who sit in three trial chambers of three judges and one appeals chamber of five judges, and there is a pool of *ad litem* (for the suit) judges. The regular judges were elected by the UN General Assembly from a list of candidates nominated by the Security Council. The Prosecutor was appointed by the Security Council on nomination by the Secretary-General. Under the Statute of the Court, the Prosecutor is authorized to initiate investigations ex officio or on the basis of information obtained from any source. The Prosecutor assesses the information obtained or received and decides whether there is a sufficient basis to proceed.[91] The ICTY itself adopted Rules of Procedure and Evidence for the Tribunal.[92]

The United States had substantial control over the process of creating the ICTY. As a permanent member of the Security Council, the United States had the veto power to block its creation had it wished to do so. Similarly, since the judges were nominated by the Security Council before being elected by the General Assembly, and the Prosecutor was appointed by the Council on nomination by the Secretary-General, the United States was in a position to insist that all the key personnel of the Tribunal were acceptable to it. Also, the United States could ensure that the Court's subject matter jurisdiction was limited to grave breaches of the Geneva Conventions of 1949, violations of the laws or customs of war, genocide, and crimes against humanity, and that the definitions of those crimes in the Court's Statute were satisfactory to it. Equally important, the competence of the ICTY is geographically limited, under Article 1 of the Court's Statute, to the prosecution of "persons responsible for serious violations of international humanitarian law committed in the territory of the former Yugoslavia since 1991 in accordance with the provisions of the present Statute." Because of this geographical limitation the United States could reasonably assume that there was little or no risk that US nationals or US troops could be subject to prosecution before the Tribunal. Surprisingly, as we saw in chapter 4, this assumption proved false when there were allegations made to the ICTY Prosecutor that US and other NATO forces had committed crimes within the Tribunal's jurisdiction during their air war in Kosovo and Serbia, even though it was ultimately determined that there was no basis to proceed with prosecution.

US comfort with its ability to control the selection of key personnel of the Tribunal may be one reason why the ICTY has such extraordinary powers. The concept of "complementarity" is often used to denote the relationship between international and national courts. The ICTY Statute provides for primacy of the Tribunal's jurisdiction over that of national courts. Hence, if it appears to the ICTY Prosecutor that a crime within the Tribunal's jurisdiction is or has been the subject of investigation or criminal proceedings in a national court, the Prosecutor may propose that the appropriate trial chamber of the ICTY formally request the national court to defer to the competence of the Tribunal. Such deferral may only be requested if the national proceedings: (i) characterize the act(s) under investigation as an ordinary crime; (ii) exhibit a lack of impartiality or independence or are designed to shield the accused from international criminal responsibility; or (iii) concern matters closely related to significant factual or legal questions that may have implications for investigations or prosecutions before the Tribunal. Should a state fail to respond adequately to a request for deferral, the trial chamber may request the president to report the failure to the Security Council, which then would decide what measures, if any, would be taken against the defaulting state. More generally, it should be noted, because the Security Council was acting under its Chapter VII powers in establishing the Tribunal, there is an international obligation on all member states of the United Nations to cooperate with the Tribunal to secure the arrest of persons indicted by the Tribunal, an obligation that the Council may enforce by coercive measures should it wish to do so.

Although the Security Council has not yet acted against states not cooperating with the ICTY, the United States has applied economic pressure against the states of the former Yugoslavia, especially Serbia and Montenegro, to induce them to cooperate with the Tribunal.[93] Pressure from the United States contributed to the decision of the Serbian government to hand over the former Yugoslav president, Slobodan Milosevic, to the ICTY. Still at large, however, are Radovan Karadzic and Ratko Mladic, leaders of Bosnia's Serbs during the Bosnian war from 1992 to 1995, who are the Tribunal's most wanted suspects. The US Department of State has offered rewards up to $5 million for information leading to the arrest or conviction of persons indicted by the ICTY, including Milosevic, Karadzic, and Mladic.

Rwanda has an unhappy history of recurrent outbreaks of ethnic conflict between the Hutus, who have constituted approximately 85 percent of the population, and the Tutsis, less than 15 percent. In April 1994, in response to the assassination of President Juvenal Habyarimana of Rwanda, Hutu extremist troops, militia, and mobs engaged in genocidal attacks against the Tutsi minority and Hutu moderates. Between April and July 1994, at least half a million and perhaps 800,000 or more Tutsis and moderate Hutus were killed. Unhappily, largely because of the unwillingness of the military powers, including the United States, to get involved, the United Nations took no action to prevent the slaughter. President Bill Clinton later apologized for US inaction. After the fighting ceased, and because of charges of "Eurocentrism" from less developed countries, especially in Africa, there was increased pressure on the Security Council to set up an international criminal tribunal along the lines of the Yugoslav model. Accordingly, on November 8, 1994, the Security Council decided to set up an ad hoc tribunal similar to the ICTY to prosecute persons responsible for genocide and other serious violations of international humanitarian law in the territory of Rwanda during 1994.[94] Ironically, although the government of Rwanda had initially requested that an international criminal tribunal for Rwanda be created, it ultimately voted against the Security Council resolution establishing the Tribunal, in part because the statute annexed to the resolution did not authorize the death penalty to be imposed on those convicted of genocide by the Tribunal. As a result of this sentiment, Rwanda has instituted its own program of wholesale arrest and detention of genocide suspects. Throughout the late 1990s approximately 125,000 persons – roughly 10 percent of the adult male Hutu population – were detained. National trials have gone forward, and in some genocide cases, the death penalty has been carried out.

The International Criminal Tribunal for Rwanda is closely modeled after the ICTY. There are, however, some salient differences. The conflict in Rwanda was essentially internal, whereas the conflict in the former Yugoslavia was in part international. As a result, the competence of the ICTR covers crimes commonly committed within a single territory, namely, genocide, crimes against humanity, and serious violations of common Article 3 of the Geneva Conventions of 1949 and Additional Protocol II of 1977, but not grave breaches of the Geneva Conventions or war crimes under the 1907 Hague Convention, because the latter apply only to international conflicts. Like the ICTY the ICTR has a presidency, a Registrar and several trial chambers of three judges. But the ICTY and the ICTR share the same appeals chamber, where the ICTR has two judges, and initially both tribunals were served by a single prosecutor, though currently each has its own.

The ICTR had a rocky start. After the Security Council selected Arusha, Tanzania, as the site for the Tribunal in February 1995, the severe financial crisis of the United Nations delayed construction of the ICTR's facilities and the hiring of staff, including investigators and prosecutors. The Tribunal nonetheless did manage to hold its first sessions in Arusha and indicted eight persons on December 12, 1995. Charges of mismanagement and neglect of the Tribunal's operations then surfaced, and the Prosecutor and the Registrar resigned under pressure on February 25, 1997. Since the change of administration, the operations of the Tribunal have improved, and it has succeeded in bringing to trial major figures in the past Rwanda government.

The United States cooperated with the ICTR in turning over a suspect to the Tribunal in March 2000, which was the first and so far the only instance of transfer of an indicted criminal by the United States to an international criminal tribunal. It did so, however, only after a US Court of Appeals, by a divided vote, affirmed the denial of the accused's petition for a writ of habeas corpus and cleared the way for his rendition.[95]

According to the US Ambassador-at-Large for War Crimes Issues, Pierre-Richard Prosper, as of February 28, 2002, at the ICTY 117 persons had been indicted, 67 had been brought into custody, 26 had been convicted, and 5 acquitted; 11 were currently awaiting trial, and 1 was awaiting the judgment of the Tribunal. At the ICTR 76 had been indicted, 57 had been brought into custody, 8 had been convicted and 1 acquitted; 17 were currently standing trial.[96] Ambassador Prosper stated that the United States "remains proud of its leadership in supporting the two ad hoc Tribunals and will continue to do so in the future." At the same time he reported that the United States was "urging both Tribunals to begin to aggressively focus on the endgame and conclude their work by 2007–2008, a timeframe that we have stressed and to which officials from both Tribunals have referred." He also claimed that "[i]n both Tribunals at times, the professionalism of some of the personnel has been called into question with allegations of mismanagement and abuse. And in both Tribunals, the process, at times, has been costly, has lacked efficiency, has been too slow, and has been too removed from the everyday experience of the people and the victims."

In short, it appears clear that the present US view of the two ad hoc tribunals is mixed. No such ambivalence exists with respect to the International Criminal Court.

The International Criminal Court The eighteen judges of the International Criminal Court have been selected and the Prosecutor, Luis Moreno Ocampo, an Argentine human rights lawyer who prosecuted in the 1980s military leaders accused of torture and murder in his country, has been sworn in before the Court. Although the ICC is modeled after the tribunals for the former Yugoslavia and Rwanda, it was created not by the Security Council but by an international treaty, the Rome Statute.[97] On March 11, 2003, it held its opening session in The Hague as the world's first permanent tribunal to try war crimes. As of July 1, 2003, 139 countries had signed and 90 had ratified the Rome Statute. The ICC reportedly has received about 400 credible complaints from around the world, and the Prosecutor (an American) has begun an investigation into accusations that Ugandan warlords abducted children to serve as soldiers and sex slaves for a rebel army.

Under Article 5 of the Rome Statute, the jurisdiction of the ICC is "limited to the most serious crimes of concern to the international community as a whole." These crimes include (i) the crime of genocide; (ii) crimes against humanity; and (iii) war crimes. In addition, the crime of aggression will be within the Court's jurisdiction, but this jurisdiction will be exercised only if the states parties are able to agree on a definition of the crime and on the conditions that would have to be fulfilled before the ICC could exercise jurisdiction over it. Should such agreement be reached, it would then be necessary to adopt a provision on aggression under the articles on amendment of the Statute. The United States unsuccessfully opposed the inclusion of aggression as one of the crimes within the Court's jurisdiction.

As we have already seen, the United States is adamantly opposed to the ICC, and has taken a number of extraordinary steps in an effort to ensure that no US national, especially military personnel, will be subject to the Court's jurisdiction. These steps include threatening to veto UN peacekeeping operations unless the Security Council adopts a resolution granting Americans involved in these peacekeeping operations immunity from the Court's jurisdiction, and pressuring countries to conclude bilateral so-called "Article 98 agreements" in which both parties agreed not to surrender the other's nationals to the Court.[98]

The US Congress has also expressed its opposition to the ICC in the strongest possible terms. The American Service Members Protection Act[99] contains a number of provisions prohibiting US cooperation with the Court, prohibits US military assistance to any country that is a party to the ICC Statute (with an exception for NATO members and specified close military allies) unless the country has concluded an Article 98 agreement with the United States, and even goes so far as to authorize the president to "use all means necessary and appropriate" to bring about the release of certain "covered persons" detained or imprisoned by or on behalf of the ICC (with resultant jokes about a "Hague Rescue Rapid Deployment Force").

A discussion of the reasons advanced by the United States to support its opposition to the ICC is beyond the scope of this chapter.[100] It is clear, however, that a major reason for the US opposition is its concern that its military personnel and government officials will be subject to politically motivated prosecutions. Other commentators have argued that the protections against such prosecutions in the Rome Statute are adequate to ensure that it operates responsibly.[101] Once the Court begins fully to operate, we should learn which view is correct. For the moment, however, the United States has rejected a revolutionary effort to enhance the rule of law in international affairs.

Hybrid courts

Hybrid courts are a recent addition to the kinds of tribunals that may be available for the trial of alleged perpetrators of war crimes, crimes against humanity, and genocide. The archetype for hybrid courts is the tribunal set up, with UN backing, in Sierra Leone.[102] The backdrop to the hybrid court in Sierra Leone, as we saw in chapter 4, is a political situation rife with corruption and mismanagement that degenerated into an extraordinarily brutal civil war involving the cutting off of limbs and other mutilations of women and children and the intervention of outside forces, especially from Liberia. After years of fighting, peace was finally imposed in Sierra Leone when, in May 2000, rebel forces took 500 UN peacekeepers hostage, prompting intervention by British soldiers. For its part, the UN Security Council adopted a resolution authorizing the Secretary-General to begin negotiations with the government of Sierra Leone toward the creation of a special court that would have subject matter jurisdiction over crimes against humanity, war crimes, and other serious violations of the law of armed conflict. A bilateral agreement between the United Nations and the government of Sierra Leone, as well as a statute for the special court, was signed in Freetown, the capital of Sierra Leone, on January 16, 2002.

Under the court's statute, there is a three-judge trial chamber and a five-judge appellate chamber. The government of Sierra Leone appoints one judge to the trial chamber and the UN Secretary-General appoints two. The appellate chamber has two judges picked by the government of Sierra Leone and three selected by the Secretary-General. Further, after consultation with the government of Sierra Leone, the

Secretary-General appoints the prosecutor. The judges of the court as well as its prosecutor (an American) have been selected, and accused persons have been brought before the tribunal.[103] The tribunal has also indicted Charles Taylor, president of Liberia until he stepped down in August 2003.

After long and tortuous negotiations that at one point broke down entirely, the United Nations and Cambodia concluded a framework agreement on June 6, 2003, to establish a hybrid court to prosecute members of the Khmers Rouges, the Marxist insurrectionaries who ruled Cambodia from 1975 until 1978, for crimes committed while they were in power. It remains to be seen whether the court will be both effective and just.[104]

The United States has been a strong supporter of both the Sierra Leone court and the efforts to establish a mechanism to prosecute the Khmers Rouges.

Notes

1. For further discussion, see John F. Murphy, *International Crimes, in* THE UNITED NATIONS AND INTERNATIONAL LAW 362 (Christopher C. Joyner ed., 1997).
2. Georg Schwarzenberger, *The Problem of an International Criminal Law*, 3 CURRENT LEG. PROBS. 263, 295 (1950).
3. *Id.*
4. *Id.* at 268.
5. *Id.* at 270.
6. ALFRED RUBIN, THE LAW OF PIRACY 328 (1988).
7. *Harvard Research on International Law: Jurisdiction with Respect to Crime*, 29 AM. J. INT'L L., Supp. 1, 435 (1935).
8. Paul Schiff Berman, *The Globalization of Jurisdiction*, 151 U. PA. L. REV. 311, 360 (2002).
9. See Restatement (Third) of the Foreign Relations Law of the United States, Section 404 (1987).
10. *Id.* (emphasis added).
11. See 18 USC Section 1091(d) (2000).
12. See 18 USC Section 2340 (2000).
13. See 18 USC Section 2441(b) (2000).
14. See, e.g., Art. 49 of the Geneva Convention for the Amelioration of the Condition of the Wounded and Sick in Armed Forces in the Field, Aug. 12, 1949, TIAS No. 3362.
15. William W. Burke-White, *A Community of Courts: Toward a System of International Criminal Law Enforcement*, 24 MICH. J. INT'L L. 1 (2002).
16. Henry A. Kissinger, *The Pitfalls of Universal Jurisdiction*, FOREIGN AFF., July/Aug. 2001, at 86. For a sharp contrast, see Christopher Hitchens, *Court Time for Henry*, THE NATION, Nov. 5, 2001, at 9 (arguing that the time has come for a trial of Henry Kissinger under the universality principle).
17. See Burke-White, *supra* note 15, at nn. 77–79 and accompanying text.

18. Belgium Act Concerning the Punishment of Grave Breaches of International Humanitarian Law, reproduced in 38 INT'L LEG. MATERIALS 918 (Act of June 16, 1993).
19. See Arrest Warrant of 11 April 2000 (Congo v. Belgium) (ICJ Feb. 14, 2002), reprinted in 41 INT'L LEG. MATERIALS 536 (2002).
20. See Marlise Simons, *Sharon Faces Belgian Trial After Term Ends*, NY TIMES, Feb., 13, 2003, at A12, col.1.
21. See Dan Bilefsky, *Bushes on Trial? Belgium Is Sweating Out Its Own War-Crimes Law*, WALL ST. J., March 28, 2003, at A11, col. 3.
22. See *Belgium Scales Back Its War Crimes Law Under US Pressure*, NY TIMES, Aug. 2, 2003, at A6, col. 1.
23. The second decision of the House of Lords was Regina v. Bartle, Bow Street Stipendiary Magistrate and Commissioner of Police, Ex Parte Pinochet, March 24, 1999, 2 WLR 827, 38 INT'L LEG. MATERIALS 581 (1999). Decisions rendered at various stages of this proceeding can be found in 37 INT'L LEG. MATERIALS 1302 (1998) and 38 INT'L LEG. MATERIALS 68, 430, 489, 581 (1999).
24. See, e.g., Ass'n Bar City of NY, Committees on International Human Rights and Inter-American Affairs, *The English Patient or the Spanish Prisoner?*, 55 RECORD 205 (2000); Curtis A. Bradley & Jack L. Goldsmith, *Pinochet and International Human Rights Litigation*, 97 MICH. L. REV. 2129 (1999); Ruth Wedgwood, *International Criminal Law and Augusto Pinochet*, 40 VA. J. INT'L L. 829 (2000); Hazel Fox, *The Pinochet Case No. 3*, 48 INT'L & COMP. LQ 687 (1999); Colin Warbrick, *Extradition Law Aspects of Pinochet 3*, 48 INT'L & COMP. LQ 958 (1999).
25. See Burke-White, *supra* note 15, at 20.
26. Locating the whereabouts of a suspect may be especially difficult in the event of a computer network attack. For discussion, see John F. Murphy, *Computer Network Attacks by Terrorists: Some Legal Dimensions*, *in* COMPUTER NETWORK ATTACK AND INTERNATIONAL LAW 321 (Michael H. Schmitt & Brian T. O'Donnell eds., 2002).
27. See GEOFF GILBERT, TRANSNATIONAL FUGITIVE OFFENDERS IN INTERNATIONAL LAW 1 (1998), quoting the OBSERVER, April 29, 1979, at 4.
28. Quoted in *id.* at 1.
29. For a more detailed discussion of barriers to extradition, see Murphy, *supra* note 26, at 332–37.
30. See US–Italy Extradition Treaty, Oct. 13, 1983, Art. IV, TIAS No. 10837 (entered into force Sept. 24, 1984).
31. US–Colombia Extradition Treaty, Sept. 14, 1979 (entered into force March 4, 1982), Hein's No. KAV 338.
32. See *Colombia Extradites Drug Suspect to the US, the Second in Days*, NY TIMES, Nov. 26, 1999, at A 25.
33. US–Mexico Extradition Treaty, May 4, 1978, 31 UST 5059; TIAS No. 9656, entered into force Jan 25, 1980.
34. See Rodrigo Labardini, *Mexico's Supreme Court Allows the Extradition of Mexican Nationals*, 17 INTERNATIONAL ENFORCEMENT LAW REPORTER, March 2001, at 106.
35. John Dugard & Christine Van den Wyngaert, *Reconciling Extradition with Human Rights*, 92 AM J. INT'L L. 187, 197 (1998).
36. 161 Eur. Ct. HR (Ser.A) (1989).
37. 99 INT'L L. Rev. 479 (1993).
38. Alona E. Evans, *International Procedures for the Apprehension and Rendition of Fugitive Offenders*, [1980] AM. SOC. INT'L L. PROC. 244.
39. See International Law Association: Helsinki Conference 216, 214 (1996) (Committee on Extradition and Human Rights Second Report) ("today the political offense exception is not accepted in a wide range of circumstances").

40. June 25, 1985, TIAS No. 12,050, as amended.
41. For a more detailed discussion of alternatives to extradition, see Murphy, *supra* note 26, at 337–40.
42. INS v. Doherty, 502 US 314 (1992). For discussion of this extraordinary case, see James Kelly, *The Empire Strikes Back: The Taking of Joe Doherty*, 61 FORD. L. REV. 317 (1992).
43. CHRISTOPHER L. BLAKESLEY, TERRORISM, DRUGS, INTERNATIONAL LAW, AND THE PROTECTION OF HUMAN LIBERTY 279 (1992).
44. United States v. Alvarez-Machain, 504 US 655 (1992).
45. See GILBERT, *supra* note 27, at 352–60.
46. See generally, *Agora: International Kidnapping*, 86 AM. J. INT'L L. 736 (1992); John F. Murphy & Jon Michael Dumont, *Hard Cases Make Bad Law*, *in* FESTSKRIFT TILL JACOB W. F. SUNDBERG 171 (Erik Nerep & Wiweka Warnling-Nerep eds., 1993). *Per contra*, see Malvina Halberstam, *In Defense of the Supreme Court Decision in* Alvarez-Machain, 86 AM. J. INT'L L. 736–56 (1992).
47. GILBERT, *supra* note 27, at 352.
48. Treaty to Prohibit Transborder Abductions, Nov. 23, 1994, US–Mex., 31 UST 5059, reprinted in MICHAEL ABBELL & BRUNO A. RISTAU, 4 INTERNATIONAL JUDICIAL ASSISTANCE: 13-4-1, at A-676.3 (Supp. 1995).
49. For an up-to-date listing of MLATs in force between the United States and other countries, see Mutual Legal Assistance in Criminal Matters (MLATs) and Other Agreements, *at* www.travel.state.gov/mlat.html (last visited May 11, 2003).
50. Michael Tigar & Austin Doyle, *International Exchange of Information in Criminal Cases*, MICH. YB INT'L LEG. STUD., TRANSNATIONAL ASPECTS OF CRIMINAL PROCEDURE 61 (1983).
51. For discussion of some of these admissibility issues, see JOHN F. MURPHY, PUNISHING INTERNATIONAL TERRORISTS 96–100 (1985).
52. Much of the discussion that follows is drawn from my article *International Law and the War on Terrorism: The Road Ahead*, in 32 ISRAEL YB HUM. RTS. 117 (2003). A slightly revised version of this article appears as a chapter in INTERNATIONAL LAW AND THE WAR ON TERROR 853 (Fred Borch and Paul S. Wilson eds., 2003).
53. For discussion, see, e.g., *id.*
54. For discussion of many of these fields of law, see the symposium on *Law and the War on Terrorism*, 25 HARV. JL & PUB. POL'Y 399–834 (2002).
55. For discussion of the many problems faced in attempting to reach agreement on a definition of terrorism, see John F. Murphy, *Defining International Terrorism: A Way Out of the Quagmire*, 19 ISRAEL YB HUM. RTS. 13 (1990).
56. 18 USC Section 2331(1).
57. UN Doc. A/C. 6/L. 850 (1972).
58. The conventions include the Convention on Offenses and Certain Other Acts Committed on Board Aircraft (1963); Convention for the Suppression of Unlawful Seizure of Aircraft (1970); Convention for the Suppression of Unlawful Acts against the Safety of Civil Aviation (1971); Convention on the Prevention and Punishment of Crimes against Internationally Protected Persons, including Diplomatic Agents (1973); International Convention against the Taking of Hostages (1979); Convention on the Physical Protection of Nuclear Material (1979); Protocol for the Suppression of Unlawful Acts of Violence at Airports Serving International Civil Aviation, supplementary to the Convention for the Suppression of Unlawful Acts against the Safety of Maritime Navigation (1988); Protocol for the Suppression of Unlawful Acts against the Safety of Fixed Platforms Located on the Continental Shelf (1988); Convention on the Marking of Plastic Explosives for the Purpose of Detection (1991); International

Convention for the Suppression of Terrorist Bombing (1997); and International Convention for the Suppression of the Financing of Terrorism (1999). The texts of these conventions may be found in UNITED NATIONS, INTERNATIONAL INSTRUMENTS RELATED TO THE PREVENTION AND SUPPRESSION OF INTERNATIONAL TERRORISM 2–131 (2001).

59. John F. Murphy, *The Need for International Cooperation in Combating Terrorism*, 13 TERRORISM: AN INTERNATIONAL JOURNAL 381 (1990).
60. See, e.g., Samuel M. Witten, *Current Developments: The International Convention for the Suppression of Terrorist Bombing*, 92 AM. J. INT'L L. 774 (1998).
61. Hans Corell, *Possibilities and Limitations of International Sanctions Against Terrorism, in* COUNTERING TERRORISM THROUGH INTERNATIONAL COOPERATION 243, 253 (Alex P. Schmidt ed., 2001).
62. Clifton M. Johnson, *Introductory Note to the International Convention for the Suppression of the Financing of Terrorism*, 39 INT'L LEG. MATERIALS 268 (2000).
63. Rohan Ferera, *International Legal Framework for Co-operation in Combating Terrorism – the Role of the UN Ad Hoc Committee on Measures to Eliminate International Terrorism, in* COUNTERING TERRORISM, *supra* note 61, at 284.
64. SC Res. 1373, UN SCOR, 56th Sess. UN Doc. S/1373 (2001).
65. *Id.*, para. 3(a)–(g).
66. *Id.*, para 8.
67. At least this was the case when I last examined the data. See MURPHY, *supra* note 51, at 110–15.
68. See, e.g., Measures to Eliminate International Terrorism: Report of the Secretary-General, UN GAOR, 55th Sess., Agenda item 166, UN Doc. A/55/179 (July 26, 2000).
69. Presentation by Ambassador Greenstock, Chairman of the Counter-Terrorism Committee (CTC) at the Symposium: Combating International Terrorism: The Contribution of the United Nations, held in Vienna on 3–4 June 2002, *at* http:// www.un.org/docs/sc/committees/1373/viennanotes.htm (visited on June 12, 2002).
70. Nicholas Rostow, *Before and After: The Changed UN Response to Terrorism since September 11th*, 35 CORNELL INT'L LJ 475, 483 (2002).
71. Presentation by Ambassador Greenstock, *supra* note 69, at 2.
72. The US report is attached as an annex to Letter dated 19 December 2001 from the Chairman of the Security Council Committee Established Pursuant to Resolution 1373 (2001) Concerning Counter-terrorism Addressed to the President of the Security Council, S2001/1220 (Dec. 21, 2001), *at* http://www.un.org/docs/sc/committees/1373/ (Jan. 15, 2003). The information regarding US prosecutions appears at page 22.
73. In his presentation, Ambassador Greenstock suggested that the Centre for International Crime Prevention might provide "model law and guidance on implementation" for the other eleven antiterrorist conventions. See Presentation by Ambassador Greenstock, *supra* note 69.
74. See Security Council Committee Established Pursuant to Resolution 1373 (2001) Concerning Counter-terrorism, Special Meeting with International, Regional, and Subregional Organizations, provisional summary record of the first part of the 57th meeting, S/Ac. 40.SR.57 (March 18, 2003), at 2.
75. Military Order of Nov. 13, 2001 – Detention, Treatment, and Trial of Certain Noncitizens in the War Against Terrorism, 66 Fed. Reg. 57, 833 (Nov. 13, 2001).
76. See, e.g., Harold Hongju Koh, *The Case Against Military Commissions*, 96 AM. J. INT'L L. 337 (2002). For a general discussion and debate on this issue, see *Agora: Military Commissions*, 96 AM. J. INT'L L. 320–58 (2002).

77. Military Comm'n Order No. 1 (Dep't of Defense Mar. 21, 2002), *at* http://defenselink.mil/news/mar2002/d20020321ord.pdf.
78. See, e.g., Laura A. Dickinson, *Using Legal Process to Fight Terrorism: Detentions, Military Commissions, International Tribunals, and the Rule of Law*, 75 S. CAL. L. REV. 1407, 1417–18 (2002).
79. See Sam Dillon & Donald G. McNeil Jr., *Spain Sets Hurdle for Extraditions*, NY TIMES, Nov. 24, 2001, at A1, col. 3.
80. Convention Relative to the Treatment of Prisoners of War, Aug. 12, 1949, 6 UST 3316, 75 UNTS 135.
81. Ari Fleischer, Special White House Announcement Re: Application of Geneva Conventions in Afghanistan (Feb. 7, 2002), *available in* LEXIS, Legis Library, Fednew File; see also White House Fact Sheet: Status of Detainees at Guantánamo (Feb. 7, 2002), *at* http://www.whitehouse.gov/news/releases/2002/02--13.html.
82. George Aldrich, a former Deputy Legal Adviser of the US Department of State, has expressed surprise at this failure. See George H. Aldrich, *The Taliban, Al Qaeda, and the Determination of Illegal Combatants*, 96 AM. J. INT'L L. 891, 892 (2002).
83. Fleischer, *supra* note 81.
84. Aldrich, *supra* note 82, at 896–98.
85. *Id.* at 895.
86. See, e.g., Ruth Wedgwood, *Al Qaeda, Terrorism, and Military Commissions*, 96 AM. J. INT'L L. 328, 335 (2002).
87. See Coalition of Clergy v. Bush, 189 F. Supp. 2d 1036 (CD Cal. 2002) (dismissing petition for writ of habeas corpus for Al Qaeda and Taliban detainees at Camp X-Ray in Cuba); Rasul v. Bush, 215 F. Supp. 2d 55 (DC 2002) (holding that US courts have no jurisdiction over detainees at Guantánamo Bay in Cuba); Al Odah Khaled A. F. v. United States, 321 F. 3d 1134 (DC Cir. 2003) (holding that detainees at Guantánamo did not have an action under the Alien Tort Claims Act). For an academic opinion that the detainees are within federal court jurisdiction, see Jordan J. Paust, *Antiterrorism Military Commissions: The Ad Hoc DOD Rules of Procedure*, 23 MICH. J. INT'L L. 677 (2002). The same author alleges that US court decisions denying habeas corpus review to detainees in Cuba violate international law. See Jordan J. Paust, *Antiterrorism Military Commissions: Courting Illegality*, 23 MICH. J. INT'L L. 1 (2001).
88. UN Doc. S/25274 at 16, para. 56 (1993).
89. SC Res. 808 (Feb. 22, 1993).
90. Report of the Secretary-General Pursuant to Paragraph 2 of Security Council Resolution 808 (1993), UN Doc. S/25704, Corr. 1 and Add. 1 (1993).
91. Art. 18(1), Statute of the International Criminal Tribunal for the Former Yugoslavia (as Amended), UN SC Res. 827 (1993), as amended by UN Doc. S/Res/1166 (1998). See also UN Doc. S/25704 (1993).
92. For the text of the Rules see 33 INT'L LEG. MATERIALS 484 (1994).
93. See *Serbia and Montenegro Meet Test for War Crimes Tribunal, US Says*, NY TIMES, June 17, 2003, at A4, col. 5.
94. SC Res. 955 (Nov. 8, 1994), 33 INT'L LEG. MATERIALS 1598 (1994).
95. Ntakirutimana v. Reno, 184 F. 3d 419 (5th Cir. 1999), cert. denied, 528 US 1135 (2000).
96. Pierre-Richard Prosper, Ambassador-at-Large for War Crimes Issues, Statement before the House International Relations Committee, Feb. 28, 2002, *at* http://www.state.gov/s/wci/rls/rm/2002/8571.htm.
97. Rome Statute of the International Criminal Court, UN Doc. A/CONF. 183/9, 37 INT'L LEG. MATERIALS 999 (1998).

98. Art. 98(2) of the Rome Statute provides: "The Court may not proceed with a request for surrender which would require the requested State to act inconsistently with its obligations under international agreements pursuant to which the consent of a sending State is required to surrender a person of that State to the Court, unless the Court can first obtain the cooperation of the sending State for the giving of consent for the surrender."
99. 22 USCA Sections 7421–7433 (2003).
100. For a recent summary of these reasons and other arguments against the ICC, see DAVID DAVENPORT, THE NEW INTERNATIONAL CRIMINAL COURT: RUSH TO JUSTICE? (2002).
101. See especially LEILA NADYA SADAT, THE INTERNATIONAL CRIMINAL COURT AND THE TRANSFORMATION OF INTERNATIONAL LAW (2002). For my views, see John F. Murphy, *The Quivering Gulliver: US Views on a Permanent International Criminal Court*, 34 INT'L L. 45 (2000).
102. For discussion and analysis of the Sierra Leone tribunal, see, e.g., Celina Schocken, *The Special Court for Sierra Leone: Overview and Recommendation*, 20 BERKELEY J. INT'L L. 436 (2002).
103. See Bruce Zagaris, *Sierra Leone Tribunal Starts Proceedings*, 19 INT'L ENFORCEMENT L. REP. 199 (May 2003).
104. See Bruce Zagaris, *UN and Cambodia Finally Reach Agreement on Prosecuting Khmer Rouge*, 19 INT'L ENFORCEMENT L. REP. 194 (May 2003).

9 Human rights and international environmental issues

In various places in this study we have had occasion to consider human rights issues arising out of US actions and the reaction thereto. In chapter 8, for example, we noted a number of human rights issues arising out of US efforts to obtain custody of alleged perpetrators of international crimes, and a major part of the criticism of the US plan to use military commissions to try detainees at Guantánamo Bay in Cuba is based on the perception that the commissions will not afford the due process rights to defendants required by international human rights law or by the law of armed conflict. In chapter 2 we examined the Senate's use of federalism clauses, declarations of non-self-executing status, and reservations to provisions inconsistent with state law as part of the process of giving its consent to US ratification of human rights treaties. The result of this process has been that the human rights treaties to which the United States is a party have had no significant impact on US law, contrary to one of the primary goals of such treaties, which is to change and improve the domestic law of states parties.

The focus in this chapter is somewhat different. It is to explore some of the difficulties the United States has had in its dealings with international institutions which have responsibility to promote and ensure respect for human rights, especially the United Nations. In recent years the relationship between the United States and these international institutions has become increasingly contentious. The first part of this chapter also sets forth a brief overview of the highly contentious subject of the US war on terrorism and human rights. The second part of this chapter briefly examines another highly contentious subject: the US refusal to become a party to either the Kyoto Protocol on climate change or the Convention on Biological Diversity. Here the United States finds itself out of step with most other nations of the world.

Human rights

The High Commissioner for Human Rights

The High Commissioner for Human Rights is the UN official with principal responsibility for human rights. The High Commissioner is appointed by the Secretary-General with the approval of the General Assembly for a four-year term with the possibility of one renewal. The original mandate of the High Commissioner was set forth in a 1993 General Assembly resolution.[1] As noted by Henry Steiner and Philip Alston, the primary tasks of the High Commissioner are

> to promote and protect the effective enjoyment of civil, cultural, economic, political and social rights, including the right to development; to provide advisory services and technical and financial assistance in the field of human rights to states that request them; to coordinate UN education and public information programmes in the field of human rights; to play an active role in removing the obstacles to the full realization of human rights; and to enhance international cooperation for the promotion and protection of human rights.[2]

The United States had long been a strong supporter of proposals to create the position of High Commissioner for Human Rights.

The first High Commissioner was José Ayala-Lasso, of Ecuador, who served from 1994–97. The shortness of his tenure may have been based in part on the widespread perception that he was ineffective in the post.

Mary Robinson, a former president of Ireland, succeeded Ayala-Lasso as High Commissioner and because of her involvement in international human rights causes, her credentials for the job were impressive. US President Bill Clinton called Robinson a "splendid choice" and offered her the full support of his administration.[3] By the end of her first term, however, Robinson's relationship with the US government had soured considerably, and rather than serving out her full second four-year term, Robinson announced that in September 2002 she would step down as High Commissioner for Human Rights. (She was succeeded in office by Sergio Vieira de Mello, a Brazilian, on September 12, 2002. On May 23, 2003, however, Vieira de Mello was appointed to serve as the UN Secretary-General's Special Representative in Iraq for a four-month period, and was killed in a bombing of UN headquarters in Baghdad in August.)

According to media reports, Robinson's conflicts with the United States were primarily in three areas: (i) her views on the Israel–Palestine conflict; (ii) her defense and allegedly detached way in which she presided over the Durban "World Conference against Racism"; and (iii) her criticism of US conduct in its war against terror, especially her condemnation of US treatment of prisoners in Camp X-Ray at Guantánamo Bay.[4] Also, throughout her tenure, Robinson was one of the most prominent critics of US administration of the death penalty, and critical comments she made about the US "unsigning" of the ICC Statute, as well as her refusal to consider reforms of the UN Human Rights Commission's election process – an issue we consider in the next section of this chapter – exacerbated tensions with the Bush administration.

The World Conference against Racism, and Robinson's role in it, are worthy of further examination. It was held in Durban, South Africa, on August 31–September 9, 2001, concluding two days prior to the fateful Al Qaeda attack on September 11. Although the United States government had originally planned to have Secretary of State Colin Powell participate in the conference, in the end the United States withdrew from the conference because it was unable to prevent the proceedings from turning into an "anti-American, anti-Israeli circus."[5] According to Tom Lantos, a Democrat congressman from California, and member of the House International Relations Committee, who participated as part of the US delegation to the conference, "much of the responsibility for the debacle rests on the shoulders of UN High Commissioner for Human Rights Mary Robinson, who, in her role as secretary-general of the conference, failed to keep the conference on track."[6] Lantos was especially critical of Robinson's alleged failure to take forceful action at a preliminary meeting held in Tehran, where the Iranian government barred Israeli passport holders and Jewish nongovernmental organizations, as well as Australia and New Zealand, two strong supporters of Israel, from attending. At the end of the Tehran meeting, according to Lantos, "Robinson made no visible effort to confront the breakdown that had occurred in the global dialogue on race that she had done so much to nurture."[7]

To be sure, Lantos does not assign sole or even primary blame of the breakdown in the Durban conference to Robinson. Primary blame he assigns to several member states of the Organization of the Islamic Conference (OIC), and he is critical as well of the Bush administration for its unilateral approach to world problems – although not, in this case, to the race issue – the radicalism of many foreign NGOs at the conference, the allegedly inadequate response thereto by US-based NGOs, and the unwillingness of European allies to take a strong stand. Moreover, some commentators have come to Robinson's defense and responded to Lantos's criticisms,[8] leveling a few of their own while defending the results of the conference.

The critical point, however, is not the quality of the results of the conference or of Robinson's performance at it. It is rather that the United States came into serious conflict with the UN official with primary responsibility for human rights, an official who was the US favorite candidate for the job. The United States has recently had similar if not more severe difficulties with the UN organ with primary responsibility for human rights, the UN Commission on Human Rights.

The UN Commission on Human Rights

The United Nations Commission on Human Rights was established in 1946. Currently consisting of fifty-three member states elected for three-year terms by the Economic and Social Council (ECOSOC), it meets in Geneva from mid-March to late April. The Commission, following the tendency of the United Nations to operate through regional groupings, has five such groups: Asia, Africa, Eastern Europe, Latin America, Western Europe, and Others. The Others group includes Canada, Australia, and New Zealand, and, in practice, the United States. This mode of operation has excluded Israel, which geographically should fall within Asia, hence denying it the possibility of being elected to the Commission.

For its part the United States had served on the Commission for every year since it was created until 2001. In that year, for the first time, the United States failed to get the requisite number of votes to be elected to the Commission, although the State Department reportedly believed before the election that it had enough confirmed "Yes" votes to ensure that the United States would be elected.[9]

As a practical matter, the United States was unable to determine which countries failed to vote for it after assuring the United States they would do so, because, under the Commission's procedure, the vote is by secret ballot. Nor was there any agreement among "expert" witnesses testifying before the Subcommittee on International Operations and Terrorism of the Senate Committee on Foreign Relations on the reasons for the US failure to get elected.[10] Various reasons were advanced. They included, among others, US policies on the Middle East; US opposition to the Kyoto Protocol, the International Criminal Court, the Landmines Treaty, and to making AIDS drugs freely available; the desire of EU member states to increase trade with some of the countries that were the object of US efforts to censure in the Commission; and the alleged US tendency to politicize the issue of human rights, introducing annual resolutions at the Commission denouncing China or Cuba while resisting any criticism of Israel.

The next year the United States regained its accustomed seat on the Commission. The election procedures of the Commission, however, have come under sharp criticism. Critics have noted, for example, that there is something egregiously wrong with a procedure that elects the representative of Libya, a state with a woeful human rights record and a supporter of terrorism, as chair of the Commission, and, as members of the Commission, such egregious violators of human rights as Cuba, Sudan, and Syria. As noted previously, one difficulty the United States had with Mary Robinson was her unwillingness to consider reforms of the Commission's election procedures that would exclude certain states from eligibility to be elected based on their poor human rights records.

Current election procedures may have contributed to an increasingly unsatisfactory performance by the Commission. Vieira de Mello, Robinson's successor as the UN High Commissioner for Human Rights, criticized the Commission for its unwillingness to consider the human rights situation in Iraq under Saddam Hussein's regime.[11] In a scathing critique of the spring 2003 session of the Commission, as well as of the recent human rights record of the United Nations as a whole, Anne Bayefsky noted, among other things, that the Commission rejected a resolution that would have criticized the current situation in Zimbabwe, and eliminated the position of rapporteur on human rights in Sudan – despite a report of the UN rapporteur on torture informing Commission members of the Sudanese practice of "cross-amputation," that is, amputation of right hand and left foot, for armed robbery, and various cases of women being stoned to death for alleged adultery.[12]

Hence the United States has had major problems in its dealings with the UN official with primary responsibility for human rights and with the UN organ with primary responsibility for human rights. It has had similar problems with treaty bodies established by two of the primary human rights treaties it has ratified: the Human Rights Committee, established by the International Covenant on Civil and Political Rights, and the Committee on the Elimination of Racial Discrimination, set up by the International Convention on the Elimination of All Forms of Racial Discrimination.

The Human Rights Committee

Earlier in this study we have briefly noted some of the problems the United States has had with the Human Rights Committee. In chapter 1, for example, we examined the strong reaction of the United States to the Committee's view, expressed in its General Comment No. 24 on reservations to the Covenant,[13] that states parties to the Covenant may not make reservations to provisions therein that represent customary international law. Also, in chapter 2, we pointed out that the Committee, in its consideration of the US report on the measures it has taken to give effect to the rights recognized in the Covenant, expressed its "regrets" on the extent of the US reservations.[14] These are not the only problems, however, that the United States has had with the Committee.

In particular, the United States had major problems with other views of the Committee expressed in General Comment No. 24, which it expressed in observations submitted to the Committee.[15] Commenting on the Committee's claim that it had the competence to address the legality of states parties' reservations, the United States argued that the Covenant did not "impose on States Parties an obligation to give effect to the Committee's interpretations or confer on the Committee the power to render definitive or binding interpretations of the Covenant." The United States also rejected the determination of the Committee that "[t]he normal consequence of an unacceptable reservation is not that the Covenant will not be in effect at all for a reserving party. Rather, such a reservation will generally be severable, in the sense that the Covenant will be operative for the reserving party without benefit of the reservation."[16] In the view of the United States, this conclusion is "completely at odds with established legal practice and principles . . . The reservations contained in the United States instrument of ratification are integral parts of its consent to be bound by the Covenant and are not severable. If it were to be determined that any one or more of them were ineffective, the ratification as a whole could thereby be nullified."[17]

In its General Comment No. 24 the Committee had also implicitly criticized the US declaration accompanying its ratification that the substantive articles of the Covenant were not self-executing, thereby ensuring that the Covenant could not be the basis for a lawsuit in US courts, as well as the US practice of reserving to any provision of the Covenant that was inconsistent with existing US federal or state law. Specifically, the Committee had stated in General Comment No. 24 that, with regard to implementing the Covenant in domestic law, domestic laws "may need to be altered properly to reflect the requirements of the Covenant; and mechanisms at the domestic level will be needed to allow the Covenant rights to be enforceable at the local level."[18] In its observations, the United States (along with the United Kingdom) met the criticisms (which had also been advanced by scholars and other commentators) head-on:

First, this statement may be cited as an assertion that States Parties *must* allow suits in domestic courts based directly on the provisions of the Covenant. Some countries do in fact have such a scheme of "self-executing" treaties. In other countries, however, existing domestic law already provides the substantive rights reflected in the Covenant as well as multiple possibilities for suit to enforce those rights. Where these existing rights and mechanisms are in fact adequate to the purposes of the Covenant, it seems most unlikely that the Committee intends to insist that the Covenant be directly actionable in court or that States must adopt legislation to implement the Covenant.

Second, paragraph 12 states that "[r]eservations often reveal a tendency of States not to want to change a particular law." Some may view this statement as sweepingly critical of any reservation whatsoever which is made to conform to existing law. Of course, since this is the motive for a large majority of the reservations made by States in all cases, it is difficult to say that this is inappropriate in principle. Indeed, one might say that the more seriously a State Party takes into account the necessity of providing strictly for domestic implementation of its international obligations, the more likely it is that some reservations may be taken along these lines.[19]

As every state party is obligated to do under Article 40 of the Covenant, the United States submitted, on August 24, 1994, its report on measures it had taken to give effect to the rights recognized in the Covenant and on progress made in giving effect to the enjoyment of those rights to the Human Rights Committee.[20] The report contains a voluminous discussion of the political and legal structure in the United States for the protection of human rights, as well as a detailed setting forth of US law and practice. In its Concluding Observations on the US report, however, the Committee expresses its "regrets . . . that, while containing comprehensive information on the laws and regulations giving effect to the rights provided in the Covenant at the federal level, the report contained few references to the implementation of Covenant rights at the state level."[21] More significantly, the Committee declared the US reservations to Article 6(5) and Article 7 of the Covenant, both of which relate to the death penalty,[22] "incompatible with the object and purpose of the Covenant."[23] In both reservations the United States is proclaiming its willingness to be bound only by the constraints of the US Constitution and not by the provisions of the Covenant.[24] The US willingness, however, to execute persons under the age of eighteen (as long as they are sixteen or older) is opposed by an overwhelming majority of other countries and as a consequence some argue that such executions violate norms of customary international law.[25] The United States has consistently rejected such arguments. The issue is unlikely to be resolved by any third-party decision maker.

Nor is the issue of the validity of the Human Rights Committee's conclusion that US reservations to Article 6(5) and Article 7 of the Covenant are incompatible with the object and purpose of the Covenant likely to be resolved by a third-party decision maker. Assuming *arguendo*, however, that the Committee's conclusion is right, and that, as argued by the US government, the reservations to the Covenant are not severable, the United States is arguably not a party to the Covenant.[26] Not surprisingly, the Committee, in its "Suggestions and Recommendations" section, recommends that the United States "review its reservations, declarations and understandings with a view to withdrawing them, in particular reservations to article 6, paragraph 5, and article 7 of the Covenant."

Lastly, the Committee identified a major problem facing US implementation of the Covenant – the unwillingness of the federal government to impose constraints on the states in their handling of human rights issues through the treaty process. The Committee warns of the potential for what it believes to be "unsatisfactory application of the Covenant throughout the country," especially in light of the federal system prevailing in the United States in which "the states of the union retain extensive jurisdiction over the application of criminal and family law in particular" and "the absence of formal mechanisms between the federal and state levels to ensure appropriate implementation of the Covenant rights."[27]

The Committee on the Elimination of Racial Discrimination

The United States signed the International Convention on the Elimination of All Forms of Racial Discrimination (Race Convention)[28] on September 28, 1966, but did not deposit its instrument of accession until October 21, 1994. The Convention entered into force for the United States on November 20, 1994.[29] It is not surprising that the United States took almost thirty years to become a party to the Convention when one considers how sensitive a subject race is in the United States.

The United States submitted three reservations along with its instrument of accession.[30] All are worthy of note and provide as follows:

(1) That the Constitution and laws of the United States contain extensive protections of individual freedom of speech, expression and association. Accordingly, the United States does not accept any obligation under this Convention, in particular under Articles 4 and 7, to restrict those rights, through the adoption of legislation or any other measures, to the extent that they are protected by the Constitution and laws of the United States.
(2) That the Constitution and laws of the United States establish extensive protections against discrimination, reaching significant areas of non-governmental activity. Individual privacy and freedom from governmental interference in private conduct, however, are also recognized as among the fundamental values which shape our free and democratic society. The United States understands that the identification of the rights protected under the Convention by reference in Article 1 to fields of "public life" reflects a similar distinction between spheres of public conduct that are customarily the subject of governmental regulation, and spheres of private conduct that are not. To the extent, however, that the Convention calls for a broader regulation of private conduct, the United States does not accept any obligation under this Convention

to enact legislation or take other measures under paragraph (1) of Article 2, subparagraphs (1)(c) and (d) of Article 2, Article 3 and Article 5 with respect to private conduct except as mandated by the Constitution and laws of the United States.

(3) That with reference to Article 22 of the Convention, before any dispute to which the United States is a party may be submitted to the jurisdiction of the International Court of Justice under this article, the specific consent of the United States is required in each case.

Article 4 of the Convention requires states parties to punish not only incitement to racial discrimination but also the dissemination of ideas based on racial superiority or hatred. It also enjoins states parties, however, to do so "with due respect to the principles embodied in the Universal Declaration of Human Rights and the rights expressly set forth in this Convention." Article 19 of the Universal Declaration of Human Rights provides, in pertinent part, that "[e]veryone has the right to freedom of opinion and expression," and Article 5(d)(viii) of the Declaration requires states parties to guarantee equality before the law with respect to the "right to freedom of opinion and expression." A number of states parties, including Austria, Belgium, France, Italy, and the United Kingdom, accordingly refrained from submitting reservations to Article 4 and instead submitted declarations setting forth their interpretation of Article 4 as not requiring any action that would violate the right to freedom of speech. The First Amendment to the US Constitution sets forth a more stringent protection of freedom of speech than that applied in other democracies, and, as a consequence, the United States had no choice but to submit a reservation to Article 4 of the Convention.[31]

The second US reservation to the Convention, rejecting any obligation to regulate "private" conduct, reflects the struggle Congress and the Supreme Court have had in determining where to draw the line between purely private conduct (which should not and perhaps constitutionally cannot be subject to governmental regulation) and the kinds of individual conduct which can. In its report to the Committee on the Elimination of Racial Discrimination, the United States summarizes the key legislation and court decisions as of the year 2000.[32]

The third US reservation was in keeping with the "longstanding policy," discussed elsewhere in this study, of rejecting compromissory clauses in human rights treaties referring disputes arising under the treaty to the International Court of Justice and requiring instead US consent on an individual dispute, ad hoc basis.[33]

Article 20 of the Convention takes an unusual approach to reservations. Unlike the International Covenant on Civil and Political Rights, which contains no provision regarding reservations, the Race Convention, in

Article 20(1), directs the Secretary-General to circulate to all states parties any reservations submitted, and provides that any state objecting to the reservation must notify the Secretary-General, within ninety days of receiving a copy of the reservation, that it does not accept it. Also, Article 20(2) states that a reservation incompatible with the object and purpose of the Convention "shall not be permitted, nor shall a reservation the effect of which would inhibit the operation of any of the bodies established by this Convention be allowed. A reservation shall be considered incompatible or inhibitive if at least two-thirds of the States Parties to this Convention object to it." No such determination has ever been made.

In its "Concluding Observations" on the US report,[34] the Committee expresses its concern with "the absence of specific legislation implementing the provisions of the Convention in domestic laws, and recommends that the State party undertakes the necessary measures to ensure the consistent application of the provisions of the Convention at all levels of government."[35] It then expresses its particular concern with the US free speech reservation to Article 4. In its view "the prohibition of dissemination of all ideas based upon racial superiority or hatred is compatible with the right to freedom of opinion and expression, given that a citizen's exercise of this right carries special duties and responsibilities, among which is the obligation not to disseminate racist ideas."[36] The Committee similarly rejects the position of the United States that "the prohibition and punishment of purely private conduct lie beyond the scope of governmental regulation, even in situations where the personal freedom is exercised in a discriminatory manner."[37]

Other "concerns" expressed by the Committee mirror some issues that are highly controversial in the purely domestic US context. These include the resistance to outlaw practices and legislation that are discriminatory not in purpose, but in effect (disparate impact); the high incarceration rate of minorities, especially African-Americans and Hispanics; the high correlation between race, both of the victim and the defendant, and the imposition of the death penalty in several US states; and the US position that the Convention permits but does not require states parties to adopt affirmative action policies.

Like those of the Human Rights Committee, the "Concluding Observations" of the Committee on the Elimination of Racial Discrimination are not binding on the United States and therefore create no legal obligation that they be carried out. Clearly, there is a substantial difference of opinion between the United States and the Committee over what the Convention should or does require. In light of this sharp difference, the political impact of the Committee's observations are likely to be limited as well.

Significantly, the Race Convention establishes perhaps the most elaborate set of rule of law procedures for monitoring states parties' performance and inducing their compliance with the Convention's norms. In addition to requiring states parties to submit periodic reports to the Committee on the Elimination of Racial Discrimination (Article 9) – a minimal compliance procedure found in almost all the major international human rights treaties – the Convention provides for (i) an interstate complaint procedure and the appointment of an ad hoc conciliation commission (Articles 11 and 12); (ii) subject to a declaration by the state party concerned accepting the competence of the Committee to do so, the submission of "communications" to the Committee from individuals within the state party's jurisdiction complaining to be victims of a violation by that state party of any of the rights set forth in the Convention (Article 14); and (iii) reference of a dispute with respect to the interpretation or application of the Convention, which is not settled by negotiation or by the procedures provided by the Convention, by any of the parties to the dispute to the International Court of Justice (Article 22). However, the United States made a reservation to Article 22, and has declined to make the necessary declaration under Article 14 to permit individuals to submit communications (i.e., petitions) to the Committee. These more far-reaching procedures have generally not been employed. Indeed, no interstate complaint has ever been brought under any of the UN treaty-based procedures. The individual complaints procedure of the Race Convention has been used sparingly, with only nine complaints having been received as of February 2000, and only three of them resulting in a determination that a violation had occurred.[38] No disputes over the interpretation or application of the Race Convention have been referred to the International Court of Justice.

The war on terrorism and international human rights

At this writing the US government has announced plans to try six suspected Al Qaeda terrorists in military tribunals in Guantánamo Bay. The reaction of the European Commission, the executive organ of the European Union, was sharp, warning that applying the death penalty to any of the suspects detained at the US base in Guantánamo Bay would risk undermining support for the US-led war on terrorism.[39]

The concern that the war on terrorism is being waged in a way that violates fundamental human rights, however, encompasses much more than the issue of the military tribunals, and has engendered an increasingly ferocious debate in the United States.[40] By and large the debate has centered on US law and practice, including the Constitution, and, increasingly, it is a debate that is being fought in the courts as persons arrested or detained in the war on terrorism have mounted court challenges. Significantly, as noted by George Harris, after September 11, "the government's anti-terrorism effort has shifted its focus from prosecution to prevention. The primary goal is no longer conviction but detention and interrogation." Some of the tools employed to further this goal include "material witness warrants, secret deportation proceedings and, relying on the president's war power, military detention of those designated as 'unlawful enemy combatants.'"[41]

A current cause célèbre is the case of José Padilla. Padilla, a US citizen, was initially arrested on a material witness warrant in May 2002, as he disembarked from an aircraft at Chicago O'Hare International Airport. Shortly thereafter, however, he was transferred into the custody of the Department of Defense and held in a navy brig in Charleston, South Carolina, as an "enemy combatant"[42] who was plotting a so-called "dirty bomb" (a conventional explosive wrapped in radioactive material) attack on the United States. In the US government's view, since Padilla was being held as an "enemy combatant" pursuant to the president's war power, his detention is not subject to habeas corpus review, and he has no right to counsel. The District Court for the Southern District of New York rejected that view, and held that Padilla has the right to consult with counsel and to submit facts and argument in support of his petition for habeas corpus.[43]

The *Padilla* court's decision, which at this writing is on appeal, was regarded by some as a victory for the due process rights of those detained in the war on terrorism. This may have been a pyrrhic victory, however, since the court affirmed the president's right to detain in military custody US citizens captured on US soil outside any combat zone. Moreover, the court's standard for the validity of such detention was "whether there was some evidence to support [the president's] conclusion" to that effect.[44] In the words of George Harris, then, "[t]he *Padilla* decision thus comes very close to saying that the executive can imprison indefinitely anyone whom it has some basis to suspect of associating with terrorists. 'Some evidence' of associating with Al Qaeda is a far cry from probable cause to believe that a crime has been committed, let alone proof beyond a reasonable doubt."[45]

The court's decision in *Padilla* may be compared with the decision of the Court of Appeals for the Fourth Circuit in *Hamdi v. Rumsfeld*,[46] where the court denied counsel to another US citizen detained as an "enemy combatant." Unlike Padilla, Hamdi was taken prisoner in Afghanistan, a war zone, rather than in the United States. The court in *Hamdi*, however, expressly eschewed "any broad or categorical holdings on enemy combatant designations" and noted that it had "no occasion, for example, to address the designation as an enemy combatant of an American citizen captured on American soil or the role that counsel might play in such a proceeding."[47]

Neither the *Padilla* nor the *Hamdi* court decision discusses the relevance, if any, of international human rights law to the cases before them. A memorandum amicus curiae of law professors currently in preparation will raise some of these issues before the Court of Appeals for the Second Circuit in the *Padilla* appeal. As we saw above, Padilla, at least at the district court level, was granted some due process rights. The same may not be said of the detainees at Guantánamo Bay. In their cases, as previously noted, US courts have ruled that they have no jurisdiction to entertain habeas corpus appeals.

International human rights law, however, both treaty-based and customary, prohibits arbitrary detention and requires judicial review of detention. Article 9(1) of the International Covenant on Civil and Political Rights, for example, provides: "Everyone has the right to liberty and security of person. No one shall be subject to arbitrary arrest or detention. No one shall be deprived of his liberty except on such grounds and in accordance with such procedure as are established by law." Article 9(4) of the Covenant further requires that "[a]nyone who is deprived of his liberty by arrest or detention shall be entitled to take proceedings before a court, in order that the court may decide without delay on the lawfulness of his detention and order his release if the detention is not lawful." Also, Article 14 of the Covenant guarantees a variety of due process rights, including "a fair and public hearing by a competent tribunal established by law." Article 4 of the Covenant allows a state party to take measures derogating from their obligations under the Covenant, but only "[i]n time of public emergency which threatens the life of the nation and the existence of which is officially proclaimed" and "to the extent strictly required by the exigencies of the situation." But the United States government has taken no steps toward such a derogation of its obligations under the Covenant.

Should a court, such as the Second Circuit in the *Padilla* case, decide to address these and other provisions of the Covenant, it would have to resolve such issues as whether the US declaration that the Covenant is non-self-executing rules out its being the basis of a court challenge to US government action and whether customary international human rights law can be the basis for such a challenge. A discussion of these issues is beyond the scope of this chapter, but at the least they constitute a formidable barrier to a successful challenge to US detentions in the war on terrorism in a US court.

As suggested by George Harris, the issue now at the forefront of the debate in the United States is: "must we as a nation tolerate diminished civil liberties, political freedom and privacy in order to protect ourselves against the threat of terrorism that has now hit home with such devastating force?"[48] However this issue may ultimately be resolved in the United States, it appears increasingly clear that for other liberal democratic states, none of which, to be sure, has suffered an attack as devastating as that of September 11, the answer is no.

International environmental issues

As we move from human rights to international environmental issues, it is worth noting in passing that there are efforts under way to achieve recognition of a human right to a safe environment. At this juncture there is no international human rights treaty setting forth such a right, but a Draft Declaration of Principles on Human Rights and the Environment was produced in 1994 by a UN group of experts on human rights and environmental protection.[49] In the UN human rights context, a draft declaration has often served as a transitional step toward a binding international human rights treaty. Draft declarations may also play a role in the process of creating customary international law, as may the presence of specific human rights, in this case environmental rights, in national constitutions.[50]

It is commonplace, of course, to recognize that, in a globalizing world, environmental problems cannot be solved by individual state action. Hence, states agree through the treaty process to collective action that they believe is in their self-interest, for example, "to limit their use of ozone-depleting substances or to impose restrictions on the import and export of endangered species."[51] The United States has become a party to several (although relatively few) such treaties. It has decided, however, that it is not in its interest to become a party to two treaties that many other countries in the world view as having cardinal importance: the Kyoto Protocol to the United Nations Framework Convention on Climate Change (Kyoto Protocol)[52] and the Convention on Biological Diversity (Biological Diversity Convention).[53]

The Kyoto Protocol

During the 1980s there was increasing concern with global warming, or climate change, and the adverse effects it was alleged to have. As a consequence, in 1988, the United Nations Environment Programme established the Intergovernmental Panel on Climate Change (IPCC), which was to assess available scientific data on climate change, especially change allegedly induced by human action. The IPCC is open to all members of the United Nations; it does not itself carry out research, but rather bases its assessment mainly on peer-reviewed and published scientific/technical literature. The IPCC issued a report in 1991 claiming that greenhouse gases, comprising carbon dioxide, methane, and others, could potentially cause serious climate disruptions.[54]

Not everyone agreed with the IPCC's assessment. In the words of a 1998 leading US law school coursebook, "[t]here is significant scientific uncertainty about whether global warming will occur, how much global warming will occur, and what the local and regional distributions of the effects of global warming will be. Moreover, there is uncertainty about the benefits and costs of actions to prevent global warming and about the sufficiency of adaptive responses to global warming."[55]

Nonetheless, in 1992, at the United Nations Conference on Environment and Development in Rio de Janeiro, 167 states adopted the Framework Convention on Climate Change (Framework Convention).[56] The United States became a party to the Framework Convention on October 15, 1992. Article 2 of the Convention commits the parties to the "stabilization of greenhouse gas concentrations in the atmosphere at a level that would prevent dangerous anthropogenic interference with the climate system." The Convention does not, however, impose any binding limits on emissions. This failure led to several conferences of the parties to the Framework Convention with a view to concluding a Protocol. But prior to the convening of the fourth conference in Kyoto, Japan, in 1997, the European Union announced its proposal for the Protocol, which called for a 15 percent reduction of the three major greenhouse gases (carbon dioxide, methane, nitrous oxide) from 1990 levels by the year 2010. The United States promptly denounced the target as "unrealistic and unachievable." This led to the passage, by a margin of ninety-five to none in July 1997, of the US Senate's so-called, after its sponsors, "Byrd-Hagel" Resolution, which directed the President not to sign any emissions reduction agreement that (i) did not also require developing countries to reduce or limit emissions or (ii) that would result in serious harm to the US economy.[57]

In December 1997, in Kyoto, Japan, over 160 parties to the Framework Agreement adopted the Kyoto Protocol,[58] which, for the first time, established legally binding limits for industrialized countries on emissions of carbon dioxide and other greenhouse gases.[59] No such legally binding limits were established for developing countries, leaving China and India – very large polluters – free from restraint. The Clinton administration nonetheless signed the Protocol on December 11, 1998, and strongly supported it. By contrast, the Bush administration announced that the Protocol was "fundamentally flawed." In its view, the Protocol was ineffective because of the exclusion of developing countries; its "precipitous" targets for the reduction of emissions were unattainable, even if the parties included all the mitigation activities that the United States wanted, such as trading in emission permits; and there were risks of "significant harm" to the US and global economies. The administration cited models suggesting a drop in US gross domestic product (GDP) of at least 1 to 2 percent by 2010, and up to 4 percent if certain trading provisions were not adopted.[60] There also was no change in the attitude of the US Senate, so that there was no chance of ratification in any event.

Once again, the United States finds itself in a distinct minority in refusing to ratify a treaty. As of May 2003, 109 states had ratified the Kyoto Protocol, including all member states of the European Union.[61]

It does not necessarily follow, however, that the United States is wrong in having decided not to ratify the Protocol. Critics of the Protocol note that the annual emissions of developing countries such as China, India, and Brazil are projected to surpass annual emissions of the developed countries early in this century. The states parties also failed to agree on a mechanism to monitor compliance and on the trading of emission permits. The United States is a strong supporter of emissions trading on the ground that it would allow reductions to take place in a more cost-effective manner. Emissions trading would allow the United States to buy credits from other developed countries, which are willing to reduce greenhouse emissions further than the Protocol requires, to achieve its own (US) reduction target and a net global lessening. The United States also would like to get credits by assisting other countries to reduce their emissions. The developing countries object to emissions trading because it would allow wealthy countries to buy their way out of their obligations to reduce greenhouse emissions at home. For its part the European Union wants to limit the developed countries' right to buy credits in other countries to 50 percent of the state's total obligation.

Bruce Yandle and Stuart Buck have accused the European Union countries of having a (not so) hidden agenda on their part with respect to the United States.[62] For example, Yandle and Buck point out, the Protocol allows countries to "band together in voluntary associations in order to have their emissions considered collectively – a 'bubble' scenario that is widely understood as applying primarily, if not solely, to the European Union. If the EU has its emissions considered as a whole, the individual countries comprising the EU have a great deal more flexibility in meeting any individual emissions targets, without necessarily having to explicitly 'trade' emissions rights."[63]

Yandle and Buck also note that the EU member states stand to benefit considerably by the Kyoto Protocol's choice of 1990 as the baseline year for measuring any emissions reductions. This is because several important EU member states had reduced their carbon dioxide emissions considerably between 1990 and 1997. This meant that they would in effect get "credit" for reductions they had already made for other reasons. By contrast, the United States and some other developed countries had increased their carbon emissions between 1990 and 1997, which meant that their burden under the Protocol would be comparatively much greater. (For example, in 1990, West Germany had just reunited with East Germany, with its enormous environmental problems.)

At the Kyoto conference the United States attempted to get "sink" credit for 20 percent of the estimated 288 million tons of carbon absorbed each year by US forests. But the European Union strongly opposed any credit for carbon sinks, at least in part because the EU countries have less land available for reforestation efforts. According to Yandle and Buck, "the EU was not motivated just by jealousy over the United States' territory available for forestation. It was also inspired by a desire to punish the United States for not having enough market-stifling command-and-control regulation. To quote a report in *The Economist*, '[s]ome European ministers made it clear that they wanted Americans to feel some economic pain more than they wanted a workable agreement.'"[64]

There appears to be increasingly convincing evidence that global warming or climate change poses a real danger to the environment and that the emission of greenhouse gases is a major contributing factor. According to a 2001 report of the IPCC, for example, there is a better than a two in three chance that most of the global warming over the past fifty years has been caused by the increase in greenhouse gas concentrations.[65] There is serious dispute, however, over whether the Kyoto Protocol, even if fully implemented, would be an effective method for combating global warming. And, as we have seen, there is also a serious issue as to whether "various nations and corporations have tried to influence Kyoto's terms to serve their own parochial interests at the expense of the public good."[66]

Biodiversity

There has long been a concern with protecting particular species of fauna and flora. More recently, however, this concern has broadened to focus on the conservation of the biological diversity of natural systems, that is, the health of ecosystems.[67] "Biological diversity" has been defined as "a broad catchall term including the interconnected and related concepts of genetic diversity . . . ; species or ecological diversity . . . ; and habitat or natural diversity."[68] In the view of some, "the preservation of biological diversity is arguably the most serious problem facing the nations of the earth."[69]

In 1987, the United Nations Environmental Programme began work on an "umbrella convention" to address biological diversity issues. The result was the Convention on Biological Diversity,[70] which was adopted at the United Nations Conference on Environment and Development in Rio de Janeiro in 1992, and entered into force on December 29, 1993. As of June 9, 2003, there were 188 parties to the Convention.[71] The United States has signed the Convention but has not ratified it.

The Convention provides for, among other things, the development of national strategies, plans, and programs to protect biological diversity, conservation measures, environmental impact assessments of projects for adverse effects on biological diversity, and national reports on implementing measures and the effectiveness of these measures.[72] The United States refused to sign the Convention. Among the reasons for this refusal were: First and foremost, Articles 16(3) and 19(2) of the Convention would require a transfer of technology, thereby risking the loss of intellectual property protection and possibly encouraging global pirating. Second, there were concerns about how the Convention would be financed. Third, the Convention created disincentives to the development of new biotechnology products.[73] These reasons reflected criticisms from biotechnology companies and their supporters, who contended that certain elements of the Convention seemed to call for the compulsory licensing of intellectual property, and that the grant of a sovereign property right in genetic material would discourage pharmaceutical research and thus would result in fewer drugs being developed. Supporters of the Convention argued that there could be no long-term pharmaceutical research without the Convention because, without conservation incentives for the developing countries, there would be very little diversity left.[74]

In a response to the Democrats' attack on President Bush's negotiating position leading up to the Rio Conference, then Senate Minority Leader Robert Dole set forth a number of arguments that, one may surmise, still animate critics of the Biological Diversity Convention, including the current Bush administration. According to Dole:

> Environmental laws and regulations governing nearly every aspect of life in America are stronger in the United States than they are in any other country in the world. We have laws on air emissions, water discharges, filling and dredging wetlands and waterways, disposal of every type of waste from common household garbage to toxic chemicals to radioactive waste. We regulate almost to the absurd, demanding asbestos which has been safely sealed in place instead be disrupted and removed at enormous cost. We demand toxic waste be removed

from leaking dump sites and transferred to exotic space age dumps which also leak, a move that generates huge profits to lawyers and little, if any, benefit to the environment.

Unfortunately, those who have criticized the President of the United States . . . fail to tell us the basic position of the two sides in the . . . negotiations. The United States wants to have a cooperative agreement whereby all nations of the world commit themselves to undertake the same type of aggressive environmental controls that the United States has taken. Conversely, the Third World has viewed these negotiations as a cash cow. For a price, they have said, we might be able to interest them in being concerned about the environment.[75]

When it came into office in 1993, the Clinton administration signed the Convention on Biological Diversity and issued an interpretive statement expressing the US understanding that "the Convention requires all Parties to ensure that access or transfer of technology is consistent with the adequate and effective protection of intellectual property rights."[76] This understanding was not sufficient to meet the concerns of the critics of the Convention.

Dole's statement, which was directed at the critics of the US position on both the Convention on Biological Diversity and the Kyoto Protocol, as well as other environmental treaties, reflects several themes explored in this study. Dole's suggestion that US environmental laws and regulations are "stronger in the United States than they are in any other country in the world" is an example of the US attitude of "exceptionalism." It also is arguably an example of US provincialism or ignorance, since some European laws on the environment have long been stronger than those of the United States. Dole's attack on the "Third World" illustrates an increasing US distrust of international institutions and conferences where the developing countries have a substantial numerical dominance and are insisting that their interests be taken into account.

Perhaps because of this increasing distrust of international institutions, Dole's statement emphasizes *national* action to protect the environment – both action the United States is taking and action developing countries (according to Dole) should take. A recent commentary postulates that "the United States has certainly participated more actively in the international environmental arena than its treaty record would suggest."[77] This participation, according to the commentary, has been through non-treaty methods where the United States can control the rules of the game. These methods include broad interpretations of US environmental statutes so as to apply their terms extraterritorially and efforts in such international economic institutions as the International Monetary Fund, the World Bank, and the World Trade Organization, where the United States wields considerable influence, either because of weighted voting procedures or strong economic clout, to ensure that these institutions factor environmental considerations into their operations. In the view of the authors of the commentary, "the trends suggest that US domestic action and international environmental law and policy seem to be converging around a pair of overarching legal principles: the *precautionary principle*, i.e., that nations should act to prevent ecological harm even in the absence of full scientific certainty, and the *equivalence principle*, i.e., that environmental harm caused within a nation's borders should be treated equally, as a legal matter, to damage caused outside of a nation's political boundaries."[78] The conclusion of the authors is that "the United States seems to be implicitly recognizing through its actions what it will not recognize explicitly in treaties."[79] It is unclear when or whether the United States will move beyond recognition through unilateral, national action and engage in international cooperation toward the same ends. The authors suggest that, "barring an unexpected environmental crisis, it will most likely be some time before the United States participates fully and it will also take time for judicial and legislative processes to catch up with some of the principles currently being developed in international environmental law." Daniel Bodansky has predicted that "the coming generation of environmental problems will probably require more expeditious and flexible lawmaking approaches, which do not depend on consensus among states."[80] The United States at present might support the view that national action should be the more expeditious and flexible lawmaking approach of choice. Others might argue that global environmental institutions with binding decision-making powers should be created. Bodansky concludes:

> When states have common interests, and the issues involved are relatively technical, states might agree to establish institutions with flexible, non-consensus decision-making procedures, as they have done in the ozone regime. In such cases, general consent confers legitimacy initially, and technical expertise helps maintain this legitimacy on a continuing basis. But this approach is unlikely to work for problems such as climate change, where states have a much wider range of interests, and the issues involved are highly political. This is a sobering conclusion, but one that clarifies the challenges that lie ahead for international environmental law.[81]

Notes

1. GA Res. 48/141 (1993).
2. Henry J. Steiner & Philip Alston, International Human Rights in Context 519 (2d ed., 2000).
3. Kareem Fahim, *The Education of Mary Robinson*, The Village Voice, *at* http://www.villagevoice.com/issues/0217/fahim.php.

4. Ian Williams, *Mary Robinson Interview*, SALON MAGAZINE, *at* http://www.salon.com/people/interview/2002/07/26/mary_robinson.
5. Tom Lantos, *The Durban Debacle: An Insider's View of the UN World Conference Against Racism*, 26 FLETCHER F. WORLD AFF. 31 (2002).
6. *Id.* at 32.
7. *Id.* at 36.
8. See especially Gay McDougall, *The World Conference Against Racism: Through a Wider Lens*, 26 FLETCHER F. WORLD AFF. 135 (2002).
9. See *The UN Human Rights Commission: The Road Ahead*, Hearing Before the Subcommittee on International Operations and Terrorism of the Senate Committee on Foreign Relations, May 24, 2001, *at* http://frwebgate.access.gpo.gov/cgi-bin/getdoc.cgi?dbname=f:73071 wais.
10. See *id.*
11. Sergio Vieira de Mello, *Only Member States Can Make the UN Work*, WALL ST. J., April 21, 2003, at A12, col. 5.
12. Anne Bayefsky, *Human Wrongs*, WALL ST. J., April 28, 2003, at A12, col. 3.
13. General Comment No. 24, General Comment on Issues Relating to Reservations Made Upon Ratification or Accession to the Covenant or the Optional Protocols Thereto, or in Relation to Declarations under Article 41 of the Covenant, UN Doc. CCPR/C21/Rev.1/Add.6 (1994). General Comment No. 24 may most conveniently be found in 15 HUM. RTS. LJ 464 (1994).
14. Consideration of Reports Submitted by States Parties Under Article 40 of the Covenant: Comments of the Human Rights Committee, 53d Sess., 1413th mtg., at 4, UN Doc. CCPR/C79/Add.50 (1995).
15. Observations by the Governments of the United States and the United Kingdom on General Comment No. 24 (52) relating to reservations. These observations may most conveniently be found in 16 HUM. RTS. LJ 422 (1995).
16. See General Comment No. 24, *supra* note 13, para. 18, 15 HUM. RTS. LJ at 467.
17. See Observations by the Governments of the United States and the United Kingdom, *supra* note 15, 16 HUM. RTS. LJ at 423.
18. See General Comment No. 24, *supra* note 13, para. 12, 15 HUM. RTS. LJ at 466.
19. Observations by the Governments of the United States and the United Kingdom, *supra* note 15, 16 HUM. RTS. LJ at 423.
20. See US Department of State, Civil and Political Rights in the United States: Initial Report of the United States of America to the UN Human Rights Committee under the International Covenant on Civil and Political Rights (July 1994).
21. Concluding Observations of the Human Rights Committee: United States of America, paragraph 267, 53rd Sess. of Committee, UN Doc. CCPR/C/79/Add. 50 (1995).
22. Art. 6(5) of the Covenant provides: "Sentence of death shall not be imposed for crimes committed by persons below eighteen years of age and shall not be carried out on pregnant women." The US reservation to this provision states that "the United States reserves the right, subject to its Constitutional constraints, to impose capital punishment on any person (other than a pregnant woman) duly convicted under existing or future laws permitting the imposition of capital punishment, including such punishment for crimes committed by persons below eighteen years of age." Art. 7 of the Covenant provides: "No one shall be subjected to torture or to cruel, inhuman or degrading treatment or punishment. In particular, no one shall be subjected without his free consent to medical or scientific experimentation." The US reservation to Art. 7 states: "the United States considers itself bound by Article 7 to the extent that 'cruel,

inhuman or degrading treatment or punishment' means the cruel and unusual treatment or punishment prohibited by the Fifth, Eighth and/or Fourteenth Amendments to the Constitution of the United States."

23. Concluding Observations, *supra* note 21, para. 279.
24. Prior to the United States becoming a party to the Covenant in 1992, the US Supreme Court held that the execution of persons younger than sixteen at the time of their offenses was an unconstitutional violation of the Eighth Amendment to the Constitution, which prohibits cruel and unusual punishment. Thompson v. Oklahoma, 487 US 815 (1988). The very next year, however, the Court upheld the death penalty for defendants aged sixteen and seventeen against claims that their execution would violate the Eighth Amendment. Stanford v. Kentucky, 492 US 361 (1989).
25. As of 1999, reportedly only eight countries, including the United States, had carried out executions of persons under the age of eighteen during the 1990s. These seven other countries were Iran, Iraq, Bangladesh, Nigeria, Pakistan, Saudi Arabia, and Yemen. Christopher Hitchins, *Old Enough to Die*, VANITY FAIR, June 1999, at 78.
26. For discussion of this possibility, see William A. Schabas, *Invalid Reservations to the International Covenant on Civil and Political Rights: Is the United States Still a Party?*, 21 BROOKLYN J. INT'L L. 277 (1995).
27. Concluding Observations, *supra* note 21, para. 271.
28. International Convention on the Elimination of All Forms of Racial Discrimination, concluded in New York, May 7, 1966, entered into force, Jan. 4, 1969. 660 UNTS 195.
29. UN High Commissioner for Human Rights Treaty Body Database, *at* http://www.unhchr.ch/tbs/doc.nsf/RepStatfrset?OpenFrameSet.
30. International Convention on the Elimination of All Forms of Racial Discrimination, 140 Cong. Rec. S7634-02 (daily ed., June 24, 1994).
31. For a comparison of the US approach to hate speech with international norms on the subject, see Elizabeth F. Defeis, *Freedom of Speech and International Norms: A Response to Hate Speech*, 29 STAN. J. INT'L L. 57 (1992).
32. Reports Submitted by States Parties Under Article 9 of the Convention: United States of America, CERD/C/351/ADD.1, Oct. 10, 2000, paras. 156–163.
33. *Id.* at para. 164.
34. Concluding Observations of the Committee on the Elimination of Racial Discrimination: United States of America, Aug. 8, 2001, A/56/18, paras. 380–407.
35. *Id.* at para. 390.
36. *Id.* at para. 391.
37. *Id.* at para. 392.
38. See STEINER & ALSTON, *supra* note 2, at 777.
39. FINANCIAL TIMES, July5/July 6, 2003, at 1, col. 1.
40. For an excellent examination of some of the more salient aspects of this debate, see George C. Harris, *Terrorism and the Constitution: Sacrificing Civil Liberties in the Name of National Security*, 36 CORNELL INT'L LJ 135 (2003) (book review).
41. *Id.* at 146–47.
42. For a discussion of the factual background to this case, see Padilla *ex rel.* Newman v. Bush, 233 F. Supp. 2d 564 (SDNY 2002).
43. *Id.* at 569.
44. *Id.* at 608.
45. Harris, *supra* note 40, at 149.

46. Hamdi v. Rumsfeld, 316 F. 3d 450 (4th Cir. 2003), *rehearing denied* Hamdi v. Rumsfeld, 2003 WL 21540768 (4th Cir. July 9, 2003).
47. *Id.* at 465.
48. Harris, *supra* note 40, at 135.
49. For discussion of this effort, see Neil A. F. Popovic, *In Pursuit of Environmental Human Rights: Commentary on the Draft Declaration of Principles on Human Rights and the Environment*, 27 COLUM. HUM. RTS. L. REV. 487 (1996).
50. For a compilation of some national constitutions that have granted protection of environmental rights, see EDITH BROWN WEISS ET AL., INTERNATIONAL ENVIRONMENTAL LAW AND POLICY 415–17 (1998).
51. Daniel Bodansky, *The Legitimacy of International Governance: A Coming Challenge for International Environmental Law?*, 93 AM. J. INT'L L. 596, 604 (1999).
52. Conference of the Parties to the Framework Convention on Climate Change: Kyoto Protocol to the United Nations Framework Convention on Climate Change, 37 INT'L LEG. MATERIALS 22 (1998).
53. Convention on Biological Diversity, 31 INT'L LEG. MATERIALS 818 (1992).
54. IPCC, CLIMATE CHANGE (1991).
55. See BROWN WEISS ET AL., *supra* note 50, at 678.
56. Framework Convention on Climate Change, 31 INT'L LEG. MATERIALS 849 (1992).
57. S. Res. 98, 105th Congress – 1997.
58. Kyoto Protocol, UN Doc. FCCC/CP/1997/L.7/Add. 2, 37 INT'L LEG. MATERIALS 22 (1998).
59. For a summary of the primary provisions of the Protocol, see Clare Breidenich et al., *Current Development: The Kyoto Protocol to the United Nations Framework Convention on Climate Change*, 92 AM. J. INT'L L. 315 (1998).
60. www. state.gov/documents/organization/4584.pdf.
61. http://unfccc.int/resource/kpstats.pdf.
62. Bruce Yandle & Stuart Buck, *Bootleggers, Baptists, and the Global Warming Battle*, 26 HARV. ENVTL. L. REV. 177 (2002).
63. *Id.* at 182.
64. *Id.* at 222.
65. See Vanessa Houlder, *Climate Change Could Be Next Legal Battlefield*, FINANCIAL TIMES, July 14, 2003, at 10, col. 1.
66. Yandle & Buck, *supra* note 62, at 180.
67. BROWN WEISS ET AL., *supra* note 50, at 927.
68. From the US Council on Environmental Quality's Eleventh Annual Report (1985), as quoted in *id.* at 927–28.
69. *Id.* at 928.
70. Convention on Biological Diversity, 31 INT'L LEG. MATERIALS 818 (1992).
71. http://untreaty.un.org/ENGLISH/bible/englishinternetbible/partI/chapterXXVII/treaty33.asp.
72. See Daniel M. Bodansky, *International Law and the Protection of Biological Diversity*, 28 VAND. J. TRANSNAT'L L. 623, 627 (1995).
73. See United States: Declaration Made at the United Nations Environment Programme Conference for the Adoption of the Agreed Text of the Convention on Biological Diversity, 31 INT'L LEG. MATERIALS 848 (1992).
74. See Daniel T. Jenks, *The Convention on Biological Diversity – An Efficient Framework for the Preservation of Life on Earth?*, 15 NW. J. INT'L & BUS. 636 (1995).
75. 138 Cong. Rec. Section 4896 (daily ed. April 7, 1992) (statement of Senator Dole).
76. See US Treaty Doc. 103–20, Nov. 16, 1993, VI–VIII.

77. Cyril Kormos, Brett Groskos, and Russell A. Mittermeier, *US Participation in International Environmental Law and Policy*, 13 GEO. INT'L ENVTL L. REV. 661, 691 (2001).
78. *Id.* at 665.
79. *Id.* at 692.
80. Bodansky, *supra* note 51, at 606.
81. *Id.* at 624.

10 Summary and conclusions, and some possible future scenarios

The United States has had considerable difficulty in adhering to the rule of law in its conduct of foreign affairs. However, there also have been occasions when the United States has taken the lead in supporting the rule of law in resolving some of the major international issues. There has been, in other words, a substantial degree of inconsistency in the US record.

This chapter consists of two parts: a summary and conclusions, based on an examination of the preceding nine chapters; and some possible future scenarios relevant to the United States and the rule of law in international affairs.

Summary and conclusions

Deviations from the rule of law

US deviations from the rule of law, especially in recent years, have been numerous. These deviations have taken a variety of forms, and some of them have engendered considerable controversy. Some might cite the treaties that the United States has rejected in the face of overwhelming support from most other countries, including most particularly close US allies. These include, among others, the Statute of the International Criminal Court, the Landmines Treaty, the Comprehensive Nuclear Test Ban Treaty, the Kyoto Treaty, the Biological Diversity Treaty, the Law of the Sea Treaty, and the proposed Protocol to the Biological Weapons Convention. The United States also has been called to task for withdrawing from the ABM Treaty, although it did so in accordance with the terms of the treaty, and for refusing to explore means to eliminate or at least limit the global illicit trade in small arms and light weapons.

This charge is not well founded. In the voluntarist system that characterizes the international legal process, each state is entitled to decide whether becoming or remaining a party to a particular treaty is in its national interest. Its failure to do so may legitimately be criticized as a policy decision, but it is not inconsistent with the rule of law in international affairs. Indeed, if there are compelling reasons for a state not to become a party to a treaty, its refusal to sign the treaty supports the rule of law.

The United States has, however, taken steps that undermine the effectiveness of treaties that it has ratified. Some examples are its refusal (until recently) to pay its UN dues, in the face of a clear obligation under the UN Charter that it do so; its use of reservations to the Civil and Political Rights Covenant and the Race Convention to ensure that no change in US law and practice would be required, contrary to the object and purpose of human rights treaties to bring change (and improvement) in the law of state parties; its enactment of implementing legislation for the Chemical Weapons Convention that contains limitations on verification efforts by the Organization for the Prohibition of Chemical Weapons that undermine these efforts and are incompatible with US obligations under the Convention; its failure to comply (along with all the other nuclear powers) with its obligations under Article VI of the NPT to seek an early end to the nuclear arms race and to pursue nuclear disarmament; and, most controversially, its violation of UN Charter norms on the use of force in Kosovo (along with other NATO members) and against Iraq. As we have seen, according to one commentator – Michael Glennon – US use of force in Kosovo and against Iraq was the final "death knell" for international law norms on the use of force. For reasons set forth in chapter 4, I believe that Glennon's thesis is not well founded.

When the United States has become a party to a major multilateral treaty, it often has refused to choose or has reserved to procedures under the treaty for ensuring that states parties carry out their obligations. The United States reserved to the compromissory clauses in both the Genocide Convention and the Race Convention providing for reference of disputes to the International Court of Justice. It has also declined to agree to procedures allowing its nationals to submit petitions to the committees with responsibility for overseeing implementation of the Civil and Political Rights Covenant and the Race Convention, alleging that the United States has failed to carry out its obligations under these treaties.

One clear obstacle to the United States ratifying major multilateral treaties is the perception in some circles that the United States can gain some of the benefits of these treaties without incurring the burdens of becoming a party to them. For example, the United States has often cited provisions of the Law of the Sea Convention or the Convention on the Law of Treaties as constituting customary international law in debates on legal issues. One burden the United States avoids by not becoming a party to these and similar treaties is a binding third-party resolution of the issue that might be contrary to the US position.

Increasingly, the United States is becoming suspicious of binding third-party dispute settlement. One reason is that the United States has not fared very well in proceedings before the International Court of Justice and its record in the World Trade Organization and NAFTA is mixed. In chapter 7 we explored US positions before the International Court of Justice. We saw there the US government's perception that several of the judges on the ICJ were biased against the United States and generally lacked professional integrity. This perception, which many in the United States argue is not well-founded, has had serious implications for the US position on the International Criminal Court and the Law of the Sea Tribunal. Even with respect to dispute settlement procedures strongly promoted by the United States, such as those of the World Trade Organization or the NAFTA, some in the United States are having second thoughts.

As an alternative to binding international treaties and third-party dispute settlement, the United States appears to favor less formal procedures because of the flexibility they afford. The ambiguity of the customary international law process allows the United States to promote its version of contemporary international law norms without an internationally agreed written document setting forth with precision an agreed process for the creation of such norms. Similarly, in negotiations, the United States may be able to maximize its considerable leverage to achieve the result it desires. In the international economic area, the United States has lately emphasized bilateral or regional free trade and investment agreements, as have the European Union and other major Western countries – in the face of criticisms that these agreements undermine efforts under WTO auspices to reach global agreements on these subjects. On the other hand, others point out that bilateral and regional agreements may actually facilitate the conclusion of global agreements.

As we saw in chapter 4, the United States is especially leery of constraints that international law and institutions may place on its use of force to protect against what it regards as threats to its national security. Hence the vehemence of the US response to the International Court of Justice's decisions in *Nicaragua v. United States* and to France's blockage of US and British efforts to secure a favorable vote in the Security Council for the use of force against Iraq.

The terrorist attacks on September 11, 2001, greatly heightened US concern with threats to its national security. This heightened concern has in turn led the United States to take, or propose, actions that are problematic under international law. US detention of alleged Taliban and Al Qaeda members at Guantánamo Bay, and the proposal to submit them for trial before military commissions, for example, have prompted well-founded charges that the United States has violated its obligations under the law of armed conflict and international human rights law. More generally, US treatment of individuals suspected of committing or planning terrorist attacks against the United States or US nationals has raised charges of violations of international human rights law. The doctrine of "preemption," set forth in the National Security Strategy of the United States document issued by the White House in September 2002, proposes the use of armed force against terrorist groups and "rogue states" seeking to develop weapons of mass destruction before they can attack the United States, and has been subject to cogent challenge from various quarters, especially as it relates to rogue states.

As we have seen in the preceding chapters, the validity of many of the charges against US actions is debatable. Moreover, there is considerable value in US efforts to adhere as closely as possible to the rule of law, even if, as in the case of the regime change in Iraq, it may ultimately not have been successful in fulfilling all of its international law obligations. One must also keep in mind that, even after September 11, there are numerous instances where the United States has closely followed the rule of law.

Adherence to the rule of law

Even before the attacks of September 11, the United States had taken a lead role in the development of antiterrorism conventions, culminating in the conclusion of the Terrorist Bombing and Terrorist Financing Conventions in the late 1990s. After September 11, the United States was instrumental in the Security Council's adoption of Resolution 1373, which made mandatory, even for non-parties, many of the provisions of the Terrorism Financing Convention and which, most significantly, created the Counter-Terrorism Committee to monitor implementation of the resolution. US representatives have been highly active participants in ensuring that the Committee performs its task effectively.

Despite criticisms from the Bush administration of some aspects, the United States has been a strong supporter, especially financially, of the Yugoslav and Rwanda Tribunals. Similar support has been forthcoming for the hybrid court in Sierra Leone and for efforts to establish a mechanism to prosecute the Khmers Rouges in Cambodia.

The United States was also a model practitioner of the rule of law approach when, in direct response to the September 11 attacks, it first demanded that the Taliban in Afghanistan take certain actions against the Al Qaeda in their midst, and, after the Taliban refused to do so, informed the Security Council that it was exercising its "inherent right of individual and collective self-defense" and only then, along with the

United Kingdom, launched air attacks against Al Qaeda and Taliban targets in Afghanistan. Although some (including this writer) would have preferred that the United States secure a Security Council resolution expressly authorizing the use of force in Afghanistan, such a resolution was not required by the Charter, and earlier Council resolutions reacting to the September 11 attacks had expressly referred to the right of self-defense.

Even with respect to the invasion of Iraq, the United States closely followed the rule of law, even though it was ultimately unsuccessful in this endeavor. Despite, according to news reports, strong opposition to doing so from some members of the Bush administration, the United States went back to the Security Council and succeeded in obtaining the passage of Resolution 1441. The passage of this resolution at a minimum strengthened the US and British argument that a further failure by the Saddam Hussein regime to fulfill its obligations under Resolution 687 to destroy its weapons of mass destruction would in effect authorize the use of force against Iraq. Moreover, despite their position that a further resolution of the Council was not legally required, the United States and the United Kingdom sought such a resolution through negotiations.

The United States has been a strong supporter of the rule of law in the World Trade Organization and in the NAFTA arrangements. So far, the United States has called for reforms in the dispute settlement processes of the WTO and NAFTA rather than revocation of their basic mandates.

Some reasons for US difficulties

Robert Kagan, first in an essay[1] and then in a book,[2] has advanced a thesis that has attracted a great deal of attention. According to Kagan, the current tension between the United States and Europe has not come about primarily because of the foreign policy of the Bush administration but is rooted in American power and European weakness. The US "superpower" status, especially in the military realm, with its global reach, has thrust it into a Hobbesian world of threats and violence, beginning with the Cold War period. By contrast, in part because of the US security guarantee against Soviet aggression, Europe was able, through the European Union and other projects, to tame the dangers and instabilities of power politics in a democratic, Kantian zone of peace. Europe has devised a political order in which power is subdued and the use of force banished. At the same time, Kagan alleges, Europe has made itself militarily weak, as its member states are unable to confront the anarchical dangers of the wider world. As a result, the United States is relatively more willing to use force than Europe, as Europe seeks peace through law and diplomacy, and there is a growing divergence in strategic views, eroding solidarity. This divergence of view came into sharp focus in the debate over Iraq, because Europe, except for the United Kingdom, lacked the power to eradicate the threat of Iraq's weapons of mass destruction and therefore favored engagement and diplomacy rather than force.

There is a measure of truth in Kagan's thesis. However, as noted by one reviewer of his book,[3] his thesis is a caricature. There is, first, the question of what one means by "Europe." US Secretary of Defense Donald Rumsfeld made a distinction between "Old Europe," with French and German dominance, and "New Europe," that is, Spain and central and eastern European states which will be joining the European Union in 2004. Members of the "New Europe," such as Poland, are less averse to using force (Poland was a member of the "coalition of the willing" in the attack on Iraq). But "Old Europe" is hardly a monolith, as the United Kingdom and France have nuclear armed forces, Germany has the largest armed forces, and Spain and Italy, along with the United Kingdom, were members of the "coalition of the willing" that supported the attack against Iraq. Moreover, as we have seen throughout this study, even the Bush administration has participated actively in the international legal process when it has decided that it would be in its interest to do so.

There is no doubt that European states are much stronger proponents of international law and institutions than is the United States. In the European Union, member states have created a new legal order that is not quite a state, but more than just a new legal order in international law.[4] It is a new legal order, moreover, whose law, in case of conflict with national law, enjoys supremacy. Member states of an expanded version of "Europe," including Russia, have also agreed to be bound by the European Convention on Human Rights, to allow their nationals to complain directly to the European Court of Human Rights of alleged violations of the Convention, and to carry out decisions of the court that go against them. Such limitations on sovereignty are simply an inconceivable prospect to most Americans.

The reasons that such limitations on US sovereignty are inconceivable to most Americans are many and varied. In some part they are based on the US attitudes of triumphalism, exceptionalism, and provincialism explored throughout this study. More fundamentally, they reflect an historical distrust of power, especially of centralized power. This distrust of centralized power in the purely US context is even more pronounced when it comes to power centers outside US territory. Hence, the United States favors international institutions and organs, such as the UN Security Council, the Yugoslav and Rwanda Tribunals, and the International Monetary Fund and the World Bank, where it enjoys a substantial measure of influence. In sharp contrast, it strongly opposes the International Criminal Court, which has established a new legal order where US nationals and officials could be tried by an international court over which the United States, as a non-party, will exercise no control. As a result, the United States has been accused of being a country that views international law and institutions as something to be inflicted on other people. In my view the record does not support this thesis.

The future: some possible scenarios

It is hazardous to predict what future lies ahead for the United States and the rule of law in international affairs. What may be stated is that the current situation will change. Whether it will change in favor of greater or lesser US adherence to the rule of law in international affairs is the question. In the remainder of this chapter, we explore two possible future scenarios. The first scenario envisages the United States increasing its adherence to the rule of law in international affairs.The second would see the United States draw back further from the international legal order and rely primarily on the application of national law and procedure and on unilateral action to resolve international problems.

Greater adherence

At this writing, the UN headquarters in Iraq has suffered a terrorist bombing attack that killed Sergio Vieira de Mello, the chief UN representative in Iraq and the UN High Commissioner for Human Rights, and at least twenty-three others. The bombing disrupted desperately needed international relief efforts and was the latest of a series of setbacks for the US and British efforts in Iraq. It has prompted more calls for the United States to "rethink" its approach to postwar Iraq, including its unwillingness to allow the United Nations to play a larger role.[5] There are reports that the United States will agree to an enhanced role for the United Nations in Iraq, although this would not include UN peacekeepers, since the United States insists that keeping or enforcing the peace is a role reserved for coalition forces.[6]

There are also strong indications that the United States will rethink its approach to Afghanistan, where the government in Kabul is having trouble subduing a growing insurgency[7] and NATO peacekeepers (called ISAF) are confined to Kabul. Europe, it should be noted, has provided the bulk of the peacekeeping troops in Kabul, which are under the command of a German NATO officer. The 5,000 or so NATO peacekeepers operate separately from the 12,000-strong coalition forces still in the country. So far, the United States and others have resisted expanding the mandate of ISAF beyond Kabul, and the result has been that the real power in the provinces lies with the warlords.[8] The economy is racked by drought and the drug trade, and well under $1billion of the $4.5 billion promised at the 2002 Tokyo conference has arrived in Afghanistan.

Despite President George W. Bush's preelection rhetoric, the Bush administration is involved in "nation building" with a vengeance.

Despite the Bush administration's aversion to peacekeeping operations and engagement in civil wars or internal conflicts, especially in Africa, the United States recently forced Charles Taylor, the dictator president of Liberia, to step down and go into exile in Nigeria (thus perhaps protecting him from the indictment of the hybrid court in Sierra Leone for war crimes). After much hesitation, the United States also supported the deployment in Liberia of a 3,000-strong West African peacekeeping force by sending 200 marines ashore to secure the port, patrol the air, and protect aid deliveries. Three American warships patrolled close to the Liberian coast.[9] The success (or lack thereof) of the Liberian mission may determine whether the United States will be more supportive of UN or UN-approved peacekeeping missions in the future. A successful conclusion of recent promising efforts to end the murderous war in the Democratic Republic of the Congo would also be helpful.

If there is to be a peaceful settlement of the current crisis between the United States and North Korea, it will have to involve binding international agreements with effective verification procedures and a role for IAEA inspectors. Clyde Prestowitz has suggested that "we should negotiate a new deal that both guarantees the security of the country from outside attack and assures it sufficient electricity and food; sign a peace treaty to conclude the Korean War and accord the North formal diplomatic recognition; and support South Korea's efforts at developing trade and investment with the North and at economic development."[10] He further points out that the United States and South Korea have differed dramatically on how this crisis should be resolved, with South Korea favoring a European- and Asian-style approach of prolonged negotiations and diplomatic efforts to integrate the North and South Korean economies rather than the US confrontational style.[11]

More generally, the crises in Iraq, Afghanistan, Liberia, and the Democratic Republic of the Congo, the Israeli–Palestinian impasse, and the threat of worldwide attacks by Al Qaeda and other terrorist groups may lead the United States to do some hard thinking about how to maintain international peace and security in the post-September 11 milieu. In particular, it will have to decide on the proper role to be played by the United Nations, regional agencies such as the European Union, NATO, the Organization of American States, and the African Union, ad hoc arrangements like coalitions of the willing, and unilateral initiatives. These questions are likely (but by no means certain) to lead to the conclusion that the magnitude of the task of keeping the peace is so great that greater reliance on international institutions is necessary. This conclusion in turn could lead to a determination to ensure that these international institutions are capable of fulfilling their tasks effectively.

Ironically, at a time when the United States has strained relations with many of its European allies, US relations with Russia and China are greatly improved. In part this may be because Russia and China face greater threats from Muslim fundamentalism than do most European states. In any event improved relations among three of the Security Council's permanent members may afford an opportunity to revisit the issue of the collective security system envisaged by Chapter VII of the UN Charter.

The future of Europe and of its alliance with the United States are bound to be a matter of high priority. If nothing else, the growing economic clout of the European Union assures close US attention. In addition, despite Kagan's thesis, the European Union is moving to develop a unified foreign and security policy, and it will be a policy that eventually will have a significant military component. As Tony Blair, the UK Prime Minister, has asserted, "Whatever its origin, Europe today is no longer just about peace. It is about projecting collective power."[12] In light of the European attitudes noted by Kagan, it is highly likely that a significant component of this projection of collective power will be support for the rule of law in international affairs.

As to whether the United States will eventually accept new initiatives in the international legal process like the International Criminal Court, the answer is likely to depend on how well these initiatives work, and what risk they might pose to the United States. Although the United States currently considers the International Criminal Court a grave threat to its vital interests, it is much more likely that the greatest risk facing the Court is that it will be unable to function effectively. If the Court can overcome the obstacles facing it, and succeed in bringing some perpetrators of genocide, war crimes, and crimes against humanity to justice, or at least serve as a stimulant to nation-states to exercise jurisdiction over these crimes, the United States may reassess its current position on the Court. Similarly, if negotiations succeed in resolving the North Korea crisis peacefully, the United States may finally become a party to the Landmines Treaty – since the key reason for US unwillingness to join relates to the current defense needs of its forces in South Korea. Finally, if the scientific evidence demonstrates an ever greater risk of climate change, the United States may return to negotiations over the Kyoto Treaty with a view to revisions that will make the treaty acceptable to it, including the inclusion of large polluters such as China and India. The same may be said with respect to the Biological Diversity Treaty.

More favorable US attitudes on binding third-party dispute settlement will also depend on these procedures functioning justly and effectively. It is difficult to envisage a dramatic increase in the US use of the International Court of Justice, but in the absence of the Court handing down future politically charged decisions, the United States may continue to agree to refer disputes to the Court on an ad hoc basis, perhaps with the use of the chamber procedures. If there is agreement on improvements in WTO and NAFTA dispute settlement procedures, it is likely that the United States will continue to favor this method of settlement for trade and investment disputes. For reasons discussed earlier, it is unlikely that the United States would ever agree to courts along the lines of the European Court of Justice or the European Court of Human Rights.

Lastly, if it is to adhere more closely to the rule of law in international affairs, the United States will have to come to grips with the reality that the international legal process now involves many more actors than just the governments of nation-states. At a minimum it will have to factor into the mix more effectively the interests of and the pressures brought to bear by nongovernmental organizations, multinational corporations, states in the United States, and prominent individuals. In short, the United States government will have to cope better with the "democratization" of US foreign policy.

Less adherence

A markedly reduced US adherence to the rule of law in international affairs would probably result only from an outbreak of major new threats to US national security. Successful new attacks in the United States, for example, by Al Qaeda or other terrorists would likely result in US measures that would clearly be incompatible with international human rights law and perhaps the law of armed conflict as well. If there was a strong suspicion that such attacks were aided and abetted by a state sponsor (as was the case with Afghanistan), or were ordered by a state, there might well be a major armed attack against such a state, even in the absence of evidence sufficient to support an attack on grounds of self-defense or based on a Security Council resolution authorizing such an attack. In such a Hobbesian world, preemptive armed attacks might become the order of the day.

Less dramatically, reduced US adherence to the rule of law might come about if, at least in the US perception, international institutions perform in an unsatisfactory fashion. Current US perceptions of the International Criminal Court could be confirmed if the Court either became highly politicized and supported clearly unfounded charges or simply performed in an incompetent fashion. Similarly, if the International Court of Justice were to hand down a decision, for example, that the bombing by certain NATO states in Serbia over Kosovo violated international law norms, the result would probably be even less US involvement with the Court. Also, if WTO or NAFTA panels were to rule against the United States in a series of high-profile cases, it might cause the United States to abandon its support for binding third-party dispute settlement in trade and investment disputes, especially if there was a strong reaction from the US Congress.

Which scenario, then, is more likely? My best guess is that the greater adherence scenario is, if only because the nature of the problems facing us require for their resolution the kind of cooperative effort that is conducive to the rule of law in international affairs. The chances for a successful rule of law in international affairs, however, will be greatly enhanced if the United States is "present at the creation" of improved international institutions and an enhanced international legal process, as it was at the end of World War II. A "new world order" will not come about automatically. It will require hard work and commitment, and the United States assuming a leadership but not a dominating role. The prize could be a world more along the lines of the one envisaged by the drafters of the UN Charter. It would be worth the struggle.

Notes

1. See R. Kagan, *Power and Weakness*, 113 Pol'y Rev, June/July 2002, at 3.
2. Robert Kagan, Of Paradise and Power (2003).
3. Ivo H. Daalder, *Of Paradise and Power: America and Europe in the New World Order*, NY Times, March 5, 2003, at E1, col. 2.
4. Compare the description of the legal order of the (then) European Communities by the European Court of Justice in Van Gend en Loos v. Nederlandse Administratie der Belastingen, 26/62, [1963] ECR 1, [1963] CMLR 105 ("new legal order in international law") with its later formulation in Costa v. ENEL, 6/64, [1964] ECR 1141, [1964] CMLR 425 ("By contrast with ordinary international treaties, the EEC Treaty has created its own legal system which, on the entry into force of the treaty, became an integral part of the legal systems of the Member States and which their courts are bound to apply").
5. See, e.g., *The Baghdad Bombing; A Mission Imperiled*, NY Times, Aug. 20, 2003, at A20, col. 1.

6. See Christopher Cooper & Gary Fields, *US and Its Allies Discuss Ways to Elevate Role of UN in Iraq*, WALL ST. J., Aug. 21, 2003, at A4, col. 5.
7. See David Rohde, *Nine Afghan Police Officers Are Killed in Attack by Insurgents*, NY TIMES, Aug. 20, 2003, at A3, col. 1.
8. See *Afghanistan: Not a Dress Rehearsal*, THE ECONOMIST, Aug. 16, 2003, at 35.
9. See, e.g., *Liberia: Goodbye to All That?*, THE ECONOMIST, Aug. 16, 2003, at 39.
10. CLYDE PRESTOWITZ, ROGUE NATION: AMERICAN UNILATERALISM AND THE FAILURE OF GOOD INTENTIONS 278 (2003).
11. *Id.* at 177–80, 245–48.
12. Quoted in *id.*, at 239.

Index